Also in the Variorum Collected Studies Series

STEPHAN KUTTNER
Medieval Councils, Decretals and Collections of Canon Law

KENNETH PENNINGTON
Popes, Canonists and Texts, 1150–1550

JAMES A. BRUNDAGE
Sex, Law and Marriage in the Middle Ages

ADAM VETULANI
Sur Gratien et les Décrétales

ROBERT SOMERVILLE
The Papacy, Council and Canon Law in the 11th–12th Centuries

BRIAN TIERNEY
Rights, Laws and Infallibility in Medieval Thought

RICHARD KAY
Councils and Clerical Culture in the Medieval West

ROBERT FEENSTRA
Legal Scholarship and Doctrines of Private Law, 13th–18th Centuries

JOHN GILCHRIST
Canon Law in the Age of Reform, 11th–12th Centuries

ROGER REYNOLDS
Law and Liturgy in the Latin Church, 5th–12th Centuries

C.R. CHENEY
The English Church and its Laws, 12th–14th Centuries

WALTER ULLMANN
Law and Jurisdiction in the Middle Ages

JANE E. SAYERS
Law and Records in Medieval England: Studies on the Medieval Papacy, Monasteries and Records

VARIORUM COLLECTED STUDIES SERIES

Decretals and the Creation of 'New Law' in the Twelfth Century

FOR ANNE

Charles Duggan

Decretals and the Creation of 'New Law' in the Twelfth Century

Judges, Judgements, Equity and Law

Routledge
Taylor & Francis Group
LONDON AND NEW YORK

First published 1998 in the Variorum Collected Studies Series by Ashgate Publishing

Published 2017 by Routledge
2 Park Square, Milton Park, Abingdon, Oxon OX14 4RN
52 Vanderbilt Avenue, New York, NY 10017

Routledge is an imprint of the Taylor & Francis Group, an informa business

British Library CIP Data
Duggan, Charles
Decretals and the Creation of New Law in the Twelfth Century: Judges, Judgements, Equity and Law. (Collected Studies Series CS607)
1. Canon Law – History, I. Title
262.9'09021

US Library of Congress CIP Data
The Library of Congress Catalog Card Number is pre-assigned as:
98–070353

ISBN 13: 978-0-86078-680-1 (hbk)

VARIORUM COLLECTED STUDIES SERIES CS607

CONTENTS

This volume contains x + 346 pages

INTRODUCTION

Whereas an earlier volume of sixteen studies appeared with the sub-title 'The Becket dispute and the Decretal Collections', the present complementary group of nine studies sets the European context of the formation and consolidation of *ius novum*, the 'new law' of the Western Church, based primarily on papal consultations and specific cases, and informed by the academic learning of the schools, where canon law was taught as a scholarly discipline. The professional and creative role of papal judges delegate in the making of the 'new law' was fundamental to this process. The first study analyses the role of judges delegate in the formation and application of the new principles of law and jurisprudence which the practice of local courts and appeals to the papacy brought into being. Without the involvement and cooperation of local ecclesiatical judges—bishops, deans, archdeacons, abbots, and others—the 'new law' might have remained a largely academic and didactic exercise. But, in the event, its reception and application in countless and widely-dispersed cases produced a fundamental evolution in legal consciousness and professional codification. Not only did the judges delegate articulate the 'new law' and ensure its enforcement and further development, but their concern with authority and correct procedure resulted in the creation and continuing evolution of decretal collections, from early primitive collections to the more professional systematic collections, leading finally through Bernard of Pavia's *Compilatio Prima* (1190) to the official code of 1234.

In England, this doctrinal and jurisdictional revolution was the essential context of the Becket dispute and its aftermath, and it is significant how widely-diffused references to aspects and echoes of the Becket dispute are found in the decretal collections (**II**). Indeed, the creative and formative role of English judges and canonical collectors in the application and development of the general and official law is exemplified in Study **III**, which provides a calendar of fifty-four decretals received by the archbishop of York (either alone or with a colleague). This English initiative is recorded in the early primitive collection at Alcobaça (*Alcobacensis prima)*, a compilation of Portuguese provenance which affords clear evidence, not only of the reception of English canonical sources in the Iberian peninsula, but also of the existence of an exceptionally early Exeter collection (here called Exeter/1 Alc.), dating from the 1160s to the early 1170s.

No less significant is the extent to which the 'new law' involved and affected all levels of Western Christian society. In Study **IV** attention is focussed on numerous cases or disputes involving English magnates. Many such cases concerned the marriage law and the inheritance of family estates. But, although English canonists were clearly precocious in their canonical interests, their professional expertise and codification, England was by no means unique in its reception and application of the 'new law'.

In exemplification, three further studies (**V–VII**) reflect the wider European context of the learned law and its regional aspects, respectively in Hungary (**V**), Italy (**VI**), and Spain (**VII**). A striking feature of these regional examples is the degree of legal expertise and sophistication assumed in the recipient judges, though it is perhaps significant that the decretals to Hungary are at some points more explicitly instructive in their statement of judicial principles and due legal process, informed by the learning, procedure, and language of the Roman Civil Law, reflecting perhaps a comparatively less professional stage of development and experience of the Hungarian Church in this respect at that time. By the end of the twelfth century the *ius commune* of the Church was firmly established as a Europe-wide institution, effectively expressing and enforcing the judicial authority of the pope. But as the authority of the papal decretal grew and broadened in its application, so did the opportunity for abuse. Study **VIII** deals specifically with the problem of forgery.

But perhaps no single problem was more frequently recorded than questions relating to the definition, canonical status, and binding character of marriage. The progressive establishment of general laws concerning betrothal and matrimony provided many potential grounds for litigation, honest and dishonest alike. The concluding study (**IX**) examines the papal response to the numerous complex cases arising from conflict between marriage law and secular conventions. In reaching a canonical ruling in delicate and difficult marriage disputes, a compassionate concern was shown, notably by Alexander III, for the parties themselves, but notably also for children involved in the decisions. In this delicate context, the pope's 'authority as judge and teacher was exercised with discretion and pastoral care'.[1]

My grateful thanks are due to the following publishers for their kind permission to reprint these studies: the University of Pennsylvania Press; Éditions Universitaires, Paris; Accademia Senese degli Intronati, Siena; the Vatican Press; Márton Áron Kiadó, Budapest; the Ecclesiastical History Society; Hahnsche Buchhandlung, Hanover; Leuven University Press; and Herder Editrice e Libreria, Rome; and especially to my wife, Dr Anne Duggan, for collaboration in all aspects of this volume.

Charles Duggan

King's College London
November, 1997

---

1 **IX** 86.

PUBLISHER'S NOTE

The articles in this volume, as in all others in the Collected Studies Series, have not been given a new, continuous pagination. In order to avoid confusion, and to facilitate their use where these same studies have been referred to elsewhere, the original pagination has been maintained wherever possible.

Each article has been given a Roman numeral in order of appearance, as listed in the Contents. This number is repeated on each page and quoted in the index entries.

I

Papal Judges Delegate and the Making of the "NewLaw" in the Twelfth Century

The Foundation of the "New Law"

In the exercise of power in twelfth-century Europe, no claims to primacy of authority and jurisdiction equalled those of the papacy in their universality and essentially spiritual nature. The fundamental basis of papal claims to universal jurisdiction lay centuries earlier in the doctrine of Petrine supremacy, the superiority of Peter among the apostles. From the fourth and fifth centuries, following the imperial acceptance of Christianity, this theological concept was interwoven with the jurisprudence and judicial procedures of Roman Civil Law, and from this union flowed the Romano-canonical procedures of the papal curia, and of the canonists and ecclesiastical judges of later centuries. Already in the pontificate of Gelasius I (†496), the judicial primacy of the pope was asserted in the right of all Christians to appeal to him—the origin of the doctrine of the pope as Universal Ordinary—the source of authority to whom every Christian could refer as to his own diocesan bishop.[1] Across the centuries, later popes consolidated and built on these foundations, most decisively in the pontificates

1. The papal assertion of an ultimate authority in matters of jurisdiction, and especially in the receipt and resolution of appeals, was expressed in a letter of Gelasius I (492–96) to the bishops of Dacia, from which a brief excerpt was transmitted to Gratian's *Decretum* (see n. 2), Causa 11, qu. 3, c. 17: "Cuncta per mundum novit ecclesia, quod sacrosancta Romana ecclesia fas de omnibus habet iudicandi, neque cuiquam de eius liceat iudicare iudicio. Siquidem ad illam de qualibet mundi parte appellandum est; ab illa autem nemo est appellare permissus"—excerpt from *Valde mirati*, Philipp Jaffé, *Regesta pontificum romanorum ad annum 1198*, ed. F. Kaltenbrunner (anno 64–590), P. W. Ewald (anno 590–882), and S. Loewenfeld (anno 882–1198), 2 vols. (Leipzig, 1885–88), 1:664, *anno* 493. There are two versions of the letter in Mansi 8:49–71: "Gelasius episcopus urbis Romae ad Dardanos"; cf. cols 54: "Non reticemus," and 66: "Non plane tacemur." Cf. also Frederic W. Maitland, *Roman Canon Law in the Church of England* (London, 1898), p. 104 and nn. 1, 2 and Jane E. Sayers, *Papal Judges Delegate in the Province of Canterbury 1198–1254* (Oxford, 1971), pp. 5–6. Thanks are due to my wife, Dr. Anne Duggan, for exceptional help in preparing this paper.

of Gregory VII (†1085), Alexander III (†1181), and Innocent III (†1216); the evolution of canon law and its codification ran parallel with the development of these doctrines. In this long and complex process, two factors are essential points of reference here: the centralizing and decisive impact of the "Gregorian Reform" from the late eleventh century onward, and the publication of Gratian's *Decretum* (*ex* 1139), which marked the dividing point between *ius antiquum* and *ius novum,* the old law and the new.[2]

On the one hand, the *Decretum* provided an authoritative summary of the old law—the culmination of centuries of development—combining papal, scriptural, patristic and conciliar rulings, texts from Roman law, the laws of secular kingdoms, and many other sources. On the other hand, it became the basis for the development of new law, defined in recent conciliar legislation and, still more significantly, in papal decretal letters addressed to many thousands of recipients throughout Latin Christendom. More than any other book in the history of canon law, it helped to create a new ethos of learned law and to establish new standards of professional conduct in ecclesiastical courts. Although never officially promulgated, it swiftly became the standard work of reference in the courts and in the schools, and provided the theoretical framework and the technical instructions necessary for the conduct of judicial cases throughout the Latin Church. One distinction in part 1, for example, defines the authority of decretal letters and the necessary obedience to papal rulings: decretals have authority even if not included in the canonical corpus; all sanctions of the apostolic see must be observed; whatever the Roman Church decrees must be observed by all; and so forth.[3] And one *quaestio* in part 2 has the character of a judicial handbook *in statu nascendi,* assembling statements of principle, procedure and practical guidance on the proper stages of litigation, supported by both canonical and civilian authorities. The final recension of this section includes decretals attributed to popes from the first century onwards (some in fact retraceable to the ninth-century Pseudo-Isidore), texts from Roman Law, including the Theodosian Code and the Digest,[4] Gratian's own *dicta,*

2. For the most accessible edition, see *Corpus Iuris canonici,* ed. Emil Friedberg, 2 vols. (Leipzig, 1879–81), 1.

3. *Decretum,* Dist. 19, cc. 1, 2, 4 et al.

4. *Decretum,* Causa 2, q. 6. Cf. Stephan Kuttner, *New Studies on the Roman Law in Gratian's Decretum* Canon Law Studies (Washington, DC, 1953, reprint from *Seminar* 11 [1953], 12–50); cf. Gabriel le Bras, Charles Lefebvre and Jacqueline Rambaud, *L'âge classique, 1140–1378: sources et théorie du droit* (Paris, 1965), pp. 119–28: Les additions, 3, Les textes du droit romain; Charles Munier, "Droit canonique et droit romain d'après Gratien et les-décrétistes," in Munier, *Vie conciliaire et collections canoniques en Occident, IVe–XIIe siècle* (London, Variorum Reprints 1987), no. 20.

and passages of precise and practical instruction. Both the basic principle of the right of appeal and aspects of the judicial process are emphasized in Gratian's rubrics—all have the right of appeal to the apostolic see, as if to a mother; the hearing of an appeal belongs to the one to whom it was made; and appeals are permissible before pronouncement of sentence[5]—to which Gratian's own *dictum* gave still further precision: an appellant must make his appeal, and set out to prosecute it within five days. Moreover, following chapter 31 on letters dimissory (*apostoli*: the formal notification issued by the judge from whom an appeal is made to the one who takes cognizance of it), Gratian inserted a series of standard letters relating to various kinds of appeal.

> The form of *apostoli* is this: "I En., bishop of the holy church of Bologna, by these apostoli, send you Roland, priest and chaplain of San Apollinare, to the apostolic see, to which you appealed from my judgment."
>
> The form of appeal is this: "I, Adelinus, unworthy minister of the church of S. Regina, feeling myself oppressed by the lord Walter, archbishop of the holy church of Ravenna, appeal to the Roman see, and request *apostoli*."
>
> The form of appeal after sentence will be: "I, A(delinus), unworthy minister of the church of S. Regina, appeal to the Roman see against the sentence of lord Walter, archbishop of the holy church of Ravenna, unjustly laid on me on Wednesday, 30 April, in the year of the Lord 1105,[6] and request *apostoli*."
>
> If one or two wish to appeal on behalf of several, they shall appeal in this form: "We, G. and P., acting for the canons of the holy church of B., feeling ourselves oppressed (or against the sentence *etc*), appeal to the Roman see, and request *apostoli*."[7]

Compiled in Bologna, the dominant law school in Europe at that time, the *Decretum* established itself immediately as the basis of canonical jurisprudence throughout the Western Church. During the following twenty years or so (1140–60), its ideas were disseminated to receptive ecclesiastical administrators throughout Europe. The *Decretum* was used by John of Salisbury, for instance, in the composition of legal letters for archbishop Theobald of Canterbury in the 1150s.[8] Without the general reception of this law book, recognized as authoritative by teachers and practitioners of

5. *Decretum,* Causa 2, q. 6, cc. 6, 8, 12 and 21. Rufinus (1157–59) prefaced his commentary on this section with a series of questions. "What is an appeal, who can appeal, by whom and to whom should an appeal be made, when and how often, how and within what time?" *Rufinus von Bologna: Summa decretorum,* ed. Heinrich Singer (Paderborn, 1902; repr. Aalen, 1963), pp. 251–53.

6. This date is inaccurate: 30 April 1105 was a Sunday.

7. *Decretum, post* Causa 2, q. 6, c. 31 (ed. Friedberg, p. 478).

8. *The Letters of John of Salisbury,* I: *The Early Letters,* ed. and trans. W. J. Millor and Harold E. Butler (London, 1955; reissued, Oxford, 1986), p. xx note 1.

the law, and of the general principles of jurisprudence which it contained, the remarkable growth of the appellate jurisdiction of the papacy, and the complementary system of judges delegate which supported it, would have been almost inconceivable in the form in which they developed through the second half of the twelfth century.

At the heart of the new law stood the papal decretal. Decretal letters were commissions to judges delegate, or replies to questions submitted to the pope for guidance on points of law or procedure, the resolution of specific disputes or problems, and a host of consultations of all kinds.[9] Gratian had defined the authority of decretal letters as equal to that of conciliar canons,[10] to which the canonist Rufinus (1157–59) simply added "because of the primacy of the Roman Church."[11] Later, in the early thirteenth century, the Bolognese canonist Tancred expressed the matter succinctly: "Rome is the fatherland of all—*patria omnium*—and the pope is judge ordinary for every individual."[12] Decretal letters were therefore the expression of the pope's superior jurisdiction in Christian society and also the means of its execution—with the judges delegate as executors—but they were essentially reactive, issued in response to judicial appeals or requests for clarification of points of law.

The right of appeal to the pope was universal and unrestricted. At any stage in a dispute, with or without an initial process in a local court,[13] an aggrieved party could appeal to the pope, who issued in response a commission to two or more local judges to hear and terminate the case, or bring the parties to an amicable settlement in their presence. Through this procedure, ever widening networks of connexion were established between the periphery and the center, between the curia and the provinces. It is sometimes supposed that the systematic development of the pope's appel-

9. In Stephen of Tournai's familiar definition (c. 1160–1170), "a decretal is a papal rescript to any bishop or ecclesiastical judge, who has consulted the Roman Church on any doubtful matter," *Die Summa des Stephanus Tornacensis über das Decretum Gratiani*, ed. J. F. von Schulte (Giessen, 1891), p. 2: "Decretalis epistola est, quam dominus apostolicus aliquo episcopo vel alio iudice ecclesiastico super aliqua causa dubitante et ecclesiam Romanam consulente rescribit et ei transmittit." Cf. Charles Duggan, *Twelfth-Century Decretal Collections and Their Importance in English History* (London, 1963), p. 32 and note 4.

10. "Decretales epistolae canonibus conciliorum pari iure exequantur," *Decretum*, Dist. 20.

11. *Rufinus*, p. 42, ". . . hic de momento decretalium epistolarum tractat, ostendens eas eiusdem auctoritatis fore, cuius et canones, propter primatum Romane ecclesie." These matters are more fully discussed in Duggan, *Twelfth-Century Decretal Collections*, pp. 34–39.

12. Maitland, *Roman Canon Law*, p. 104 n. 2, citing Cambridge, Gonville and Caius College, MS 85, fol. 7: "ille est iudex ordinarius rei apud quem ille reus domicilium habet. . . . Item Roma est patria omnium [*Digest*, 50.1.33] et dominus papa iudex est ordinarius singulorum, ut ix. qu. iii. cuncta per orbem [*Decretum*, C.9, qu. 3, c. 17]." *

13. Sayers, *Papal Judges Delegate*, pp. 5–8.

late jurisdiction was inimical to the traditional rights and jurisdiction of diocesan bishops, but its effectiveness was in fact dependent on the active collaboration of local ecclesiastics such as bishops, archdeacons, deans, abbots, and priors. Some of the English bishops acquired a high reputation as papal judges delegate. Bartholomew of Exeter and Roger of Worcester, for instance, "the twin lights of the English Church" in Alexander III's familiar evaluation, were the most frequently appointed judges delegate of their generation.[14] No fully comprehensive survey of papal commissions to judges delegate is possible for the twelfth century, since the papal registers for the period are mostly lost. But their receipt and transcription are abundantly recorded in local archives, from which many volumes of *Papsturkunden* have been printed, notably for the various regions of France, for England, Spain, Portugal, Germany, and the military orders; a vast number of papal letters of all kinds to Italian recipients are registered in several volumes of the *Italia Pontificia*. The archival records of cathedral chapters and religious houses throughout Europe preserve rich evidence of commissions to judges delegate, their procedures, and judicial settlements. And from these it is frequently possible to trace the origin, process, and outcome of the various stages of litigation and series of disputes through prolonged periods of time. Such records reveal with unusual clarity and completeness the process by which the papal judges were appointed and discharged their duties.

The Standardization of the Process

The papal commissions of delegation empowered the judges to summon the parties, examine witnesses, evaluate the evidence, and reach a judgment by the pope's authority, and mandate the execution of sentence by the local ordinary. On the conclusion of the case, the judges issued letters to the parties and reported all details to the pope. The appeal therefore set in motion an interactive chain of juridical authority, from litigant to pope,

14. In evident recognition of the rapid expansion of delegated jurisdiction in the twelfth century and of the bishops' outstanding share in the process, almost every published biography of English bishops in the period now includes a chapter on the bishop in question, as judge delegate, as well as scattered references to his judicial activities. Cf. Dom Adrian Morey, *Bartholomew of Exeter. Bishop and Canonist: A study in the Twelfth Century* (Cambridge, 1937), esp. ch. 4, "The Bishop as Judge Delegate"; Morey and C. N. L. Brooke, *Gilbert Foliot and His Letters* (Cambridge, 1965), pp. 230–44; Mary G. Cheney, *Roger, Bishop of Worcester, 1164–79* (Oxford, 1980), esp. chs. 4, "The Judge-Delegate," and 5, "The Bishop and the Law"; and Duggan, *Decretal Collections*, passim.

from the pope to the judges, from the judges to the local bishop, and from the judges back to the pope. If difficult or unusual questions were raised in the course of litigation, the judges could seek clarification from the pope. Each stage was conducted in accordance with universally applied norms derived from Gratian and professional commentaries and formularies specifically compiled for this purpose, pervasively influenced by the processes of Roman civil law.[15] Even before the composition of such strictly canonical formularies, handbooks on civilian procedure, like the *pseudo-Ulpianus de edendo,* were widely used by ecclesiastical lawyers in the formulation and presentation of cases in church courts.[16]

The universal reception of the *Decretum* and the adoption of Romano-canonical procedure by the papal chancery, the canonists, and the judges delegate decisively shaped the exercise of judicial authority in the Church. Gratian established general principles of ecclesiastical law which could be applied universally, *mutatis mutandis,* throughout Christendom. The Romano-canonical process created new standards for the conduct of cases, the submission of evidence, and the interrogation of witnesses.[17] Although local customs sometimes remained intact, the new law helped to break down regional barriers and establish a common law, the *ius commune* of the whole Church. Bishops, archdeacons, and local officials could not ignore these developments, for their own local authority and jurisdiction were

15. Sayers, *Papal Judges Delegate,* ch. 12, "The Procedure of the Courts of Judges Delegate"; Wacław Uruszczak, "Les juges délégués du pape et la procédure romano-canonique à Reims dans la seconde moitié du xiie siècle," *Tijdschrift voor Rechtsgeschiedenis,* 53 (1985), 27–41; Ludwig Falkenstein, "Appellationen an den Papst und Delegationsgerichtsbarkeit am Beispiel Alexanders III. und Heinrichs von Frankreich," *Zeitschrift für Kirchengeschichte,* 97 (1986), 36–65; cf. the summary of the formulary "A. B. C. Judices" in the Appendix, below. For a short overall survey, cf. G. G. Pavloff, *Papal Judges Delegate at the Time of the Corpus Iuris Canonici,* Canon Law Studies (Washington DC, 1963). On papal rescripts and the canonists, see now the exhaustive treatment of judges delegate in Harry Dondorp, "Review of Papal Rescripts in the Canonists' Teaching," *ZRG Kan.Abt,* 76 (1990), 172–253; 77 (1991), 32–109; on judges delegate specifically see 51–60.

16. Francis de Zulueta and Peter Stein, *The Teaching of Roman Law in England Around 1200,* Selden Society, Supplementary Series 8 (London, 1990), p. xli; cf. Linda Fowler-Magerl, *Repertorium zur Frühzeit der gelehrten Rechte. Ordo iudiciorum vel ordo iudiciarius: Begriff und Literaturgattung,* Ius Commune: Veröffentlichungen des Max-Planck-Instituts für Europäische Rechtsgeschichte, Frankfurt am Main, Texte und Monographien, 19 (Frankfurt am Main, 1984), pp. 65ff.

17. Stephan Kuttner, "The Revival of Jurisprudence," in *Renaissance and Renewal in the Twelfth Century,* ed. Robert L. Benson and Giles Constable (Cambridge, MA, 1982), pp. 299–323; Richard H. Helmholz, "Canonists and Standards of Impartiality for Papal Judges Delegate," in Helmholz, *Canon Law and the Law of England* (London, 1987), pp. 21–39; Stanley Chodorow, "Dishonest Litigation in the Church Courts," in *Law, Church and Society: Essays in Honor of Stephan Kuttner,* ed. Kenneth Pennington and Robert Somerville (Philadelphia, 1977), pp. 187–206.

undermined and open to criticism and review if their subjects found them wanting in due process or in the law itself. But the judges delegate were not simply passive agents of papal authority. Their judgments helped to shape the law in their own regions; their questions to the *curia* elicited definitions on difficult or contentious points of law or procedure; and the collections of decretals compiled in the households of notable English judges delegate provided the sources from which the new decretal law of the entire Latin Church derived.

The decretal *Quamvis simus,* addressed by Alexander III to bishop Richard of Winchester in 1177, affords a perfect example both of papal responses to multiple consultations on points of principle and procedure, and their dismemberment and incorporation in professional collections. The letter deals with eight points, later distributed according to subject matter in the systematic collections. In the primitive Bridlington collection (*ex* 1181), the letter is still preserved as an entity under the general rubric *Quot iudicibus et in quibus delegatus possit delegare,* but it is subdivided into eight distinct topics, each with its individual rubric. The first six deal with judges delegate and the judicial process, as briefly summarized here:

(a) *Delegatus condelegato causam delegare potest etiam si hoc in litteris non apponatur, sed non appellatione remota:* a delegate can sub-delegate to one or more others, to hear and resolve the matter at issue, or to hear statements and take evidence, while reserving judgment to himself. Everything is subject to his will and satisfaction, though he cannot delegate a case *appellatione postposita,* even if it was commissioned to him *appellatione remota*—without leave of appeal. And if a case is commissioned to two judges, one of them can commit judgment to his colleague or to another, even if the commission does not state that one can proceed without the other.

(b) *Si quis crimen obicit testi, qui contra eum producitur:* if anyone imputes a crime against witnesses brought against him, of such a nature that he could prevent their bearing witness in a civil case, his objection shall be heard; and if it can be proved in civil process, the witnesses cannot be admitted to give testimony against him, but neither should they be punished because of it.

(c) *Inhibita appellatione, deferendum est appellationi facte ex incidenti questione, sine qua principalis causa non poterit terminari:* the question is: should a case be left undecided, when appeal has been made on an incidental question, even though the principal matter was commissioned without leave of appeal? The pope replies that, if the question arising is such that the principal issue cannot be decided without it, the hearing of the whole case should be intermitted in deference to the appeal, until the superior judge, to whom appeal was made, decides otherwise about the whole affair—*aliter de tota causa disponat.*

(d) *Si diverse littere impetrantur diversis iudicibus, priores preiudicant:* if a litigant secures letters of commission from the apostolic see, and his adversary has the same matter commissioned to other judges, the former should proceed to hearing and settlement, unless the later letters mention the earlier commission. Otherwise, the later letters have no force of law. But if the earlier commission is mentioned in the later, the case is thereby removed from the earlier judges, since the later were not obtained by fraud—*non sint tacita veritate impetrate*. Moreover, if a case is commissioned in the presence and with the assent of the parties, of whom one has the case later committed to another, concealing the earlier commission and not informing his adversary, the party guilty of such deceit and fraud should be condemned to pay the expenses thereby incurred by his opponent.

(e) *Nullus cogitur ad ferendum testimonium:* the Roman Church has not been accustomed (*minime consuevit*) to compel anyone to bear witness to the truth.

(f) *Delegatus potest sententiam executioni mandare, si ordinarius noluerit:* if the diocesan bishop neglects to mandate execution of the sentence imposed by the judge delegate, the latter, by virtue of his delegation by the Roman pontiff, has full power to order its execution.[18]

This letter is of exceptional interest, not only for the precise and technical nature of its juridical instructions and for the light it throws on the process of judicial consultation between bishops and the papal curia, but also for the identity of its recipient. The bishop of Winchester, who had no doubt submitted a list of questions arising from the conduct of delegated jurisdiction, was none other than Richard of Ilchester, who had been foremost among Henry II's secular administrators during and after the Becket dispute, and was engaged in the royal administration of Normandy when he received it.[19] Here is an example of a 'royalist bishop' actively participating in the advancement of canon law in England and beyond. *Quamvis simus* soon entered the canonical tradition: after its appearance in the Bridlington Collection, it appears dismembered in seven parts in the *Appendix* and *Bamberg* collections,[20] and in nine segments in Bernard of

18. Oxford, Bodleian MS 357, fol. 85v (Bridl. 23). For the component parts, cf. *JL* 14156 (parts a, b, d–f, h), 14152 (part c), 14154 (part g). Full details of all decretal collections cited in this essay, their manuscripts, printed analyses and relevant studies are provided in *Decretales ineditae saeculi xii* (cf. n. 30, below).

19. With his former colleagues in the royal administation, John of Oxford and Geoffrey Ridel, he was elected bishop in 1173, and consecrated in 1174: Charles Duggan, "Richard of Ilchester, Royal Servant and Bishop," *Transactions of the Royal Historical Society*, 5th Series, 16 (1965), 1–21, esp. pp. 16–20.

20. The parts are distributed in *Appendix* and *Bambergensis* as follows (in each case, two of the original chapters appear as one): *Appendix* (Mansi, 22: 248–453, 7.8, 8.6, 10.31, 7.9, 8.6, 7.10, 15.6, 39.2); *Bambergensis* (Walter Deeters, *Die Bambergensisgruppe der Dekretalensammlungen des 12. Jhdts.*: Inaugural Dissertation . . . der Philos. Fakultät der Rheinischen Friedrich Wilhelms-Universität [Bonn 1956]: 33.8, 39.5, 42.31, 33.9, 39.5, 33.10, 44.4, 22.1). Cf. Charles

Pavia's *Compilatio prima*,[21] from which four segments were received into the *Decretales* of 1234.[22] In this way the responses to questions raised by one local ecclesiastic came to form part of the general law promulgated by Gregory IX.

The Making of the "New Law": Cases

The canonical developments of the mid-twelfth century were such that very few bishops were unaffected by them. Whether actively or passively engaged in the process, ecclesiastical administrators of all kinds were drawn into the new legal structure as judges or litigants, and a knowledge of the law and expertise in its procedures became essential accomplishments. Not all bishops were trained lawyers, but most found it necessary to recruit *iuris periti* to their households. Archbishop Roger of York, for example, employed the eminent Roman lawyer Vacarius, who played a leading role in the advancement of Roman Law in England. Vacarius himself appears in decretal letters and in litigation.[23]

More than fifty decretals to Roger survive in the collections, their interests ranging from dynastic questions in the English state to the Canterbury-York dispute for primacy in the English Church; the status and rights of churches, clerics, and religious; marriage disputes involving English magnates; religious orders and their houses; and judicial and procedural questions.[24] The York decretals show very clearly the juridically complex and sophisticated nature of the procedures involved in the discharge of papal mandates. The commission *Cum iam pridem* to arch-

---

Duggan, "English Canonists and the *Appendix Concilii Lateranensis*, with an Analysis of the St. John's, Cambridge, MS 148," *Traditio* 18 (1962), 459–68; repr. in Duggan, *Canon Law in Medieval England: The Becket Dispute and Decretal Collections* (London, 1982), no. 8.

21. *1 Comp.* (= *Quinque compilationes antiquae nec non collectio canonum Lipsiensis*, ed. Emil Friedberg [Leipzig, 1882; repr. Graz, 1956], pp. 1–65), 1.21.7, 2.13.13, 2.20.34, 1.2.3, 2.13.13 + 2.14.1, 1.21.8, 3.33.10, 1.20.4.

22. *Corpus iuris canonici*, 2 (cited as *X*), 1.29.6, 1.3.3, 2.38.8, 1.28.3. For this tradition, see below, pp. 184–85. Sections of the letter were entered under three different numbers in Jaffé's *Regesta*, nos. 14156 + 14152 + 14154.

23. Cf. Peter Stein, "Vacarius and the Civil Law," in Stein, *The Character and Influence of the Roman Civil Law: Historical Essays* (London, Hambledon Press, 1988), pp. 167–85; Stein, "Vacarius and the Civil Law in England" and "The Liber pauperum," in de Zulueta and Stein, *Roman Law in England*, pp. xxii–vii and xxviii–xxxvii. Cf. Cheney, *Roger, Bishop of Worcester*, pp. 361–62 n. 87; and below, p. 189 n. 50.

24. Charles Duggan, "Decretals of Alexander III to England," *Miscellanea Rolando Bandinelli, Papa Alessandro III*, ed. Filippo Liotta (Siena, 1986), pp. 85–151.

bishop Roger, Bartholomew of Exeter, and the abbot of Ford (or Rufford) records charges against the prior of Bridlington on grounds of immorality and uncanonical election. The case had been commissioned previously to the bishop of Durham and the abbot of Fountains, who exonerated the prior and reported back to the pope. But the charges were later repeated in person to the pope by canon Walter, who alleged that the judges had not conducted the case in due legal form, and listed various other malpractices. Unwilling to leave the matter in silence or re-open the case once settled, the pope re-commissioned the case with a long and complex series of instructions, ordered the new judges to discover how the earlier judges had proceeded, and laid down the following alternatives:

> (a) If they find that the judges absolved the prior before hearing the brothers, they must ensure that Walter's expenses are paid by the church, hear the case in all the matters mentioned and reach a fair judgment.
>
> (b) If they find that the judges received the canons' oath and then absolved the prior, that decision is upheld.
>
> (c) If the prior excommunicated any of the canons after Walter placed them under the protection of the Roman Church and the pope, the sentence is not to hold, unless the prior was absolved by the judges (as they reported to the pope).
>
> (d) If the prior establishes his case, the judges must strictly forbid him to use that opportunity to molest or oppress any of the brothers, and ensure that Walter and his associates remain in peace, unless they have presumed to trouble him again, after he was lawfully absolved.
>
> (e) If the prior refuses to answer or submit to their judgment, they are to suspend him by apostolic authority and forbid the brethren to obey him.
>
> (f) And if the prior wishes to appeal, the judges will hear all the charges and exceptions, hear witnesses, place their sworn testimony under seal, send them to the pope, and fix a term for both parties to appear before him. Sufficient expenses are to be provided from the church for the canons to appear against the prior.[25]

The Bridlington case records appeals by a religious community against their superior. But while the right of appeal could be a protection for the oppressed, it could be used also to evade legitimate authority. In a clear

25. Duggan, "Decretals of Alexander III," p. 123: *WH* (= number assigned by Walter Holtzmann in his projected *Regesta decretalium saeculi XII,* in process of completion by Stanley Chodorow and Charles Duggan), 250; *JL* (= Jaffé, *Regesta Pontificum Romanorum ad annum 1198* 13891, 1161–81 (? 1174–80); pd *Claustr.* (= Ferdinand Schönsteiner, "Die Collectio Claustroneoburgensis," *Jahrbuch des Stiftes Klosterneuburg* ii [1909], 1–154), p. 205; cf. Walter Ullmann, "A Forgotten Dispute at Bridlington and its Canonistic Setting," *Yorkshire Archaeological Journal* 148 (1951), 469–73.

and brief directive, *Relatum est auribus,* the pope condemned in general terms the abuse of the process by persons in the York diocese who launch an appeal to evade the archbishop's jurisdiction, when they have in fact no complaint.[26] The remedy of appeal was devised to relieve the oppressed—*ad oppressorum levamen est inventum.* Therefore, if any of Roger's subjects wish to appeal on any matter, he must compel them by apostolic authority to prosecute their appeal within a year, in person or through a suitable representative, or stand to his judgment, unless they can show clear and reasonable cause for failing to do so. Elsewhere, in *Proposuit nobis G.,* the pope ruled that an appeal in one case does not make the appellant less answerable in others in which an appeal has not been made. But, since the judge seems suspect to the appellant, he should not compel the latter to answer in other cases while the first is still pending, except for a crime so grave and manifest that he may rightly be condemned ipso facto.[27] Again, in *Super eo quod,* in reply to Roger's enquiry about the respect due to an appeal launched by one party in fear of a report that his adversary had secured papal letters, the pope ruled that deference should not be paid to an appeal seemingly launched to frustrate the legal process.[28] And the problem of forgery[29] was the subject of *Si quis obiciat,* a brief fragment which states that if a litigant alleges forgery and wishes to prove it, but claims that his proofs are overseas, he should be allowed deferment, and he can appeal, if it is refused, even if appeal was forbidden on the principal question.[30]

The Making of the "New Law": Decretal Collections

These few examples merely suggest the comprehensive range of the delegates' jurisdiction, and record their initiative in seeking authoritative papal

26. Duggan, "Decretals of Alexander III," p. 141: *WH* 874, *JL*—, 1159–81; pd *Claustr.,* p. 194.

27. Duggan, "Decretals of Alexander III," p. 136: *WH* 749, *JL* 14350, 1159–81; pd *X,* 2.28.4.

28. Duggan, "Decretals of Alexander III," p. 145: *WH* 1009, *JL* 14163, 1159–81; pd *2 Comp., Quinque compilationes antiquae,* p. 77 and Mansi, 21: 1097.

29. Cf. Charles Duggan, "*Improba pestis falsitatis:* Forgeries and the Problem of Forgery in Twelfth Century Decretal Collections (With Special References to English Cases)," in *Fälschungen im Mittelalter,* ed. Horst Fuhrmann, *MGH, Schriften* 33/2 (Hanover, 1988), pp. 319–61.

30. *Si quis obiciat:* Duggan, "Decretals of Alexander III," p. 142: *WH* 914, *JL*—, 1164–81, pd *Decretales ineditae* (= *Decretales ineditae saeculi XII,* ed. et rev. Stanley Chodorow and Charles Duggan, from the papers of Walther Holtzmann, Monumenta Iuris Canonici, Series B: Corpus Collectionum, 4 [Città del Vaticano, 1982]), pp. 128–29 no. 74. The fragment is probably a re-wording of an excerpt from *In eminenti,* to Roger of York: *WH* 552, *JL* 14350, 1164–81, pd. *1 Comp.* 2.20.40.

instructions, definitions, and decisions, thus actively sharing in the judicial process. But the English judges delegate went an important stage further, and played a creative and dominant role in the formation of the first post-Gratian decretal collections. These early collections were essentially a reflection of judge-delegate activity, both recording the commissions of the judges and providing a corpus of precedents for their successors. The first traces of their activities can be seen in the many individual texts of all kinds inserted by canonists in Gratian manuscripts—the so-called *paleae,* and the creation of early *Dekretanhänge,* or appendices to Gratian, which were compiled as small independent supplements to the *Decretum.*

The practical and professional purpose of these early additions is evident. The earliest extant primitive collection is the short *Wigorniensis altera,* composed in the household of Roger of Worcester, one of the most famous judges delegate of Alexander III's pontificate. At least three of its texts are found also in earlier *Dekretanhänge,* and only one is dated *post* 1174.[31] From the same source came the crucially important Worcester collection itself (*Wigorniensis,* 1181).[32] No decretal collection records more clearly the appointment, functions and procedures of judges delegate in the period. It is a large, professionally organized compilation of 274 numbered items, arranged by subject matter in seven books, and provided with numerous rubrics, summarizing the essential points of canonical interest in the subsections of the longer decretals. It lacks only the principle of decretal dissection to make it fully systematic, but the apparatus of rubrics compensates for that deficiency. The first four books deal respectively with marriage questions, the status and privileges of religious, of the clergy, and of churches. Of exceptional significance are the last three books, directed specifically to the work of judges delegate, the judicial process, appeals, and "instruction of judges in diverse cases," as their titles and contents make clear:

31. Duggan, *Twelfth-Century Decretal Collections,* pp. 69–71; analysis, pp. 152–154 and plate I: an emended analysis of the collection is in preparation.

32. Hans-Eberhard Lohmann, "Die Collectio Wigorniensis (Collectio Londinensis Regia): Ein Beitrag zur Quellengeschichte des kanonischen Rechts im 12. Jahrhundert," *ZRG KanAbt.* 22 (1933), 35–187. For Holtzmann's classification of decretal collections into primitive and systematic categories, see *Studies in the Collections of Twelfth-Century Decretals,* from the papers of Walther Holtzmann, ed. Christopher R. Cheney and Mary G. Cheney, Monumenta Iuris Canonici, Series B: Corpus collectionum, 3 (Città del Vaticano, 1979), pp. xxxi–xxxii. Following the work of Jacoba Hanenburg ("Decretals and Decretal Collections in the Second Half of the Twelfth-Century," *Tijdschrift voor Rechtsgeschiedenis* 34 [1966], 522–99, esp. pp. 591–92) and Peter Landau ("Die Entstehung der systematischen Dekretalensammlungen und die europäische Kanonistik des 12. Jahrhunderts," *ZRG KanAbt.* 65 [1979]), 120–48), however, the "Worcester" group, which Holtzmann called primitive, has been re-classified as systematic, because its members are professional works, devised in books according to subject matter.

Book V. de casibus, in quibus non est deferendum appellationibus (13 chapters).
Book VI. de casibus, in quibus est deferendum appellationibus, etiam si causa sit appellatione remota commissa (4 chapters).
Book VII. ad informandum iudices in diversis casibus quandoque emergentibus (81 chapters).[33]

The Worcester collection was the work of experienced canonists in the circles of the two most famous judges delegate of the period, Bartholomew of Exeter and Roger of Worcester, together with their familiar colleagues Baldwin of Ford, Adam of Evesham,[34] Robert of Kenilworth, and others. Baldwin succeeded Roger at Worcester and archbishop Richard at Canterbury, and these successive stages of his promotion are reflected by the insertion of later decretals to him in these offices, entered by different hands in the manuscript volume. It was from collections of this kind, and especially from the "Worcester" tradition itself, that the later systematic traditions evolved. And, since the decretals dealt with actual cases or answered questions on which bishops and judges required authoritative definitions, they constituted a source of living law, shaped to the pressures and preoccupations of contemporary society. In the execution of their office the papal judges delegate controlled the direction of the evolving law by their handling of the cases, the questions of principle and procedure which they raised, the manner in which they recorded the latest definitions and decisions, and in all such practical and professional ways.

The importance of the new law was quickly recognized in Bologna, where the doctors of the schools sought the latest decretals to supplement their teaching in precisely the same way that professors in law schools today gather and cite the latest laws in their treatment of legislation and judicial decision. But although decretal letters were sent to all parts of the Church, the initiatives taken by English judges delegate in the 1160s and 1170s proved decisive in the formation and consolidation of the new law. The sources from which the Worcester collection (*Wigorniensis*) was compiled were also the seed bed from which the later fully systematic collections were primarily made, first in the *Appendix concilii Lateranensis*[35] assembled in

33. Ibid., pp. 119–23, 123–24, and 125–49.

34. On commissions to Adam of Evesham, and a final report by Adam to the pope, see Katherine Christensen, "'Rescriptum auctoritatis vestre': a judge-delegate's report to pope Alexander III," in *The Two Laws: Studies in Medieval legal history dedicated to Stephan Kuttner,* ed. Laurent Mayali and Stephanie A. J. Tibbetts, Studies in Medieval and Early Modern Canon Law, 1 (Washington DC, 1990), pp. 40–54.

35. So called because the decretals are appended to a copy of the decrees of the Third Lateran Council of 1179 in some early manuscripts.

Oxford or Lincoln from 1184, and then in the closely-related *Bambergensis*,[36] made at Tours, also from 1184. Both compilations were associated with the professional teaching of canon law in the Angevin Empire, respectively in England and Touraine, and mark the reception of the latest decretal law into the academic tradition. From these two sources, the English material was received by the great Bolognese canonist Bernard of Pavia, whose "Leipzig" collection (*post* 1185) formed the basis of his *Compilatio prima* (*post* 1188), which established the form and structure of later collections of decretal law.[37] Bernard's was the first of the "five ancient collections," of which two (Peter of Benevento's *Compilatio tertia* and Tancred's *Compilatio quinta*) were promulgated by popes Innocent III and Honorius III in 1210 and 1226 respectively.[38] From these momentous achievements, it was but a small step to the compilation by Raymund of Peñafort, under papal auspices, of the *Liber Extra* or *Decretales* of Gregory IX in 1234.[39] With characteristic insight, Maitland recognized long ago the essential links in this chain:

> One small step will be taken by Innocent III., another small step by Honorius III., . . . and then Gregory IX. will issue a code of some two thousand sections. The Englishmen who gave Alexander III. the opportunity for issuing a hundred and eighty decretals of permanent importance contributed an ample share to the plentitude of power.[40]

In the state of historical knowledge at that time, Maitland could not know the precise nature of the crucially creative role of the English judges delegate and the canonists in their circles in the genesis of post-Gratian decretal collections, and through them their influence on the later official collections. Indeed, as noted already, the entire professional transmission of the decretals was influenced by the English judges and collectors. In Holtzmann's statistical survey,[41] the total number of decretals in all known collections for the period from 1145 to 1198 was 1055, of which 509 were received in England and 33 in the English king's continental lands; 199 were

36. So called because the manuscript survived in the Staatsbibliothek in Bamberg.

37. Divided into five books, each devoted to a specific topic: *iudex, iudicium, clerus, connubium, crimen*. Indeed, Bernard's earlier collection, *Parisiensis secunda* (the first extant systematic collection, c. 1177–78) had already revealed the influence of the English primitive collections.

38. The "Leipzig" collection and the "five ancient compilations" (*prima, secunda, tertia, quarta,* and *quinta*) are analysed in Friedberg, *Quinque compilationes antiquae*.

39. ed. Friedberg, *Corpus Iuris canonici*, 2.

40. Maitland, *Roman Canon Law*, p. 130.

41. Walther Holtzmann, "Über eine Ausgabe der päpstlichen Dekretalen des 12. Jahrhunderts," *Nachrichten Akad. Göttingen* (1945), 15–36, esp. p. 34 Anh. 1.

received in Italy, including the Norman territories in the south; 133 in the French king's lands; 13 in Germany; and a total of only 7 in Scotland and Ireland.[42] Although these statistics now need minor modifications, they remain valid in their broad implications. The predominance of English decretals in the collections was a consequence not simply of the admittedly large number of decretals received in England, but far more significantly of the creative role of the English judges delegate.

The Judge Delegate's Jurisdiction

The delegate's jurisdiction extended to every level and branch of Western Christian society, from kings, prelates, and magnates, to monastic and religious communities, to simple clerks, and lay men and women. In the course of the great rebellion of 1173–74, for example, King Henry II of England was threatened with interdict if he failed to restore the wife and fiancée respectively of his two eldest sons, Henry and Richard. Margaret and Alice, daughters of Louis VII of France, had been detained by Henry II in retaliation for his sons' involvement in the revolt. Following the complaint of the French king, Alexander III sent the decretal *Non est vobis* to the entire clerical order in the English king's lands, both in England and on the continent, announcing that he had commissioned the archbishop of Tarantaise, the bishop of Clermont, and the prior of Chartreuse (or the prior of Mont Dieu) to admonish the English king to restore Margaret and Alice within forty days of receiving the papal letter.[43] If he failed to do so, divine office should be suspended in the provinces in which they were detained or to which transferred, except for the baptism of infants and penance for the dying, until they were restored. The pope ordered the recipients to induce the king to comply, or to enforce the sentence with-

42. The relatively small number of decretals to French recipients in the collections is *prima facie* surprising, in view of the close relations between the French Church and the Roman curia, notably during the period of Alexander's exile in France from early April 1162 until September 1165, in the course of which he summoned a council at Tours in 1163, and the papal curia functioned at Sens, 1163–65. Indeed, the non-canonical archives in France for the period are rich in records of papal *privilegia*, letters of confirmation of rights, and other letters, many explicitly recording litigation in the presence of papal judges delegate, whose commissions have not survived. In contrast, the almost total absence of decretals to German recipients (only three from Alexander III), in the collections, is easily explained by the emperor's support for a series of anti-popes, following Alexander's election in 1159, until his reconciliation with Frederick I at Venice in 1177, a crucial and formative period in the origin and evolution of decretal collections.

43. *WH* 669, *JL* 12248, 1173 *ex.*

out contradiction or appeal. In the event, Henry II survived the rebellion with his authority enhanced, and it is unlikely that the commissioners—all residents of Henry's continental lands—were able to execute the mandate. The French king's daughters were still in King Henry's company when he returned to England in 1174.[44] Nevertheless, the principle that interdict might be imposed on a whole province for one person's offence was noted in a marginal comment in one English decretal collection—*Ecce quod pro delicto unius tota terra interdicitur*[45]—and a truncated version of the letter was transmitted through the systematic collections from *Bambergensis* to the *Decretales,*[46] no doubt because of the important disciplinary principle involved.

At the lower end of the scale, the "poor clerk" R. took his tearful complaint in person to pope Lucius III at Verona in 1184—*Constitutus in presentia nostra R. pauper clericus lacrimabili conquestione monstravit. . . .* He had obtained the church of Ham[47] in due canonical order, through presentation by the patron and institution by the diocesan bishop, but the clerk H. (or G.), through concealment of the truth, secured papal letters to the bishop of Ely and the abbot of Crowland, who summoned R. to appear before them in a place several days' journey from his church. When his adversary claimed that he had himself been presented to the church first, and the judges unjustly harassed R. with frequent and peremptory citations and many labors and expenses, the latter appealed to the pope. The distinguished canonist bishop Bartholomew of Exeter supported R.'s claims, and assured the pope of their truthfulness, recording that he had himself instituted R. first, and that the latter had been excessively burdened by the earlier judges. The pope therefore ordered the abbot of Ford (Baldwin, later bishop of Worcester and archbishop of Canterbury) and the archdea-

44. For relevant details, cf. Charles Duggan, "English secular magnates in the decretal collections," *Monumenta Iuris Canonici,* Series C, Subsidia, 9 (1992), pp. 595–96.

45. Oxford, Bodleian MS, Tanner 8, p. 696b; cf. Walther Holtzmann, "Die Dekretalensammlungen des 12. Jahrhunderts, I: Die Sammlung Tanner," *Festschrift zur Feier des 200jährigen Bestehens der Akad. der Wissenschaften in Göttingen, phil.-hist. Klasse* (1951), 7.5.20, p. 138.

46. Bamb. 50.34; *X,* 4.1.11. For the full text, derived from a manuscript of St-Victor, in Paris, see André Duchesne, *Historiae Francorum Scriptores* 4 (Paris, 1641) 769, Mansi, 21: 1032, *PL,* 200: 965.

47. *WH* 180, *JL*—, 1184. Pd in Heinrich Singer, "Neue Beiträge über die Dekretalensammlungen vor und nach Bernhard von Pavia," *Sitzungsberichte der Kais. Akad. der Wissenschaften in Wien,* phil.-hist. Kl., 171.1 (1913), 233. Holtzmann considered the place-name of the church in question so corruptly transmitted (ham., ham., n.) that an accurate identification was unlikely, but a very probable location is that of the church of St Pancras in Ham, within the limits of modern Plymouth, almost on the border of Devon and Cornwall, the respective areas of jurisdiction of the archdeacons of Totnes (Devon) and Cornwall in the decretal.

cons of Totnes and Cornwall to restore everything as it was before his adversary's appeal. If they determine that R. was canonically instituted first—as indeed was the case, on the evidence of his own statement and that of the bishop—they are to restrain his adversary from troubling him, impose perpetual silence on the former in respect of the church, and set moderate expenses, to be paid to R. No letters may be effective in prejudice of this decision.

The judges perhaps had little difficulty in executing this mandate, but sometimes the cases presented for their judgment involved very powerful persons and institutions. The stages of a protracted dispute between archbishop Roger of York and the prior and canons of the Augustinian house at Guisborough in Yorkshire are recorded in two decretals of Alexander III and in archival records. The earlier letter, *Dilecti filii nostri,* is of interest for its meticulous instructions to the judges delegate, the bishop of Exeter and the dean of Lincoln. The prior and canons of Guisborough had complained that Roger had suspended the prior after appeal, interdicted their churches, and declared the canons excommunicate if they obeyed the prior. The pope ordered the judges to summon the parties within thirty days when requested to do so. If they found the facts as stated, they must publicly declare that the prior and canons were not bound by the archbishop's sentence, "because if the matter so appeared to us, we would certainly have done the same"—*quia, si nobis constaret, nos hoc idem proculdubio fecissemus.* They must make a full and careful report to the pope, and admonish those who know the truth to tell it and not fail to bear witness through fear or favor of the archbishop or anyone else. The canons had also complained that the archbishop oppressed their vicars and clerics with undue exactions, and granted their churches to his relations. All of this was clearly contrary to the canons and damaging to his reputation. The judges must investigate the truth of the charges. If they find the facts as stated, such grants must be revoked by papal authority, unless the canons maliciously delayed to make appointments; the churches must be restored to the prior and canons, and their vicars and clerics must keep their oaths, unless unjustly extorted by the prior. The judges must order the archbishop to refrain from undue oppressions and exactions, and inform the pope of the truth of all these matters without delay. With unusual emphasis and directness, the pope mandated the judges to ensure that the case was not unduly prolonged by over-refined examination, as many judges did—*sicut a multis fieri solet.* The simple and pure fact itself must be investigated, according to the form of the canons and the institutes of the fathers. If the archbishop were unwilling to appear or obey their judgment, the judges should proceed with the affair, unless he had a canonical excuse.[48]

But in a later commission, *Ex transmissa nobis conquestione,*[49] to bishop John of Chichester and the abbots of Ford and Evesham, the pope replied to a complaint by the prior and canons that, after a papal sentence in their favour concerning the church of Kirklevington, the archbishop had placed the clerk W. de Ridale in their chapel after appeal to the pope and without their knowledge, excommunicated two of the canons, without summons, conviction, or confession, and finally deposed and excommunicated the prior, interdicted divine office for the whole convent unless they showed him obedience and reverence, interdicted their churches, and excommunicated the chaplains who sang in their churches and the parishioners if they paid tithes or oblations to the canons. The pope could not overlook such serious matters. The judges must summon the parties, diligently investigate the matter, *omni gratia et favore postponente.* If the charges brought by the canons are proved, the judges must correct what the archbishop has done after appeal, in respect of deposition, excommunication and interdict, tithes, oblations, and other rights. The judges must forbid the archbishop to harm or oppress the prior and canons in their persons or property.

This case had in fact arisen from Roger of York's attempts to circumvent the grant of Kirklevington and its chapels made to Guisborough Priory by Robert de Brus by appointing his own nominees. The decretals cited here are eloquent witness to his aggressive and intimidating tactics. In the event, an unsatisfactory compromise was worked out in 1180 in the presence of the papal legate Alexius, who had come to Britain to settle, among other things, the even more weighty question of the status of the see of St Andrew's (over which Roger also claimed jurisdiction).[50]

48. *Papal Decretals Relating to the Diocese of Lincoln in the Twelfth Century,* ed. Walther Holtzmann and Eric W. Kemp, Lincoln Record Society 47 (Hereford, 1954), pp. 30–33 at p. 30: ". . . provisuri attentius, ne ita subtiliter, sicut a multis fieri solet, cuiusmodi actio intendatur, inquiratis sed simpliciter et pure factum ipsum et rei veritatem secundum formam canonum et sanctorum patrum instituta investigetis."

49. *Cartularium prioratus de Gyseburne,* ed. W. Brown, Surtees Society 89 (1899), 2: 81 no. 718; cf. *Papsturkunden in England,* 1. ed. Walther Holtzmann, Abhandlungen der Akademie der Wissenschaften zu Göttingen, phil.-hist. Klasse, New Ser. 25 (Berlin, 1930), pp. 443–45 no. 173.

50. I am indebted to Dr. Marie Lovat for advice on the closing stages of this tortuous litigation. The whole process of this and other related cases will be treated in her forthcoming edition of the *York Acta*; meanwhile, cf. *Cartularium de Gyseburne* 2: 46–49 nos 182–84. The archbishop secured a life interest in Kirklevington. See also Raymonde Foreville, *L'Église et la royauté en Angleterre sous Henri II Plantagenet* (Paris, 1943), p. 472. It is a matter of some interest that the compromise was witnessed by Masters Vacarius and Ambrose, both eminent Roman lawyers, among others.

At the other end of the country, another powerful Augustinian house was engaged in a long and acrimonious dispute with the knight Joel of Vautort and his nephew over the *ius patronatus* of the church of Sutton.[51] Two decretals *Ex parte nobilis* and *Cum nuntius canonicorum* record the successive stages in the litigation, and the judges' final settlement is recorded in the Plympton cartulary. According to Joel's report, the parties were brought before the diocesan bishop (Bartholomew of Exeter), but, believing himself oppressed, Joel placed himself and his lands under the protection of St Peter and the pope. Thereupon the bishop allegedly placed all the churches in Joel's lands under interdict, after appeal—which the pope can scarcely believe—with the result that the bodies of parishioners, who had meanwhile died, remained unburied. In *Ex parte nobilis,* the pope ordered archbishop Richard of Canterbury to summon the parties and investigate the matter. If he found that interdict was imposed after appeal, he should publicly declare the sentence void and order the bodies to be buried, unless they were of persons excommunicated or interdicted individually—*nominatim*. Then he should hear the case and reach a judicial verdict, notwithstanding any papal letters impeding truth and justice. If he found that the churches were interdicted before appeal, he should secure sufficient surety from Joel to accept his judgment, then release the churches from the sentence, notwithstanding any contradiction or appeal, and proceed to hear all aspects of the case and bring it to a conclusion, without leave of appeal.

The matter was not immediately resolved, as the commission *Cum nuntius canonicorum* to archbishop Richard of Canterbury and bishop Roger of Worcester makes clear. A messenger from each side appeared in the pope's presence—*in nostra essent presentia constituti*. The canons' messenger produced a copy of a charter (*rescriptum*), which the former bishop of Exeter, William Warelwast, had allegedly granted in their favor against the claims of Reginald, Joel's grandfather. The knight's messenger asserted, in contrast, that he and his predecessors had freely held the right of patronage at that time, that it lawfully belonged to him, and disclaimed all previous knowledge of the document now produced. Since neither side had come prepared to pursue the case, the pope could not fittingly bring it to a conclusion, and therefore he committed it to Richard and Roger, confident in their prudence and honesty. They should summon the parties, and, if authentic letters established that the church was adjudged to the canons, they

51. Now St. Andrew's in Plymouth.

should impose perpetual silence on Joel in respect of it, and confirm the sentence of interdict placed on his lands by bishop Bartholomew because of the loss and injury sustained by the canons. If the knight did not comply with these orders, they should excommunicate him, notwithstanding any letters secured by concealment of the truth. The outcome of the dispute is not recorded in the decretal collections, but the judges' notification of settlement survives among extracts from a lost Plympton cartulary in a seventeenth-century manuscript. The notification rehearses the details of the case, with the additional note that Joel informed the pope that the *ius patronatus* of the church belonged to him and his nephew, whose guardian he was. After the fourth peremptory edict, Joel failed to appear in response to their summons and was judged contumacious. The judges examined authentic letters and seals with the advice of bishop Bartholomew, and by papal authority imposed silence on Joel and those who acted in his name in this matter.[52]

The Guisborough-York and Plympton-Vautort cases exemplify the sophistication and complexity of ecclesiastical cases in the period and the ability of judges delegate to summon very powerful persons before their tribunals. But the delegate's jurisdiction stretched even beyond the confines of the kingdom in which a case was brought. In November–December 1181, pope Lucius III sent letters respectively to John of Oxford, bishop of Norwich, and archbishop Richard of Canterbury, both on behalf of the plaintiff Master Stephen of Blois, concerning sureties which he had given respectively for Master G. de Insula and Master Peter of Blois, the archbishop's chancellor at the time of the Lateran Council (March, 1179),[53] which the bishop of Norwich attended.[54] Stephen complained that he had guaranteed payment of debts incurred by G. de Insula on his departure from Bologna—*in recessu suo a Bononia*—and by Master Stephen. Neither had paid the debt, meanwhile much augmented, and Stephen was harassed by the creditors. The pope mandated the recipient in each case to compel the debtor to release Stephen from the bond if the charges were confirmed; if the debtor denied the debt or interest, he should be compelled to swear

52. For a full discussion of the texts, and the background to the case, see *Decretales ineditae*, pp. 73–77 no 43a; cf. also Cheney, *Roger, Bishop of Worcester*, pp. 95, 143–44, 186, 283–84, 334–35 and 344.

53. R. W. Southern, "Peter of Blois: a Twelfth-Century Humanist?" in Southern, *Medieval Humanism* (New York, 1970), pp. 105–32; cf. Christopher R. Cheney, *English Bishops' Chanceries, 1100–1250* (Manchester, 1950), pp. 33–35.

54. To bishop John of Norwich: *WH* 161, *JL*—, Nov.–Dec. 1181; the letter is known only from the Rochester decretal collection (*Roff.* 121); cf. now *Decretales ineditae*, pp. 113–114 no. 16. To Richard of Canterbury: *WH* 162, *JL* 14963, Nov.–Dec. 1181; transmitted to *X*, 3.22.3.

an oath, notwithstanding custom which is contrary to law—*consuetudine que legi contraria est non obstante, iuramentum calumpnie subire cogatur.* Moreover, since it would be difficult for Stephen to bring his witnesses to England, the respective commissioners (Norwich and Canterbury) should instruct the Bolognese judges to act in their place (*vice tua*), examine and thoroughly question the witnesses, and send back their sealed depositions, indicating what trust should be placed in the witnesses or depositions. If the accused disdain to appear or stand to judgment, they should be deprived of their ecclesiastical benefices, and their incomes assigned to the payment of the debts until the creditors were satisfied. This notable case involving the well-known Peter of Blois reflects the international character of the new law in a striking way. In it the guarantor of debts incurred in Italy seeks relief through an appeal to the pope, which involves collaboration between two judges in England and colleagues in Bologna, who are given the responsibility of establishing the veracity of the plaintiff's allegations. A more revealing example of the supranational character of the new law can scarcely be imagined.

By virtue of his papal commission, the judge delegate's jurisdiction extended to all levels and classes of society. The magnates in their marriages, dynastic interests, and inheritances, their patronage of churches, tithes, and numerous matters were subject to the delegates' rulings in the event of disputes arising.[55] The question of legitimacy in marriage, though essentially a spiritual and religious question, entailed vital political and material interests of property and inheritance. The pontificate of Alexander III was of crucial importance in the development of the Church's doctrine of marriage, and many of Alexander III's commissions dealt with aspects of this question.[56] But the cases themselves reflect the dynastic and political interests which lay behind the doctrinal issues: the dispute between Richard of Anstey and Mabel de Francheville related to the Sackville inheritance; that between Francus de Bohun and Ralph de Arderne recorded one stage in the prolonged Bohun-Arderne dispute which was not finally settled until 1199; and that relating to the marriage of William FitzGodric and Aubrey de Lisours related to the Lacy of Pontefract inheritance.[57] These cases and

55. Cf. Duggan, "English Secular Magnates," pp. 605–10.

56. Charles Donahue, "The Policy of Alexander III's Consent Theory of Marriage," *Proceedings of the Fourth International Congress of Medieval Canon Law, Toronto, 1972*, ed. Stephan Kuttner, Monumenta iuris canonici, Series C: Subsidia 5 (Città del Vaticano, 1976), pp. 251–281.

57. *Letters of John of Salisbury*, 1:227–237 no. 31; P. M. Barnes, "The Anstey Case" in *Medieval Miscellany for Doris Stenton*, Pipe Roll Society, New Series 36 (London, 1962), pp. 1–

numerous others were argued in the delegates' presence on the basis of the canonical and doctrinal principles underlying the Church's law of marriage, but it is evident that great political and material interests in English society were at issue.

Indeed, at the highest level, the crisis of conflicting jurisdictions in England between papal and royal power is most clearly recorded in the dispute between Henry II and Becket, focused in the sixteen clauses framed by Henry II's lawyers at Clarendon in 1164. Among these, the third clause, relating to criminous clerks, attracted most controversy then, and has continued to do so in historical debate. But the eighth clause, concerning appeals, was far more important both in doctrine and in practice, since it sought to establish an invariable procedure whereby appeals should progress from the archdeacon's court to the bishop's, and thence to that of the archbishop; if the latter proves remiss in doing justice, the case should go to the king, to be decided thereafter in the archbishop's court by the king's order in such a way that it should go no further without royal assent.[58] The clause struck at the heart of papal appellate jurisdiction, and therefore also at that of the judges delegate, and would have curtailed the most active and creative function of papal authority in the period had it been implemented. But the post-Becket settlement at Avranches in 1172 with the legates Albert and Theodwin, to the effect that appeals would go freely to the pope except that suspect appellants would swear that no harm to the king or the kingdom would result thereby, ensured that the system would develop without further hindrance.[59]

Eventually the flood of appeals was so great that Gregory VIII, the former chancellor Albert de Morra,[60] sought to curtail them. In failing health, Gregory reigned as pope less than two months (21 October to 17 December 1187), and in the general letter *Vel ex malitia* to all archbishops

24; Charles Duggan, "Equity and Compassion in Papal Marriage Decretals to England," in *Love and Marriage in the Twelfth Century*, ed. Willy Van Hoecke and Andries Welkenhuysen (Leuven, 1981), pp. 68–70; cf. Duggan, "English Secular Magnates," pp. 606–9; *Decretales ineditae*, pp. 123–125 no. 71.

58. *Councils and Synods with Other Documents Relating to the English Church, A.D. 871–1204*, ed. Dorothy Whitelock, Martin Brett and Christopher N. L. Brooke (Oxford, 1981), I/2, p. 880.

59. Ibid., pp. 942–956. For the papal confirmation of the agreement (2 Sept. 1172), see p. 955: "Appellationes autem ad sedem apostolicam factas nec impedies nec impediri permittes, quin libere fiant in ecclesiasticis causis ad Romanam ecclesiam bona fide, absque fraude et malo ingenio, et per Romanum pontificem tractentur et suum consequantur effectum: ita tamen ut si qui tibi suspecti fuerint, securitatem faciant quod malum tuum vel regni non querent"; cf. p. 949 no. 5.

60. See below, at n. 65.

and bishops, he spoke of his own physical frailty—*imbecillitate proprii corporis laborantes,* the malice of litigants, and the failure of the recipient prelates—*ex . . . defectu vestro.*[61] He could not properly attend to all matters arising, nor hear the complaints of those rushing upon him from all sides. Burdened with matters of middling importance, he could not deal with more weighty questions. He therefore set out a series of rulings to limit recourse to the curia to such issues, leaving other questions for settlement in the dioceses in which they arose. For example, cases relating to matters of less than twenty marks value should be resolved in their diocese of origin, cases should not needlessly be appealed to the curia, nor should litigants compel their adversaries to journey to the curia, when the case will be sent back to their area for settlement. Nevertheless, whenever litigants have a just cause for appeal to the pope, the prelates should not neglect to provide them with letters dimissory, containing a full record of the process. The import of the letter was in effect to buttress the traditional hierarchy of jurisdictions in the Church, and to curtail the abuse of the appellate system, while maintaining the pope's authority in appropriate cases.

Conclusion

As suggested at the outset, the development of the judge-delegate system recorded a remarkable development both in papal jurisdiction and the concept of the authority of the law itself, which could not have occurred without the interaction and collaboration of three sets of participants: the litigants who appealed, the popes who responded, and the delegated judges who received and executed their commissions. In this way, the new canon law responded to the changing circumstances of contemporary society and to the demand for clarity, authority, and consistency in the application of norms of behavior throughout the Western Church. It was an expression both of papal authority and of the authority of law itself, but it was also a reflection of a widespread desire to substitute lawful process for arbitrary judgment: to place the authority of the law above that of the person. Appeals to the Roman curia offered a relief from oppression, bias, or illegality,

61. A problem arises in the verbal transmission of this letter: the version of the phrase in the canonical tradition is *ex . . . defectu nostro* (*1 Comp.*, 2.20.47, p. 24), suggesting admission of neglect by the pope himself; the version in the archival tradition (in MSS in Alençon and Paris) is *ex . . . defectu vestro: Papsturkunden in Frankreich,* ed. Johannes Ramackers, new series 2: *Normandie* [Göttingen, 1937], p. 383).

whether real or imagined. The appellate process was itself inevitably open to abuse and exploitation, and both popes and jurists were much concerned with misuse of the system and laid down safeguards to counteract it. But when lawfully and conscientiously applied, the system afforded protection to the weak against the powerful and the reform of long-standing abuses. In the exercise of power in twelfth-century society, the rapid growth of the learned law, both Civil and canon, created new forms and procedures for defending rights and challenging existing power structures. Religious could sue their superiors, clerks could counter the biased or autocratic jurisdiction of their bishops, churches could protect their interests against oppressive lords, and monks and clergy could seek redress of grievance through an objective forum rather than the arbitrary judgment of their prelates. The extraordinary popularity of the appeals procedure is proof of its relevance to the needs of the period. The process was activated from the periphery, not from the center, by litigants not by judges. It was to some extent subversive of established hierarchies. As Alexander III expressed it, "appeals were created for the relief of oppression," and the aggrieved could invoke the process of the law to make the balance of power less uneven.

Simultaneously, these developments brought into existence a new and learned elite, and created a new profession, open to talent and less dependent on birth and privilege. Education, knowledge, and mastery of the processes and procedures of the law opened new paths to influence and status. What distinguished Romano-canonical process from the regional laws of Europe was its universality, its basis in written codes (Gratian's *Decretum* and later the Gregorian *Decretales,* and Justinian's *Corpus iuris civilis*), and its requirement of men skilled in the law for its effectiveness. It is called "the learned law" with good reason. Its practitioners were trained in its procedures and learned in its lore, and litigants were represented in the process by skilled advocates. The demands of the system filled the law schools in Bologna, Oxford, Montpellier, Paris, and elsewhere, produced a new professional elite, and its international character offered career paths across Europe. Gerard Pucelle (later bishop of Coventry) founded a school of canon law in Cologne; Master Ralph of Sarre (in Kent) taught at Reims where he later became dean;[62] the English canonists Gilbert and Alan taught at Bologna and assembled collections of Innocent III's decre-

62. Cf. Ludwig Falkenstein, "Zu Entstehungsort und Redaktor der Collectio Brugensis," *Proceedings of the Eighth International Congress of Medieval Canon Law, San Diego, University of California at La Jolla, 21–27 August 1988,* ed. Stanley Chodorow, Monumenta iuris canonici, Series C: Subsidia 9 (Città del Vaticano, 1992), pp. 117–62 at pp. 140–144, and n. 108.

tals, used by John the Welshman in compiling the *Compilatio Secunda*, the second of the "five ancient collections," from which the Gregorian *Decretales* of 1234 descended.

Appendix: The Judge Delegate Formulary *A. B. C. judices*[63]

The development of the legal learning and professional expertise of judges delegate ran parallel with that of officials in the papal chancery, in the reception of Roman law, and the adoption of Romano-canonical procedures.[64] It was most clearly marked in the Chancery by the evolution of the functions of the chancellor, the notary, the corrector of apostolic letters, and in the development of the *Audientia litterarum contradictarum* under such eminent chancellors as Albert de Morra, legate to the English king in the post-Becket settlement in 1172 and later pope Gregory VIII (1187).[65] The professional learning and its practical application by English canonists and judges are reflected in their construction and use of procedural treatises and *ordines*—notably the Anglo-Norman *Incerti auctoris ordo iudiciorum* (the pseudo-*Ulpianus de edendo*), *c.* 1140, the *Olim edebatur actio* (a post-1177 expansion), the *Ordo iudiciarius* (1182–85), attributed to a canonist in the circle of archbishop John Cumin of Dublin, and William Longchamp's *Practica legum et decretorum* (post-1183).[66] At a practical level, the exercise of the judge delegate's power is continuously recorded in the numerous commissions and their gradual incorporation in canonical collections, but its scope and application are most professionally recorded in judge-delegate formularies. No extant English formularies for the specific guidance of judges

63. For the full Latin text, see F. Donald Logan, "An Early Thirteenth-Century Formulary," *Studia Gratiana* 14 (1967): *Collectanea Stephan Kuttner*, 4: 75–87; cf. n. 67 below.

64. de Zulueta and Stein, *Roman law in England*, p. xix, "This was developed by cooperation between civil lawyers and canonists; at first the civil lawyers took the leading role, but by the end of the century the canonists had largely taken over."

65. Brigitte Meduna, *Studien zum Formular der päpstlichen Justizbriefe von Alexander III. bis Innocenz III. (1159–1216): die* non obstantibus-*Formel*, Österreichischen Akademie der Wissenschaften (Vienna, 1989), pp. 9–13, 23–39, 126–170, *et passim*.

66. de Zulueta and Stein, *Roman law in England*, pp. xl–xliii: Procedural works. For the work of the Anglo-Norman canonists, see Stephan Kuttner and Eleanor Rathbone, "Anglo-Norman Canonists of the Twelfth Century: an Introductory Study," *Traditio* 7 (1949–51), 279–358; Charles Duggan, "The Reception of Canon Law in England in the Later Twelfth Century," *Proceedings of the Second International Congress of Medieval Canon Law, Toronto, 1962*, ed. Stephan Kuttner and J. Joseph Ryan, Monumenta iuris canonici, Series C: Subsidia 1 (Città del Vaticano, 1965), pp. 359–390, esp. pp. 371–377.

delegate pre-date the closing years of the twelfth century, since no predecessor of Innocent III (1198–1216) is named in them, but it is almost certain that earlier versions preceded the first known survivals. Several copies of the group *A. B. C. judices* (briefly analysed below) are found in codices now widely dispersed in manuscript libraries.[67] The provenance of the collection is certainly English, since the custom of the English Church is mentioned in one formula—"tam quia forma rescripti, licet consonet canonibus, tamen consueto cursui et Anglicane ecclesie consuetudini refragatur,"[68] but the extant versions record variants and additions to a common stock—manuscripts in the Vatican and at Montecassino, for instance, include additions of Bolognese material, in evidence of the expansion of an English archetype from Italian sources.

The formulary, briefly summarized below, contains a series of standard letters relating to a range of possible stages in a hypothetical action between two parties, variously identified, concerning title to a certain church, which has been delegated by the pope (identified as "Innocent" in forms 1,14 and 15) to the judges A., B., and C.

1. *Form of the first citation on receipt of the papal mandate*. The judges A. B. C. to the rector T. of a certain church: on receipt of the mandate, the judges set a time and place for the rector of the church in question to appear before them.

2. *Form of the second citation, the first peremptory summons*. The judges to the defendant: on his failure to appear or send a suitable *responsalis*, the judges issue a second citation, the first peremptory.

3. *Form of excuse*. The clerk N. to the judges A. B. C.: he could not appear when summoned, since he was judge in another case, for which he had set the date before citation in the present litigation.

4. *Form of third citation, the second peremptory summons*. The judges to the

67. For the extant manuscripts, now in London (British Library and Lambeth Palace), Cambridge (Gonville and Caius College), Baltimore, the Vatican, Montecassino, and Oxford (Bodley), see Logan, "An Early Thirteenth-Century Formulary," pp. 77–79 and Sayers, *Papal Judges Delegate*, pp. 45–49. The British Library copy is in a volume including the early English primitive decretal collection *Regalis:* cf. Duggan, *Decretal Collections*, p. 82 n. 1.

68. Logan, "An Early Thirteenth-Century Formulary," pp. 77 and 85–86 no. 14. The English origins of the formulary are further supported by incidental references in some of the manuscripts. The Baltimore MS includes Oxford and Northampton references, suggesting "an origin in the nascent university," while the Bodley MS seems clearly based on actual cases, with references to named persons, offices and places, pointing to Cirencester as the likely place of origin (Sayers, *Papal Judges Delegate*, pp. 46–59). A formulary from Canterbury, edited in Jane E. Sayers, "A Judge Delegate Formulary from Canterbury," *Bulletin of the Institute of Historical Research*, 35 (1962), 198–211, is in matter and style of presentation comparable to the *A. B. C. judices* analysed here, but it is a fuller and later work in 30 forms, possibly post 1227 in completion, and influenced by Tancred's *Ordo iudiciarius* (c. 1216: Sayers, "A Judge Delegate Formulary," p. 200).

defendant: the judges issue a third citation, the second peremptory, and warn him that they will proceed with the case, if he fails to appear.

5. *Form of the third peremptory summons, for a person of rank.* The judges to the defendant: in consideration of the defendant's status, the judges can issue a third peremptory summons.

6. *Form of the letter of commission by a judge.* The judge A. to his fellow judges B. and C.: since he is prevented by other commitments from being present in the case between N. and H., he commissions one of his clerks to act in his place, except for the formal presentation of the case and definitive judgment.

7. *Form of a judge's letter of excuse for absence.* The judge C. to his fellow judges A. and B.: he notifies his colleagues that he cannot be present to hear the case committed jointly to them. They are to proceed with their commission, and he is informing the parties.

8. *Form of letter by which the defendant appoints a proctor.* The clerk N. to the judges A. B. C.: since he cannot be present, he commissions a proctor E. (the bearer of his letter) with full powers to act for him, and he is informing the other party.

9. *Form of letter to the judge ordinary ordering execution of an interlocutory sentence.* The judges delegate to the judge ordinary: on N's failure to appear in response to several letters and a peremptory summons, the judges issue an interlocutory judgment against him (after taking counsel), and give possession of the church to his adversary H., pending final judgment, the question of right being reserved—*causa rei servanda*. By the authority of the pope committed to them, they mandate the ordinary not to defer execution of their sentence.

10. *Request to the judges delegate on behalf of a litigant.* To the judges B. and C.: an unidentified source requests the judges to listen earnestly to the plea of H., the bearer the letter.

11. *Form of letter recording a settlement made by the litigants.* General notification by the judges A. B. C. in the case between the clerks N. and H.: the parsonage to remain with H., but N. to have the vicarage, in return for an annual payment.

12. *Form of letter of execution of a definitive sentence.* The judges delegate to the judge ordinary: having fully considered all the evidence presented by N., they adjudge the church to him, and order the judge ordinary to execute the judgment without delay.

13. *Charter containing the judgment* de re iudicata. Formal instrument containing the final sentence.

14. *Form of reference to the pope on a doubtful matter.* The judges A. B. C. to the pope (Innocent III): the judges report their examination carried out by his authority. After examination of witnesses of both sides, their claims and objections, and consultations with legal experts, they decided to refer the matter to the pope, with the form of the rescript and the testimony and allegations of both sides, to secure an equitable judgment from him; and they set a date for both sides to appear in his presence.

15. *Form of letter mandating the judge ordinary to execute the sentence, including the financial penalty imposed on the loser.*

[16. *Form of letter of revocation sent by judges delegate to earlier judges.* Masters C. and D. to bishop A. and abbot B.: on receipt of Pope Innocent's commission, they request bishop A. and abbot B. to withdraw from the hearing and execution of the case between N. and H., which has been transferred to them by papal mandate.][69]

Errata:

p. 173, note 4., *New Studies in Gratian's Decretum,*Canon Law ... *should read* *New Studies in Gratian's Decretum*, Canon Law ...

p. 175, note 12., cuncta per orbem *should read* Cuncta per orbem

p. 198, line 22 to 23, the question of right being reserved *should read* in order to protect its integrity

p.198, line 23, *causa rei servanda should read causa rei servande*

69. Logan, "An Early Thirteenth-Century Formulary," p. 77 n. 4. On all procedural matters, see now Linda Fowler-Magerl, *Ordines iudiciarii and Libelli de Ordine ludiciorum (from the middle of the twelfth to the end of the fifteenth century)*. Typologie des Sources du Moyen Age Occidental (Turnhout, 1994).

II

ST THOMAS OF CANTERBURY AND ASPECTS OF THE BECKET DISPUTE IN THE DECRETAL COLLECTIONS

Decretals and decretal collections have a special importance for the twelfth-century English Church, precisely because of the uniquely-important contribution which English bishops and canonists made to the law of the universal Church at that time, exceeding in this context that of their contemporaries elsewhere. The fruits of their labours produced a fleeting 'English period' in the history of medieval canon law, when English collectors were in advance of their continental colleagues, and more prolific, and therefore left a lasting imprint on the law of the Western Church. At the heart of this matter lie the origins, course and aftermath of the Becket Dispute. Earlier theories of a somewhat isolated and ill-instructed Church, brought up-to-date by a posthumous victory following Thomas's martyrdom, were misconceived. The Becket Dispute is fully explicable only if the dynamic forces within the English Church throughout the period are perceived, and its creative role in the formation of 'new law', dating from the reception of Gratian's *Decretum* (*c*. 1140). Historians have long recognized a close relationship between the Becket question and the evidence in the early decretal collections, though its nature is still debated.[1] The present paper brings together the surprisingly large number of decretals which refer to Thomas in person, or to major themes of the crisis in which he was involved.

In a broad but nevertheless crucial sense the entire corpus of twelfth-century decretals is relevant to the history of the English Church in the pontificate of Alexander III (1159-81), and of the Becket dispute within that period. More than a third of all decretals in the surviving collections were sent by Alexander to English recipients, nearly 400 in a total of about 1100; more than half of all extant primitive collections of the first phase, dating from the mid-1170s forward, were made by English collectors dependent chiefly on letters received in England; many of the continental primitive collections were partly derived from English sources; and the most formative transitional collection from the primitive to the systematic tradition, the *Appendix concilii Lateranensis*, was almost certainly of English authorship.[2] Reciprocal interchange between the Roman curia and the English episcopate, and between England and the continental schools of theology and canon law, had profoundly influenced the life of the English Church in the reign of Stephen and the early years of Henry II's rule.[3] The presence of Alexander III in exile in northern France from 1162 made access to the curia from

England more easy, and English bishops played a leading role at the council of Tours in May 1163.[4] Paradoxically, the crisis in England between Thomas and Henry II, and the rivalry between Thomas and Roger of York, still further promoted these increasingly close relations. The quarrel itself entailed a voluminous correspondence with the pope, and the process of consultative and appellate recourse to the curia made further progress.[5] Shortly after Thomas passed into exile, Roger of Worcester secured a series of permanently important canonical rulings from Alexander at Sens in November 1164, while a member of the mission presenting Henry II's case to the pope; and he secured others of similar importance in the years 1167-69, when he was himself in exile.[6] Doubtless, the years of crisis checked to some extent the flow of routine appeals, above all in the harshly oppressive final phase in 1169-70, but they did not cease altogether. Indeed it can now be argued that the tentative origins of the English collections can be rediscovered in the years of Becket's exile, most clearly in the work of bishop Bartholomew and his circle at Exeter.[7] In the years after Becket's death in 1170 and the compromise of Avranches in 1172, Roger and Bartholomew were the most eminent judges delegate in England, the 'twin lights of the English Church' in the pope's estimation, and the record of their exceptional importance is attested in both the sources and the construction of the English collections.[8]

Most of the forty-six letters calendared below (nos **1-6**, **7a**, **7b**, **8-45**) are decretals of Alexander III to English recipients. All were incorporated in decretal collections, but some are also found in non-canonical sources. An attempt has been made to place them here in chronological order, but the dates are uncertain in some cases, and subject to later revision. Two earlier letters are included for their relevance to themes of Becket's career: Gregory I's instructions to St Augustine on the projected organization of the English Church (**1**), and a letter of Leo IX to Eadwige of Canterbury, on the criminous but penitent clerk Andrew (**2**). The letter of Adrian IV to archbishop Theobald (**3**), concerning the Cistercian monks of Boxley and tithe payment, is included since it has been wrongly assigned to Alexander III and archbishop Thomas in the past. Letters **4-39** were all issued within the limits of Alexander's pontificate. With three exceptions (**11**, **18** and **19**), all were sent by the pope himself: one is a letter of the papal vicar Walter of Albano, on the penitent subdeacon Peter (**11**); one was written to Alexander by Henry II, to avert the potentially harmful consequences of Becket's murder for his own reputation (**18**); and one by archbishop Rotrou of Rouen, declining to impose an interdict on Henry II's continental lands (**19**). An important letter to John of St Andrews, on the immunity of clerks who are merely tonsured, was sent by either Alexander or his successor Lucius III (**40**). A supplement of five decretals comprises letters of Alexander to Richard of Canterbury, mostly concerning the archbishop's jurisdiction (**41-45**: the exception is **44**, relating to Jews); they are included here since they have sometimes been assigned to Thomas in the past, and appear so in editions and registers. It is a matter of interest that eight of the 46 letters are printed in the recent *Decretales ineditae saeculi XII*, six for the first time (**9**, **12**, **22**, **26**, **32** and **40**; the exceptions being **25** and **35**). Six of the letters were re-discovered in the Cottonian and Peterhouse collections (**9**, **12** and **22** in both; **25** and **26** in *Cott.* only; and **40** in *Pet.* and *Bridl.*), which have proven rich sources of previously-unknown English and continental decretals. Two are found in the Bridlington collection (**35** and **40**), and one in the Italian St Florian collection (**32**), where it derives from an English source in the Norwich diocese.

It is possible that Thomas was himself the recipient of a small number of the early letters of Alexander III listed below: one concerning the alleged son of a priest, holding a certain church (**4**), and conceivably another, to the archbishop of Canterbury and his suffragans, on the problem of priests' sons succeeding to their fathers' churches (**7b**). He was very probably a co-recipient, with Bartholomew of Exeter, of a letter on the Exeter canons who leased out capitular lands to the chapter's detriment(**8**); he is named in a letter to Bartholomew, concerning the latter's dispute with clerks in the Barnstaple archdeaconry, the letter dating from the period of his exile, but with retrospective reference to his jurisdiction while still in England (**10**); and a charter of an un-named archbishop of Canterbury, cited in a dispute over the church of Grafton in Oxfordshire, may have been his (**13**).

A mandate of Alexander to all the bishops of England on 19 May 1168 deplores the evil custom that had grown up in England in 'this time of trouble' between the king and Thomas, whereby churches and benefices were improperly granted by laymen (**14**); and Thomas is included by common form in the general address of a St Albans privilege of 17 November 1168-69 (**15**). He is named and his defence of Church freedom elaborated in the papal sentences imposed on Gilbert of London and other bishops of the Canterbury province, and on Roger of York and Hugh of Durham, for their roles in the coronation of the Young King on 14 June 1170 (**16** and **17**); and his allegedly provocative behaviour is criticized in the king's letter of self-exculpation following the murder (**18**). Though not specifically naming Thomas, the archbishop of Roucn's letter refusing to lay interdict on Henry II's continental lands arose from this context (**19**); and it is very probable that Richard Barre secured his release from the fealty which Geoffrey Ridel had improperly exacted from him, while he was himself on royal business in the curia (20). The purgation of Roger of York in respect of his role in the Young King's coronation and his possible complicity in Thomas's murder was assigned to Rotrou of Rouen and Thibaud of Amiens (21); and the cardinal legates Albert and Theodwin were commissioned to investigate the request of the Canterbury monks for Thomas's canonization (22). On 31 January 1172, the pope explained to Bartholomew of Exeter the degrees of complicity in Thomas's murder, and the appropriate penances (23); and between late 1171 and early 1173, he provisionally restored to Roger of York the right to have his cross borne before him 'per totam Angliam' (24). Thomas the Martyr is named in a mandate to an unidentified bishop and Richard of Ilchester, exempting Silvester, treasurer of Lisieux, from the importunity of a London Jew (25). The actions of Jocelin of Salisbury while excommunicate, to be annulled by the legates Albert and Theodwin, relate to the sentences laid on him by Thomas and the pope (26). The letters of canonization, dispatched by Alexander in March 1173, were addressed to the prior and monks of Canterbury, all the faithful, and the prelates, clergy and people of England (27 and 28). At some uncertain date after the canonization, the pope condemned the improper expulsion of a clerk from the church of St Hippolytus at Dinsley, while St Thomas the Martyr was in exile (29); and two letters, in 1174 and 1174-75, relate to the filling of vacancies in English bishoprics and abbeys, in the general settlement of the English Church following the compromise (30 and 31). Excommunications imposed on clerks by Thomas are cited in letters concerning the church of Bungay and the canons of Pentney in 1174-76, earl Hugh of Norfolk being involved in each case (32 and 33). And in a letter to Richard of Canterbury in 1176-77, Alexander reproached him for failing to sustain the defence of the Church's freedom, for which his glorious predecessor Thomas was martyred (34).

Many decretals record the intervention or interest of the English king, and reveal his concern either with general areas of jurisdiction or rights in particular cases. The relatively small number of such letters selected here relate directly to the course of his quarrel with Becket, or enunciate with striking clarity some of the central issues around which the controversy turned. Three letters of Alexander III were addressed to the king in person, and one was sent by the king to the pope. Of exceptional interest is the recently-discovered decretal in defence of clerical privilege, arising from the case of an accused subdeacon who had appealed to the pope (9); a famous letter defines the papal doctrine on the *ius patronatus*, and its submission to ecclesiastical judgment when in dispute (38); and a third records the rejection of king Henry's request to the pope on behalf of a knight in a patronage dispute over a certain church (37). The king's defensive letter to the pope on hearing of Becket's murder has been noted above (18). In 1161, with Canterbury vacant, Alexander had given Roger of York permission to crown the king's eldest son, when requested to do so (6). Several letters from the following years touch on problems arising in the course of the dispute between Henry and Thomas: already mentioned are the mandate on lay abuse of patronage in 'this time of trouble' (14), the letters of suspension or excommunication of the prelates who had participated in the Young King's coronation (16 and 17), and the archbishop of Rouen's refusal to interdict Henry's lands on the continent (19). The mandate exempting archdeacon Silvester of Lisieux from the importunity of a London Jew records the reason for Silvester's financial difficulty: king Henry had appropriated his prebend at Waltham when he followed St Thomas the Martyr into exile (25). And it is possible that royal patronage is implied in the legate Pierleoni's report in 1177 that his wish to condemn the forger Hugh of Southwell was deflected by powerful people - 'magnarum personarum supplicatione'(35).

In his letters of condemnation of the prelates who were present at the Young King's coronation in June 1170, Alexander III referred to the written constitutions, or wicked statutes, which king Henry had proposed against the Church's freedom (16 and 17), and spoke in similar terms in October 1171 in his commission to Rouen and Amiens to deal with Roger of York's purgation (21). These were clear allusions to the constitutions of Clarendon of January 1164, in which Henry sought to define in sixteen clauses his jurisdictional rights vis-à-vis the Church, the *avitae consuetudines,* the customs which his grandfather Henry I had allegedly, and in most cases in fact, enjoyed.[9] From the Church's viewpoint, the most important constitution was almost certainly clause 8, which sought to subject to the king's will the appellate jurisdiction of church courts, at the point of reference from England to the papal curia. The selection of decretals listed here, though relatively few in number, bear witness* to the fundamental importance of this issue, the only one which was explicitly cited in the compromise at Avranches in May 1172.

Seven of the listed decretals throw light on the most familiar and fiercely contested constitution, clause 3, relating to criminous clerks: more than a century earlier, the priest Andrew had committed a murder and secured absolution from Leo IX, *c.* 1049-50, in a letter believed until recently to have been sent to Bartholomew of Exeter by Alexander III (2); Alexander wrote to the king himself in defence of the subdeacon I., whom the royal bailiffs wished to arrest and draw to secular judgment on a charge of murder (9); the papal vicar Walter imposed sentence on the subdeacon Peter, who had committed a murder and had come, like the priest Andrew and the subdeacon I., in person to the curia (11); Alexander's instructions to Bartholomew of Exeter, on the degrees of complicity in Thomas's murder, included guilty clerks (23); and he mandated an appropriate

* bear *should read* bears

sentence on the forger Hugh of Southwell, whose judgment by the legate had been prevented (**35**); the bishops of London and Worcester were commissioned by the pope in the case of a clerk suspected of causing the death of William Sarracenus (**36**); and Alexander or his successor Lucius III instructed John of St Andrews on criminous clerks who were merely tonsured (**40**).

The sensitive matter of advowsons was treated at Clarendon in clause 1, which stated that cases concerning advowsons were matters for the king's court.[10] The contrary view was expressed by Alexander III in a letter to the king (**38**), and in another to the bishops of England or France (**39**): these letters were most probably from the closing years of Alexander's pontificate, *c.* 1179; and he rejected a request by the king on behalf of a certain knight in a patronage dispute (**37**). As noted above, the pope had mandated the English bishops during Becket's exile to annul the uncanonical grants of churches and ecclesiastical benefices by lay persons (**14**). The rights of patrons, and the granting or seizing of benefices, were in contention in several decretals: concerning a vicarage in the church of Grafton (**13**); the uncanonical exaction of fealty by Geoffrey Ridel from Richard Barre in return for a benefice (**20**); the king's appropriation of the prebend of Waltham when Silvester of Lisieux followed Thomas into exile (**25**); and the despoilment of the clerk Ralph of the church at Dinsley by lay pressure (**29**).

Two further clauses from the Clarendon constitutions find echoes in the decretals below. The pope's rebuke to archbishop Richard for confirming episcopal elections in the royal chamber (**34**), possibly in 1176-77, reflects the king's success in maintaining his rights as expressed in clause 12; and his letter to the prelates of France, England and Scotland, forbidding all knowing association with excommunicates, through fear or favour of their princes or of any mortal person (**12**), may reflect his concern with the sentences imposed on English magnates and royal officials by Becket in the course of the dispute, a practice condemned by clause 7, if lacking royal consent.

The claims of York for independence and equal status with Canterbury gave rise to many papal rulings, and several letters reflecting the origins and course of this rivalry were received into the collections: the letter of Gregory I to St Augustine on the future organization of the English Church (**1**); an excerpt from an early privilege of Alexander III, repeating his predecessors' confirmation of York's rights (**5**); his concession during the Canterbury vacancy after Theobald's death that Roger could crown king Henry's eldest son, when asked to do so (**6**); the sentences on the prelates who were present when he later crowned the Young Henry, contrary to papal orders, when Becket was in exile (**16** and **17**); and the concession, which Roger provisionally recovered after Thomas's death, that he could have his cross borne before him throughout England (**24**).[11]

Several letters record the commissions of papal legates to England, or to the continental possessions of the English king: the letter suspending Roger of York and Hugh of Durham laments the frustration of legates sent at Becket's request (**17**); the legates Albert and Theodwin, appointed to effect the reconciliation which was achieved at Avranches in May 1172, were mandated to investigate the requests for Thomas's canonization (**22**), and to annul the ordinations and grants of Jocelin of Salisbury while excommunicated (**26**); their reports are mentioned in the letters announcing the canonization (**27** and **28**); and the cardinal legate Hugh Pierleoni, in England in 1175-76, reported to the pope the case of the forger Hugh of Southwell (**35**). A letter to archbishop Richard, listed here because it has been wrongly assigned to Thomas in the past, treats of his rights as papal legate for his province (**45**).

Among the notable persons who appear in the letters are R. Foliot (**13**), Richard Barre and Geoffrey Ridel (**20**), earl Hugh of Norfolk (**16**, **32** and **33**), Richard de Lovetot (**29**), Wimer (**32**), master Hugh of Southwell (**35**), William Sarracenus (**36**) and the knight R. (**37**). Churches mentioned include Boxley (**3**), Grafton (**13**), Waltham (**25**), St Hippolytus at Dinsley (**29**), Bungay (**32**), Epperstone and Shelford (**35**) and *Bliburg* (**37**). In one way or another, as recipients or concerned parties, religious houses are involved in seven decretals (**3**, **13**, **15**, **22**, **27**, **31** and **33**); the problem of priests' sons is raised in three letters (**4**, **7a** and **7b**) and a canon's son appears in another (John, bishop-elect of Chichester, **30**). Excommunications are frequently mentioned (**11**, **12**, **14**, **15**, **16**, **18**, **26**, **32**, **33**, **34** and **39**; cf. suspension, **17**; interdict, **19** and **33**). Three letters deal with Thomas's canonization (**22**, **27** and **28**); and six provide important* insights into procedural and jurisdictional problems (**10**, **34**, **36**, **41**, **42**, **43** and **45**), but the last four were addressed to Richard.

CALENDAR OF LETTERS

1

Gregory I to Augustine, bishop of the English. 22 June 601

Cum certum sit pro omnipotenti Deo ... multiplicius (vel *multipliciter) insudare. Et quia (nova) Anglorum ecclesia ... regna pertingant. [Deus te incolumem custodiat, reverentissime frater. Data die x. kalendarum Iuliarum imperante domino nostro Mauricio Tiberio piissimo Augusto anno xviiii. post consulatum eiusdem domni anno xviii. indictione iiii.]*

The pope grants the use of the pallium to Augustine, to be worn only in the solemnities of the Mass, with authority over twelve bishops whom he will ordain. Future bishops of the city of London will be consecrated by their own synod and receive the pallium from the apostolic see. Augustine will send a

* six *should read* seven

worthy person of his choice to be bishop of the city of York, who will likewise ordain twelve bishops, when the city and its region have been won to God's word, and will enjoy metropolitan rank. York will receive the pallium, yet be subject to Augustine in his lifetime; but after his death, York will not be subject to London. Thereafter, there will be that distinction of honour between London and York that he shall have precedence whose consecration was earlier. Augustine himself will have authority not only over his own bishops and those of York, but over all the priests of Britain.

WH 222, *JE* 1829, 22 June 601. Pd *App*. 44.1; *Cass*. 55..1; abbrev.: *1 Comp.Ag*., 1.25.1; *X* 1.33.1; *Gregorii I pape Registrum Epistolarum*, edd. P. Ewald and L. Hartmann, *Monumenta Germaniae Historica, Epp*. 2 (1899), 311-12: Liber xi no. 39; and Bede's *Ecclesiastical History of the English People*, edd. B. Colgrave and R.A.B. Mynors, Oxford Medieval Texts (1969), 104-06, 1.29, with the concluding salutation and date.

This famous letter of Gregory I to St Augustine on the future organization of the English Church proved of interest to the compiler of the seminal systematic decretal collection *App*., as the opening item in title 44: 'De preeminentia *Lundoniensis et Eboracensis (episcopi) et de privilegiis generaliter vel specialiter indultis etc.'; and thereafter in *Bamb*. 47, *Lips*. 56 and *Cass*. 55, with the heading 'De preeminentia Lundoniensis et Eboracensis.' In *Tann*. 6.7, the title was adjusted to 'De preeminentia Eboracensis et Cantuariensis archiepiscoporum', in recognition of the realities of the twelfth-century English Church (on the respective claims of Canterbury, York and London in the twelfth century, see R. Foreville, *L'Église et la royauté en Angleterre sous Henri II Plantagenet, 1154-89*, Paris 1943, 26-76, 231-40 and 504-16; and A. Morey and C.N.L. Brooke, *Gilbert Foliot and his letters*, Cambridge 1965, 149-62). The letter was not received in English primitive collections before the mid-1190s, in *Cott*. 7,53 and *Pet*. 3.28, and not at all in French and Spanish primitive collections, but was included in the early Italian collections *Flor*. 125, *Duac*. 60 and *Cus*. 141.

2

Leo IX to archbishop Eadwige of Canterbury. *c*. 1049-50

Hunc Andream presbiterum vestrum in homicidii crimine lapsum ... Calixtus noster antecessor in decretis suis sic promulgauit: Errant, inquit, qui putant ... a malis abstineat. [Peccator post penitentiam ... iam vivit deo per Ihesum Christum dominum nostrum.]

The priest Andrew had committed a murder and completed seven years of severe penance. In view of the pain of his sorrow more than the span of time, he was absolved by the pope, who sends him back to be restored to his priesthood. Those who think such restoration unfitting can learn from the holy fathers, among whom pope Calixtus decreed that those are in error who think that a guilty priest cannot minister to the Lord after a suitable penance, provided that he amends his life and avoids evil. [After penance, the sinner is not the man he was; he was dead in sin, but now lives in God through Christ.]

WH 539 (*olim* 737), *JL* 13912 (*sub annis* 1159-81), *c*. 1049-50. Full text in Oxford, Bodl. MS Barlow 37 (6464) fol. 13r-v; and Durham Cathedral MS C.III.1, fol. 63v, *marg. infer*., at Gratian D.50, c.37. Pd *App*. 26.13 (*Presbiterum etiam*, to the bishop of Exeter); *1 Abr*. 2.11.4 (*Hunc Andream, sine inscriptione)*.

* episcopi *should read* episcoporum

No collection records the correct address or complete text of this letter. There is no inscription in some collections; in others the sender is Alexander III or 'Idem'; and the recipient appears in some as the bishop of Exeter. The opening occurs variously as *Hunc Andream* or *Presbiterum*. The letter in fact dates from the mid-eleventh century, when it was sent by Leo IX to archbishop Eadwige of Canterbury, c. 1049-50, with the concluding passage 'Peccator post ... dominum nostrum', which is not found in the collections. Its internal reference to pope Calixtus is a pseudo-Isidorian derivation (*Pseudo-Calixtus* I, ep. 2, c. 20: *Decretales Pseudo-Isidorianae*, ed. P. Hinschius, [Leipzig 1863], 142); for the resolution of these problems, see S. Kuttner, 'The decretal "Presbiterum" [*JL* 13912]: a letter of Leo IX', *BMCL* 5 [1975], 133-35).

3

Adrian IV to archbishop Theobald of Canterbury. 1154-59

Commissum nobis a Deo ... illibata conservare. Pervenit quidem ad nos quod monachi de Boxle ecclesie sancte Marie ... absque diminutione persolvi.

The monks of Boxley do not pay tithes in full to the church of St Mary in whose parish they live, and they refuse to pay them. The archbishop must compel them to pay in full the tithes which had previously been paid, before they dwelt there, even for cultivated lands on which buildings had formerly stood. Likewise, the former tithes must be paid without reduction for pastures now brought to fertility.

WH 134, *JL* 11660 (*sub annis* 1162-70), 1154-59. Pd *App*. 13.12; *Cass*. 35.13; *1 Comp.Ag*. 3.26.18; *X* 3.30.4; and *Materials TB*, 5.129 no. 66 (*sub anno* 1164, with n. 'no date discoverable').

The decretal is found also with the opening *Commisse*. It is attributed frequently to Alexander III and archbishop Thomas, called 'beatus' in some collections. But its doctrine on Cistercian tithe payment agrees with that of Adrian IV, which Alexander reversed in the first year of his pontificate (cf. Duggan, *Decretals of Alexander III*, 122-23). It was in fact addressed to archbishop Theobald, and almost certainly by Adrian IV (who is named in *1 Berol*. 52: 'Idem' *post* 'Adrianus'; *Cus*. 26; *2 Par*. 56.4; *Oriel* 13.15; *Brug*. 17.12; and *Frcf*. 20.15), and concerns the Cistercian abbey of Boxley in Kent.

4

Alexander III to archbishop Theobald or Thomas of Canterbury. 1159-October 1164

Helias iste ad nostram presentiam accedens (vel accusationes) monstravit ... ab ecclesia removeas.

Elias has accused the priest R. of holding a church, although it is said that he was born in the priesthood. The sacred canons declare that none born in the priesthood should be advanced to holy orders, or for any reason admitted to churches, unless they have taken the religious habit and lived worthy lives in the cloister. If it is shown that R. was born in the priesthood, the archbishop should remove him from the church.

WH 538, *JL* --, 1159-November 1164. Pd *1 Abr*. 2.15.1.

The two earliest texts (*3 Cant*. 12 and *1 Dun*. 3.32) supply the initial T. for the recipient archbishop, identifying either Theobald or Thomas; they have also the variant *accusationes* in the opening sentence. Alexander's ruling in this letter is explicitly based on earlier canons (cf. Councils: Melfi, *anno* 1089, can. 14; Clermont, *anno* 1095, can. 25; Lateran II, *anno* 1139, can. 21: Mansi, 20.724 and 818, and 21.531), cf. *Suggestum est nobis, infra* 7, and is consistent with that in other mandates sent to England in the early years of his pontificate. It is therefore possible that *Helias iste* is one of the rare decretals to Thomas preserved in the collections, but it is virtually certain that he would not have received such a commission after his departure for exile on 1 November 1164.

5

Alexander III to archbishop Roger of York 22 January 1161

[In hunc modum plures Romani pontifices a tempore beati Gregorii scripserunt:] Antiquam Eboracensis ecclesie dignitatem auctore Deo conservare cupientes ... a Romano pontifice consecrari.

Wishing to preserve the ancient dignity of York, the pope confirms his predecessors' ruling that Canterbury may not exact obedience from York, nor should York make such profession, and repeats pope Gregory's prohibition of the subjection of York to Canterbury (*olim* London). The distinction of honour between them is decided by priority of consecration. If Canterbury withholds consecration from York, the latter can be consecrated by his suffragans or by the Roman pontiff.

WH 88, *JL* 12749 (*sub anno* 1176), 22 January 1161. Pd *App*.44.2; *Cass*. 55.2; Diceto, 1.406 (*sub anno* 1176); *Materials TB*, 5.132 no. 68 *sub anno* 1164).

This passage appears in *App.*, *Bamb.*, *Lips.*, *Cass.*, *Tann.* and other collections, immediately following *Cum certum sit*, in titles relating to the pre-eminence of London or Canterbury and York (cf. *supra* 1). It is placed by Diceto (1.405-06) after an account of the disorderly contention between the partisans of Canterbury and York at the legatine council of London on 14 March 1176, with cardinal Hugo Pierleoni presiding, and is therefore repeated under 1176 in *JL*. The editor of the Becket correspondence questioned the letter's authenticity (*Materials TB*, 5.132 no. 68: 'The occasion and date of this letter do not appear ... on the whole the piece looks more like a statement on the part of York than like an utterance of Alexander'). It also occurs with the address 'Universis suffraganeis Cantuariensis ecclesie'; and is falsely attributed to Celestine III in *Alan.app.* 72. It is in fact an excerpt from Alexander III's privilege to Roger of York on 22 January 1161 (cf. *PU England*, 2.291 no. 105: and for earlier popes, Calixtus II, *JL* 6831; Honorius II, *JL* 7227; Innocent II, *PU England*, 2.148-50 no. 13; Eugenius III, *ibid.*, 231-33 no. 66; and Adrian IV, *ibid.*, 262-64 no. 86); the transmission of the privilege is indicated in the phrase 'In hunc modum ... scripserunt', with which the excerpt is prefaced in several decretal collections and in non-canonical sources (cf. Duggan, *Decretals of Alexander III*, 119 no. 88; see also *supra* 1 and *infra* 24).

6

Alexander III to archbishop Roger of York. 17 or 20 June 1161

Quanto per carissimum filium nostrum Henricum illustrem regem Anglorum ... commoneas exhibere. Datum Rome apud sanctam Mariam novam xv. (vel xii.) kal. Julii.

In recognition of king Henry's help for God's Church in its extreme necessity, and of his constant devotion, the pope wishes to increase his honour, and exalt the king and his people, He therefore grants, after consulting his brethren, the king's request that his eldest son Henry shall be crowned in England. He mandates the archbishop of York, since it pertains to his office, to place the crown by apostolic authority on the head of the king's firstborn son, when required by the king to do so, and confirms in advance the archbishop's action. The archbishop will also show the son due reverence and subjection, saving his father's mandate, and will admonish others to do likewise.

WH 772, *JL* 11353 (*sub anno* 1167), 17 or 20 June 1161. Pd *Cass.* 55.4; *Materials TB*, 6.206-07 no. 310 and n. (*sub anno* 1167); A. Duggan (Heslin), 'The coronation of the Young King', *SCH* 2 (1965), 177-78.

The date of this decretal occurs variously as 17 or 20 June. It was assigned formerly to the year 1167 or even to 1170, with Becket in exile, but is correctly dated 1161, in the vacancy following Theobald's death (see A. Duggan, *SCH* 2.165-78). It was presumbly this letter which was discussed by Henry II and* Becket on the occasion of their reconciliation at Fréteval on 22 July 1170, with reference to the Young King's coronation by the archbishop of York on 14 June 1170, and its precedents and prohibition, as recorded in Thomas's report to the pope (*Miserationis oculo, Materials TB*, 7.326-38 no. 684, at 331: 'Constabat enim eas (litteras), quando Cantuariensis ecclesia vacabat, eo proposito fuisse impetratas'; cf. Duggan, *Decretals of Alexander III*, 137 no. 772; and for the papal letters of condemnation of the prelates who took part in the coronation ceremony, cf. *Oportuerat vos* and *Licet nobis commendabiles, infra* 16 and 17).

7

Alexander III to (a) the bishops of Salisbury and Exeter
(b) the archbishop of Canterbury and his suffragans 1161-81 (? 1161-64x70 or 1174-81)

(a) To Salisbury and Exeter	**(b) To Canterbury and suffragans**
Suggestum est nobis quod J., dicatur filius sacerdotis et in sacerdotio genitus, ecclesiam in qua pater suus dicitur personatum habuisse sibi paterna successione usurpare presumit. Unde quoniam sacris canonibus prohibitum est ne quis heredit-ario iure ecclesiastica beneficia possidere presumat, nec hii qui in sacerdotio geniti sunt, nisi	*Suggestum est nobis quod quidam cum in sacerdotio geniti ecclesias in quibus patres sui dicuntur personatus habuisse sibi paterna successione usurpare presumunt. Unde quoniam sacris canonibus prohibitum est ne qui heredit-ario iure ecclesiastica beneficia possidere presumant, nec hii qui in sacerdotio geniti sunt, nisi*

* presumbly *should read* presumably

probate vixerint in claustro monachorum vel canonicorum regularium ad sacros ordines debent promoveri, fraternitati vestre per apostolica scripta precipiendo mandamus quatinus rem ipsam cum omni diligentia inquiratis et, si manifestum et publicum fuerit patrem predicti J. prefate ecclesie personatum gessisse, ipsum ab eadem ecclesia si eam iam adeptus est <appellatione remota penitus> excludatis, nec ad eius gubernationem assumatur. Nolumus enim ut propterea causa in iudicium deducatur vel testes super hoc proferantur, dummodo hoc manifestum existat.

probate vixerint in claustro monachorum vel canonicorum regularium ad sacros ordines debeant promoveri, vobis per apostolica scripta precipiendo mandamus quatinus rem ipsam cum omni diligentia inquiratis et, si manifestum et publicum fuerit patres eorum ecclesiarum personatus gessisse, ipsos ab eisdem ecclesiis si eas iam adepti sunt appellatione remota penitus excludatis, nec ad earum gubernationem ulterius assumantur. Nolumus enim ut propterea causa in iudicium deducatur vel testes admittantur, cum hoc manifestum existat.

(a) The pope has learned that J., who is alleged to be the son of a priest and born in the priesthood, has usurped by hereditary succession the parsonage which his father held. The sacred canons forbid such possession of ecclesiastical benefices; nor should such sons be advanced to holy orders, unless they have first lived worthily in a house of monks or regular canons. The recipients must examine the charge. If it is public and manifest that J.'s father held the parsonage, he must be removed from the church if he has already acquired it, and not accepted for its charge in the future. The pope does not wish the matter to be brought to legal process, or witnesses received, if the offence is manifest. (b) The pope issues a general mandate to the archbishop of Canterbury and his suffragans, to the same effect and in similar language, not arising from a specific case.

(a) *WH* 1003, *JL* 14097, 1160-64 (1159-81). Pd *Claustr.* 139; *App.* 19.7; (b) *WH* 1005, *JL* 13815, *post* 1161 (1159-81). Pd *1 Dert.* 30; *Cass.* 33.11; *1 Comp. Ag.* 1.9.12; *X* 1.17.10.

Letter (a) is first found in the Canterbury and Durham collections (*3 Cant.* 15 and *1 Dun.* 3.40), and thereafter in six English collections and one Norman collection (*1 Rot.* 8.1). Letter (b) first appears in the Spanish and Bridlington archetypes and in *Wig.*, in which latter it is abbreviated, beginning at *Cum sacris canonibus;* thereafter the truncated version *Quoniam sacris* was transmitted through nine systematic collections to *X* 1.17.10. Only *Wig.* has both versions (*Wig.* 3.23 and 24), the truncated version of (b) appearing among it additions to the family archetype. The two letters have a clear textual relationship. The language of (a), arising from a particular case, seems more coherent; the concluding sentence in (b) is less appropriate to a general injunction. It is possible that a case commissioned to Salisbury and Exeter provided the occasion or model for a general mandate to the whole Canterbury province; it is also possible that (b) is a canonist's adaptation of the more circumstantial (a). If (b) is in fact an authentic text, itwasconceivably sent to Theobald or Thomas and the

Canterbury suffragans (1159-70), though most decretals of Alexander III to Canterbury and its suffragans were sent to Richard (1174-81).

The date of the letters is uncertain, but their doctrine and expression are consistent with the early years of Alexander's pontificate, as in *Helias iste*, to Theobald or Thomas (*supra* 4). At least two further decretals of Alexander to English prelates define the probationary period required before priests' sons could be ordained, but their dates are uncertain (*Ad audientiam nostram*, *WH* 29, *JL* 14223, 1163-75, to Gilbert of London and at least one other recipient; and *Quod super his*, *WH* 823, *JL* 13869, 1159-81, to Hugh of Durham. The requirement is also found in decretals of later popes. On the other hand, a decretal to Roger of Worcester, dated 26 November 1164, condemned both the hereditary possession of churches by the sons of priests or parsons and their illicit ordination after institution, without reference to the probationary period (*Inter ceteras*, *WH* 589, *JL* 12254); and many of Alexander's later letters to English prelates, arising from actual cases, deal with hereditary possession, without reference to the incumbents' ordination (cf. *Decretales ineditae*, 79-80 no. 45, 103-04 no. 59, and 133-35 no. 78; on the pope's allusion to the sacred canons, cf. also *Helias iste* (*supra* 4), and the councils of Poitiers [1078: can. 8; *X* 1.17.1; Mansi, 20.498-99] and Lateran II [1139: can. 16; Mansi, 21.530]). The letter requires further investigation.

8

Alexander III to the archbishop (probably Thomas) of Canterbury and bishop Bartholomew of Exeter. 1162-64 (1162-81)

Ad audientiam nostram noveritis pervenisse quod quidam de canonicis Exoniensis ecclesie ... incommoditas provenire.

Certain canons of Exeter have let out chapter lands on perpetual leases for money payments, without consulting their fellow-canons and to the chapter's detriment. The pope orders the recipients to revoke the leases in legal form, if the charges are true; if the lands cannot otherwise be recovered, they must compel the canons responsible to pay back the money they received, to prevent more serious damage to the church if the leases are allowed to remain.

WH 30, *JL* 17624 (*sub annis* 1191-98), 1162-64 (1162-81). Pd *Brug.* 17.10; *2 Comp.Ag.* 3.10.2; *X* 3.13.9.

This letter was probably sent to archbishop Thomas of Canterbury and bishop Bartholomew of Exeter in the early and reforming years of Bartholomew's episcopate, before Thomas's departure for exile on 1 November 1164; it is found within a sequence of Exeter decretals in *1 Alc.*, several of which can be positively dated in the 1160s (see Duggan, *Decretals of Alexander III*, 101-02 no. 78). An earlier attribution of the decretal to Celestine III was shown by Lohmann to be incorrect ('Die Collectio Wigorniensis', 79).

9

Alexander III to Henry II. (1162-65) 1160-76

Quanto superni dextera conditoris te ampliori potentia decoravit ... regie tuitionis presidium exhibere. Lator autem presentium subdiaconus I. nomine ... ordine iudiciario experiantur.

In proportion to the greater power with which God has endowed him, the king should be subject to Him with greater devotion, and restrain his ministers from actions which undoubtedly lead to harm. In nothing can he give more offence to God than by molesting churches or ecclesiastics, either himself or through his agents, whereas he is bound by the power entrusted to him to afford them his royal protection. The subdeacon I. has approached the pope in person, and reported that certain people suspected him of murdering a peasant, as he was passing one evening through a certain district at the same time as themselves. The king's ministers therefore wished to arrest him and draw him to secular judgment. But since the subdeacon is subject to ecclesiastical judgment by reason of his status, the king should not allow his bailiffs to seize him or draw him to secular judgment in despite of ecclesiastical privilege, even if he were guilty, which the pope does not believe is evident. The pope mandates the king, with respect for the divine majesty and for the honour of God's holy church, strictly to forbid his bailiffs and agents to lay hands on the subdeacon, or arraign him in a secular court. If any should wish to accuse him in this matter, they may do so before an ecclesiastical judge.

WH 774, *JL* --, (1162-65) 1160-76. *Cott.* 5.27 and *Pet.* 4.38 only. Pd *Decretales ineditae 59-60 no. 35.*

This mandate, until recently unknown, is of evident interest for the history of clerical privilege, and for the dispute between Henry II and Becket on that issue. Arising from an actual case of alleged murder, the papal mandate is addressed to the king. Although there is no evidence within it to date the letter more precisely than by Alexander III's pontificate, it belongs very probably to the earlier years. It makes no allusion to the dispute which developed with increasing sharpness from late 1163; and a papal letter in these terms is inconceivable after the compromise between Henry II and the legate Pierleoni in 1175-76, which is therefore its *terminus ad quem*. The record that the suspect clerk was able to visit the pope in person points to a period after Alexander III's arrival in northern France in 1162 and before his departure in 1165, conceivably in the first year of Becket's archiepiscopate (see *Decretales ineditae*, 60).

10

Alexander III to bishop Bartholomew of Exeter

early 1165-April 1167

Cum causa que inter te et quosdam clericos tuos de archidiaconatu Banostrapolis ... ad presentiam venerabilis fratris nostri Thome Cantuariensis archiepiscopi ... restitutionem compellas.

A dispute between the recipient and some of his clerks in the Barnstaple archdeaconry, concerning financial matters and various other complaints, was appealed to the pope from the court of archbishop Thomas of Canterbury. On the failure of the clerks to appear on the appointed day, the pope commissioned the case to bishops Henry of Winchester, Robert of Hereford and Roger of Worcester. Meanwhile, the canon P. of Plympton explained to the pope the background of the dispute: the clerks had raised the financial matter and drawn their bishop into the archbishop's court, after resisting his frequent attempts to correct their immoral lives. The pope commissioned the bishops of Winchester, Hereford and Worcester to examine the case, to hear the bishop's charges against the clerks, if they were earlier, and reach a judgment on that matter and on the financial dispute. With the commissioners' advice, the bishop should himself impose a suitable penance on the clerks, if it is established that he could have condemned them within his ordinary jurisdiction. He must compel all clerks in his diocese to live chastely or relinquish their churches and cease to celebrate. However, if it is true that the vicar of one of the clerks was removed from his church and replaced by another, while he was himself in the papal curia, the bishop must compel the substitute to restore its benefices to the church in question.

WH 217, *JL* --, early 1165-April 1167. *1 Alc.* 76 only. Pd Morey, *Bartholomew of Exeter*, 134-35, no. 9.

This decretal concerns the recalcitrant clerks of the Barnstaple archdeaconry in north Devon, and the historical details in the letter fix the dating limits from early 1165 to April 1167 (see Duggan, *Decretals of Alexander III*, 90-91 and 100-01; Morey, *op. cit.*, 92-93; and M. Cheney, *Roger, bishop of Worcester*, 331-32 no. 31).

11

Bishop Walter of Albano, papal vicar, to bishop Gilbert of London and the chapter of Rochford Hundred. 1167-73x75

Veniens ad apostolice sedis clementiam Petrus subdiaconus ... de cetero vexetis.

The subdeacon Peter had committed a murder and come to the curia for absolution. The papal vicar Walter released him from excommunication and imposed a detailed course of penance on him. He is demoted from his subdiaconal status and must in future serve as an acolyte; but, because God does not judge twice in the same matter - 'quia non iudicat Deus bis in idipsum' - the pope has by dispensation granted that he can keep his benefice in full, and he should suffer no further vexation.

WH 1057, *JL* --, 1167-73x75. *Belv.* 20 only. Pd *Gilberti ex abbate Glocestriae episcopi primum Herefordiensis deinde Londoniensis epistolae ...*, ed. J.A. Giles, 2 vols, Patres Ecclesiae Anglicanae, Oxford 1846, 2.204 no. 442.

The letter is found only in *Belv.*, in a volume of Foliot materials, and is addressed to bishop Gilbert of London and the Hundred of Rochford in the county of Essex, in the London diocese. It has a special importance in the context of the criminous clerks dispute between Henry II and Becket from 1163 onwards, above all for the papal vicar's citation of the scriptural maxim 'non iudicat Deus bis in idipsum', most familiar through its use by Becket in the controversy. Walter of Albano was made cardinal bishop by Adrian IV before 1159, and occurs in that office from February 1159 to 6 August 1177, but he had died before the Lateran Council in March 1179 (J.M. Brixius, *Die Mitglieder des Kardinalkollegiums von 1130-1181* [Berlin 1912], 60 and 118). He acted on Alexander III's behalf in northern France during the pope's exile there (cf. *JL* 10849: *Iustis petentium*, Paris, 13 April 1163), and occurs as papal vicar between 5 May 1167 and 3 February 1173 (Holtzmann, 'Die Register Papst Alexanders III in den Händen der Kanonisten', *Quellen und Forschungen aus italienischen Archiven und Bibliotheken* , 30 [1940], 24); John of Salisbury records Walter's tenure of the office, in a letter c. April-May 1168 (*Epistolae JS*, 2.552-71 ep. 272, at p. 560: 'Episcopus Albanensis domini papae vices agit in urbe'). Two decretals of Alexander III to Walter survive in the collections: *De adolescente illo, WH* 331, addressed 'Albanensi epicopo', 1167-68; and *Ex tuarum tenore, WH* 513, addressed 'W. Albanensi episcopo vicario nostro', 28 April 1168 (both are registered as a single letter in *JL* 11527, but cf. Holtzmann, 'Register', 23-25 nos 3 and 4, and idem, 'Kanonistische Ergänzungen zur Italia Pontificia', *Quellen und Forschungen*, 37 (1957), 76 nos 6 and 7). The subject matter of *Ex tuarum tenore* is strikingly similar to that of *Veniens ad apostolice:* the clerk N. was guilty of an offence of such seriousness that it would merit degradation if public; since it is secret, he should after penance be content in his present order. But, since the sin was secret, he cannot be refused promotion, if he desires it. The dating limits of *Veniens ad apostolice* are most probably 1167-73x75, the terminus ad quem being set by its presence in *Belv.* (cf. Duggan, *Decretal Collections*, 72 and 158).

12

Alexander III to the archbishops, bishops and other prelates in the kingdoms of France, England and Scotland.

1166-72 (1159-81)

Attenta diligentia et sollicitudine nos providere oportet ne grex dominicus nobis commissus spiritualis alimonie patiatur defectum ... condigne satisfacere studeant.

The pope speaks of his duty to safeguard the spiritual welfare of the Lord's flock, and to prevent the decay of ecclesiastical discipline. He is especially concerned that the recipient prelates do not place reverence for an earthly prince above the fear of God. Men's actions show how prone they are to vice and corruption, and the pope is obliged by his office to correct the excesses of all, and to be concerned more with their salvation than with favour and human glory. He mandates the recipients not to communicate knowingly with excommunicates, through favour or fear of their princes or of any mortal person, and so to share in their condemnation. If any manifestly presume to contravene this order, or can be convicted of such by their metropolitan, they are forthwith suspended from office and excommunicted, until they make suitable satisfaction to the judges who had imposed the original sentences for so great an offence.

WH 94, *JL* --, 1166-72 (1159-81). *Cott.* 3.35 and *Pet.* 2.22.1 only. Pd *Decretales ineditae*, 1-2 no. 1.

The decretal is found only in two English collections of the late twelfth century. Its immediate context has not been established, but it may be compared with the letter *Saluti regum*, which Alexander III sent to king Louis VII of France, and which deals with the same subject in comparable terms and is preserved in the Becket materials (cf. *JL* 11841, *c.* 8 October 1170; *Materials TB* , 7.381-82 no. 713 and n.: 'referred by *JL* to 1170, but may possibly be of an earlier date'). The problem of association with excommunicates had a long ancestry, both in the wider Church, notably in the period of Gregorian Reform in the eleventh century, and in the context of ducal and royal edicts in Normandy and England, to limit the excommunication of tenants-in-chief and royal familiars, as at Lillebonne in 1080, Poitiers in 1163 and Clarendon in 1164: cf. Constitutions of Clarendon, clause 7, 'Nullus qui de rege teneat in capite, vel aliquis dominicorum ministrorum eius excommunicetur, nec terre alicuius eorum sub interdicto ponantur, nisi prius rex, si in terra fuerit, conveniatur *etc.*; and Whitelock, Brett and Brooke, *Councils and Synods*, I.ii, 864-65. It was a most serious problem from the time of the sentences pronounced by Becket at Vézelay on Whit Sunday 1166 until the reconciliation at Avranches in 1172, after his death. *Attenta diligentia* could date from that period; the pope's very emphatic language suggests more than a routine concern with a familiar problem. But in the absence of more positive evidence, the letter cannot be more securely dated than by Alexander III's pontifical years.

13

Alexander III to the dean and precentor of the church of Lincoln. 1167-73x75(1159-81)

Ex conquestione W. clerici de Greftun ... severitate ecclesiastica compescatis.

The clerk W. had held the vicarage of the church of *Greftun* for an annual payment by the concession of the former abbess E., but the clerk P. presumed to molest him in respect of the vicarage, having been granted the church by the present abbess E., on the basis of a charter of the archbishop of Canterbury and a transaction with R. Foliot, which was confirmed with an oath but later quashed at the wish of both parties. The recipients must examine the truth and the form of the transaction and of R. Foliot's oath, through the spoken testimony of those who were present, and by judicial process discover the truth of the matter, notwithstanding the archbishop's charter. If the charge is substantiated, they shall admonish and if necessary compel P. to leave W. in peace in the vicarage, and exact nothing further from him.

WH 403, *JL* --, 1167-73x75 (1159-81). Pd *Sang.* 6.6.14; and *Papal decretals relating to the diocese of Lincoln in the twelfth century*, edd. W. Holtzmann and E.W. Kemp, Lincoln Record Society 1954, 34-35 no. 14.

The successive abbesses E. almost certainly identify their house as that of the Benedictine nuns at Godstow, near Oxford in the Lincoln diocese: Edith Lancelene (Ediva) was abbess from the convent's foundation in 1133, but had been succeeded by Edith secunda by 1167; the latter died *c.* 1182 (see D. Knowles, C.N.L. Brooke and V.C.M. London, *Heads of Religious Houses: England and Wales 940-1216* [Cambridge 1972], 211-12; if the present identification is correct, the decretal confirms that there were indeed two abbesses Edith, rather than one, *q.v. ibid.*). The transmission of the name of the church is uncertain (*Greston, Grefton, Graccor*), but Grafton near Oxford is the probable identification. That the dean and precentor of Lincoln were commissioned to deal with the case suggests that the mandate was issued after the death of bishop Robert de Chesney on 27 December 1166 (by which time also Edith secunda had succeeded), and before the election of Geoffrey Plantagenet, or its confirmation, respectively *c.* May 1173 and before July 1175. If these suppositions are correct, the dating limits are 1167-73x75, the dean was Adelelm, and the precentor Richard de Almeria. The dispute could then scarcely have arisen on the basis of a charter of archbishop Richard, who was not consecrated until 7 April 1174, by the pope at Anagni, and did not reach England until August. It is therefore possible that Theobald or Thomas was the archbishop whose charter was in question. With so many hypotheses undecided, the wider limits of the pope's pontifical years must be allowed for the mandate. The R. Foliot, who was a party to the transaction, was presumably not the well-known Robert Foliot, archdeacon of Oxford (from 1151) and bishop's official until his election to Hereford in late

April 1173, and one of the *eruditi* of archbishop Thomas in the early years of his exile.

14

Alexander III to all the bishops of England. 19 May 1168

Ad audientiam nostram communi fama referente ... ab omnibus evitari. Datum Beneventi xiiii. kalendas Junii.

From common rumour and the report of many the pope has learned of an evil custom that has arisen in the recipient bishops' districts after the outbreak of the present trouble between king Henry and archbishop Thomas of Canterbury, namely that lay persons throughout England grant churches and ecclesiastical benefices to whom they wish, and invest clerks at their own authority. Since this practice gravely endangers the Church's freedom, and both those who give and those who receive such grants are anathema, the pope quashes them utterly, and orders the bishops to secure without leave of appeal that all who received from lay hands churches, prebends and ecclesiastical benefices anywhere in England - 'et maxime huius turbationis tempore' - resign them into the bishops' hands, and relinquish them to those who by ecclesiastical law have the right of disposing of them. If the offenders do not comply with the bishops' warning within forty days of the receipt of the present mandate, the bishops must excommunicate them, without fear or favour or the prohibition of anyone, and ensure their avoidance as excommunicates until they have resigned the grants and made satisfaction in respect of fruits received. If the bishops themselves prove negligent or remiss in this commission, the pope excommunicates the offenders by his own authority, unless they obey his orders within the prescribed time.

WH 20, *JL* 11398, 19 May 1168. *Belv.* 21. Pd *Materials TB*, 6.419-20 no. 413 (from Becket correspondence: cf. A. Duggan, *Thomas Becket*, 243 and 282).

15

Alexander III to the archbishops, bishops and other prelates of England. 17 November 1168-69

Licet universa loca religiosa ex commissi nobis officii ... precipimus observari. Datum Beneventi xv. kal. Decembris.

It is the pope's duty to cherish all religious places, but especially those subject to St Peter and himself, *nullo mediante*. Therefore he wishes the liberties and rights of St Albans to remain whole and unharmed, especially those granted by the apostolic see and strengthened with the privileges of the Roman Church. The recipients must not in future excommunicate or interdict the monks or obedientiaries of St Albans. Since a sentence imposed by them on the parishioner of another is illegal, how much less should that be observed which is imposed on the special sons of the Roman Church, who have no bishop but the Roman pontiff. If any of them presume in this way, their action will be void and worthless. The pope wishes all privileges granted to the abbot and monks and their monastery to be confirmed, and orders the recipients to observe them inviolably.

WH 623, *JL* 13741, Benevento, 17 November 1168-69. Pd abbrev. in *Cass.* 19.8 and *1 Comp.Ag.Fr.* 3.25.4; complete (from Brussels Bibl. roy. 7965-73, fol.

198v [17th-century transcript from a St Albans cartulary]) in Holtzmann, 'Register', 85-86 no. 3, and *PU England* 3.304-05 no. 166.

This privilege to St Albans is addressed to all English prelates in 1168-69, its standard protocol therefore including archbishop Thomas in exile. It is one of three letters relating to St Albans' rights, issued by Alexander III on a single day, 17 November at Benevento (see *PU England*, 3.304-06 nos 165-67: 165, to abbot Simon and the monks of St Albans, *Licet universa loca*, parallel in subject-matter to the present letter; 166, the present letter; 167, to archbishop Roger of York and bishop Hugh of Durham, Ex commissi nobis, concerning the rights of St Albans' churches and chapels). Alexander III was at Benevento on 17 November in the three years 1167-69, but the letter *Cum monasterium vestrum*, a rebuke to the prior and monks of St Albans in respect of the vacancy following abbot Robert's death on 23 October 1166, was dated at Benevento on 1 July 1168; since one of the three letters issued on 17 November names Simon as recipient abbot, their earliest and probable date is 1168 (see *PU England*, 3.297-98 no. 155; Alexander did not reach Benevento until August 1167; abbot Simon was elected c. 21 May 1167).

16

Alexander III to bishops Gilbert of London, Jocelin of Salisbury, Bartholomew of Exeter, Richard of Chester, Walter of Rochester, Godfrey of St Asaph and Nicholas of Llandaff.

16 September 1170

Oportuerat vos, quando primum carissimus filius noster Henricus ... precipimus evitari. [Datum Ferentini decimo sexto kalendas Octobris.]

The bishops should have sought to prevent the shipwreck of ecclesiastical dignity, when king Henry first proposed that written constitutions, clearly contrary to Church freedom, should be confirmed by oath. But they placed reverence for an earthly prince above the fear of God and episcopal honour. Even if they then accepted the customs in fear and under duress, they should not have persisted in observing such usurpations until the Church's laws seem utterly proscribed in their kingdom. Their archbishop Thomas went into exile to resist these usurpations, even if through fleshly weakness he seemed at first to consent. But having then withheld their support, they recently increased his grief and assisted at the coronation of the king's son, though this conflicted with Canterbury's ancient right and the authority of both the archbishop and the pope himself. Nothing was said on that occasion about the Church's freedom, but an oath was taken to preserve the customs of the kingdom. The pope has striven to effect a reconciliation, and recognizes the king's liberality to him in many matters, but such great offences cannot be overlooked. He suspends the bishops, subjecting to anathema the bishops of London and Salisbury, the bishop of Rochester and Geoffrey Ridel, archdeacon of Canterbury, and confirms the archbishop's sentences on Robert, the archdeacon's vicar, and earl Hugh of Norfolk's clerks Nicholas, Thomas, William and the others.

WH 692, *JL* 11835, 16 September 1170. *Sang*. 3.13.9; *1 Abr*. 3.9.2. Pd *Materials TB*, 7.360-64 no. 700; Diceto, 1.340.

The letter occurs in two Anglo-Norman decretal collections and in non-canonical sources, and should be read with *Licet nobis*, to Roger of York and Hugh of Durham (*infra prox.*). Its full address is found in Diceto, which also supplies the bishops' personal names; Llandaff is omitted in Sang.; Rochester, St Asaph, and Llandaff are omitted in *1 Abr.* No copy lists the bishops in their customary order of precedence, except that London always appears first. On the coronation of the Young King, see *Quanto per carissimum* (*supra* 6); and Duggan, *Decretals of Alexander III*, 133-34 no. 618, and 137 no. 772.

17

Alexander III to archbishop Roger of York and bishop Hugh of Durham. 16 September 1170

Licet nobis commendabiles et grati in pluribus existatis ... de reddenda ratione. [Datum Ferentini decimo sexto kalendas Octobris.]

The pope rebukes the recipients for their compliance with the English king's policies in diminishing the freedom of the Church, and records the frustration of legates whom he sent in response to archbishop Thomas's requests. Specifically, in the coronation of the young king, the king's son, the recipient archbishop performed the ceremony without mention of the Church's freedom, but the preservation of the ancient customs which endanger the Church was confirmed. The archbishop's offence was all the greater being committed in the province of another, and of one suffering exile for justice. The recipients are suspended from all episcopal office.

WH 618, *JL* 11836, 16 September 1170. *Sang.* 3.13.8; *1 Abr.* 3.9.1; *2 Dun.* 4. Pd *Materials TB*, 7.364-68 no. 701 (with variant opening *Licet commendabiles nobis* and the date).

Only three decretal collections preserve this well-known letter, which should be read with *Oportuerat vos (supra prox.)*; perhaps with prudence, the Durham collection *2 Dun.* omits the bishop of Durham from the address of this papal rebuke and sentence.

18

Henry II to Alexander III. early (? January) 1171

Ob reverentiam Romane ecclesie et amorem vestrum ... me salubris consilii medicamine foveatis.

Because of his reverence for the Roman Church and the love which he has sought from the pope and preserved to the present time, the king granted to archbishop Thomas of Canterbury peace and full restoration of his possessions, in accordance with the pope's mandate, and a return to England with an honourable escort. The archbishop, however, did not take back with him the joy of peace, but fire and sword. He called in question against the king a matter concerning his realm and crown, and dared to excommunicate royal servants on all sides and without cause. Finding such provocation intolerable, these servants and others in England attacked the archbishop and killed him. The king cannot relate this matter without grief, and is deeply worried that the anger which he had long harboured against the archbishop had provided the cause of this crime. Because the king fears more for his reputation than his conscience in this deed, he seeks the pope's healing advice.

WH --, *JL* --, early (? January) 1171. *1 Abr.*, fol. 87v, addition in lower margin. Pd *Materials TB* ,7.440 no. 739 (from E. Martène and U. Durand, *Thesaurus novus anecdotorum*, 1 [Paris, 1717], 559).

This letter survives only as a late addition in the decretal collection *1 Abr.*, inserted at the foot of a folio, together with *Cum testimonium veritati* (*infra prox.*), a notification by archbishop Rotrou of Rouen of his non-compliance with the papal mandate to place a sentence of interdict on Henry II's continental lands. But in sentiment and purpose it is related to the well-known letter *Cum apud regem*, Arnulf of Lisieux to Alexander III, reporting Becket's murder in terms of regret, but also in mitigation of the king's responsibility (*Materials TB* ,7.438-39 no. 738: '... quod quidam inimici eius ... in eum irruptione facta, quod sine dolore dicere non possumus nec debemus, personam eius aggredi et trucidare crudeliter perstiterunt ... licet ipse novas inimicitias recentibus iniuriis et frequentibus maleficiis compararet, arbitrari se nominis sui famam et gloriam maledictis emulatorum respergi posse, et confingi id ex eius conscientia processisse ...'). It is probable that Arnulf's hand is seen also in the present letter.

19

Archbishop Rotrou of Rouen to all bishops and abbots of the English king's continental lands. March-mid April 1171

Cum testimonium veritati exhibere debeat unusquisque fidelis, hoc precipue a pontificibus est exigendum. Notum sit itaque serenitati vestre ... si lata esset sententia, relaxari deberet.

The archbishop informs the recipients that the archbishop of Sens has imposed an interdict on the English king's continental lands, acting on a papal mandate in which both archbishops were jointly and equally commissioned, but he did not himself assent to this action, nor does he do so now. He refused consent, in the presence of the archbishop of Sens and to his face, and refuses it still, especially since he heard the king offer to make such full satisfaction that the sentence should be lifted, if it had been imposed.

WH --, *JL* --, March-mid April 1171. *1 Abr.*, fol. 87v, addition in lower margin. Pd *Materials TB*, 7.445-46 no. 742 (from Martène, *Thesaurus novus anecdotorum*, 1.559).

This notification by archbishop Rotrou of Rouen should be read with Henry II's letter *Ob reverentiam (supra prox.)* to Alexander III, for their related context and preservation together as late additions in *1 Abr.* The pope's joint commission to William ofSens and Rotrou of Rouen, in the immediate aftermath of Becket's murder, has not survived, but is mentioned in several other letters (cf.*Vestro apostolatui*, William of Sens to Alexander III, including a report of Rotrou's non-compliance with the mandate, at Sens in the company of bishops Arnulf of Lisieux, Giles of Evreux, Roger of Worcester and many members of the English king's *familia; Miseranda rumorum*, William [? William du Puiset, son of bishop Hugh, and archdeacon of Northumberland from 1174] to bishop Hugh of Durham; *Licet presentis*, bishop Stephen of Meaux to Alexander III; and *In apostolice sedis*, Alexander III to Joscius of Tours, Tusculum 14 May 1171, including papal ratification of archbishop William's sentence of interdict: *Materials TB*, 7.440-43 no. 740, 443-45 no. 741, 446-47 no. 743, and 483-85 no. 755; for Roger of Worcester's unexpected and presumably slight role in this sequence of events, see M. Cheney, *Roger, bishop of Worcester*, 51-53). The letters of archbishop William and Alexander III make clear that the papal commission mandated either recipient to act, if the other was unable or unwilling to do so. The *terminus ad quem* of the present item can be deduced from that of *In apostolice sedis*.

20

Alexander III to Richard Barre. 1171 (1169-73)

Ex diligenti tua relatione nobis innotuit quod G. Cantuariensis archidiaconus ... valeas demonstrare.

Richard Barre has informed the pope that archdeacon Geoffrey of Canterbury induced him with many promises to do homage to him and swear fealty in return for a yearly benefice. Recognizing the illegality and danger of such a bond, Richard sought absolution from the pope and promised that he would accept nothing from the benefice. In view of his honest petition, the pope releases him from homage to the archdeacon, especially since it is contrary to both divine and human laws. He should accept a suitable penance from a bishop or discreet priest, by whose advice he should be reconciled to God. And for Richard's future protection, the pope grants him letters of absolution, to safeguard him from the snares of the wicked, and as evidence to all.

WH 407, *JL* 14176, 1171 (1169-73). Pd *Sang*. 3.9.1; *1 Comp.Ag*. 5.2.19; *X* 5.3.17; occurs otherwise only in *Frcf.Max. 12.4g*.

Richard Barre was a well-known servant of Henry II, and a trusted royal emissary in the closing years of the Becket dispute; he was archdeacon of Lisieux not later than 1173x77 (see *The letters and charters of Gilbert Foliot*, edd. A. Morey and C.N.L. Brooke, Cambridge 1967, 455 no. 420), and archdeacon of Ely from 1188x90; in 1188, he was Henry II's emissary to the emperors Frederick I and Isaac Angelus and king Bela of Hungary in the preparations for a projected crusade (see Diceto, 2.51-54). He was present in the papal curia in late 1169 and again in 1171, just after the news of Becket's murder arrived there (see *Epistolae JS*, 2.692-93 and n. 4; and *Materials TB*, 7.471-78 nos 750-51). It is possible that he secured the present letter of absolution and protection on one of these occasions, probably the later. The archdeacon of Canterbury (named G. in *Frcf.Max.*, R. in *Sang.*, H. in *X)* was Geoffrey Ridel, a leading royal agent during the dispute, the 'archidiabolus noster' of the Becket correspondence, and excommunicated twice by the archbishop (cf. C. Duggan, 'Richard of Ilchester, royal servant and bishop', *TRHS*, 5th Series, 16 [1966], 1, 2 and n. 1): he was elected bishop of Ely in late April 1173, and consecrated on 6 October 1174 (see *Cum de tua, infra* 30). The probable date of the present letter is 1171, within the limits 1169-73.

21

Alexander III to archbishop Rotrou of Rouen and bishop Thibaud of Amiens. 23 October 1171

Et ipsa loci vicinitas et fama vulgata per orbem vos ignorare non patitur ... officii sui plenitudinem incunctanter restituatis. Sane, si his exequendis ... maturius exequatur. Datum Tusculani decimo kalendas Novembris.

The wicked and inhuman crime perpetrated against the former archbishop of Canterbury, Thomas of holy memory - 'sancte recordationis', had arisen from the suspension of archbishop Roger of York from his pontifical office, since the king's indignation on hearing the sentence had prompted some of his bystanders to attack and kill Thomas in his own church. The king's envoys had been unable to persuade the pope to commission to their regions the purgation of Roger and other bishops who had been sentenced for a similar fault, and Roger claimed that the so-called emperor Frederick would not afford him safe passage, because of his devotion to the pope and the church from the beginning of the present trouble, though he was prepared to make the journey. In consideration of Roger's faith and devotion, and of his own wish to defer to the English king as far as God and justice allow, the pope commits the affair to the recipients. They are to summon the archbishop to a place on the border of the French and English kings' territories - 'in marchia', and associate with themselves religious and discreet men. With appropriate persons of his own church - two of the greater persons, or two other canons, the masters Vacarius and Angelus, or two others of equal merit, or two priors or abbots, the archbishop shall swear that he did not confirm the wicked constitutions, or promise to keep them, that he in no way wittingly provoked the king to kill or harm the archbishop, that he had not received the pope's letters forbidding him to crown the king's son, nor contrived to avoid receiving them. On these conditions they shall restore his office to him. If either of the judges cannot act in the commission, the other shall do so with religious and weighty men of the other's area.

WH 383a, *JL* 11908, 23 October 1171. *1 Par.* 171. Pd *Materials TB*, 7.498-501 no. 763.

The present letter is found only in the French decretal collection *1 Par.* (beginning *Et ipsa vicinitas*, ending at 'restituatis', and omitting the date) and in the Becket correspondence. Roger of York and his suffragan Hugh of Durham had been suspended for their part in the coronation of the Young King Henry on 14 June 1170 (see *Licet nobis commendabiles, supra* 17; cf. *Quanto per carissimum, supra* 6); it was the reaction to Becket's publication of that papal sentence on his return to England in December and of the simultaneous sentence of Gilbert of London and other bishops of the Canterbury province (see *Oportuerat vos, supra* 16), which led to his murder on 29 December (see *Ob reverentiam, supra* 18). The present mandate records Alexander III's provisions for Roger's purgation in respect of the coronation and his possible culpability in the murder; on the same day he issued cautionary instructions in a separate letter to the same commissioners (see *Quia nonnunquam, JL* 11909, *Materials TB*, 7.501-02 no. 764; for the record of Roger's purgation and the presence of the famous jurist Vacarius, see *ibid.*, 501; and for Roger's thanks to the pope and his letter to Hugh of Durham and other prelates, ibid., 502-06 nos 765 and 766). Some months later, the pope wrote again to Rotrou of Rouen and Thibaud of Amiens, mandating them to deal with the absolution of Gilbert of London and the other bishops (see *Fraternitati vestre, JL* 12143, 27 February 1172, *ibid.*, 506-09 no. 767).

22

Alexander III to the cardinal legates Albert of San Lorenzo in Lucina and Theodwin of San Vitale. **late 1171**

Dilecti filii nostri (prior) et monachi Cantuarienses ... fuerit annuendum. Preterea, memoratam ecclesiam ... in basilica beati Petri conspergi.

The prior and monks of Canterbury have urgently entreated the pope for the canonization of the martyred archbishop Thomas, whose merits are attested by the miracles which God has worked through him. With the customary discretion of the Roman Church, the pope commissions the legates to investigate the reported miracles, seeking the truth from bishops and others in the region. With their careful report, he can proceed with the canonization, if it is seen to be proper. The purgation of the cathedral, profaned by the murder, should be in accordance with the practice of St Peter's basilica, without re-dedication.

WH 356a, *JL* --, late 1171. Only in *Cott.* 4.32 and *Pet.* 3.32. Pd *Decretales ineditae*, 61-62 no. 36.

The letter is of interest both for Thomas's canonization and the process of papal authorization of canonizations (cf. C. Duggan, 'Bishop John and archdeacon Richard of Poitiers: their roles in the Becket dispute and its aftermath', in *Thomas Becket: Actes du colloque international de Sédières*, ed. R. Foreville, Paris 1975, 78-79; S. Kuttner, *The history of ideas and doctrines of canon law in the middle ages*, Variorum Reprints, London 1980, Retractationes VI, 9; *Decretales ineditae*, 62. An already-known fragment likewise addressed to Albert and Theodwin deals with the same matter as the final sentence, the reconciliation of Canterbury cathedral profaned by Becket's murder, and is perhaps an adaptation from the present commission (cf. *Mandamus vobis*, *JL* 12200, pd *Materials TB*, 7.551 no.787, *sub anno* 1173):

Dilecti filii	**Mandamus vobis**
Preterea	*Mandamus vobis quatinus*
memoratam ecclesiam	*ecclesiam Cantuarie*
que per interfectionem prefati	
archiepiscopi idem carnificum	
profanata est	
diligenter faciatis secundum	*faciatis*
quod ecclesiastica institutio	
precipit expurgari,	*reconciliari,*
ita quod	*ita tamen ut sacramentum*
dedicationis	*pristine dedicationis*
non debeat sacramentum iterari,	*non debeat iterari,*
sed aqua benedicta sicut	*sed, sicut solet fieri in*
sepe fieri solet in basilica	*ecclesia beati Petri, tantum*
beati Petri conspergi.	*aqua benedicta aspergatur.*

23

Alexander III to bishop Bartholomew of Exeter. **31 January 1172**

(a) Sicut dignum est et omni rationi consentaneum ... introitu coerceri. (b) Super eo vero quod a nobis ... sedem venire. (c) Monachi vero et canonici ...

providentia adhibenda. (d) Si vero aliquis ... excommunicationis immunis. Data Tusculani ii. kalendas Februarii.

(a) The pope distinguishes the various forms of complicity in the murder of the former archbishop of Canterbury, and the appropriate penances: of those who intended to kill him, or strike or capture him with that intention; of those who assisted the murderers; of those who incited the king; of those who, unaware of the deed, gave service to the perpetrators, knowing their disposition; of those who subsequently occupied his possessions, of those who wittingly associated with excommunicates; of those clerks who were armed participants, or who gave advice on his capture. (b) The pope likewise gives advice on students who strike one another, whether clerks or religious, of full or minor age; (c) on monks and canons regular who strike one another in their cloister; (d) on a secular doorkeeper who injures a clerk, or a lay official who lays violent hands on a clerk; and on one who injures a clerk in self defence, and one who lays violent hands on a clerk basely discovered with his wife or close female relation.

WH 929, *JL* 12180, 31 January 1172: the date occurs in *Wig.Alt.* 1 only. Pd *App.* 35.1(a), 14.7(b), 14.8(c), 14.9-10(d); *Cass.* 64.5(a), 19.9(b), 10(c), 11(d); *1 Comp.Ag.* 5.10.7(a), 5.34.2(b), 3(c), 4(d); X 5.12.6(a), 5.39.1(b), 2(c), 3(d); and part (a) in *Materials TB*, 7.534-36 no. 780, *sub anno* 1172.

This well-known letter of Alexander III on degrees of complicity in Becket's murder and their appropriate penances found a permanent place in the general canon law, all its constituent parts being transmitted into *X*, in the titles *De homicidio voluntario vel casuali* (5.12) and *De sententia excommunicationis* (5.39). The whole text is found integrally in 16 primitive and two systematic collections; parts are found in nine primitive collections and in many systematic collections; and part (a) is found also in Alan of Tewkesbury's collection of the Becket correspondence (Brit. Libr. Cotton MS Claudius B.ii, v. 103). The edited text in the Becket correspondence, depending on *Belv.* and Alan of Tewkesbury, concludes at 'introitu coerceri', the editor noting that 'the remainder of the letter deals with questions as to clerks striking each other and other such matters' (*Materials TB*, 536 n. 8).

24

Alexander III to archbishop Roger of York.

ex 1171 - mid-February 1173

A memoria nostra non excidit ... debeat habere.

In the first year of Alexander's pontificate, Roger had sent him a copy of letters of Honorius II granting Roger's predecessors and their successors the right to have their cross carried before them throughout England - 'per totam Angliam', and Alexander confirmed this. But Thomas of Canterbury - 'sancte et venerande memorie' - later objected to this as diminishing his right and dignity, and appealed to the apostolic see, claiming that the right had not been allowed to Roger or his predecessors. Alexander therefore forbad Roger to have his cross carried before him in the Canterbury province, pending an investigation of the question. Whereupon Roger, through the clerks I. and A., objected that he had been despoiled of a right before a judicial enquiry. Alexander now decrees that the letters of prohibition issued at Thomas's request are not to be prejudicial to the exercise of rights granted by the apostolic see and exercised by Roger and his predecessors. The right of carrying his cross throughout England will hold until the matter is definitively decided.

WH 1, *JL* 12530, ex 1171-mid-February 1173. Archival copies: PRO Ancient Corres-pondence, I no. 1; York Cathedral Library *Registrum magnum album*, part I, fol. 47v. Pd *App*. 50.37; *Cass*. 55.3; 2 *Comp.Ag*. 2.9.1; *X* 2.16.1; *Historians of the church of York and its archbishops*, ed. J. Raine, Rolls Series, 3 vols., 1879-94, 3.73-74 no. 57 (*inter* 1170-75?); *Materials TB*, 7.568-69 no. 798 (*sub annis* 1175-76); see Duggan, *Decretals of Alexander III*, 114-15 no. 1.

At least 18 copies of this interim concession survive in archival and canonical sources: in the PRO Ancient Correspondence, in the *Registrum Magnum Album (RMA)* in the York archives, in Alan of Tewkesbury's collection of Becket correspondence, and in 15 decretal collections, from *App.Cr.* to a shortened and edited version in *X*. Even the earliest decretal collections containing the letter post-date the deaths of Alexander III and Roger of York in 1181. The text, date and historical context of the letter, all raise difficult problems. The *incipit* occurs as *A memoria nostra* (which is probably correct), *A memoria vestra* (which is irreconcilable with the single recipient and internal syntax), *Memoria nostra* and *Memoriam nostram* (vel *vestram*). The text in *RMA* has an obvious error, where the pope's former concession, to which Thomas subsequently objected, is stated as confirmed by the present letter - 'tibi scripti presentis munimine confirmamus' (*recte*: 'tibi scripti nostri munimine confirmavimus'); the text in *App.Cr.* is defective in its several inconsistencies of singular and plural forms applied to the recipient; the version in *AlanT* seems more reliable, except for its incorrect *incipit*.

The date is given as 1170-75(?) in *RMA*, as *c*. 1175 in *JL* and *WH*, and as 1175-76 in *Materials TB*. Since the text was clearly written after Becket's death on 29 December 1170, its earliest possible date is 1171; and its general and provisional form is unlikely to post-date the precise commission of Alexander III to bishops Jocelin of Salisbury and Hugh of Durham on 6 October 1174, mandating them to convene the archbishops of Canterbury and York after peace has been restored between Henry II and his son, investigate the issues dividing them 'super iure primatie et de cruce ferenda', forward the depositions to the pope and fix a term for the archbishops to appear before him (see *Cum summi pontificatus: PU England*, 2.332-33 no. 141; indeed the mandate refers to an earlier commission on the same point to the same recipients - 'sicut iam pridem ita et nunc experientie vestre committimus audiendam', which would bring back the *terminus ad quem* to June 1174 at the latest). It has been argued on grounds of historical probablility that 1173 is a more likely date, in the Canterbury vacancy following Thomas's death, but after Roger's purgation on 13 December 1171, and after Thomas's canonization on 21 February 1173, in view of the pope's description of him as 'sancte et venerande memorie' (see Foreville, *L'Église et la royauté*, 518 and n. 2; cf. G.F. Scammell, *Hugh du Puiset, bishop of Durham*, Cambridge 1956, 73). The phrase in fact suggests a date before the canonization, not after it. Several letters of Alexander III in 1171 in the aftermath of the murder already speak of Thomas as 'sancte recordationis', and others in 1172 as 'recolende et sancte memorie', or 'sanctus et reverendus vir' (cf. *Patrologiae cursus completus, series latina*, ed. J.P. Migne, Paris 1855, 200.725-27, 730-31, 735-36, 872-74 and 894-95 nos. 788-90, 794, 798, 995 and 1014; and E.W. Kemp, *Canonization and authority in the Western Church*, Oxford 1948, 87-89). In the letters of March 1173 announcing the canonization and thereafter, Alexander most commonly wrote 'sanctus Thomas', 'beatus Thomas', 'sanctus Thomas martyr', or 'gloriosus et inclitus martyr Thomas' (cf. 25, 27, 28, 29, 32, 33 and 34 *infra*). The probable dating limits for *A memoria nostra* are therefore *ex* 1171 - mid-February 1173.

The letter of Honorius II, a copy of which Roger of York had sent to Alexander III in the first year of his pontificate, was presumably *Quemadmodum vestrum*, to William of Corbeil, archbishop of Canterbury, all the bishops of England and king Henry I, on 9 December 1125 (see *Historians of the Church of York*, 3.50 no. 33). It ordered them to permit the archbishop of York to have his cross carried before him, according to the ancient custom of the Church of York, and to crown the king. It did not include the phrase 'per totam Angliam', nor did Alexander's reply to Roger's petition, in *Quanto personam* on 28 January 1161 (*ibid.*, 69-70 no. 53, Anagni, 28 January 1160-61, but the former year is an improbably early date), nor did the closely parallel version of *Quanto personam* preserved in the Becket materials with the date Montpellier, 13 July 1162 (*JL* 10742, *Materials TB*, 5.21-22 no. 13). It may be surmised that the reissue of *Quanto personam* was in response to Roger's heightened concern with his prerogatives and status, following the election and consecration of Thomas to Canterbury, on 23 May and 3 June 1162 respectively. The increasing tension between them was sharply expressed at the council of Tours in the pope's presence in May 1163, and in the presence of king Henry II at Westminster in October (R.W. Eyton, *Court, household, and itinerary of king Henry II*, London 1878, 64: 1 October; but now cf. F. Barlow, *Thomas Becket*, London 1986, 95: 13 October).

Six letters in particular record the course of the dispute on the cross-bearing issue between the council of Westminster and 21 January 1164, in which period also the conflict between Thomas and the king reached a crisis at the council of Clarendon, from 13 January 1164. Sometime after the council of Westminster, the unidentified writer of *Comitem Flandrensem* reported to Thomas that the pope was dispatching a Templar to act on his behalf in seeking to avert contention, and that he was instructing Roger not to presume to have his cross borne before him in the Canterbury diocese pending a decision (*ibid.*, 58-61 no. 36); and in *Pro illa animi*, the pope informed Roger that he had inspected his predecessors' rescripts and recalled that he had previously granted him the right to have his cross borne before him 'per totam Angliam', but, since a still-unresolved dispute had arisen on this matter, he must not exercise that right in the meanwhile (*ibid.*, 67-68 no. 41). In fact, in the extant letters to this point, Alexander had not used the words which he now 'remembered', and their entry into the dispute may date from this time. It was perhaps in response to complaints from Thomas and Gilbert of London that the pope's ruling against Roger hardened, perhaps also in reaction to the more fundamental crisis in England. In *Venerande pater*, Thomas complained of Roger's provocative behaviour in the southern province - 'contra crucem crucem erexit, cruces crucem opposuit, Christum significans esse divisum, crucis scandalum suscitavit' (*ibid.*, 44-46 no. 27); and in *Ut ostium cardine* he was strongly supported by Gilbert, recently transferred from Hereford and shortly to emerge as his most bitter opponent (*ibid.*, 46-47 no. 28; and Morey and Brooke, *Letters and charters of Gilbert Foliot*, 191-92 no. 146). In *Querimonias adversus* to Thomas on 21 January 1164, Alexander explained that his early letters to York had not included the disputed phrase, and cited the more generally framed concession of *Quanto personam* in its 13 July 1162 version: it was through forgetfulness that he had used those words, not intentionally - 'unde ex oblivione potius quam ex industria contingit quod verbum illud, scilicet *per totam Angliam* postreme littere continebant. Non enim tenorem priorum litterarum concessionis nostre memoriter tenebamus' (*ibid.*, 69 no. 43, *JL* 10996). And in *Decet prudentiam* he more strictly forbad Roger to have his cross carried before him in the southern province, pending a decision, if he wished to avoid the risk of permanent deprivation of the right (*ibid.*, 68 no. 42, *JL* 10742).

The claims of York were re-asserted at a time of acute danger for Thomas at the council of Northampton in October 1164, but in his years of exile the conflict focussed on more substantial problems, which culminated in the Young King's coronation by Roger on 14 June 1170, and in the chain of events which led to Thomas's death and Roger's suspension (see *Quanto per carissimum, Licet nobis commendabiles*, and *Et ipsa loci vicinitas*, 6, 17 and 21 *supra*). In the more favourable circumstances of reconciliation after Thomas's death, most probably between Roger's rehabilitation and Thomas's canonization, and possibly after the compromise of Avranches on 12 May 1172, Roger advanced once more his claim to have his cross borne before him 'per totam Angliam'. This is the almost certain context of *A memoria nostra*, with Alexander once more conceding the claim, pending a final ruling. But the election of Richard to Canterbury in 1173 and his consecration by the pope on 7 April 1174, followed by a spate of papal confirmations of Canterbury's rights, re-awakened the contention. Alexander's commission to Jocelin of Salisbury and Hugh of Durham on 6 October 1174 was not fulfilled, perhaps through Jocelin's incapacity and Hugh's disfavour with the king (see Scammell, *Hugh du Puiset*, 73-74). The issue was raised at Richard's provincial council of Westminster on 18 May 1175, and an agreement was reached between Richard and Roger after the legate Pierleoni's arrival in England in late October 1175, when they agreed to accept the judgment of the archbishop of Rouen and other nearby bishops of the kingdom of France, on the cross-bearing issue and other disputes between them; and this concord was confirmed for a five-year period at the council of Winchester on 15 August 1176 (see *Gesta regis Henrici secundi*, ed. W. Stubbs, Rolls Series 1867, 1.89, 104-05 and 118-19; and *Chronica magistri Rogeri de Houedene*, ed. W. Stubbs, Rolls Series 1868-71, 2.77, 85-86 and 99). Roger of York died on 21 November 1181, and his see was still vacant when Henry II died in 1189. Later echoes of the dispute were recorded in a lost letter of Innocent III and in Honorius III's *Decet prudentiam* on 6 February 1217-18 mandating archbishop Gray of York - 'ad exemplar igitur felicis memorie Alexandri et Innocentii predecessorum nostrorum' - not to have his cross borne before him in the Canterbury province (see *Historians of the Church of York*, 113 no. 81; cf. *The Letters of Pope Innocent III*, edd. C.R. Cheney and M.G. Cheney, Oxford 1967, 189 no. 1154).

It remains surprising that, after Becket's death, and during the process of his canonization, Alexander III once more believed that he had granted to York the full concession 'per totam Angliam' in the first year of his rule, on the basis of Honorius II's grant of 1125, since neither he nor Honorius had done so, especially since he had made the same mistake in 1163, had then been persuaded of his error, and took explicit pains to correct his language and explain to Thomas that he had written the words 'ex oblivione potius quam ex industria'. The authenticity of the letter in its surviving form merits further study.

25

Alexander III to an unidentified bishop and Richard of Ilchester, archdeacon of Poitiers. July 1172 - 21 February 1173

Conquerente nobis dilecto filio nostro Silvestro thesaurario Lexoviensis ecclesie ... noscitur excusare.

When preparing to follow the glorious martyr archbishop Thomas of Canterbury into exile, Silvester, treasurer of Lisieux, incurred a debt with a London Jew, for which he provided security from one year's income from his prebend at Waltham. But king Henry II appropriated the prebend and forbad the treasurer or his guarantors to repay either principle or interest upon the Jew's demand. When the king restored the prebend to Silvester, the Jew refused to accept the prebendal income for a single year on the terms of the original agreement. The pope now orders the recipients to free Silvester and his guarantors from liability for the augmented interest - 'quia non debet reus iudicari, quem impossibilitas noscitur excusare'.

WH 140, *JL* --, July 1172 - 21 February 1173. *Cott.* 5.53 only. Pd *Decretales ineditae*, 117-19 no. 68; W. Holtzmann, 'Zur päpstlichen Gesetzgebung über die Juden im 12. Jahrhundert', *Festschrift Guido Kisch* (Stuttgart 1955), 229.

The name of the recipient bishop cannot be read in the single extant copy in the mutilated *Cott.* manuscript. Holtzmann proposed that he was Norman, but an English bishop (possibly Gilbert of London) was a more likely choice. Silvester occurs in papal correspondence from the early 1160s to the late 1170s (see *Decretales ineditae*, 40-41 no. 22, 43 no. 24, and 117-19 no. 68; and his activities in his uncle's diocese in the years 1161-79 are recorded in *The Letters of Arnulf of Lisieux*, ed. F. Barlow, Camden Society, Third Series, 61 (1939), introduction *passim*, and 54-55, 146, 199-201 and 203). The present letter was almost certainly issued after the Compromise of Avranches on 21 May 1172, but before Thomas's canonization on 21 February 1173; its *terminus ad quem* could not be much later than Richard of Ilchester's election as bishop of Winchester in April/May 1173 (see *Decretales ineditae*, 118-19). The concluding phrase of the decretal is a citation from Roman law: 'Impossibilium nulla obligatio est': *Digest*, 50.17 *de div. regulis iuris antiqui* 185.

26

Alexander III to the cardinal legates Albert of San Lorenzo in Lucina and Theodwin of San Vitale. 1172-73

Qui a gremio sancte matris ecclesie pro suis excessibus ... in irritum revocetis.

Those who are excommunicated for their excesses cannot dispose of ecclesiastical properties or confer ordinations. Therefore the pope orders the legates to annul and declare void all ordinations, grants and concessions, in respect of prebends and other ecclesiastical benefices, conferred by the bishop of Salisbury, in person or through other ecclesiastics, while he was under sentence of excommunication.

WH 802, *JL* --, 1172-73. Only in *Cott.* 6.101. Pd *Decretales ineditae*, 63-64 no. 37.

Bishop Jocelin of Salisbury was excommunicated three times in the course of the Becket dispute: by archbishop Thomas on Whit Sunday 1166 and in 1169, and by Alexander III on 16 September 1170, for his presence at the coronation of the Young King on 14 June in that year (see D. Knowles, 'Archbishop Thomas Becket: a character study', Raleigh Lecture for 1949, in *Proceedings of the British Academy*, 35. 177-205; reprinted in *The Historian and Character*, edd. C.N.L. Brooke *et al.*, Cambridge 1963, 98-128, at 118-21; and *Oportuerat vos, supra* 16. His purgation was assigned to the legates Albert and Theodwin, the papal commissioners entrusted with the negotiations which led to the Compromise of Avranches in May 1172, and it was made within the limits 30 March 1172 and early 1173, perhaps later than March (see *Decretales ineditae*, 63-64).

27

Alexander III to the prior and monks of the church of Canterbury. 12 March 1173

Gaudendum est universitati fidelium de mirabilibus ... piis orationibus impetrare. Datum Signie iiii. idus Martii.

All the faithful must rejoice at the wonders wrought by St Thomas, former archbishop, but the recipients should experience a greater joy, since they have witnessed his miracles, and their church is adorned with his holy remains. In consideration of Thomas's glorious merits in his lifetime and in the certain knowledge of his miracles, learned from common report and the witness of the cardinal legates Albert and Theodwin and many others, the pope pronounced his canonization on Ash Wednesday in an assembly of clergy and laity, and declared him numbered in the college of holy martyrs. The recipients and all the faithful of England shall yearly celebrate the day of the martyr's passion; and for the proper reverence of his holy remains, it shall be borne in procession on some important feast day, and laid in the altar or placed in a raised reliquary, and prayers shall be offered to God, seeking Thomas's intercession for the salvation of the faithful and the peace of the universal Church.

WH 525, *JL* 12201, Segni, 12 March 1173. *Belv*. 26; and Becket correspondence. Pd *Materials TB*, 7.545-46 no. 784 (cf. *Redolet Anglia, infra prox.*).

28

Alexander III (a) to all the faithful; (b) to the archbishops, bishops and other prelates, and all the clergy and people of England. 13 March 1173

Redolet Anglia fragrantia et virtute ... apud Dominum intercedat. Datum Signie iii. idus Martii.

Although no one who contemplated the life and glorious death of St Thomas, former archbishop of Canterbury, could doubt his holiness, nevertheless our Saviour and Redeemer attested his heavenly triumph by the wonderful miracles wrought after his death. The many reports of these miracles were confirmed for the pope by the cardinal legates Albert and Theodwin from local evidence and many witnesses, and on this basis the pope canonized him on Ash Wednesday in the presence of a great congregation of clergy and laity, after consulting his brethren. The recipients shall solemnize annually the day of Thomas's death, and seek his intercession with the Lord on our behalf.

WH 850, *JL* 12204, Segni, 13 March 1173. Pd *Materials TB*, 7.547-48 no. 785 (*sub anno* 12 March 1173).

The famous letter of canonization was issued in many copies, and survives widely in international archives. The decretal collections preserve the variant addresses cited above, and the date 13 March 1173 at Segni (*1 Dert.* 58 and *Eber.* 16.5 wrongly have Anagni), while *Materials TB* has 12 March (cf. *JL* 12203 and 12218, the latter to archbishop William of Sens, 2 April 1173 at Anagni; and *Gaudendum est, supra prox.*).

29

Alexander III to bishop Roger of Worcester and prior Robert of Kenilworth March 1173-early 1179

Conquestus est nobis Radulfus clericus lator presentium quod, cum ecclesiam sancti Ypoliti de Dinnesleia ... permittatis turbari.

The clerk Ralph has complained that, after he had canonically acquired and peacefully held the church of St Hippolytus at Dinsley, Richard de Lovetot forced him to relinquish it, while St Thomas the Martyr was in exile, and he did not dare to object. If the recipients find that Ralph was canonically instituted in the church, and despoiled by lay pressure without judgment and just cause, they must ensure that the church is restored to him, together with the incomes meanwhile received, unless it can be shown that he abjured it voluntarily later; and they must not permit him to be disturbed illegally.

WH 153, *JL* 14049, March 1173-early 1179. Pd *Brug*. 31.1; 2 *Comp.Ag.Fr.*, 2.7.2 (very corrupt text).

The correct address is found only in two early collections, *1 Alc.* 65 and *Wig.* 7.66; elsewhere it occurs without an inscription, or addressed to the bishop of Paris, the abbot of St Rémi and the dean of Meaux. The church of St Hippolytus gave its name to the Hertfordshire village Ippollitts, once part of the manor of Dinsley (on Richard de Lovetot [or Luvetot] and his family connexions with Dinsley, see M. Cheney, *Roger, bishop of Worcester*, 327-28 no. 23, the present decretal). The brothers Richard and Nigel de Lovetot are familiar in feudal and fiscal records of the 1160s. That Richard was succeeded by his son William in accounting for the honour of Belvoir in the pipe roll 17 Henry II, for 1170-71, gave rise to the supposition that Richard died in 1171 (see *Early Yorkshire Charters*, ed. W. Farrer, 3 [1916], 5-6). But a Richard de Lovetot appears high in the long list of prisoners captured by Henry II at Dol on 26 August 1173 (eighth in order in a list headed by earl Hugh of Chester and Ralph of Fougères); and the names of Richard's son William and his widow Emma appear in the lists of fines for forest offences (a penalty frequently imposed on those who had acted against Henry in the rising of 1173-74) in the roll for 22 Henry II, for 1175-76, William's fine being entered for Dinsley in the county of Hertford; and Emma also accounted in the same year for permission to marry. The Richard de Lovetot who is recorded accounting for his father's estate from 25 Henry II, for 1178-79, was the son of Nigel and the earlier Richard's nephew. It is conceivable that he was the Richard de Lovetot in the list of prisoners in 1173, but circumstantially less likely. It seems probable that the Richard of the decretal was Nigel's brother, and that he died sometime between 26 August 1173 and 1176 (cf. Pipe Rolls *16 Henry II*, 54; *17 Henry II*, 96; *22 Henry II*, 7,93,94; *25 Henry II*, 34, 81; *Liber Rubeus de Scaccario: Red Book of the Exchequer*, ed. H.Hall (Rolls Series,

1896), 19, 26, 430, 689, 700. The dating limits of the decretal are Thomas's canonization in February 1173 and early 1179, after Roger of Worcester departed from England for the last time.

30

Alexander III to John, bishop-elect of Chichester
28 April-August 1174

Cum de tua et aliorum electione qui sunt in quibusdam ecclesiis Anglicanis electi ... commodum et honorem.

Objection has been raised in the papal curia concerning the election of the recipient and of others to English churches. It was said that he has a defect in the eye, and is the son of a canon. In view of the recipient's personal qualities, the pope has by dispensation ordered archbishop Richard of Canterbury, apostolic legate, not to defer his promotion on grounds of his birth. As far as the defect in his eye is concerned, the pope has ordered the archbishop to act as seems best, with the advice of his suffragans, and especially of the bishops of Exeter and Worcester. The elect should with humility and devotion seek from the archbishop what the pope has granted by dispensation and with loving care.

WH 226, *JL* 12367, 28 April-August 1174. Pd *App.* 40.3; *Cass.* 40.7; *1 Comp.Ag.* 1.12.3; *X* 1.20.2.

The dean of Chichester, John Greenford, was elected bishop in late April 1173, but was not consecrated until 6 October 1174. Richard, prior of Dover, was elected to Canterbury on 3 June 1173, consecrated by the pope at Anagni on 7 April 1174, and appointed apostolic legate on 28 April. Five other elections were made in 1173: Richard of Ilchester to Winchester; Geoffrey Ridel to Ely; Geoffrey Plantagenet to Lincoln; Robert Foliot to Hereford; and Reginald FitzJocelin to Bath. Various objections were raised to all seven elections, notably by the Young King Henry in the opening phase of the 1173-74 revolt. This is the context of the present mandate. (On the background and outcome of the seven elections of 1173, see *Materials TB*, 7.552-57 nos 798-92; *Letters and charters of Gilbert Foliot*, 291-302 nos 220-28 and comments; *Epistolae JS*, 2.760-85 nos 311-21; and Foreville, *L'Église et la royauté*, 375-84). With the exception of the Lincoln election, all were confirmed and the elect consecrated in 1174; Geoffrey's election to Lincoln was defective on grounds of illegitimacy and age: it was not confirmed until *ante* July 1175, and in the event he was never consecrated to Lincoln, and resigned on 6 January 1182. The details for John and Richard fix the limits of the decretal as 28 April-*c.* August 1174 (cf. M. Cheney, *Roger, bishop of Worcester*, 332 no. 32 and 214-15); for John's career as dean and bishop of Chichester, see *The acta of the bishops of Chichester, 1075-1207*, ed. H. Mayr-Harting, Canterbury and York Society, 130 [1962], *passim*). The mandate attests Alexander III's high regard for Bartholomew of Exeter and Roger of Worcester (see Duggan, *Decretals of Alexander III to England*, 97-100).

31

Alexander III to all religious brothers and sisters in monasteries and houses of regulars in the province of Canterbury, lacking superiors. 28 April 1174-April/May 1175

Cum ex defectu pastorum sacris Dei ecclesiis multa provenire soleant detrimenta, expedit nobis sollicite providere ne pastoribus et prelatis diutius careatis, quia tunc grex dominicus morsibus luporum exponitur, cum destituitur providentia et sollicitudine pastorali. Inde est quod cum velimus ... auctoritate compellat.

Because of the harm that comes to God's churches through lack of pastors, the pope orders the individual convents, when required by archbishop Richard of Canterbury, apostolic legate, or even before that, to agree on a suitable person, elect him as pastor and present him to the archbishop, according to custom and reason, so that he can go forward to confirm or reject as is fitting. They should know that the pope has ordered the archbishop to compel them to comply, if they are negligent in this matter.

WH 239, *JL* --, 28 April 1174-April/May 1175. Pd *Wig*. 2.19; *Claustr*. 108.

The mandate is preserved only in six collections, and the full text is found only in the Canterbury MS *1 Cant*. 6; elsewhere the arenga is abbreviated. The archbishop's initial R. is found in *1 Cant*. and *1 Rot*. 7.3, though the latter by scribal error describes him as *archd*. The *terminus a quo* is decided by Richard of Canterbury's appointment as legate on 28 April 1174. The implementation of the papal mandate is recorded in the council at Woodstock in the opening days of July 1175, in the presence of Henry II, the Young King Henry, the archbishop, bishops and a large concourse of abbots (cf. *Gesta Regis Henrici secundi*, 1.92-93, about 1 July: '... et fere omnes abbates totius Angliae Cantuariensis diocesis ibi convenerant; et ibidem magnum coram predictis regibus celebraverunt concilium de pastoribus eligandis et instituendis per abbatias, quae tunc vacabant per Angliam, et de pastore eligendo ad sedem pontificalem Norwicensis ecclesiae'; and Diceto, 1.401-02, 8 July). Diceto provides a list of eleven Benedictine abbeys in question, and the records of these houses show that their abbots had died or been deposed, and had been succeeded by the following dates respectively: St Augustine's, Canterbury, Clarembald intruded 1163 and deposed 1173, Roger elected 1175; Battle, Walter died 1171, Odo elected 1175; Hyde, Selida/Salidas died 1171, Thomas elected 1175; Abingdon, *in commendam* to bishop Godfrey of St Asaph 1165-75, Roger elected 1175; Westminster, Laurence died 1173, Walter elected 1175; St Benet of Hulme, William II died 1168, Thomas elected 1175; Thorney, Walter II died 1169, Solomon elected 1176; Crowland, Edward died 1173, Robert elected 1175; Shrewsbury, Adam deposed 1175, Ralph elected 1175; Abbotsbury, details uncertain but vacant in 1175, ? Ralph occurs late twelfth century; Muchelney, vacant 'a morte abbatis' (? Hugh I, 1172-73), still vacant 1175, Hugh (? II) occurs 1175. Battle, Abingdon and Muchelney are recorded in the king's hands in 1171-75, 1164-65 and ? from 1172-73 respectively. The *Gesta regis Henrici secundi* and Roger of Howden's *Chronica* omit Shrewsbury from the list, and add the Augustinian house of Grimsby, which was vacant in 1175, when Thomas was probably elected (cf. *Gesta regis Henrici secundi*, 1.91-92: 'erant autem tunc temporis duodecim abbatie vacantes per Angliam in Cantuariensi diocesi'; *Chronica magistri Rogeri de Houedene*, 2.79; and *Heads of religious houses*, 36, 29, 82, 25, 77, 68, 75, 42, 71, 23, 57, 189).

32

Alexander III to bishops Bartholomew of Exeter and Roger of Worcester. **March 1174-1175x76**

(a) *Conquestus est nobis magister Thomas clericus comitis Hugonis ... fine debito terminetis.* (b) *Ad hec nobis noveritis intimatum ... mereatur absolvi. Si autem uterque vestrum his exequendis etc.*

(a) Master Thomas, clerk of earl Hugh of Norfolk, has complained that the priest Wimer damaged houses on the land of his church at Bungay, and carried off church property to the value of forty marks. If the charge is established, the recipients must compel Wimer to make good Thomas's loss, restore all that was taken, and make appropriate satisfaction. Then, if he wishes his case to be tested, the recipients shall hear it and reach a conclusion. (b) It is also alleged that Wimer continued to celebrate divine office after papal prohibition, and that St Thomas the Martyr therefore excommunicated him on papal orders. Although neither pope nor archbishop absolved him, he was released after the martyr's death, by bishop William of Norwich, now deceased. If these charges are true, the recipients must reimpose the sentence, until he is released by papal authority.

WH 151, *JL* --, March 1174-1175x76. *Flor.* 168 only. *Decretales ineditae*, 92-93 no. 51.

This letter is one of a group of five decretals found only in the St Florian collection (Flor. 168-72, fol. 179v a-b), which relate to the church of Bungay in Suffolk, and involve the priest or chaplain Wimer and master Thomas, clerk of earl Hugh of Norfolk. Wimer was an important royal administrator, sheriff of Norfolk and Suffolk from 1170, and itinerant justice in 1172-73. Together with Walter of Grimsby, he was a bearer of the oppressive constitutions which Henry II sent to Englnd *c.* October/November 1169 (see D. Knowles, A.J. Duggan and C.N.L. Brooke, 'Henry II's supplement to the Constitutions of Clarendon', *EHR*, 87 [1972], 757-71, at 759 and 765), and his excommunication by archbishop Thomas is recorded in the letter *Lamentati sumus*, to the sub-prior William and the convent of Canterbury, *post* 18 November in the same year (*Materials TB*, 7.97-100 no. 573, at p. 99). Thomas, a clerk of earl Hugh of Norfolk, likewise appears in a list of persons excommunicated by Alexander III in the letter *Oportuerat vos*, to Gilbert of London and other bishops, on 16 September 1170 (*ibid.*, 360-64 no. 700 at p. 363; cf. *supra* 16). The death of bishop William of Norwich occurred on 17 January 1174, his successor John of Oxford was consecrated on 14 December 1175, and earl Hugh of Norfolk died before Christmas 1176, which dates provide the limits for the present mandate. The links of the Bungay decretals with the Becket dispute and its aftermath, their overlapping interests with the well-known Pentney affair (see *Ad aures nostras*, *infra* 33), and with the political crisis of 1173-74, as well as the technical interest of their discovery in a collection of the Italian family, are discussed in *Decretales ineditae*, 83-85.

33

Alexander III to archbishop Richard of Canterbury.
7 April 1174-1175x76 (1174-81)

Ad aures nostras noveris pervenisse quod, cum terra nobilis viri Hugonis comitis ... appellatione cessante reducas.

St Thomas the Martyr, when in exile, had excommunicated certain clerks who had celebrated divine office after the lands of earl Hugh of Norfolk had been placed under interdict, as a result of his injury to the canons of Pentney. On their request for absolution, when he was about to return from exile, Thomas enjoined on them a year's abstinence from celebration while he consulted the pope, but his martyrdom intervened. The pope now mandates the recipient to suspend the clerks from office and benefice, without leave of appeal, since they continued to celebrate as before; and they must not be restored without papal orders. The recipient must depose from office those whom he knows to have been instigators of the offence, and excommunicate them if they resist his sentence.

WH 44, *JL* 14316, 7 April 1174-1175x76 (1174-81). Pd *Lips*. 11.28; *Brug*. 12.9; and *Epistolae GF*, 2.70-71 no. 348; and *Materials TB*, 7.417-18 no. 728.

A series of letters relating to the dispute between earl Hugh of Norfolk and the Augustinian canons of Pentney is printed in *Materials TB*, 6.543-62 nos 481-90; cf. *ibid*., 7.149; *Letters and charters of Gilbert Foliot*, 210-14; and M. Cheney, *Roger, bishop of Worcester*, 321 no. 10; see also *Oportuerat vos (supra 16)* for Thomas's sentence on earl Hugh's clerks. The Pentney case is discussed in Foreville, *L'Église et la royauté*, 206-09; D. Knowles, *The episcopal colleagues of archbishop Thomas Becket*, Cambridge 1951, 127-29; and Morey and Brooke, *Gilbert Foliot and his letters*, 184-85 n. 2. For the comparable context of the Bungay dispute, see *Conquestus est nobis* (*supra* 32).

34

Alexander III to archbishop Richard of Canterbury, apostolic legate. **early 1176-mid 1177 (1176-81)**

(a) Qua fronte nos super articulis iuris consulere valeas non videmus ... respondebimus. Sane si quis pro contumacia ... pareat equitati. (b) De his etiam qui se conqueruntur ... duxerint appellandum. (c) Si super eo vero quod defuncto aliquo ... ecclesiastice sepulture.

(a) The pope cannot see how the archbishop has the affrontery to consult him on points of law, since in matters known to him and perfectly clear he is said to pervert the course of law, and evidently act against the liberty of the Church, for which his glorious predecessor Thomas did not fear to suffer martyrdom. For he is said to confirm episcopal elections, not in the church as is proper, nor in his own chamber or palace, but in the very camera regis, contrary to law and the pontifical office. Nevertheless, the pope is sending his reply, lest he seem to deny assent to the archbishop's petitions. If anyone is bound by interdict or excommunication for contumacy or any other reason, and offers to accept judgment on that matter, the judge can absolve him, lest he should die excommunicate, even if his adversary objects to his absolution. But he must first give assurance that he will acccept judgment in the presence of the pope, if his opponent prefers, or of a papal commissioner, or of someone on whom both parties have agreed. (b) The same applies to those who complain that they have been unreasonably excommunicated, even if the judges who imposed the sentence think that appeal should be made to the pope. (c) Sometimes when a debtor dies, religious or ecclesiastics or even secular persons demand that the debts are paid before the body is buried, and make an appeal. The pope rules that, if the deceased did not provide for the settlement of debts when disposing of his goods, and a surety is not given for their payment by his heir or relations, the body should not be handed over for ecclesiastical burial after appeal.

WH 755, *JL* 14312, early 1176-mid 1177 (1176-81). Pd *App*. 31.2(a), 31.3(b), 43.3(c); *Cass*. 51.38; *1 Comp.Ag*. 2.20.41; *X* 2.28.25.

The *arenga* of this letter expresses the pope's concern with the rights of the Church in the matter of episcopal elections; but in the compromise which followed the investiture conflict in England in the reign of Henry I, when Anselm was archbishop of Canterbruy, the Church's claims had not in fact been secured, and elections had been subject to royal direction and consent (Whitelock, Brett and Brooke, *Councils and Synods*, 1.ii, 649, 651, 656-61, 690-93 and 707). The interests and intentions of Henry II had been made clear in clause 12 of the Constitutions of Clarendon in 1164: 'Cum vacaverit archiepiscopatus vel abbatia vel prioratus de dominio regis, debet esse in manu ipsius et inde percipiet omnes redditus et exitus sicut dominicos. Et cum ventum fuerit ad consulendum ecclesiae, debet dominus rex mandare potiores personas ecclesiae et in capella ipsius domini regis debet fieri electio, assensu domini regis et consilio personarum regni etc.', *ibid*., 867-69); and the elections of 1173, to fill up the vacancies which had accumulated during the Becket dispute and its aftermath, clearly reflected the royal will in most cases. The king's own son alleged to Alexander III that the persecutors of the martyr were being promoted to ecclesiastical honours and that the elections were not canonically free (cf. Duggan, 'Richard of Ilchester', 13-14). Nevertheless, in the period of reconciliation after the compromise of Avranches, Alexander confirmed the elections, following due consideration (cf. *supra* 30). The rebuke delivered to archbishop Richard in the present decretal was therefore prompted by elections after 1174, when Richard's own election was confirmed. Adam was consecrated for St Asaph on 12 October 1175, John of Oxford for Norwich on 14 December 1175, Peter de Leia for St Davids on 7 November 1176 and Guy for Bangor on 22 May 1177; after more than two years interval in which no elections took place, Baldwin was consecrated for Worcester on 10 August 1180, and Seffrid for Chichester on 16 September 1180. It is unlikely that *Qua fronte* was a belated rebuke by Alexander in response to the promotions of Baldwin (a distinguished canonist) and Seffrid. The elections between late 1175 and mid-1177, including *that royal administrator John of Oxford (the hated 'jurator' of the Becket correspondence, present at the schismatic council of Würzburg in 1165, and excommunicated by Becket at Vézelay on 12 June 1166 [cf. Duggan, 'Richard of Ilchester', 1-2]), are therefore the likely context. In view of the pope's opening comments, it is not surprising that *Qua fronte* does not occur in early derivations from Canterbury archives.

* including that royal administrator *should read* including that of the royal administrator

35

Alexander III to archbishop Roger of York and bishop Hugh of Durham. **(*post* April) 1177**

Ex constanti relatione dilecti filii nostri Hugonis sancti Angeli diaconi cardinalis ... penitentie emendare.

From the report of Cardinal Hugh of Sant' Angelo, and from letters which the cardinal has shown him, the pope has learned that master Hugh of Southwell had presented forged letters to archbishop Roger of York. When Hugh denied the charge, which was proven by a sufficient number of witnesses, the cardinal wished to condemn him as a forger, whereupon Hugh appealed to the pope. Yielding to the intervention of powerful people - 'magnarum personarum supplicatione inductus', the legate deferred to the appeal. The pope does not approve of this deferment and wishes to impose a deterrent punishment; he orders the recipients to despoil Hugh of the churches of Epperstone and Shelford, impose perpetual silence on him in respect of the churches, whoever may object - 'nullius contradictione vel appellatione obstante', and confine him in some monastery, where he can make amends for his wrong-doing.

WH 404, *JL* --, (*post* April) 1177. *Bridl.* 152 only. Pd Scammell, *Hugh du Puiset*, 251-52; *Decretales ineditae*, 130-32 no. 76.

The decretal is found only in the Bridlington collection, where its full text is embodied within an executory report by the two recipient prelates to bishop Roger of Worcester. Cardinal Hugh Pierleoni was papal legate in England for several months from 1175 until late June-early July 1176, but apparently did not arrive back in the papal curia until April 1177, which is therefore the earliest date of the decretal. Master Hugh of Southwell is known from other sources, and the powerful patronage he enjoyed is evident from the present letter, but his last appearance in witness lists is in late May 1177, which matches the details of the present case (cf. M. Cheney, *Roger, bishop of Worcester*, 340 no. 47A). Pierleoni's legation marked an important stage in the process of reconciliation after Becket's death, begun at Savigny and Avranches in 1172 (see Whitelock, Brett and Brooke, *Councils and Synods*, 1.ii, 993-1010; Foreville, *L'Église et la royauté*, 431-39; and Diceto, 1.410. Among the problems resolved in 1176 was that of criminous clerks (cf. *supra* 2, 9 and 11; *infra* 36 and 40): the king conceded the principle of clerical immunity, in return for the exclusion of forest offences and matters involving lay fee. The present decretal is of evident canonical importance, both for its subject-matter and the form of its entry in the Bridlington collection, since it is clearly derived from the records of English judges delegate and throws light on the sources used by English collectors (cf. *Decretales ineditae*, 131-32; and Duggan, *Decretals of Alexander III*, 125-26 no. 404).

36

Alexander III to the bishops of London and Worcester.
mid 1176-early 1179 (1164x81)

Significatum est nobis quod cum inter Willelmum Sarracenum et G. (vel *E.*) *clericum iurgia mota fuissent ... nostra auctoritate spolietis.*

In the strife which arose between William Sarracenus and a certain clerk (G. or E.), the latter threatened, as many persons testified, to take action which would endanger William's life. When in the same year William was atrociously wounded and died, it was believed by some that the clerk was responsible, and he was thereby defamed. The pope wishes neither the innocent to be condemned nor the guilty to remain unpunished. He therefore mandates the recipients to impose canonical purgation on the clerk, without leave of objection or appeal, if he cannot be convicted in their presence by suitable persons and yet is publicly defamed. If the clerk fails in the purgation, or can be convicted by judicial process in the commissioners' presence, they must suspend him perpetually from the service of the altar, and despoil him of his benefice by papal authority.

WH 960, *JL* --, mid 1176-early 1179 (1164x81). Pd *Claustr.* 198; *Brug.* 42.5.

The decretal survives only in ten collections of English, Anglo-Norman or French provenance, and was not received in the main systematic transmission leading to *1 Comp.* and *X*. The address to London and Worcester is found in the earliest copies, though some later collections have Norwich and London; the printed text from *Brug.* is certainly incorrect in its address to Toledo. The presence of the letter in the *Wig.* archetype (cf. *Claustr.* and *Wig.* 7.7) supports its attribution to bishops Gilbert of London and Roger of Worcester. In all probability, the letter postdates the agreement on criminous clerks reached between Henry II and the legate Pierleoni in 1176, which would on this assumption provide its *terminus a quo*; its likely final date is set by bishop Roger's departure from England in early 1179, and death in August of that year (see M. Cheney, *Roger, bishop of Worcester*, 361 no.86; and *ibid.*, 141 and 183-84).

37

Alexander III to Henry II. **1159-81**

Magnificentie tue litteras, quas pro R. milite super iure patronatus ecclesie de Bliburg. ... in posterum non generetur.

The English king has written to the pope on behalf of the knight R., concerning the right of patronage of the church of *Bliburg*. The pope has received the letter with appropriate favour, and considered the king's request as far as is acceptable to God and right conduct, but it is contrary to the statutes of the holy fathers for clerks to be removed on a patronage issue from churches which they have canonically obtained. He cannot therefore in conscience grant his favour to the knight in this matter.

WH 639, *JL* 13726, 1159-81. Pd *App.* 50.32; *Cass.* 53.22; *1 Comp.Ag.Fr.* 3.33.26.

The decretal first appears in collections made after the death of Alexander III in 1181: in the final title of *App.Cr.* and in *Bamb.* 44.22, and thereafter only in six systematic collections. It is always found immediately preceding *Relatum est auribus* (*infra* 39), except in *1 Rot.* (12.5), which omits the latter. The place of the church in question occurs as *Bliburg, Bligurgis, Blilourg, Buburg, Liburgis and Ligurgis*, of which *Bliburg* is the most likely form, suggesting Blyborough, near Blyton in Lincolnshire, Blythburgh in Suffolk, or less probably Blyth in Nottinghamshire, but the identity of the place, or that of the knight, is not yet established. Holtzmann noted Blyborough as a possible identification, but without supporting evidence. The record of the English king petitioning the pope on behalf of an individual feudal tenant suggests an exceptional royal interest, which both Blythburgh manor and and the chapel of Blyth reveal in the period. Blythburgh was a royal manor in Edward the Confessor's reign and at the time of the Domesday Inquest. Grants of the manor or its church were made successively by Henry I, Stephen and Henry II: Henry I gave the church and its belongings to the Augustinian house of St Osyth, in connexion with the foundation of Blythburgh Priory and with the support of the Claverings who were the lords of the manor, c. 1120; in 1137-47, Stephen granted the manor to John, son of Robert de Chesney, and Henry II gave it to William de Chesney, John's brother and heir, in 1157-58. William died in 1174, whereupon the lands passed to his daughter Margaret and her husband, Hugh de Cressi. A charter granted by Hugh in 1186-89 was attested by archbishops Walter of Rouen and Baldwin of Canterbury, bishop Hugh of Lincoln, dean Hubert Walter of York, and earl William of Arundel. The close royal and court connexions with Blythburgh are therefore evident, but its principal feudal tenants in the period of the decretal (1159-81) were William and Hugh, whereas the knight claiming patronage of the church of *Bliburg* is consistently designated R. in the collections. On the other hand, various knights R. appear among the major benefactors of Blythburgh Priory: Robert de Money, for instance, whose family held lands in the Blythburgh hamlet of *Bregge*, was a feudal tenant of earl Hugh of Norfolk in 1166, and was succeeded by his son Roger (I am indebted to Dr Harper-Bill for the comment that no document gives any hint of a patronage dispute at Blythburgh in the period; cf. C. Harper-Bill, *Blythburgh Priory cartulary*, 1 [1980] and 2 [1981], Suffolk Record Society: Suffolk Charters [2 and 3], 1. 6-7, 12, 54-56 nos. 60, 61, 62; 2. 239 no. 483; *et passim;* and *Victoria County History of the County of Suffolk*, ed. W. Page, 2 vols. [London 1911 and 1907], 1. 420 and 2. 91-94). The royal chapel of Blyth (*Blide, Blida*) in Nottinghamshire is an improbable identification: the *capellaria* was granted by Stephen to Lincoln cathedral, and by Henry II to Walter of Coutances, royal clerk and administrator, bishop of Lincoln (1183-85), and archbishop of Rouen (from 1185); Rouen cathedral acquired the *capellaria* after Walter's translation (J.H. Denton, *English Royal Free Chapels, 1100-1399* [Manchester University Press 1970], 75-76). Richard of Lindsey acquired lands at Blyth, as a result of his marriage (K.J. Stringer, *Earl David of Huntingdon, 1152-1219* [Edinburgh University Press 1985], 160 and 309 n. 61). The historical context of the decretal requires further study.

38

Alexander III to Henry II. **? *c.* 1179 (1159-81)**

Quanto te superna providentia maioris honoris et gratie privilegio decoravit ... solummodo terminari.

The pope reminds the king that he should love religious men with a more generous affection, in proportion to the honour and favour which divine providence has conferred on him. Suits involving the patronage of churches are so closely linked with ecclesiastical matters that they cannot be determined except by ecclesiastical judgment, or resolved except by an ecclesiastical judge.

WH 775, *JL* 13727, ? *c.* 1179 (1159-81). Pd *App.* 47.4; *1 Comp.Ag.* 2.1.5; abbrev.: *X* 2.1.3.

This important and much-discussed decretal occurs with various opening phrases: *Quanto te superna* (vel *divina* vel *fraterna); Quanto divina;* and *Noverit igitur discretio (*the shortened form 'causa patronatus ... terminari' is found in the commentary *De iure naturali:* K.W. Nörr, 'Die Summen De iure naturali und De multiplici iuris divisione', *ZRG Kan. Abt.*, 48 (1962), 145 no. 7). The significance of Alexander's statement is made clear by comparison with the first clause of Henry II's Constitutions of Clarendon in 1164: 'De advocatione et presentatione ecclesiarum, si controversia emerserit inter laicos, vel inter clericos et laicos, vel inter clericos, in curia domini regis tractetur et terminetur' (for the historical context of the disputed jurisdiction over advowsons, see M. Cheney, 'The compromise of Avranches of 1172 and the spread of canon law in England', *EHR*, 56 (1941), 190-95, and *Roger, bishop of Worcester*, 142-48 and 165; J.W. Gray, 'The ius presentandi in England from the Constitutions of Clarendon to Bracton', *EHR*, 67 (1952), 481-509, esp. 481-90; W.L. Warren, *Henry II* (London 1973), 542-46; Whitelock, Brett and Brooke, *Councils and Synods*, 1.ii, 856-57 and 886-87; the most expert study of the whole question is now in Landau, *Ius patronatus, passim;* for *Quanto te*, see 206-10).

39

Alexander III to the archbishops and bishops of England (or France) ? *c.* 1179 (1159-81)

(a) Relatum est auribus nostris quod nonnulli ambitione nimia tracti ... teneri astrictos. (b) Ad hoc, quoniam quidam laici ... faciatis attentius evitari.

(a) Impelled by excessive ambition, some clerks in the recipients' districts presume to acquire the patronage of churches and ecclesiastical benefices in the secular court, taking advantage of lay recognition or secular power, without seeking the bishop's hearing. Such persons are unworthy of the name or rights of pastor, and the recipients must deprive them of office and benefice, without leave of appeal, if they do not resign such acquisitions when ordered to do so, unless they are shielded by prescription or episcopal concession. And if they still do not comply, they must be excommunicated until they make fitting satisfaction. (b) Some laymen deprive churches of lands and possessions to constrain ecclesiastics to litigate in the secular court. The recipients must publicly prohibit such actions under pain of perpetual anathema. Anyone who manifestly contemns their prohibition shall be excommunicated, without leave of appeal, and avoided as excommunicate until he makes proper satisfaction.

WH 871, *JL* 13744, 1159-81. Pd *App*, 50.33 (a) and 34 (b); *Cass.* 53.23; *1 Comp.Ag.* 3.33.27; *X* 3.38.21.

The decretal begins with *Nostris est auribus intimatum* in *App.*, and appears in no primitive collection and no source earlier than Lucius III's pontificate, 1181-85. Its provenance is uncertain: it is addressed to French prelates (*per Galliam)* in *App., Cass., Tann.* 6.2.33, *Frcf.Frcf.* 51.32 and *Sang.* 7.47; and to English prelates (*per Angliam*) in *Bamb.* 44.23, *Lips.* 52.30, *Frcf.Rot.Max.* 51.32, *1 Comp.Ag.* 3.33.27 and *X* 3.38.21. The transmission of the text suggests a single source, rather than two parallel letters to France and England respectively, as do the variant inscriptions within the single *Frcf.* family. The English attribution is more probable (cf. M. Cheney, 'The compromise of Avranches', 194-95), and is perhaps supported by the adjacent occurrence of the present decretal and *Magnificentie tue* (*supra* 37), Alexander III to Henry II, likewise on the ius patronatus, in every collection in which both letters appear.

40

Alexander III or Lucius III to bishop John of St Andrews.
1180-82

Quia nos duxit tua fraternitas consulendos si clerici tantummodo tonsuram habentes ... ut merito utramque penam inducat.

The bishop has asked the pope if clerks who are merely tonsured should be judged by the Church or by a lay court, and how they should be punished, if they have been convicted of murder or other crimes, or have lawfully confessed. The pope replies that by reason of their clerical status they are exempt from secular jurisdiction and, while they still bear the tonsure, should be judged only by the Church. If they are convicted or confess, they should suffer an appropriate ecclesiastical punishment, not a secular one, unless the crime was so grave - 'nisi crimen adeo grave fuerit' - that it merits both penalties.

WH 1038, *JL* --, 1180-82. *Bridl.* 146 and *Pet.* 4.39 only. Pd *Decretales ineditae*, 143-44 no. 83.

The importance of this letter for Scottish history and also by implication for the Becket dispute is discussed in *Decretales ineditae*, 143-44. Its dating limits are fixed by John's consecration to St Andrews in 1180 and the appointment of papal legates in 1182 to examine the rival claims of John and Hugh. The sender is not named in either collection, but the presence of the letter in the Bridlington collection created an assumption that he was most probably Alexander III, since no decretals of later popes were identified in the main transcription, though Lucius III's name is written once in red in the margin (cf. Duggan, *Decretal Collections*, 91-92). But there is in fact more evidence to attribute decretals in the collection to Lucius III than was previously thought (as will be shown in a forthcoming analysis of *Bridl.*, *Reg.*, *Claud.*, *Chelt.*, *Cott.* and *Pet.* in Duggan, *MIC*, in preparation), and it is possible that the present letter was sent by him, rather than Alexander III in the closing year of his pontificate. As far as its canonical doctrine is concerned, it should be noted that the decretal speaks of clerks who are merely tonsured, and therefore not in holy orders, and that its final sentence echoes the language of well-known decretist commentaries (cf. Rufinus, *Summa decretorum*, at C. XI qu. 1, ed. H. Singer (Giessen, 1891), 309: 'si adeo horrendum crimen fuerit').

SUPPLEMENT

This final sequence of five decretals, mostly dealing with aspects of the archbishop of Canterbury's jurisdictional rights, were almost certainly addressed to archbishop Richard. They are appended here, since all have appeared in* collections or works of reference as letters received by Becket, in some instances even in twelfth-century manuscripts of Becket correspondence, in modern editions and in *JL*.

*to archbishop Richard *should read* to archbishop Richard, to Richard and his suffragans, or to his suffragans. They are appended here, since all have appeared in collections or works of reference as letters or linked with Becket

41

Alexander III to archbishop Richard of Canterbury, apostolic legate. **14 May 1174 (or 1176)**

Relatum est auribus nostris quod, si quando episcopi suffraganei tui ... videris statuendum.

Sometimes the suffragan bishops and archdeacons of the recipient's province appeal to the pope on some specific matter, and place their dioceses and archdeaconries under papal protection; and since they set a year for the term of the appeal, they prevent him dealing with their own excesses and those of their subjects in the meanwhile, and make all his justice void and suspended. The pope grants that the archbishop in no way loses his jurisdiction over the suits and manifest excesses of his subjects through such an appeal, except for the matter of the appeal itself, and he can decide on them whatever seems just to him.

WH 876, *JL* 11661 (*sub annis* 1162-70), 14 May 1174 (or 1176). Pd *App.* 10.30; *Cass.* 51.29; *1 Comp.Ag.Fr.* 2.20.25; and *Materials TB*, 5.128-29 no. 65.

This letter and *Significavit nobis (infra prox.)*, to all suffragans of the church of Canterbury, must be taken together. The parallel letters often appear together in decretal collections, and occur also in the Becket correspondence, which supplies the date Anagni, 14 May, for *Significavit nobis*. The letters have sometimes been attributed incorrectly to archbishop Thomas (as in *JL* and *Materials TB)*, but the pope was not at Anagni on 14 May in any year during Thomas's archiepiscopate, nor is the problem of jurisdiction in question appropriate to Thomas in exile (cf. S. Chodorow, 'A group of decretals by Alexander III', *BMCL* 3 [1973], 53 no.8, *Significavit nobis).* Moreover, Richard's initial R. is attached to the archbishop in at least one copy of each of the parallel letters. Richard was present in person in the curia at Anagni on 14 May 1174, which supports the assignment of the letters to that year, but their phrasing implies a period of resistance to his own jurisdiction, whereas he had been only recently consecrated and appointed legate by the pope, on 7 April and 28 April respectively. The letters may well record Richard's concern to secure his jurisdictional authority in this respect, as in many others, at the outset of his rule, but the alternative possibility of 1176 must be allowed.

42

Alexander III to all the suffragans of the church of Canterbury. **14 May 1174 (or 1176)**

Significavit nobis venerabilis frater noster Ricardus Cantuariensis archiepiscopus, apostolice sedis legatus ... ad rectitudinis tramitem revocare. [Datum Anagnie secundo idus Maii.]

When the suffragans or their archdeacons appeal from the archbishop's presence to the pope on a specific matter, they place their dioceses and archdeaconries under papal protection, and by setting the term of appeal at a year allow him to take cognizance neither of their own past excesses or new ones, nor of the offences of their subjects, and they suspend and make nugatory all his justice in the meanwhile. Manifest offences must not remain uncorrected through the pretext of appeal, nor must their subjects rejoice with impunity in their excesses. The recipients must not by the device of papal protection and appeal try to impede the archbishop from taking cognizance of their subjects' suits and excesses. He can punish their subjects appropriately, with due warning, and he can correct the suffragans' own excesses, if manifest and notorious, except those issues on which the appeal was made. He can put right whatever has been done unjustly.

WH 983, *JL* 12378 (14 April 1174), 14 May 1174 (or 1176). Pd *Claustr.* 117; *App.* 10.24; *Cass.* 51.22; *1 Comp.Ag.Fr.* 2.20.24; *Materials TB,* 6.400-01 no. 408, with the date.

The context and date are discussed for the parallel letter to archbishop Richard *Relatum est auribus (supra prox).*

43

Alexander III to archbishop (probably Richard) of Canterbury. April 1174-1176x77 (1162-79)

Cum teneamur consultationibus singulorum ... diligimus caritate. Quoniam nos consulere voluisti utrum si eorum qui appellant ... facere licebit.

The pope has a general duty to respond to those who consult him, but he replies all the more willingly to the archbishop, because of the greater affection in which he holds him. The archbishop has asked if he can correct the situation when the possession of an appellant to the pope has been disturbed. The pope replies that the archbishop can deal with that matter within his ordinary jurisdiction, if it is referred to him, the subject of the appeal itself being intermitted.

WH 316, *JL* 13809 (*sub annis* 1159-81), April 1174-1176x77 (1162-79). Pd *App.* 10.23; *Cass.* 51.21; *1 Comp.Ag.* 2.20.23; *X* 2.28.17.

The recipient archbishop has not been identified, but he was probably Richard. The warmth of the pope's affection expressed in the letter - 'quanto personam tuam abundantiori diligimus caritate' - suggests Thomas rather than Richard, but the nature of the enquiry fits better into the early years of the latter's archiepiscopate, when many comparable problems were referred to Alexander III for guidance (cf. 41 and 42 *supra;* see also M. Cheney, 'The council of Westminster 1175: new light on an old source', *SCH* 11 (1975), 61-68); the importance of *Cum teneamur* in the history of tuitorial appeals is discussed in Norma Adams and Charles Donahue, *Select Cases from the ecclesiastical courts of the diocese of Canterbury, c. 1200-1301,* Selden Society, 95 (1981 for 1978-79), 64-66. On the other hand, the pope's later dissatisfaction with Richard's compliance with royal practices, notably in the matter of episcopal elections in the *camera regis,* makes it unlikely that the letter was issued many years after Richard's elevation; it is improbable that Alexander wrote to Richard in such affectionate terms after the stern rebuke with which he opened *Qua fronte,* c. 1176-77 (*supra* 34).

44

Alexander III to Richard archbishop of Canterbury, apostolic legate, and his suffragans. 28 April 1174-March 1179

Non sine multa admiratione auditur et creditur quod Iudei ... senteniam proferatis.

The pope has heard that Jews occupy parish churches in the recipients' province, by purchase or contract or even in pledge. Since the incomes due are not paid, the churches are said to be already ruined. The recipients should be prompt to correct whatever is hostile to divine majesty and alien to Christian institutions. They must therefore first seek king Henry's favour, and then strictly compel any Jews who hold parish churches by such means in their province to relinquish them; or, if Jews retain parishes which they have already acquired or so acquire in the future, the recipients must compel them to pay the customary incomes due to the churches. The faithful must be strictly bound by anathema not to pay homage or fealty to Jews. The recipients must excommunicate without leave of appeal any who act against their prohibition.

WH 673, *JL* 13976 (*sub annis* 1159-81), 28 April 1174-March 1179. Pd *Claustr*. 168; *App*. 20.3; *Cass*. 54.3.

The decretal is addressed to 'beatus Thomas' in *App*., but Thomas was legate only from 2 May 1166, while in exile, and the address is an obvious later construction; the letter was almost certainly sent to Richard (for possible links with Richard's provincial council in May 1175, see M. Cheney, 'The council of Westminster 1175'; see also W. Holtzmann, *Festschrift Guido Kisch*, 222 no 5, the present decretal, and no. 6: *Cum in Cantuariensi*, *WH* 255 (b), *JL* 13976, Alexander III to archbishop Richard). The *terminus ad quem* of the decretal is provided by Alexander III's legislation on the Jews in the Lateran Council in March 1179 (cap. 26: *Judei sive Saraceni);*

45

Alexander III to all the suffragans of the church of Canterbury.
1175-81 (28 April 1174-1181)

Cum non ignoretis venerabilem fratrem nostrum R(icardum) Cantuariensem archiepiscopum vobis non solum metropolitico sed etiam legationis iure preesse ... possit transferre.

Archbishop Richard of Canterbury has both metropolitical and legatine authority over the recipients, but some of them claim that he ought in neither capacity to hear cases from their dioceses, except on appeal. While this is true of his rights as metropolitan, as legate he represents the pope in his province, and in this status he can and should hear all cases brought to him from their dioceses, either on appeal or on the complaint of any who approach him. Therefore they must leave to his judgment any matters taken to him, and they must neither deter nor obstruct any clerk or layman who wishes to refer his cause to the archbishop.

WH 275, *JL* 11665 (*sub annis* 1166-70), 1175-81 (28 April 1174-1181). Pd *App*. 44.3 = 50.66; *Cass*. 41.1; *1 Comp.Ag*. 1.22.1; *X* 1.30.1; and *Materials TB*, 5.297-98 no. 159 (*sub anno* 1166).

The decretal is dated 1166-70 in *JL* and 1166 in *Materials TB*, on the erroneous assumption that Thomas was the archbishop concerned, the letter being found in Alan of Tewkesbury's collection of Becket correspondence (Brit. Libr. MS Claudius B.ii, 2.101). The archbishop was Richard, in or after 1175; the context and subject-matter support this view (cf. 40, 41 and 42 *supra)*, and his initial R. is found in *Font*. 2.52.

ABBREVIATIONS

Canones-Sammlungen = E. Friedberg, *Die Canones-Sammlungen zwischen Gratian und Bernhard von Pavia*, Leipzig 1897 (repr. Graz 1956).

Decretales ineditae = S. Chodorow and C. Duggan, from the papers of W. Holtzmann, *Decretales ineditae saeculi XII*, Città del Vaticano 1982 (*MIC*, 4).

Diceto = *Radulfi de Diceto decani Lundoniensis opera historica*, ed. W. Stubbs, London 1878 (Rolls Series 68).

Duggan, *Decretals of Alexander III* = C. Duggan, 'Decretals of Alexander III to England',*Rolando Bandinelli Papa Alessandro III* (Accademia Senese degli Intronati), ed. F. Liotta, Siena 1986, 85-151.

Duggan, *Decretal Collections* = C. Duggan, *Twelfth-Century decretal collections and their importance in English history*, London 1963 (University of London Historical Studies, 12).

EHR = *English Historical Review*.

Epistolae JS = *The Letters of John of Salisbury*, 2, edd. W.J. Millor and C.N.L. Brooke, Oxford Medieval Texts 1979.

Holtzmann-Cheney = C.R. Cheney and M.G. Cheney, from the papers of W. Holtzmann, *Studies in the collections of twelfth-century decretals*, Città del Vaticano 1979 (*MIC*, 3).

JE, *JL* = P. Jaffé: 2nd ed. S. Loewenfeld, F. Kaltenbrunner and P. Ewald, *Regesta pontificum romanorum*, Leipzig 1885-1888.

Mansi = J.D. Mansi, *Sanctorum conciliorum nova et amplissima collectio*, Firenze 1759 - Venezia 1798.

Materials TB = J.C. Robertson and J.B. Sheppard, *Materials for the history of Thomas Becket, archbishop of Canterbury*, London 1875-85 (Rolls Series, 67).

MIC = *Monumenta Iuris Canonici, Series B: Corpus Collectionum*, Città del Vaticano.

Pd = printed in

PU England = W. Holtzmann, *Papsturkunden in England*, I-III, Berlin 1930-31, 1935-36, Göttingen 1952 (Abhandlungen der Akademie der Wissenschaften in Göttingen, NF 25, Dritte F. 14-15, 33).

SCH = *Studies in Church History*.

SG = *Studia Gratiana*.

Singer, *Neue Beiträge* = H. Singer, *Neue Beiträge über die Dekretalen-Sammlungen vor und nach Bernhard von Pavia*, Wien 1914 (Sitzungsberichte der Kais. Akademie der Wissenschaften in Wien, philos.-histor. Klasse, 171).

TRHS = *Transactions of the Royal Historical Society*.

WH = Walther Holtzmann, *Regesta decretalium saeculi XII*.

ZRG Kan. Abt = *Zeitschrift der Savigny-Stiftung für Rechtsgeschichte, Kanonistische Abteilung*.

SIGLA OF DECRETAL COLLECTIONS

1 Abr. = *Abrincensis Prima*: Singer, *Neue Beiträge*, 355-400.
Alan.app. = *Coll. Alani*, R. von Heckel, in *ZRG Kan. Abt.*, 29 (1940)

226-334 (app.: 309-334).

1 Alc. = *Alcobacensis prima:* Holtzmann-Cheney, 8-25; Duggan, in *SG* 14 (1967), 51-71; idem, *Decretals of Alexander III*, 89-108.

App. = *Appendix Concilii Lateranensis:*

Cr. = editio princeps: P. Crabbe, *Concilia omnia tam generalia quam particularia* (2nd edn. Cologne 1551), 2.820-944; Mansi, 22.248-453.

Bamb. = *Bambergensis:* W. Deeters, *Die Bambergensisgruppe der Dekretalen-sammlungen des 12. Jhdts.*, Bonn 1956 (Inaugural Dissertation ... der Philos. Fakultät die Rheinischen Friedrich Wilhelms-Universität).

Belv. = *Belverensis:* Duggan, *Decretal Collections*, 71-73, 154-62, (numerical concordance with *WH:* 212).

Bridl. = *Bridlingtonensis:* Oxford, Bodleian Library, MS Bodley 357 (S.C. 2452), fols. 80r-133v.

Brug. = *Brugensis: Canones-Sammlungen* 136-70.

1, 3 Cant. = *Cantuariensis prima, tertia:* Duggan, *Decretal Collections*, 73-76, 162-71, and pl. III, (numerical concordance with *WH:* 212).

Cass. = *Casselana:* J.H. Boehmer, *Corpus iuris canonici*, II (Halle 1747); Deeters, *Bambergensisgruppe*, 7-9.

Claustr. = *Claustroneoburgensis:* F. Schönsteiner, in *Jahrbuch des Stiftes Klosterneuburg*, 2 (1909), 1-154.

1, 2 Comp. = *Compilatio prima, secunda:*

Ag. = Antonio Agustin, *Antiquae collctiones decretalium*, Lerida 1576; reissued in *Opera omnia*, IV, Lucca 1769.

Fr. = E. Friedberg, *Quinque compilationes antiquae necnon collectio canonum Lipsiensis*, Leipzig 1882 (repr. Graz 1956).

Cott. = *Cottoniana:* London, British Library, MS Cotton Vitellius E.xiii, fols. 204r-288r.

Cus. = *Cusana:* Holtzmann-Cheney, 66-74.

1 Dert. = *Dertusensis prima:* W. Holtzmann, in *ZRG Kan. Abt.*, 16 (1927), 39-77.

1 Dun. = *Dunelmensis prima:* Holtzmann-Cheney, 75-99; Duggan, 'A Durham canonical manuscript of the late twelfth century', *SCH* 2 (1965), 179-85.

2 Dun. = *Dunelmensis secunda:* Holtzmann-Cheney, 300-18.

Eber. = Eberbacensis: W. Holtzmann, in *ZRG* Kan. Abt., 17 (1928), 548-55.

Flor. = *Florianensis:* Holtzmann-Cheney, 43-63.

Font. = *Fontanensis:* Holtzmann-Cheney, 100-15.

Frcf. = *Francofortana:*

Frcf. = Frankfurt, Stadt- und Universitäts-bibliothek, MS Barth. 60, fols. 2r-85r: S. Kuttner, in *ZRG Kan. Abt.*, 22 (1933), 370-80.

Rot. = Paris, Bibliothèque Nationale, MS lat. 3922A, fols. 173r-209r: Holtzmann-Cheney, 160-68.

Max. = London, British Library, MS Egerton 2901, fols. 1r-97v.

Lips. = *Lipsiensis:* E. Friedberg, *Quinque compilationes antiquae*, 189-208; Deeters, *Bambergensisgruppe*, 10-11.

Oriel. = *Orielensis:* Holtzmann-Cheney, 127-31.

1 Par.	= *Parisiensis prima:Canones-Sammlungen*, 45-63.
2 Par.	= *Parisiensis secunda: Canones-Sammlungen*, 21-45.
Pet.	= *Petrihusensis:* Cambridge, Peterhouse, MSS 193, final quire; 114, first and final quires; 193, first quire; 203, final quire; 180, first and final quires.
1 Rot.	= *Rotomagensis prima:* Holtzmann-Cheney, 160-207.
Sang.	= *Sangermanensis:* Singer, *Neue Beiträge*, 68-354.
Tann.	= *Coll. Tanneri:* W. Holtzmann, in *Festschrift zur Feier des 200 jähr. Bestehens der Akad. der Wissenschaften in Göttingen*, Göttingen 1951, 83-145.
Wig.	= *Wigorniensis:* H.E. Lohmann, 'Die Collectio Wigorniensis', in *ZRG Kan. Abt.*, 22 (1933), 36-187.
Wig. alt.	= *Wigorniensis altera:* Duggan, *Decretal Collections*, 152-54 and pl. I.
X	= *Decretales Gregorii IX:* E. Friedberg, *Corpus iuris canonici*, II, Leipzig 1881.

ALPHABETICAL INDEX OF LETTERS

JAFFÉ-EWALD-LOEWENFELD REGISTER

JE

1829	1

JL		*JL*	
11353	6	13726	37
11398	14	13727	38
11660	3	13741	15
11661	41	13744	39
11665	45	13809	43
11835	16	13815	7(b)
11836	17	13912	2
11908	21	13976	44
12180	23	14849	29
12201	27	14097	7(a)
12203/4	28	14176	20
12367	30	14312	34
12378	42	14316	33
12530	24	17624	8
12749	5		

Not in *JL:* 4, 9, 10, 11, 12, 13, 18, 19, 22, 25, 26, 31, 32, 35, 36, 40.

NOTES

It is an honour and pleasure to share in this tribute to Professor Foreville, to whom all historians of the medieval English Church, and of the Becket dispute in particular, are deepley indebted. My thanks are also due to Professor Stephan Kuttner for his continued and unfailing kindness on my many visits to work on the Holtzmann papers in the Institute of Medieval Canon Law in the University of California at Berkeley, to the Central Research Fund of the University of London for generous help with travel expenses, and to my wife, Dr Anne Duggan, for much scholarly and technical advice.

The decretals cited in this study are identified by WH numbers, according to their place in Walther Holtzmann's unpublished index, the basis of numeration in the projected *Regesta decretalium saeculi XII*. For the Abbreviations' list, Sigla of decretal collections, alphabetical index of letters, and Jaffé-Ewald-Lœwenfeld Register, refer to the end of this paper.

1. Cf. M. CHENEY, *Roger, bishop of Worcester, 1164-1179*, Oxford 1980, 193-212, esp. 208-12; and C. DUGGAN, *Canon law in medieval England: the Becket dispute and decretal collections*, Variorum Reprints, London 1982, *passim* and *Addenda et corrigenda*, 1-8, esp. 2-3.

2. *Ibid.*; and HOLTZMANN-CHENEY, 116-18.

3. C. DUGGAN, 'From the Conquest to the death of John', in *The English Church and the papacy in the middle ages*, ed. C.H. Lawrence, London 1965, 84-93 (repr. in *Canon law in medieval England*, XV).

4. F. BARLOW, rev. of Duggan, *Decretal collections*, in *History* 48 (1963) 361; idem, *The English Church, 1066-1154*, London 1979, 147; R. SOMERVILLE, *Pope Alexander III and the council of Tours (1163)*, Berkeley-Los Angeles-London 1977; DUGGAN, *Decretals of Alexander III, 92-93*.

5. Anne DUGGAN, *Thomas Becket: a textual history of his letters*, Oxford 1980; and edition of letters in preparation: Oxford Medieval texts.

6. CHENEY, *Roger, bishop of Worcester*, 348 no. 61, 349-50 no. 63, and 364 no. 91.

7. DUGGAN, *Decretals of Alexander III, 89-106, esp. 90-93*.

8. *Ibid.*, 95-98.

9. D. WHITELOCK, M. BRETT and C.N.L. BROOKE, *Councils and Synods, with other documents relating to the English Church*, 1.ii (1066-1204), Oxford 1981, 855-83; C. DUGGAN, 'From the conquest to the death of John', 88-93; idem, 'The significance of the Becket dispute in the history of the English Church', *Ampleforth Journal*, 75 (1970), 365-75 (repr. in *Canon Law in medieval England*, I).

10. The definitive study on the *ius patronatus* is by P. LANDAU, *Ius patronatus: Studien zur Entwicklung des Patronats im Dekretalenrecht und der Kanonistik des 12. und 13. Jahrhunderts*, Köln/Wien 1975.

11. For a complete calendar of Alexander III's decretals to Roger of York, see DUGGAN, *Decretals of Alexander III*, 106-46.

III

DECRETALS OF ALEXANDER III TO ENGLAND

I (a) *Decretals to Exeter in 'Alcobacensis prima'*

The primitive decretal collection *Alcobacensis prima* (*1 Alc.* 1-125) survives in a Portuguese manuscript of c. 1181, which belonged in the middle ages to the Cistercian abbey of Alcobaça, and is now in the Biblioteca nacional in Lisbon (cod. Alcob. 144 [314], ff. 1v-39v). There is no doubt of the Portuguese provenance of its transcription, as distinct from the authorship of the work, since material in Latin and Portuguese was entered by a later hand on the first folio recto, and more positively since the only known copy of Alexander III's letter *Cum in quibusdam* (*1 Alc.* 45), to king Alfonso of Portugal in 1179-81, is found within the unbroken run of decretals.[1] The collection is composed almost entirely of decretals and decrees of Alexander III,[2] beginning with the canons

This study is a by-product of work in progress on twelfth-century decretal collections and on the projected *Regesta decretalium saeculi XII*. The *Regesta*, based on Walther Holtzmann's plan and papers now in the Institute of Medieval Canon Law in the University of California at Berkeley, will be published in the *Monumenta Iuris Canonici* series by the Biblioteca Apostolica Vaticana. My thanks are due to Professor Stephan Kuttner, Director of the Institute, for his unfailing generosity in the course of my many visits to Berkeley to work on the Holtzmann papers, and to the British Academy and the Central Research Fund of the University of London for their generous support for my work on the larger projects. Among scholars to whom I am most indebted in the present study are Mrs Mary Cheney, for her related publications on Roger of Worcester, and my wife, Dr Anne Duggan, for many valued suggestions.

All decretals cited in the paper are identified by *WH* numbers, according to their place in Walther Holtzmann's index, the basis of numeration in the *Regesta decretalium saeculi XII*. Where the notes for an individual decretal record the total number of systematic collections containing that item, the figure counts the *Compendiensis* and *Orielensis I* collections as separate works, but they are now classified as members *C* and *O* of the *Bambergensis* family (see HOLTZMANN-CHENEY, xvi, and *Decretales ineditae*, xx-xxi). If they are not counted separately, the totals are reduced by one in *1 Alc.* 75, 79, 80, 81, and *RY Calendar* 235, 341, 378, 443, 510, 518, 590, 772, 870, 998, and by two in *RY Calendar* 458, 461, 552, 749, 873, 880.

For the Abbreviations' list and Sigla of Decretal Collections see at the end of this paper.

[1] *PU Portugal*, 254-55 n° 81.

[2] Exceptions are *1 Alc.* 107, *Commisse* (ms. *Commissum*) *nobis*, *WH* 134, *JL* 11660, Adrian IV to archbishop Theobald (*ms.* Thomas) of Canterbury, 1154-59; 108, *Propter sollicitam*, *WH* 752, *JL* —, Eugenius III to the canon (?) 'Ric. Cic.', a privilege of doubtful authenticity, 1145-51: see *Decretales ineditae*, 119-21 n° 69.

of the Third Lateran Council of 1179 (*1 Alc.* 1-26), and continuing with papal letters thereafter to its conclusion (27-125). No pope later than Alexander III is named in the collection,[3] but its inclusion of letters from his closing years, together with the conciliar decrees, fixes the date of completion at c. 1181 or soon after. The work was originally complete, but is now defective through the loss of its second quaternion: the conciliar decrees break off in mid-*Nulla ecclesiastica* (26), and the collection resumes in mid-decretal *Meminimus nos/Super eo quod* (27).[4]

The collection is technically primitive, without division into component books or titles, and its individual decretals are mostly left intact. It is written by a single hand throughout, with no discernible interruption or plan of subject-matter arrangement, but at least two main sources have been distinguished in its composition. The first was a collection of the *Dertusensis* (Tortosa or Roman/ Spanish) filiation, closely matching *Dertusensis prima* itself (*1 Dert.*: Tortosa, Biblioteca del Cabildo, ms. 144, ff. 1-29).[5] The second was an English source not otherwise known as an entity, or conceivably a series of English proto-collections derived from the diocesan archives of archbishop Richard of Canterbury, and bishops Roger of Worcester and Bartholomew of Exeter.[6] The importance of *Alcobacensis prima* in recording the texts of English decretals otherwise lost, and better texts with fuller diplomatic details of decretals already known, was evident from earlier studies on Bartholomew of Exeter and on decretals to Lincoln,[7] and has been still further exemplified in the recent *Decretales ineditae saeculi XII*.[8] Studies on the collection itself have made familiar the pattern of

[3] Holtzmann once decided that *Graviter oculos* (*1 Alc.* 68: *WH* 537, *JL* 13743) should be assigned to Lucius III (1181-85); the full address from Alexander III in *1 Alc.*, together with the absence of any other post-Alexander decretals in the collection, argues against that view.

[4] *1 Alc.* 26 = Mansi, 22. 222, c. 8. For *1 Alc.* 27, *WH* 649, *JL* 13162, 1 and 4 Sept. 1167-69, see M. Cheney, *Roger, bishop of Worcester, 1164-79*, Oxford 1980, 172-79, 349-50 n° 63, 364 n° 91.

[5] C. Duggan, *English decretals in continental primitive collections, with special reference to the primitive collection of Alcobaça* (hereafter *Alcobaça collection*), in *SG* 14 (Collectanea Stephan Kuttner, 4), 51-71, esp. 61-68; Holtzmann-Cheney, 8-25 (analysis 16-25).

[6] Duggan, *Alcobaça collection*, 63-71 (comparative tables 69-71); Holtzmann-Cheney, 10-15; M. Cheney, *Roger, bishop of Worcester...*, 203-06.

[7] A. Morey, *Bartholomew of Exeter, bishop and canonist*, Cambridge 1937, texts: 130-31 n° 4, 133-35 n' 8 and 9; *Decretals to Lincoln*, collations: 2-3 n° 1, 6-9 n° 4, 18-19 n° 7, 28-29 n° 12, 40-41 n° 16.

[8] *Decretales ineditae*, texts and comments: 96-97 n° 54, 119-21 n° 69.

TAV. II

Saec. XIII

COURTRAI, Collezione privata Goethals, Frammenti di un ms. contenente una biografia di Tommaso di Canterbury in versi, f. 1*v*: Alessandro III si congeda da Tommaso per far ritorno dalla Francia.

(Cfr. P. MEYER, *Fragments d'une vie de Saint Thomas de Cantorbery en vers accouplés*, Paris 1885, p. 2).

assembly of the English material in it, with its distinct layers of decretals to Canterbury, Worcester and Exeter, a feature commonly found in early English collections, and in continental collections influenced by them.[9] The concentration of letters to Canterbury and Exeter respectively appeared at first most striking, but so close a relationship has recently been disclosed between one sequence of 23 decretals (*1 Alc.* 50-72) and judicial commissions to Roger of Worcester that their assembly in this form was almost certainly the work of canonists in his circle, probably in the last two years of his life, 1177-79.[10]

It does not diminish the importance of this Worcester discovery in the Alcobaça collection to re-assert the exceptional interest of its Exeter decretals. The collection when complete included a total of 17 letters to recipients in the Exeter diocese, but one is now lost with the missing quaternion (see *1 Dert.* 15: *Sicut dignum est, WH* 929, *JL* 12180, to Bartholomew of Exeter, 31 Jan. 1172). Five further letters are found in scattered units (*1 Alc.* 62: *Ex parte Ade, WH* 448, *JL* 13955, to Robert of Hereford and abbot Baldwin of Ford, 1174-80; 66: *Ad aures nostras, WH* 52, *JL* —, to Bartholomew of Exeter and Roger of Worcester, 1174-79; 85: *Si vobis constiterit, WH* 921, *JL* 13923, to the same two bishops, 1164-79 [? 1172-79]; 89: *Robertus de Ber, WH* 891, *JL* 14228 = 13930, to Exeter and St Albans, June 1167-1181; 112: *Significavit nobis Hugo, WH* 971, *JL* 13812, to Richard of Canterbury and Bartholomew of Exeter, 1174-77). At least four of these six decretals date from 1172 or later, and none can be positively dated earlier; five were joint commissions, respectively with Canterbury, Worcester (twice) and Hereford, and with Simon, abbot of St Albans. At least three relate to problems outside the Exeter diocese (*1 Alc.* 66 concerns the church of East Grinstead in Sussex; 89 responds to a complaint by Robert de Ber, presumably of Bere Regis in Dorset; 112 relates to the churches of Moreton and Whaddon in Gloucestershire); one is a famous letter to Bartholomew concerning penances appropriate for degrees of complicity in Becket's murder (*Sicut dignum est,* cf. above); one is a fragment lacking regional evidence of the patronage problem which gave rise to it (85). Only one relates to a problem in the Exeter diocese, involving the church of Cullompton in Devon, and that was commissioned to the bishop

[9] Cf. n. 6 above.
[10] CHENEY, *Roger, bishop of Worcester...*, 204-06.

of Hereford and the abbot of Ford (62). Only two were addressed to Bartholomew as sole recipient (*Sicut dignum est,* and 89).

In evident contrast, eleven decretals to Exeter appear in a single unbroken sequence (*1 Alc.* 73-83: hereafter *Exeter/1 Alc.,* see analysis and comments below).[11] The coherence of interests in this group of letters is too emphatic to reflect mere chance, or a pattern of organization devised by the collector.[12] Without exception, the mandates were sent by Alexander III to Bartholomew of Exeter, in every case but one to the bishop alone, and his colleague in that single exception was his own archbishop (78). The focus of regional interests is very sharply defined: acquisitive canons who leased out capitular lands were members of the Exeter chapter (78); the clerks whose immoral lives emboldened them to resist the bishop's discipline were of the Barnstaple archdeaconry in north Devon (76); the sub-deacons who lived the lives of married laymen were of the Exeter diocese or resident there (81). Wherever a parish church is named in these decretals, it is readily identified in Devon or Cornwall: the priest who pledged a silver chalice and half a breviary was the priest of Uffculme (75); the subdeacon who was the son of a priest, but received a compassionate papal judgment, had been presented to Aylesbeare (79); the clerk who assigned parochial tithes in settlement of a commitment arising from his sister's marriage was probably of Calstock (73); the church which a priest's son sought, as if by hereditary right, was that of Veryan (77). The Exeter master Simon Lovell, later archdeacon of Worcester, appears as the pope's informant in one decretal (77); the canon P. of Plympton acts in the papal curia, as the bishop of Exeter's proctor, in another (76). A delicate marriage commission involved the sometime sheriff of Devon, Hugh of Raleigh (83). A dispute between the wealthy Scalers family and the Cistercians of Old Warden is the only non-Exeter issue (80) raised in these decretals, at a time when the disputants' own dioceses, respectively of Ely and Lincoln, were possibly vacant through the deaths of their bishops, or in the case of Ely through his incapacity.[13]

[11] Duggan, *Alcobaça collection,* 65-67, 71 (comparative table); Holtzmann-Cheney, 10-12, (analysis of *1 Alc.* 73-83) 21-22.

[12] Holtzmann-Cheney, 10-11; Holtzmann asserted a possible Exeter origin of *1 Alc.* 73-83, but described the English letters in *1 Alc.* as « arranged ... according to the addresses ».

[13] Robert of Lincoln died probably on 27 Dec. 1166; Nigel of Ely survived until 30 May 1169, but in a declining phase of much reduced activity.

The dating of the *Exeter/1 Alc.* decretals is no less significant than the regional emphasis of their subject-matter. Five of the letters cannot be dated more narrowly than by the limits of Bartholomew's consecration and Alexander III's death, 1161-81 (73, 74, 75, 79, 81). But six can be placed with varying degrees of conviction in the first nine years of Bartholomew's episcopate, 1161-70. The Barnstaple decretal (76) was issued when Robert of Melun, bishop of Hereford, was still alive or very recently dead; the Veryan case (77) was reported when Simon Lovell was still at Exeter; both these commissions were therefore issued by 1167 at the latest. The pipe rolls show that Hugh of Raleigh ceased to be sheriff of Devon in 1167, and he apparently died c. 1169/70, which must be the ultimate date of a challenge to his marriage (83). For reasons developed below (78), it seems most likely that Becket was the archbishop of Canterbury who acted with Bartholomew against the acquisitive canons of Exeter, on which assumption their joint commission cannot be later than 1164. The complaint by the Scalers heir and widow, concerning lands pledged by Tibbald Scalers' father (80), is unlikely to postdate by many years Tibbald's succession, which may have occurred as early as c. 1160, and his possession is clear in the feudal returns of 1166. Alexander's response to a series of questions (82) put to him by Bartholomew is actually dated 1164-65 in one collection; the reliability of this evidence has been called in question, but perhaps finds some support from its present context. It is a matter of the highest interest that one of the Exeter decretals certainly, and a second most probably, involved Becket before his departure for exile in 1164, one as the archbishop from whose court a case was appealed to the pope (76), the other as joint commissioner with the diocesan bishop (78). No letter in *Exeter/1 Alc.* has yet been positively dated after 1169/70.

The evidence in *Exeter/1 Alc.* of a single and clearly focussed provenance, not simply in the invariable address of its decretals to Bartholomew, but more significantly in their consistent application to problems in the Exeter diocese, wherever the problems are identified, considered together with their dates of issue, wherever these can be determined, points to the discovery of a uniquely early collection, a palaeo-collection among English decretal sources.[14]

[14] Apart from brief appendices to Gratian's *Decretum*, significant elements in the early collections, whether English or continental, cannot easily be dated before the 1170s: the *Fragmentum Trecensis* (Troyes, Bibliothèque municipale, ms. 103,

It is possible that sub-components of *Exeter/1 Alc.* existed and circulated separately (cf. *1 Alc.* 74, 75, 81, 82, 83 = *1 Cant.* 31, 16, 27, 28, 29 = *Roff.* 97, 36, 89, 95, 96; but *1 Alc.* 73, 76-80 do not occur in *1 Cant.* or *Roff.*), and that it was itself assembled in stages over a period of time. With that caveat and with due regard for the decretals not precisely dated, it appears that *Exeter/1 Alc.* or at least a component in it dates from the years 1161 to 1169/70, and was conceivably put together as early as 1167/68. The hand of the bishop himself is not directly revealed in the collection, though it was clearly composed from a record of his commissions, nor is that of archdeacon Baldwin of Totnes (later abbot of Ford, bishop of Worcester and archbishop of Canterbury, a famous canonist and judge delegate whose influence is clear in the early 'Worcester' collections), then in the Exeter chapter.[15] One possible author was Simon Lovell, the Exeter master who is named as the pope's informant in one of the letters (77), and was promoted as archdeacon of Worcester in 1167, a date of possible significance.[16] The driving principles of a bishop deeply devoted to his pastoral and administrative duties are reflected in the Exeter decretals, which mostly respond to local problems drawn to the pope's attention. The commitment revealed in the letters matches the known reforming zeal of Bartholomew in the early years of his rule,[17] years which partly coincided with the exile of Alexander III in northern France (1162-65), with the council of Tours in 1163, and with the Becket dispute from 1163/64-1170. The reciprocal interchange between the English Church and the curia in those years, the pres-

ff. 2, 265v-266) cannot be earlier than 1173-74, since it includes the decretal *Sicut Romana ecclesia, WH* 944, *JL* 12293 = 13874, to archbishop William of Sens, 2 June 1173-74; nor can the small but influential archetype (which contains the same decretal) found in *Wig. alt.* 1-10 and *Belv.* 9-18, the earliest extant English collections (Duggan, *Decretal collections*, 69-73, 152-162), and in early continental collections: cf. *Cus.* 105-12, 114, 115, 119; et al.

[15] For Baldwin and the Worcester Collection, see H.-E. Lohmann, *Collectio Wigorniensis*, in *ZRG Kan. Abt.*, 22 (1933), 53 and n. 1; Duggan, *The Trinity collection of decretals and the early Worcester family* (hereafter *Trinity collection*), in « Traditio », 17 (1961), 506-26, esp. 514-16, 525-26.

[16] Mary Cheney named Simon Lovell in a list of possible authors of *Wigorniensis*, at Worcester in 1181 or later; others listed were Master Silvester (on whom, see H.M.R.E. Mayr-Harting, *Master Silvester and the compilation of the early English decretal collections*, London/Edinburgh 1965 [Studies in Church History, 2], 186-96), Samson of Worcester and Peter of Worthington: Cheney, *Roger, bishop of Worcester...*, 199; cf. n. 22 below.

[17] Morey, *Bartholomew of Exeter...*, 79-99: « The bishop and his diocese »; cf. 81: « his earliest activities were connected with the organization of the Chapter and his cathedral church »; and for problems with his clergy, 89-94.

ence of English bishops at the council and the impact of the council's work on the bishops, the ease of access from England to the curia, all at a period of dynamic growth in canon law, conditioned the broad pattern of development in the English Church, and provide the wider context of the local concerns which the Exeter decretals record.[18].

The Worcester component in *Alcobacensis prima* (*1 Alc.* 50-72: hereafter *Worcester/1 Alc.*) was assembled from the records of Roger of Worcester's office. It is markedly different from *Exeter/ 1 Alc.* in the wider regional context of its letters and their later date, and possibly even in its compiler's motivation.[19] The integrating factor in *Worcester/1 Alc.* is Roger's jurisdiction as a papal judge delegate, not as the bishop of Worcester, though that aspect of his work is included. Eleven of its letters were addressed to Roger (*1 Alc.* 52-56, 60, 61, 63, 65, 66, 71), alone or with colleagues, in connexion with cases in his own diocese or elsewhere, extending even to the diocese of York (53). Other decretals, not addressed to Roger, relate to churches in his diocese (50, 67), or to cases in which he was involved at some stage (51, 57, 58, 70, 72). Two have general addresses (64, 68), and copies may have come to his hand; and three (59, 62, 69) have no links yet identified with Roger or his diocese. Contrasting with the datable letters in *Exeter/ 1 Alc.*, those in *Worcester/1 Alc.* are notably later in issue: 14 of its 23 letters were issued within the period 1172-79 (50-52, 55, 57, 58, 61-63, 65, 66, 69-71); twelve of these can be dated in or after 1174, and one (71) was probably issued in 1177. No letter can be positively placed earlier than 1172, and none has been shown to postdate Roger's death in 1179. The date of completion of *Worcester/1 Alc.* is therefore 1177-79 or shortly after, mainly on a basis of commissions received by or involving Roger, or of interest to his professional staff, in the years 1174-78. It is a modest but expert collection from the opening decade of the classical age of the English judges delegate.

That the Exeter and Worcester components in *Alcobacensis prima* existed as separate collections in England, and related to

18 R. SOMERVILLE, *Pope Alexander III and the council of Tours*, Berkeley/ Los Angeles 1977, 19-62, *passim*.

19 My thanks are due to Mrs Cheney for material on Roger of Worcester and the Alcobaça collection in this paragraph: see CHENEY, *Roger, bishop of Worcester...*, 204-206, and the invaluable calendar of Roger's decretals, 317-373. The completeness of references to Roger's letters would not be possible without her work.

other collections independently of one another, is readily seen by collation. The eleven decretals in *Exeter/1 Alc.* are found as an entity in no other known collection, and two of its letters (*1 Alc.* 76, 77) are not otherwise known.[20] But some kinship is seen between the Exeter group and the 'English' family of primitive collections (e.g., *1 Alc.* 74, 81-83 = *1 Cant.* 31, 27-29 = *Roff.* 97, 89, 95, 96), most notably with the Fountains (*Font.*) and Royal (*Reg.*) collections:

1 Alc.	73	74	75	78	79	81	82	83
Font. (1)	41	39	40	—	—	42	43	44
Reg.	115	82	116	117	112	75	76+40	77

In contrast, the 23 decretals in *Worcester/1 Alc.* were later arrivals in other English primitive collections, and are almost wholly absent from the Fountains and Royal collections (*1 Alc.* 50a = *Font.* 1. 33; *1 Alc.* 69, a fragment = *Font.* 1. 10a = *Reg.* 160; no other items in *Worcester/1 Alc.* occur in *Font.* or *Reg.*). Collation with the Worcester collection (*Wigorniensis*: *Wig.*) is still more instructive. This collection was developed from an archetype (*Ex./Wig.*) in seven books, for each of which *Wig.* has a supplement of additional letters, of Worcester provenance more than any other.[21] The archetype *Ex./Wig.* was the common-stock of the so-called 'Worcester' family, but still earlier sources lay behind it: an English component (*Ex.*), perhaps of Exeter origin, and material from continental collections. It is not clear where *Ex./Wig.* was first assembled, but later recensions including *Wig.* were completed at Worcester. Both *Ex./Wig.* and *Wig.* itself postdate March 1181, and the latter was certainly finished at Worcester between 1181 and Baldwin's promotion to Canterbury in 1184 (decretals of Lucius III in the codex were inserted by later hands). Eight of the eleven decretals in *Exeter/1 Alc.* (the same eight as those collated with *Font.* and *Reg.* above) were received by *Wig.*, of which seven were derived from *Ex./Wig.*, and only one was in the *Wig.* supplement (*1 Alc.* 73 = *Wig.* 4. 46). The transmission of decretals is therefore from a source related to *Exeter/1 Alc.* to the archetype *Ex./Wig.*:

1 Alc.	73	74	75	78	79	81	82	83
Wig.	4.46	1.30	4.6	4.8	3.39=24	3.15	1.17	1.29

[20] DUGGAN, *Alcobaça Collection,* 65-67, 71 (comparative table); HOLTZMANN-CHENEY, 11.

[21] DUGGAN, *Trinity Collection*, 514-15, 525-26 (revised in DUGGAN, *Canon Law in medieval England*: *the Becket dispute and decretal collections* [collected studies], London 1982, VI, esp. 525-26 and 'Addenda et corrigenda').

But if the decretals in *Worcester/1 Alc.* are collated with *Wig.*, a contrasting channel of transmission is revealed. Fourteen of its 23 letters were received by *Wig.*, of which only three were known to the archetype *Ex./Wig.* (*1 Alc.* 51b = *Wig.* 4. 26; *1 Alc.* 57 = *Wig.* 7. 58; *1 Alc.* 69 = *Wig.* 2. 7a); and eleven appear in the *Wig.* additions. The *Wig.* additions in Book 7. 64-67 (the first additions in the book) and 81 are most striking, and the final item (81) is otherwise known only in *1 Alc.* (70).

1 Alc.	51	55	57	58	59	62	63	65	66	67	69	70	71	72
Wig.	4.26	4.40	7.58	7.64	3.29	7.65	4.41	7.66	4.50	2.33	2.7	7.81	2.37	7.67

A similar though slighter expansion from the archetype *Ex./Wig.* with decretals in *Worcester/1 Alc.* is found in the early 'Worcester' derivation in the Klosterneuburg collection (*Claustr.* 329, 331, 326, 330: not in *Ex./Wig.*):

1 Alc.	50	51	53	54	57	68	69
Claustr.	329	173	331	326	290	330	84-86+65

The summary conclusion is that, whereas the assimilation of *Exeter/1 Alc.* decretals in the Worcester collection had already occurred in its archetype *Ex./Wig.* (and probably in its remoter ancestor *Ex.*), the reception of *Worcester/1 Alc.* decretals was in the supplements. This matches the independent judgment that the core of the 'Worcester' family archetype was not in fact made at Worcester, but was more probably made at Exeter and expanded at Worcester, mainly from Roger's diocesan archives, with a few additional Exeter decretals, possibly brought in Baldwin's circle. It is perhaps significant that the two senior ecclesiastics at Worcester after August 1180 had been promoted from the Exeter chapter: the archdeacon Simon Lovell from 1167, and the bishop Baldwin from 1180.[22]

That the Exeter and Worcester groups of decretals in *1 Alc.* were previously independent collections, of which the Exeter group was the earlier, is supported by a further and distinct inference. It is known that Bartholomew of Exeter and Roger of Worcester acquired an unrivalled reputation as papal judges delegate. They

[22] Cf. n. 16 above. The canonical circle of Simon and Baldwin, first at Exeter and then at Worcester, suggests a very probable source of authorship of early collections, including *Exeter/1 Alc.*, *Ex./Wig.*, and *Wig.* But the *Wig.* codex evidently moved to Canterbury with Baldwin and his circle, and Simon remained at Worcester: DUGGAN, *Trinity Collection*, 516; MAYR-HARTING, *Master Silvester...*, 186-96; CHENEY, *Roger, bishop of Worcester...*, 198-200.

were in Alexander III's evaluation the « twin lights of the English Church », and in the embroidered eulogy of Giraldus Cambrensis they were commissioned by Alexander to resolve almost all the English cases in his time.[23] The basis of truth in Giraldus' exaggeration is that Bartholomew and Roger were apparently commissioned by Alexander more than any other delegates. On the evidence of the decretal collections, in a total of 387 of his letters to England, 71 were received by Roger and 57 by Bartholomew of which 16 were addressed to them jointly.[24] The total number of their joint commissions, known at present from all sources, is at least 23.[25]

Now, if the decretals to Bartholomew or Roger which can be dated positively before 1170 are considered, it is found that no Exeter/Worcester joint commissions occur among them. Roger then appears acting with Robert of Melun, bishop of Hereford, four times in the years 1163-67,[26] twice with Henry of Winchester in 1165-67,[27] once with Hilary of Chichester in 1164-67,[28] and as sole recipient of three decretals between 1164 and 1169.[29] In no case so far known has he been shown as acting with Bartholomew in those years. Likewise, if the Exeter decretals in *Exeter/1 Alc.* which can be fixed in the years 1161-69/70 are examined, it is seen that all but one were addressed to Bartholomew as sole recipient, the single exception being a joint commission with the archbishop of Canterbury.[30] None of the letters was addressed to Roger. Of the 23 commissions sent to Bartholomew and Roger as colleagues, ten cannot be narrowly dated and so must be provisionally assigned to 1164-78,[31] but the 13 which can be more closely dated were without exception issued between 1172 and 1178, and of these

23 J.S. Brewer, et al., *Giraldi Cambrensis opera,* VII, London 1891 (Rolls Series, 21), 57; Morey, *Bartholomew of Exeter...,* 45; Cheney, *Roger, bishop of Worcester...,* 116-17, 124, 126, 131, 133.

24 Numbers of decretals to various recipients given in this study are based on the forthcoming *Regesta decretalium saeculi XII* (from the *WH* index); cf. Morey, *Bartholomew of Exeter...,* 44-45; Cheney, *Roger, bishop of Worcester...,* 130-31.

25 Cheney, *Roger, bishop of Worcester...,* 130-31.

26 *RW Calendar,* internal refs. and mentions: 331-32 n° 31, 367-68 n[i] 100, 101, 373 n° 124.

27 *RW Calendar,* internal refs.: 321 n° 10, 331-32 n° 31.

28 *RW Calendar,* mention: 366 n° 95.

29 *RW Calendar,* decretals: 348 n° 61, 349-50 n° 63, 364 n° 91; and two non-decretals: 339 n° 46, to establish a house of canons regular at Keynsham; 350 n° 65, leave to return to his Worcester diocese if he can act freely there.

30 The exception is *1 Alc.* 78.

31 *RW Calendar,* 321 n° 9, 324 n° 16, 333 n[i] 34, 35, 336-37 n° 42, 339-40 n° 47, 358-59 n[i] 81, 82, 365 n° 92, inferred: 372 n° 122; Bartholomew's co-recipient in 361-62 n° 87 was more probably Richard of Winchester.

at least 11 date from 1174 or later.[32] The evidence points to the years 1172-78, and especially 1174-78, as the period of the famous collaboration of Bartholomew and Roger as papal delegates. This is a proposal not only of value for the dating of all Exeter/Worcester joint commissions, but of importance for the general history of the English Church. The decretal evidence is in harmony with the broader history of the English Church in those years. Bartholomew and Roger were among the English bishops most clearly concerned with canonical order and reform in the years of the emerging Becket crisis, in close liaison with the papal curia. Some of their earliest decretals date from 1164-67, though they do not appear working together on papal commissions at that time. Roger went into exile on Becket's instructions in late 1167, and did not return to England until August 1171, several months after Becket's murder. Meanwhile, Bartholomew and Henry of Winchester emerged as the most positive defenders of the Church's rights in England, the most supportive of Becket's position against the king, especially from 1169. But the aged Henry of Winchester died on 8 August 1171, about the time of Roger's return. Bartholomew was then seen as an evident symbol of the Church's interests. He was chosen to deliver the sermon at the re-dedication of Canterbury cathedral, desecrated by the archbishop's murder (29 Dec. 1170), on 21 Dec. 1171;[33] and he received the papal mandate concerning penance for the murderers and their abettors, dated 31 Jan. 1172.[34] The large numbers of Exeter and Worcester decretals, including the joint commissions, date from 1172 onwards, especially from 1174. Their historical context in the settlement at Avranches in 1172 and the forward movement of canon law in England thereafter seems clear enough.[35] In the narrower context of this present study, the evidence adduced on the joint commissions supports the conclusion that *Exeter/1 Alc.* and *Worcester/1 Alc.* once existed as independent sources, that

32 *RW Calendar*, 319-20 nⁱ 5, 6, 7, 323 n° 13 (with Clarembald of Faversham), 327, n° 22, 328 nⁱ 24, 25, 332 n° 32 (internal ref.), 332-33 n° 33 (with Clarembald of Faversham, prob. 1172), 347-48 n° 59, 362 n° 88 (with Hugh of Bury St Edmunds); mentions: 367 n° 98 (with Richard of Canterbury and Gilbert of London), 370 n° 114 (? 1173 - Sept. 1174). Two further commissions were possibly sent to Bartholomew and Roger (318 n° 3A, 323 n° 14), though the manuscripts record them to London and Exeter (1174-76) and London and Worcester (1174-78) respectively.

33 Morey, *Bartholomew of Exeter...*, 33.

34 *Sicut dignum est*, *WH* 929, *JL* 12180.

35 Duggan, *Canon law in medieval England...*, I, III, IV, 139-40, XV, 91-94 and 'Addenda et corrigenda'; cf. Cheney, *Roger, bishop of Worcester...*, 208-12.

the former was assembled in the years 1164-69/70 from Exeter archives, and that the latter was a work of wider scope, from the Worcester archives, perhaps a decade later. There are no Exeter/Worcester joint commissions in *Exeter/1 Alc.*, but two (*1 Alc.* 56, 66) are found among the many decretals from the 1170s in *Worcester/1 Alc.* The Exeter and Worcester components in *1 Alc.* recorded not only their separate places of origin, but distinctly different phases in the process of collection. The Exeter archives from the mid-1170s contained more varied decretal resources than those recorded in *Exeter/1 Alc.*, as the ancestor of the 'Worcester' family (the archetype *Ex.*, discussed above) makes clear.

I(b) *Alcobacensis prima 73-83 (here named Exeter/1 Alc.)*

The letters in the following analysis all have full addresses ('Alexander episcopus servus servorum Dei venerabili fratri [78: venerabilibus fratribus Cantuariensi archiepiscopo et] Exoniensi episcopo, salutem et apostolicam benedictionem'), with the initial B. for Bartholomew in seven items (73, 74, 77, 80-83). The precise date of Bartholomew's consecration, after the death of archbishop Theobald on 18 April 1161, is uncertain; the limits of Alexander's decretals to Bartholomew are given here as 1161-81, but it is unlikely that any were issued before 1162. It is possible that Simon Lovell was in some way linked with the authorship of *Exeter/1 Alc.*, in the mid-1160s, and perhaps also with the archetype *Ex./Wig.* at Worcester in or after 1181.

73. *Pervenit ad nos quod, cum Willelmus clericus de Calest. in minore esset etate constitutus et Girardus de Calester. sororem eiusdem ... studeat convenire.* To B(artholomew) bishop of Exeter.

When William clerk of *Calest.* was young and Girard of *Calester.* married his sister, William gave a solemn undertaking to pay Girard five shillings yearly. A dispute later arose between them, and a compromise was reached by arbitration, whereby Girard would receive parochial tithes, his own and those of his villeins, in lieu of the previously agreed sum. The pope orders the recipient to compel Girard, if the accusation is proven, to relinquish the tithes to the church, of which he is a parishioner, and make no further presumption concerning them. He must also induce William to make an amicable arrangement with Girard.

WH 720, *JL* 13918, 1161-81. *1 Alc.* 73; *Font.* 1. 41; *Reg.* 115; *Wig.* 4. 46; *Chelt.* 4. 6; *2 Dun.* 176; and ten systematic collections. Pd *Brug.* 17. 9; *X* 1. 43. 3. The place-name *Calest.* in *1 Alc.* and five other primitive collections is very probably Calstock in east Cornwall (cf. *Calestoch* in Domesday Book and in contemporary records; it derives its Cornish root from nearby Callington).

74. *Ex presentium latoris confessione percepimus quod, cum iste quandam alterius ... statuta procedas.* To B(artholomew) bishop of Exeter.

The *lator presentium* confessed to the pope that he had committed adultery with another man's wife and accepted penance, but later relapsed into the same offence; and he married the woman when her husband was dead. The recipient must carefully investigate the affair. If it is found that either party contrived in any way the husband's death, or that the man had promised to marry the woman, while her husband was still alive, the recipient must separate them without delay. But, if neither of these conditions is proved, he should proceed according to ecclesiastical custom and the canons.

WH 474, *JL* 13900, 1161-81. *1 Alc.* 74; *1 Cant.* 31; *Roff.* 97; *Font.* 1. 39; *Reg.* 82; *Wig.* 1. 30; *Claustr.* 67; *Chelt.* 9. 27; *Cott.* 2. 64; *Pet.* 1. 65; and six systematic collections. Pd *Claustr.*; *App.* 45. 2.

75. *Ex presentium latoris insinuatione accepimus quod Alexander quondam sacerdos ecclesie de Offecolon calicem quendam ... differas cohercere.* To (Bartholomew) bishop of Exeter.

A complaint was brought to the pope that Alexander, former priest of the church of *Offecolon*, had pledged a silver chalice and half a breviary belonging to the church when he was in financial straits, and had not redeemed them by the time of his death. Since it is an unworthy matter for the church to lose its possessions in this way, especially those used in the sacred ministry, the pope orders the recipient, if the charge is true, to compel Walter, Alexander's son and heir to his patrimony, to redeem the pledged possessions and restore them to the church.

WH 475, *JL* 13911, 1161-81. *1 Alc.* 75; *1 Cant.* 16; *Roff.* 36; *Font.* 1. 40; *Reg.* 116; *Trin.* 4. 6; *Wig.* 4. 6; *Claustr.* 147; *Chelt.* 8. 9; *Cott.* 4. 75; *Pet.* 3. 80; and eleven systematic collections. Pd *App.* 29. 1; *X* 3. 21. 3.

The location of the problem is Uffculme in Devon, appearing as *Offecolon* in *1 Alc.* (*Offocolo.*, *Offec.*, *Offet.*, etc. in other collections; cf. *Offecoma* in Domesday Book).

76. *Cum causa que inter te et quosdam clericos tuos de archidiaconatu Banostrapolis super quibusdam denariis ... ad presentiam venerabilis fratris nostri T(home) Cantuariensis archiepiscopi ... venerabilibus fratribus nostris Hen(rico) Wintoniensi, R(oberto) Herefordensi, et R(ogero) Wigorniensi episcopis ... restitutionem compellas.* To (Bartholomew) bishop of Exeter.

A dispute was protracted between the recipient and some of his clerks in the archdeaconry of Barnstaple, concerning financial matters and various other complaints which the bishop alleges against them, and was appealed to the pope from the court of archbishop Thomas of Canterbury. But the clerks came unprepared to make their case, and the pope set a term for both parties at the next feast of St Lucy. The bishop's proctor, the canon P. of Plympton, remained long in the curia, but the clerks did not come, and at length sent written excuses. The pope therefore commissioned the bishops Henry of Winchester, Robert of Hereford and Roger of Worcester to hear the case, but the canon of Plympton revealed to him the bishop's frequent attempts to correct the immoral lives of the clerks and their recalcitrance in resisting his admonitions. They publicly retained their concubines, celebrated divine office in defiance of his prohibition, and contumaciously refused to appear in answer. It was following this that they raised the financial matter, and drew the bishop into the archbishop's court. To avoid the pretext of appeal being exploited as a cover for immorality, the pope ordered the judges to examine the case, and to hear the bishop's charges against the clerks if they were earlier, and to reach a canonical verdict on that matter and on the money dispute. If the judges establish that the bishop could have condemned the clerks in his ordinary jurisdiction, in respect of his accusations against them, he should himself impose a proper penance upon them, with the judges' counsel. He must compel all clerks who have churches in his diocese, or who celebrate divine service there, to live chastely or relinquish their churches and cease to celebrate. But if it is true that, while the vicar of one of the clerks was in the papal curia, the bishop removed him from his church and replaced him with another, the bishop must compel the substitute to restore its benefices to the church in question.

WH 217, *JL* —, 1165-67. *1 Alc.* 76 only. Pd MOREY, *Bartholomew of Exeter...*, 134-35. The form *Banostrapolis* in *1 Alc.* identifies Barnstaple in north Devon (cf. *Barnestaple* in Domesday Book, *Bardanstapol*, etc.), one of the four archdeaconries in the Exeter diocese.

The internal references fix the early phases of litigation in the limits of Thomas of Canterbury's consecration in May 1162 and his departure for exile on 1 Nov. 1164, for he was clearly still in England when the case was taken to his court and appealed from there to the pope. The mandate to the judges delegate postdates Roger of Worcester's consecration on 23 Aug. 1164, and the final terminus of the present letter is fixed by Robert of Hereford's death on 27 Feb. 1167, or very shortly after. Since the feast of St Lucy falls on 13 Dec., the limits of the letter are early 1165 to April 1167.

77. *Ex transmissa nobis relatione dilecti filii nostri magistri Symonis Lupelli nostris est auribus intimatum quod, A. sacerdote de Helerki de hac luce subtracto, ... studeas precavere.* To B(artholomew) bishop of Exeter.

The pope has learned from Master Simon Lupellus that, when the priest A. of the church of *Helerki* died, his son presumed to claim the church and strives to secure it as if by hereditary right. Since this is clearly contrary to the rulings of the holy fathers, the pope orders the recipient to remove the son within ten days of receiving the mandate, if it is shown that A.'s son was born in the priesthood or succeeded his father in that church. Moreover, he orders the bishop not to advance to holy orders other sons of priests in his diocese, and to take every precaution to prevent them from succeeding in their fathers' churches.

WH 507, *JL* —, 1161-67. *1 Alc.* 77 only. Pd MOREY, *Bartholomew of Exeter...*, 133-34. The decretal concerns the church of Veryan in Cornwall, named here in its old Cornish form *Helerki* (*Elerchi* in Domesday Book, *Elerky* in Feet of Fines). Master Simon Lupellus was presumably Simon Lovell, a member of the Exeter chapter who was promoted as archdeacon of Worcester in 1167; in the latter appointment he worked closely with the canonist bishops Roger and Baldwin (a former colleague at Exeter, as archdeacon of Totnes). Simon's promotion fixes the limits of the present mandate at 1161-67.

78. *Ad audientiam nostram noveritis pervenisse quod quidam de canonicis Exoniensis ecclesie ... incommoditas provenire.* To (? Thomas) archbishop of Canterbury and (Bartholomew) bishop of Exeter.

The pope has heard that certain canons of Exeter have let out chapter lands on perpetual leases for money payments, without consulting their colleagues and to the chapter's detriment. The recipients are ordered to revoke the leases in legal form, if the charge is true, so that, if the leased-out lands cannot be otherwise recovered, they must compel those responsible to pay back the money they received, to prevent more serious damage to the church if the leases are allowed to remain.

WH 30, *JL* 17624, (? 1162-64) 1162-81. *1 Alc.* 78; *Reg.* 117; *Wig.* 4. 8; *Claustr.* 149; *Chelt.* 11. 3; *Cott.* 6. 100; and eleven systematic collections. Pd *Brug.* 17. 10; *X* 3. 13. 9.

The decretal is listed in *JL* under Celestine III (1191-98: from *2 Comp.* 3. 10. 2; *X* 3. 13. 9; see also *Alan.* 3. 10. 1), but is shown by the early collections to be a letter of Alexander III (see LOHMANN, *Collectio Wigorniensis...*, 79). Its presence in the *1 Alc.* group of Exeter decretals supports a still more precise dating. In view of Bartholomew's known integrity and concern for good order in his diocese, it is most unlikely that an abuse of the kind which gave rise to this letter would have arisen late in his period of office. On this assumption, the archbishop who acted with him was Thomas of Canterbury before his departure for exile on 1 Nov. 1164. An acceptance of Richard of Canterbury, Becket's successor from 1174, as Bartholomew's colleague would date the problem at least twelve years after Bartholomew's careful rule began. Moreover, the pope would not have sent a commission of this kind to Becket in exile, so its likely dating limits are mid-1162 to late October 1164. Almost certainly therefore, the letter is a rare example of a decretal to Becket.

79. *Proposuit nobis R. presentium lator quod, cum ipse ad ecclesiam de Haleberia a domino fundi fuerit presentatus ... suffragio celebrare.* To B(artholomew) bishop of Exeter.

The subdeacon R. complained to the pope that, although he was presented to the church of *Haleberia* by the *dominus fundi,* the bishop of Exeter was unwilling to consent or commit the cure of souls to him, because he was the son of a priest. The pope commends the bishop's prudence in this matter, but is moved to compassion by the clerk's needs and the burdens which he endured on his journey to the curia. It is unfitting that an ordained subdeacon, as he claims to be, should altogether lack an ecclesiastical income, and therefore the pope orders the recipient to seek within ten days of receiving the mandate a suitable priest to serve in the church in question, with the assent of the plaintiff clerk. The latter should receive half the benefice income of the church, and officiate in it in his own order — a priest cannot solemnize Mass or other divine offices alone, without the assistance of a minister.

WH 751, *JL* 14217, 1161-81. *1 Alc.* 79; *Reg.* 112; *Bridl.* 53; *Wig.* 3. 39 = 3. 24; *Claustr.* 140; *Chelt.* 12. 6; *Cott.* 6. 27; and eleven systematic collections. Pd *App.* 19. 6; *X* 1. 17. 6.
The place-name appears as *haleb'a* in *1 Alc.*, and *alesb'ia* in *Wig.*, and identifies Aylesbeare in Devon (cf. *Aylesbere* in charters); from *App.* onwards, the name was wrongly transmitted as Salesby. The decretal is found in a shortened redraft in *Bridl.*, beginning *Audivimus quod J. presentatus.*

80. *Ex transmissa conquestione T. Escalers et matris eius nobis innotuit quod pater eius, qui est ex hac luce subtractus, terram suam de Dullibam monachis de Wardun pro quadam pecunie summa ... contradicunt. Quia vero usurarum crimen deo et hominibus abhominandum existit et tanto gravius ... inquisita et cognita, si tibi constiterit quod predicti monachi ... absque difficultate restituant pacifice possidendam.* To B(artholomew) bishop of Exeter.

The plaintiff T. Escalers and his mother informed the pope that T.'s father, now dead, had pledged his estate at *Dullibam* to the monks of *Wardun* for a certain sum of money, but the monks refuse to restore the land, although they have received over and above the principal. Since the crime of usury is all the more grave in ecclesiastics and religious, the pope orders the recipient to investigate the case, and compel the monks to restore the land to T. and his mother, if he confirms that the monks have recovered their principal and expenses.

WH 501, *JL* 13998, (? 1161-66) 1161-81. *1 Alc.* 80; *Bridl.* 20; *Claud.* 20; and nine systematic collections. Pd *App.* 16. 10; *1 Comp.* 5. 15. 7.
1 Alc. is the only primitive collection to preserve the full decretal. A shortened version is found in *Bridl.*, *Claud.*, starting with an adjusted mandatory clause: « Si tibi constiterit quod monachi de Wardona ... absque difficultate restituant », and ending with the transferred phrase: « quia usurarum crimen ... existit ». The full text was received by *App.* and subsequent systematic collections.
The estate in question is Dullingham in Cambridgeshire, and the monks were the Cistercians of Old Warden in Bedfordshire. The Scalers family held lands in Cambridgeshire, where Robert de Scalers was tenant in demesne in the early twelfth century, and was perhaps dead by 1160, since his son Tibbald appears in charter evidence by that date, at the latest, and had certainly succeeded his father as tenant of Dullingham by 1166, since he occurs in the feudal returns of that year. Robert was the father and husband, and Tibbald the son, in the present decretal. Later evidence records a grant of land to the Cistercians of Old Warden from the Scalers' Dullingham estates, c. 1200. It is not clear why the present dispute was commissioned to the bishop of Exeter, except perhaps as an impartial judge between subjects of the bishops of Ely and Lincoln. The sees were simultaneously vacant between 30 May 1169 and 1173/74: Lincoln from 27 Dec. 1166; Ely from 1169. But if Tibbald had inherited his father's estate by 1160, or 1166 at the latest, it is

improbable that a dispute of this nature, involving the property rights of the heir and the widow, would have been delayed many years after Robert's death. The date of the decretal is therefore uncertain but the limits 1161 — c. 1166 can be reasonably proposed. See J. DUGDALE, *Monasticon Anglicanum,* V, London 1846, 150-51 n° 8; H. HALL, *Liber Rubeus de Scaccario,* I, London 1896 (Rolls Series), 368-69; G.H. FOWLER, *Cartulary of the abbey of Old Wardon*, Bedford 1930 (Bedford Historical Record Society, 13), 175-78 n[i] 225-31; P.M. WRIGHT, *Victoria County History of Cambridgeshire and the Isle of Ely,* VI, Oxford University Press 1978, 161.

81. *Significatum est nobis quod quidam subdiaconi in tua diocesi existentes vel commorantes matrimonia contrahere presumpserunt ... dimittere sunt cogendi.* To B(artholomew) bishop of Exeter.

It was drawn to the pope's attention that certain subdeacons of the recipient's diocese, or dwelling there, had presumed to contract marriages, and they live like laymen with their wives. Since this is contrary to canon law, the pope orders the bishop to examine carefully the manner of their lives before contracting marriage, and their probable future behaviour if they dismissed their wives. If they had lived honourably before, or were likely to live chastely if they put their so-called wives away, he must compel them to do so. But if their former lives were dissolute and they were likely to live in a worse and promiscuous manner, he can by dissimulation permit them to remain together, to avert a graver fault; but they may not minister at the altar or receive ecclesiastical benefices. If any such persons hold the parsonages of churches, they must be compelled forthwith to dismiss their wives or relinquish the churches.

WH 962, *JL* 13904, 1161-81. *1 Alc.* 81; *1 Vict.* 127; *1 Par.* 81; *1 Cant.* 27; *Roff.* 89; *Font.* 1. 42 = 3. 17; *Reg.* 75; *Bridl.* 4; *Claud.* 4; *Trin.* 3. 16; *Wig.* 3. 15; *Claustr.* 131; *Chelt.* 9. 71 = 12. 2; *Cott.* 5. 47; and twelve systematic collections. Pd *Claustr.* 131; *App.* 18. 13; *1 Comp.* 4. 6. 3.

82. (a) *Super hoc quod a nobis tua sollicitudo quesivit utrum ille scilicet qui prius cognovit ... in priori servetur.* (b) *De peregrinationis item quoque votis an elemosinis ... dispensare.* (c) *Preterea hi qui de matrimonio contrahendo ... promiserunt coniungant.* To B(artholomew) bishop of Exeter.

The pope responds to a series of questions put to him by the bishop. The latter has asked him what are the mutual obligations of a man and his wife when the man confesses in secret to illicit relations previously with the mother or sister of the woman he later married, and what advice he should be given, since the matter cannot be proved and the man does not wish to remain continent. The pope replies that the man should strive to persuade his wife to live in continence, so that they both may do so, if she is willing. But if they cannot be so persuaded, the man should render his wife her due and expiate his sin with penance. The same applies if his offence was after the marriage. The bishop has further asked if pilgrimage vows can be commuted, and be redeemed by alms or in necessity fulfilled by another. The pope replies that the decision should rest with whoever presides in the case, so that the latter should carefully consider the rank of the person and the reason for commutation, whether the pilgrimage or the compensation would be more useful and more pleasing to God, and on these considerations he should base his dispensation. Finally, if parties have promised unconditionally to contract a marriage, or have taken an oath, they should be induced by every means to fulfil their undertaking.

WH 1013 (abc), *JL* 13907+13916+13903 (? 1164-65) 1161-81. *1 Alc.* 82; *1 Vict.* 128; *1 Par.* 82+83; *1 Cant.* 28; *Roff.* 95; *1 Dun.* 2. 29; *Font.* 1. 43 = 3. 18; *Wig.* 1. 17; *Claustr.* 44+45; *Chelt* 9. 18; *Cott.* 2. 45; *Pet.* 1. 51; parts in *Cus.* 169. II (ab.); *Reg.* 76 (a), 40 (b); *Bridl.* 54 (a), 5 (bc); *Claud.* 138 (a), 5 (bc), 146 (*ex* c); sixteen systematic collections and five later primitive collections. Pd *Claustr.*; *App.* 12. 7 (a), 35. 3 (b), 6. 33 (c), 50. 43 (c); *2 Comp.* 4. 7. 1 (a); *X* 3. 34. 1 (b), 4. 1. 2 (c).
The decretal is transcribed in a single paragraph in *1 Alc.* An additional concluding passage is found in *Claud.* 146, *App. Cr.* 50. 43, *Bamb. O* 57. 32: *Si autem sibi invicem id remittere voluerint ... hoc possit in patientia tolerari*, to the effect that the parties can be permitted mutually to remit their commitment, to avert a worse contingency, as when one may marry someone whom he or she will always hate. For this item, *Bamb. O* provides the date « VI l(ibro) reg(istri) », that is 1164-65. The reliability of this date has been queried (see HOLTZMANN, *Die Register Papst Alexanders III in den Händen der Kanonisten*, Rome 1940 [Quellen und Forschungen aus italienischen Archiven und Bibliotheken, 33], 51-52, n° 32), but is perhaps supported by the early date of several letters in this sequence of Exeter decretals.

83. *Pervenit ad audientiam nostram quod Hugo de Ralega* (ms. *Relega*) *et* (*Muriel*) *uxor sua in tali sunt linea consanguinitatis coniuncti ... studeas terminare.* To B(artholomew) bishop of Exeter.

The pope has heard that Hugh de Ralega and his wife are so closely related by consanguinity that no lawful marriage is possible between them. In a matter of such discretion, he orders the bishop to summon both parties and investigate the matter, if people came forward who wish to impugn the marriage and can do so. He must discover how long the two have lived together, and whether the accusers were silent at the time of the marriage, knowing that it would take place. If they knew of the marriage then, and kept silence, it would be a serious matter to hear them now. But if it is found that the marriage was recent, or that the accusers did not hear of it in time, the bishop should hear and canonically resolve the case, taking careful account of local report and that of individuals. The pope affirms that it is better to leave united those who have been joined together contrary to men's laws, than to separate against God's law those who have been lawfully united.

WH 701, *JL* 14214, 1161-69/70. *1 Alc.* 83; *Aur.* 121; *Cus.* 173; *1 Cant.* 29; *Roff.* 96; *Font.* 1. 44; *Reg.* 77; *Bridl.* 6; *Claud.* 6; *Wig.* 1. 29; *Claustr.* 66; *Chelt.* 9. 26; *Cott.* 2. 24; *Pet.* 1. 28; and eleven systematic collections. Pd *Claustr.*; *App.* 8. 23; *1 Comp.* 4. 19. 3.

The decretal is wrongly addressed to the bishop of Winchester in *Frcf. FRM* 3. 20; it begins *Pervenit ad nostram audientiam* in *Reg.*, *Claustr.* The wife of Hugh de Ralega is identified as Muriel in *Cus.*; the initial M. occurs in many collections, but is omitted in *1 Alc.*

The case concerns the marriage of Hugh de Raleigh, sheriff of Devon in the years 1160-67. Hugh appears in the pipe rolls from the fiscal year 1159-60, and accounted as sheriff until the Michaelmas Exchequer of 1167; his successor, Robert FitzBernard, accounted for 1167-68, but Hugh continued to appear in the rolls until 1169-70. His brother Richard rendered account for him in 1170-71, and thereafter accounted for Hugh's liabilities and his own through many years. It appears that Richard inherited the estate. Hugh is also found as witness to a notification by Bartholomew of Exeter, concerning the church of Colebrook within the years 1161-69, together with Robert FitzBernard and prior Richard of Plympton, who was succeeded by John in the latter year. Since Richard de Raleigh succeeded to Hugh's estate, it appears that Hugh was without direct heir, and the challenge to his marriage may record the property interests of relations, conceivably for the dower interests of his wife. WH dated the decretal 1162-67, influenced by the dates of Hugh's tenure of office as sheriff, but the wider limits 1161-1169/70 must be allowed. See MOREY, *Bartholomew of Exeter...*, 67-68, 143-44 n° 22; PIPE ROLLS: *The Great Roll of the Pipe from the reign of Henry II*, London 1884-1925 (Pipe Roll Society): *13 Henry II* (1166-67), 168; *14 Henry II* (1167-68), 124, 127; *15 Henry II* (1168-69), 49; *16 Henry II* (1169-70), 99; *17 Henry II* (1170-71), 26.

II (a) *Decretals to Roger of York*

The many decretals to archbishop Roger of York have been largely neglected by historians of canon law in England, in contrast with those to his contemporaries in the south. Studies on the

English primitive collections have rightly emphasized the impact of leading prelates of the province of Canterbury, whose judicial commissions inspired the canonists in their circles to record and organize the papal letters which their own bishops received, to which they later added similar archival material from other dioceses, together with letters from primitive decretal collections of English or continental authorship. In this way they shared in the development of the early decretal collections. The *Alcobacensis prima,* discussed above, affords a clear example of this process of evolution in the several strata of diocesan sources from which it was partly derived, in its clusters of letters from Exeter, Worcester and Canterbury archives, brought together to form an almost wholly English entity, which was annexed in the Alcobaça collection to a member of the *Dertusensis* or Tortosa family. But it is not only in the Alcobaça collection that decretals to Canterbury, Worcester and Exeter excite attention by their numbers and concentration. It is a familiar phenomenon in the early collections.[36] In the whole corpus of Alexander III's decretals in canonical sources, more than half were addressed to English recipients — by the latest reckoning, 387 in a total of 713. The largest numbers were received by Roger of Worcester (71) and Bartholomew of Exeter (57), as noted already, and by Richard, archbishop of Canterbury (59). Gilbert of London received 24, and the famous abbots Baldwin of Ford and Adam of Evesham 13 and 9 respectively. At the other extreme, only one decretal to Geoffrey of Ely is found in the collections, and not more than four to Reginald of Bath.[37] The relationship between this statistical reckoning and the judicial commissions of the bishops and canonists whose careers helped most directly to shape the decretal collections has been much discussed. The respective totals do not necessarily reflect the proportions of letters which the individuals in fact received, but rather the extent to which their interests influenced the collections.[38] Against this backcloth, the decretals to

[36] DUGGAN, *Decretal collections*, 66-117, *passim*, 118-24, 149-51; and n. 35 above.

[37] Numbers based on the *Regesta decretalium*; cf. n. 24 above. The statistics here relate only to Alexander III's decretals. It should be noted that the total to Richard of Canterbury includes 21 which he received jointly with his suffragans. See also A. MOREY and C.N.L. BROOKE, *The letters and charters of Gilbert Foliot*, Cambridge 1967, Appendix VIII, 525-29.

[38] DUGGAN, *Decretal collections*, 118-24, 149-51.

Roger of York merit a closer evaluation, since no less than 52 letters from Alexander III to Roger appear in the collections.[39]

There is no known collection of northern provenance which points to Roger's circle as its place of authorship. Indeed, the impact of northern canonists generally on the English primitive collections is much less marked than that of their colleagues in the south. Three early collections survive in manuscripts of northern provenance, the Durham 1, Fountains and Bridlington collections. The *Dunelmensis prima*, in a Durham codex of varied canonical matter (Durham Cathedral Library, ms. C. III. 1, ff. 5v-18r: *1 Dun.*), comprises three separate elements: the first is linked with a *Decretum* appendix of Italian origin;[40] the second is more closely related in contents and arrangement to the Canterbury collection (*Cantuariensis prima, tertia*) than to any others.[41] There is no significant Durham or York element anywhere in the collection, except for two otherwise unknown items of regional interest in the third part, a privilege to Master R. of York [42] and a forged decretal to the monks of Lenton in the York diocese.[43] The Fountains collection (*Fontanensis*: *Font.*, Oxford, Bodleian Library, ms. Laud Misc. 527 [S.C. 814], ff. 24r-45v) belonged to the Cistercian abbey of Fountains. It is likewise composed of three parts of complex ancestry, deriving from sources in the Italian primitive family[44] and English sources, the latter including a relation of *Exeter/1 Alc.*, discussed with the Alcobaça collection above.[45] The second of the three parts of *Fontanensis*

[39] The calendar of Roger's decretals provided below (hereafter *RY Calendar*) includes 54 items (numbered by their place in the *Regesta decretalium*), but two (914, 916) are canonists' redrafts of material in other items (552, 443). On the other hand, a decretal of unknown provenance (*Conquerente dilecto*), *WH* 138, *JL* —, ? 1159-81: *Decretales ineditae*, 137-39 n° 80, could conceivably have been sent to Roger as one of its co-recipents.

[40] *1 Dun.* 1. 1-50: HOLTZMANN-CHENEY, 76-77, 80-85 (analysis); completed before the 1179 Lateran council.

[41] *1 Dun.* 2. 1-59: HOLTZMANN-CHENEY, 77, 79, 85-90 (analysis); concludes with the canons of the 1179 Lateran council. For *1 Dun.* 3. 1-71: HOLTZMANN-CHENEY, 77-78, 90-99 (analysis); ends with four letters of Lucius III (from 1181) in later hands. Cf. DUGGAN, *A Durham canonical manuscript of the late-twelfth century*, London/Edinburgh 1965 (Studies in Church History, 2), 179-85.

[42] *1 Dun.* 3. 61: *Sacrosancta Romana*, *WH* 892, *JL* —, 1159-81, *Decretales ineditae*, 132-33 n° 77.

[43] *1 Dun.* 3. 46: *Sancta Romana*, *WH* 892, *JL* —, 1159-81, *Decretales ineditae*, 133-35 n° 78.

[44] *Font.* 1. 1-53, 2. 1-55, 3. 1-38: HOLTZMANN-CHENEY, 100-102 (for comparison with the Italian family, 101-102), 103-15 (analysis). The compiler inserted a letter of Lucius III to the Cistercian general chapter (*Font.* 2. 25); otherwise, no part has any letters later than Alexander III.

[45] HOLTZMANN-CHENEY, 102, and *Exeter/1 Alc.* above.

opens with 25 items relating almost wholly to Cistercian privileges, mostly to the abbey of Fountains itself. Six of these letters were addressed to Roger of York (*Font. 2. 4, 5, 7, 10, 11,* 14), in four cases (*ital.*) with the bishop of Durham as co-recipient, and two further letters with general addresses (2. 8, 21) must have reached him. This is an important source of papal letters of northern provenance not known elsewhere, but it is essentially a Cistercian archive, and its tenor is sometimes hostile to Roger.[46] The Bridlington collection (*Bridlingtonensis*: *Bridl.*), belonged to the Augustinian priory at Bridlington, but its largest identified source was an archetype from the Canterbury province, which was also the primary basis of the Claudian collection (*Claudiana*: *Claud.*).[47] Within the Bridlington supplements to the archetype, there is some evidence of the use of York archives. Nine decretals to Roger occur within a run of 32 items (*Bridl.* 145, 149, 152, 160, 161, 162, 166, 174, 176).[48] Eight of these nine are rarely found in early collections (the exception is 174); four appear in no collection earlier than *Bridl.* (145, 160, 161, 162; and the fragment 176); and one is found in this collection alone (152).[49] Apart from this example, the northern collections show limited evidence of Roger's judicial concerns, or of the use made by northern canonists of their local records. They did not build on Roger's archives, as the southern collectors did on those of Richard of Canterbury, Roger of Worcester and Bartholomew of Exeter.

Nevertheless, decretals to Roger of York figure substantially in collections from 1179-81 onwards. The evidence of the French *Parisiensis prima* (*1 Par.*) is misleading: its chapters 8+9-14, 15, 16, 17, 18, 19, 20, 31+32 seem there assigned to Roger of York; but 8-14 are the single letter *Fraternitatem tuam* with an appendix of texts frequently found with it; 15, 17, 31, 32 are parts of the one decretal *Inter ceteras consultationes*; 18, 19, 20 are in reality

[46] E.g., *RY Calendar* 38, 395, 765, 773.

[47] Duggan, *Decretal collections*, 84-95, esp. 88-89. The collection contains part of a letter of Lucius III (*Bridl.* 134 [ms: 135], f. 118vb: *Si aliquis auctoritate*, excerpt from *Quesitum est a nobis*, *WH* 792, *JL* 15185 and 15170, to John of Norwich, 1181-85), and the marginal rubric « Lucius III » is misplaced nearby (at *Bridl.* 132, f. 118rb); otherwise, no item later than Alexander III has been found in it.

[48] *RY Calendar* 341, 458, 404, 59 (abbreviated in *Bridl.*), 18, 854 (fragment in *Bridl.*), 870, 518, 98. Cf. *Bridl.* ms., between ff. 121vb and 130ra; through scribal error the letters are respectively numbered one unit high (145 appears as 146, etc.).

[49] *RY Calendar* 404: *Decretales ineditae*, 130-32 n° 76.

well-known letters to Richard of Canterbury (18: *WH* 927, *JL* 13813, 1174-81; 19: *WH* 717, *JL* 13821, 1174-81; 20: *WH* 562, *JL* 13820, 1174-81).[50] A further part of *Inter ceteras* occurs as item 98, where it is assigned to John of Norwich.[51] The apparent sequence of decretals to Roger of York therefore contains only four of his letters. The first generation of Worcester family collections (from 1181) marked a more positive assimilation of Roger's decretals. The lost archetype (*Ex./Wig.*, above) included 16 York decretals,[52] to which four more were added in the Worcester (*Wig.*) expansion of the common stock.[53] It seems at first that three of the seven component books of *Wig.* open with letters to Roger, under their headings «... quarum prima destinata est Eboracensi archiepiscopo»;[54] the comment is accurate for Books 4 and 7, but the first decretal in Book 5 was sent to Hugh of Durham.[55] Thereafter, most large collections include significant numbers of York decretals. Thus, the Cotton collection (*Cottoniana*: *Cott.*, a post 1193 development from the 'Worcester' stock, with many later accessions) reveals in a preliminary survey 32 of Roger of York's decretals.[56]

All of Roger's decretals have now been printed. The recently published *Decretales ineditae saeculi XII* includes four new letters to Roger,[57] two brief canonical maxims or comments seemingly based on letters to him,[58] two new texts addressed to recipients in the York diocese (including the Lenton forgery),[59] and one decretal of unknown address, apparently relating to a church in the York

[50] *Canones-Sammlungen*, 53-54; *recte* to Richard and his suffragans.

[51] *Canones-Sammlungen*, 57. Cf. *1 Par.* 57-58: 99-105 and 107, assigned there to the abbot of St Albans; only two items to St Albans are in the group (99+100 and 107); 101-105 are components of a single letter to the archbishop of Sens (*Sicut Romana*, *JL* 12293 = 13874, 2 June 1173-74).

[52] *Wig.* 1. 33+37, 42; 2. 9, 13, 21; 3. 25; 4. 1, 5, 12; 7. 1, 3, 10, 14, 18, 23, 31+40+49.

[53] *Wig.* 4. 28, 31+32; 5. 12, 13.

[54] LOHMANN, *Collectio Wigorniensis...*, 108, 119, 125.

[55] LOHMANN, *Collectio Wigorniensis...*, 119: *Wig.* 5. 1: *Suggestum est auribus nostris*, *WH* 999, *JL* 13870, 1159-81.

[56] *Cott.* 2. 11, 18a, 21, 49; 3. 4, 6, 6d, 8, 11, 23, 42, 44, 57, 64, 67+76; 4. 12, 14, 66; 5. 4, 34; 6. 22, 42, 43, 45, 54, 57, 64, 65, 66, 70, 81; 7. 10, 32, 49, 54, 55. The two items 3. 23 and 6. 43 are a single decretal; 3. 67+76 and 6. 57 are a single decretal; 6. 22 = 6. 66. Some of the York decretals are incorrectly addressed in the ms.

[57] *Decretales ineditae*, 121-28 n' 70-73; see also 130-32 n° 76, otherwise printed only in G.V. SCAMMELL, *Hugh du Puiset, bishop of Durham*, Cambridge 1956, 251-252.

[58] *Decretales ineditae*, 128-30 n' 74, 75.

[59] *Decretales ineditae*, 132-35 n' 77, 78.

diocese, perhaps to Roger as one of its co-recipients.[60] The register of Roger's decretals given below is preliminary to a full analysis of all twelfth-century decretals to the province of York. Only letters addressed to Roger himself are listed now, but a later survey will extend the scope of reference to include decretals to other recipients which throw occasional light on Roger's lost commissions, to members of his cathedral chapter, to masters, canonists and secular litigants in his province or diocese, to his suffragan bishop Hugh of Durham, and the imposing number of decretals to northern religious houses. The total of 54 items registered includes all of Roger's decretals in collections known at present. With one possible exception (25), all were sent to Roger (1154-22 Nov. 1181) by Alexander III (1159-30 Aug. 1181), the single exception being just possibly sent by Lucius III (*el.* 1 Sept. 1181). The great majority were sent to Roger as sole recipient; seven jointly with the bishop of Durham (33, 38, 130, 395, 404, 618, 765); two with both Robert of Lincoln and Richard of Chester (98, 675a); one with Richard of Coventry/Chester (461); two with Roger of Worcester (443, 916); one with Bartholomew of Exeter and Baldwin of Ford, or the abbot of Rufford (250); and one with the dean and chapter of his own cathedral (998). The dates proposed for individual decretals sometimes differ substantially from those hitherto printed (note especially 98, 518); six or seven letters can be dated before 1170 (*53, 88,* 98, 130, *518,* 675a, *772*), of which three or possibly four (*ital.*) were not later than 1161, an exceptionally early date. At the other end of the time scale, at least 8 to 12 postdate 1172 (1, 12, 25, 231, 235, 250, 338, 404, 773, *873, 880,* 998), of which at least two (*ital.*) date from 1179-81, and a further letter could be post Aug. 1181 (25). One decretal originally assigned to Celestine III (1191-98) is correctly re-assigned to Alexander III (854).

The historical and canonical interest of Roger's decretals can be briefly summarized. A few are of the highest political importance. Two touch on Henry II's dynastic anxieties, recording respectively the pope's consent in 1161, when Canterbury was vacant, that Roger might crown the king's eldest son, when requested by Henry to do so (772), and the suspension of York and Durham in 1170 for officiating at the ceremony in the greatly altered circumstances of Becket's exile (618). Two further letters deal with aspects of the

[60] *Decretales ineditae,* 137-39 n° 80.

related Canterbury and York dispute in matters of dignity and jurisdiction, affirming in 1161 York's total immunity from Canterbury's authority (88), and c. 1175 York's right to have his cross carried before him throughout England, pending a final decision (1). An excerpt from a privilege to York is found in three related collections (253). At least 26 decretals, about half the total, deal in some way with churches, their patrons, clergy, institutions and services: seven relate significantly to patrons and the *ius patronatus* (53, 179, 590, 863, 880, 998, 1058), and others do so incidentally. The problem of hereditary claims to churches and of priests' sons succeeding in their fathers' churches gave rise to three decretals (179, 510, 863); uncanonical successions (341) or conferments (378), simony (18, 33, 235), forgery (404, 914), and expectative benefices (873) elicited others. Some letters concern particular persons, offices or churches: the rights of the archdeacon of Chester (231), the unreasonable income sought from Beverley by the archdeacon of Bedford (870), the rivalry for the next vacant archdeaconry in the Coventry diocese (461). Among churches identified in the decretals as in dispute are those of Sheriff Hutton (53), Ripley (179), Epperstone and Shelford (404), Rempstone and the chapel of Costock (443), Calverton (674), Masham, Kirkby Malzeard and Langford (998), and Wath-upon-Dearne (1058); an unnamed church is cited in another (235). The important rule that religious and clerks must not draw one another to a secular court is enforced in one decretal (840). Miscellaneous problems include the provision of a chapel for remote parishioners, cut off by winter weather (25), the seizure of property from a church cemetery (447), the absence of clerks from their dioceses (519), commutation of a pilgrimage vow (490), and the deceit of an untonsured clerk seeking a benefice (443, 916).

Six decretals to Roger arose from disputed marriages and illicit unions. Two relate to the protracted litigation concerning the dynastic marriage of William FitzGodric to Aubrey de Lisours, whose daughter when under age had been betrothed to William (12, 420; see also 235). A similar problem arose from a certain Walter's illicit relations with the mother of a girl to whom he had been betrothed (432a). One decretal concerned an invalid marriage and a consequent question of incest (43); another resulted from a clandestine marriage with the sister of the man's betrothed (854). In a mandate of great importance, Roger was ordered to issue a general prohibition against clandestine marriages in the future (990).

Thirteen decretals respond to the rights of religious orders, or relate to individual religious or problems arising for particular houses. Five letters are concerned primarily with Cistercian tithe exemption (98, 130, 395, 675a, 765), protecting incidentally the monks' servants from deprivation of the sacraments (395) and the monks and their servants from acts of violence (675a). One letter confirms the Cistercian exemption from interdict and excommunication (38); another to Roger is one of several to various recipients relating to the grange of Warsill, disputed between the archbishop and the abbot and monks of Fountains (773).[61] All these but two (98, 675a) are found uniquely in the Fountains collection,[62] one of the two (675a) being otherwise known only in an archival source (Oxford, Bodleian Library, ms. Bodley e Mus 195 [S.C. 3608], f. 120). The decretal *Fraternitatem tuam* is of exceptional interest. Its date proposed here is from c. 1160 or not many years later. Its explicit reversal of Adrian IV's limitation of tithe immunity to « new works » and its formulation of total tithe exemption for monks and canons point to Alexander's restoration of the full Cistercian privilege, but the letter does not restrict the concession to them. It embraces white and black monks, regular and secular canons. It conceivably records a transitional or tentative statement of policy from an early date in Alexander's pontificate. Likewise, the date proposed below for *Audivimus et audientes* (98), namely 1166, suggests a revision of the conventional judgment that all decretals with that incipit are of later date. The Hospitallers' privilege that their members may not leave, even for a stricter religion, is cited in one letter (18), and the rights of the Premonstratensian canons of Welbeck in their church in another (447). Other decretals deal with charges of immorality and uncanonical election against the prior of the Augustinian house at Bridlington (250), and the probably identical problem of a recalcitrant prior (338). The injunction that religious and clerics must not draw one another to secular judgment (840) has been mentioned already.

An important class of seven decretals (59, 458, 552, 590, 749, 874, 1009) and a canonist's redraft (914) deals with procedural and judicial questions, mostly involving appeals. Thus, a litigant

[61] See comment for *RY Calendar* 773, and fuller details in *Decretales ineditae*, 87-88 n° 47.

[62] *RY Calendar* 38, 130, 395, 765, 773 = *Font.* 2. 4, 7, 11, 10, 14.

may not evade the delegate's jurisdiction by appealing on an incidental question and failing to prosecute the appeal, but neither can the archbishop or other judges have a general right to decide such questions (59). Measures should be taken to avoid frustratory appeals, by compelling the appellant to prosecute his appeal within a year, or show reasonable cause for failing to do so (874). Nor should deference be paid to appeals launched through fear of letters which the litigant thinks his adversary has secured, since the motive of the appeal seems frustratory (1009). Although an appeal in one case does not make the appellant less answerable in others, the judge should not compel him to answer in other cases while the appeal is pending, unless for a manifest crime (749). Several questions arise from cases commissioned without leave of appeal (552). Thus, an appeal is not allowed in such a case, unless it was made before the appellant was cited; but an appeal should be respected if the judge has refused to accept the litigant's proofs of forgery (and deferment should be granted to one who alleges forgery, but his proofs are overseas [914]); one of two delegates jointly commissioned without leave of appeal may not proceed alone in the case, unless the commission expressly allowed that. Apart from appeals, if deception arises in connexion with the pope's own sentence, questions arising should be referred back to him (552); a judge who receives a mandate containing alternative propositions, should proceed on whichever is proved to him; and if second letters are secured in a case without mention of the first, both commissions should be suspended until the pope has been consulted (590). A judge should keep to the form laid down in a case commissioned « sub certa forma », but reasonable exceptions should be admitted and equity observed (458).

II (b) *Calendar of Roger of York's decretals*[63]

1. *A memoria nostra non excidit ... debeat habere.* To (Roger) archbishop of York, apostolic legate.

In the first year of the pope's pontificate he confirmed York's right to have his cross carried before him throughout England, but

[63] *RY Calendar*: the decretals are listed here with their *WH* numbers in the *Regesta decretalium saeculi XII.*

archbishop Thomas of Canterbury — « sancte et venerande memorie » — later objected that this was in derogation of his right and dignity. The pope rules that, pending a decision on this matter, there shall be no prejudice to the rights granted to York by his predecessors.

JL 12530, c. 1175. *Chelt.* 19. 9; *Cott.* 7. 55; *Pet.* 3. 30; eleven systematic collections and one later primitive collection. Pd *App.* 50. 37; *X* 2. 16. 1. Cf. J. RAINE, *Historians of the church of York and its archbishops*, III, London 1894 (Rolls Series), 50 n° 33; *PU England* 2. 291 n° 105 (22 Jan. 1161); and *WH* 88 below.

12. *Accessit ad presentiam nostram nobilis vir Willelmus filius Godrici ... prohiberi non possunt.* To (Roger) archbishop of York.

In the case of the nobleman William FitzGodric who married the mother of a girl to whom he was previously betrothed, the pope mandates the recipient to confirm the marriage and declare the children born of it legitimate, if the girl was not yet seven at the time of the betrothal and later refused her consent, and if William had been released from his commitment to her. But if the girl had reached the age of seven, the marriage was shameful, yet it can be tolerated if such a course of action seems prudent to the recipient, to avert the re-creation of discord between the families concerned. The union then being tolerated by the Church, the children cannot be debarred from their inheritance from either parent.

JL 13887, 1175+. *Cantab.* 86; *1 Vict.* 4; *1 Berol.* 123; *Flor.* 117; *Duac.* 52; *Cus.* 138; *Wig.* 1. 37+33; *Claustr.* 310+70; *Chelt.* 9. 37+30; *Cott.* 2. 18a; *Pet.* 1. 20a; and ten systematic collections. Pd *App.* 6. 7; *X* 4. 2. 5.

The case concerns the marriage of William FitzGodric and Aubrey de Lisours, the Lacy of Pontefract heiress, and Aubrey's daughter by her former husband FitzEustace; cf. *WH* 235 and 420 below; and *Decretales ineditae,* 123-25 n° 71.

18. *Ad audientiam apostolatus nostri pervenit quod quidam diaconus G. ... minime dubitatur.* To (Roger) archbishop of York.

The deacon G. bribed his archdeacon's nephew to promote his ordination to the priesthood, but was smitten in conscience and, taking prudent counsel, joined the Hospitallers. Now ten years later he wishes to expiate his fault by penance in a solitary place, with licence to celebrate the priestly office in secret. The pope rejects his request, citing the Hospitallers' privilege which forbids members professed in their order to leave, even for a stricter religion. He should do penance in their community, but not officiate as priest.

JL 13889, 1159-81. *Bridl.* 161; *Pet.* 4. 3; seven systematic collections and one later primitive collection. Pd *2 Comp.* 3. 18. 2; MANSI, 21. 1098. See J.D. LE ROULX, *Cartulaire général des Hospitaliers de S. Jean de Jérusalem*, I, Paris 1894, 204; cf. *JL* 9930 and 11586.

25. *Ad audientiam nostram noveris pervenisse quod villa que dicitur N. ... instituere non omittas.* Alexander III or Lucius III to (Roger) archbishop of York.

The village N. is so far distant from its parish church that heavy winter rains prevent the parishioners from travelling there to attend services at the proper time. The archbishop is ordered to allow a chapel to be provided in the village (having confirmed that the rector can secure a suitable living without its revenue), at the rector's presentation and with the canonical assent of the founder, its priest being supported by ecclesiastical incomes in the village.

JL 13884, 1159-81/2. *App. Lp.* 47. 14; *Bamb.* 14. 6; *Erl.* 16. 1; *Lips.* 19. 9; *Tann.* 6. 3. 26; *1 Comp.* 3. 35. 2; *Sang.* 7. 50; *X* 3. 48. 3. Pd *X*.

The address of the letter is uncertain. Friedberg and *JL* accepted Alexander III as sender, from the inscription « Idem » following c. 23 of the 1179 Lateran Council in *1 Comp.* and *X*. WH preferred the evidence of *Bamb.* and *Erl.* which have « Idem » following a decretal of Lucius III to the archbishop of Tours (*WH* 62, *JL* 15198, 1184-85), and of *Lips.*, *Tann.*, and *Sang.*, which name Lucius III; and he assigned the decretal to 1181-85. The letter made a late entry into the collections. It is found in no primitive collections, and in the *App.* group it appears only in *App. Lp.*, as the penultimate chapter, without an inscription; in the *Bamb.* group it appears only in *B*, with « Idem » following the decretal of Lucius III. Thereafter it is assigned to Lucius III in *Lips*, *Tann.*, and *Sang.* An ambiguity may result from the entry in *Bamb. B.* On historical grounds, the attribution to Alexander III is more likely. Lucius was not elected until 1 Sept. 1181, and Roger of York died less than two months later, on November 22, after which the see of York was vacant for ten years. An exchange of correspondence between Lucius and an archbishop of York was extremely unlikely. It is possible that Lucius wrote on a problem submitted to his predecessor, or that he replied to a letter written by Roger in the closing weeks of his life. It is unlikely that a reply to such a letter would have reached York before Roger's death. The latest possible date of the decretal is January 1182.

33. *Ad audientiam nostram pervenisse noscatis quod cum aliqui in parrochiis vestris decedunt ... a vobis requiretur.* To (Roger) archbishop of York and (Hugh) bishop of Durham.

The pope mandates the recipients strictly to ensure that priests and clerics in their jurisdiction refrain from their sacrilegious cupidity in exacting payments from the goods of deceased persons before permitting their burial. Such exactions are in conflict with patristic institutes and with the pope's own decree in the council of Tours. They may take nothing more than that which the deceased or their relations freely wished to give. Future offences will be punished by the pope, and the recipients of the mandate will be called to account for them.

JL —, 1163-79. *Chelt.* 14. 11; *Cott.* 4. 66; *Pet.* 3. 71; *Tann.* 2. 1. 13; *Sang.* 2. 1. 15; *1 Abr.* 2. 1. 4. Pd *Sang.* The decree referred to by the pope is Tours (1163), c. 6: MANSI, 21. 1178; cf. Lateran (1179), c. 7; MANSI, 22. 221-22.

38. *Ad audientiam nostam pervenit unde miramur plurimum et movemur ... animo tolerare. Dat' Anagnie vi. kal. Decembris.* To (Roger) archbishop of York and (Hugh) bishop of Durham.

The pope has heard that the recipients do not hesitate to pervert the meaning of the apostolic privilege to Cistercians which exempts their churches from interdict and their monks and *conversi* from excommunication, except for the evident fault of abbot and brethren. The recipients are strictly forbidden to allege such fault if the abbot and brethren cultivate land or retain possessions after papal prohibition. If they wish to show malice in this way, the pope will not bear it in patience.

JL —, 26 Nov. 1159-79. *Font.* 2. 4 only. Pd *PU England* 3. 385-86 n° 252.

43. *Ad aures nostras noveris pervenisse quod cum quidam vir parrochianus tuus mulierem quandam ... probatur incestum.* To the archbishop of York (or Genoa, or Ravenna).

A certain man in the archbishop's jurisdiction married a woman who was later shown to have known his cousin, both before and after the marriage. The pope grants his wish to marry another, since that was no true marriage, unless he committed incest with her after he knew of her sin with his cousin.

JL 14164, 1159-81. *Wig.* 1. 42; *Claustr.* 313; *Chelt.* 9. 40; *Cott.* 2. 49; *Pet.* 1. 55; nine systematic collections and one later primitive collection. Pd *Claustr.* 313; *Brug.* 49. 28; *2 Comp.* 4. 13. 1; MANSI, 21. 1099 and 1104.
The address is uncertain, since the decretal is variously found with inscriptions to the abbot of Cassino, and the archbishops of Ravenna, Genoa, and York. The attribution to the abbot of Cassino in the Worcester family collections conflicts with the text, which requires a recipient bishop; that to Ravenna occurs only in the *1 Comp. Rot.* 4. 14. 3. The address to Genoa is found only in the *Frcf.* collections, where it may be a scribal error: the corrector in *Frcf. Rot.* 4. 16 has written «vacat» by the archbishop of Genoa's name. The attribution to York occurs in *Tann.* 7. 8. 14, *Sang.* 8. 85, and *1 Abr.* 8. 6. 9. WH left the matter open, but the inscription to York seems most reliable.

53. *Ad aures nostras pervenit quod G. quondam Eboracensis abbas patronatum ecclesie de Hotun ... denunties non tenere.* To (Roger) archbishop of York.

The former abbot G. of York granted the patronage of the church of Hotun to a certain knight B. The church belonged to the monastery, and the abbot granted it unlawfully — « de voluntate potius quam de iure ». The pope orders the archbishop to revoke the grant, since the patronage of churches should be transferred from laymen to churches, rather than from churches to laymen.

JL —, 1159-81 (? 1159-60). *Cott.* 6. 64; *Tann.* 6. 3. 4. Pd *Decretales ineditae,* 121-123 n° 70.
The case is discussed in *Decretales ineditae,* where the church is identified as that of Sheriff Hutton, the abbey as St Mary at York, the abbot as Geoffrey, and the knight as Bertram de Bulmer.

59. *Ad aures nostras te significante pervenit quod cum interdum tibi vel aliis ...* (*Postulabas tibi ...*) *... dilationibus fatigari.* To (Roger) archbishop of York.

When cases are commissioned to the recipient or to others, without leave of appeal, one of the parties may seek to evade jurisdiction by appealing on incidental questions and not fixing a term. The pope refuses the archbishop's request that the right of deciding such questions be granted to himself and other judges. But a suitable term should be set, and judgment should be reached on both principal and incidental questions, if the appeal is not prosecuted within the time.

JL 13876, 1159-81. *Bridl.* 160; *Claud.* 108; *Chelt.* 19. 2; *Cott.* 3. 44; *Pet.* 2. 17. 1; seven systematic collections and one later primitive collection. Pd *X* 2. 28. 33.

The text begins at *Postulabas tibi* in *Bridl.* and *Chelt.*, and is abbreviated in *X* to *Ad aures nostras. Appellanti ... iudicio delegati.*

88. *Antiquam Eboracensis ecclesie dignitatem ... pontifice consecrari.* To (Roger) archbishop of York.

Wishing to preserve the ancient dignity of York, the pope confirms his predecessors' ruling that Canterbury may not exact obedience from York, nor should York make such profession, and repeats pope Gregory's prohibition of the subjection of York to Canterbury (*olim* London). The distinction of honour between them is decided by priority of consecration. If Canterbury withholds consecration from an elect of York, the latter can be consecrated by his suffragans or by the Roman pontiff.

JL 12749, 22 Jan. 1161. *Cott.* 7. 54; *Pet.* 3. 29 (the folios are severely damaged in *Cott.* and *Pet.*, with the loss of most of the text); nine systematic collections and one later primitive collection. Pd *App.* 44. 2; *Cass.* 55. 2.
The passage is excerpted from a York privilege (see *PU England* 2. 291 n° 105; for earlier related texts, cf. *JE* 1829; *JL* 6831, 7227; *PU England* 2. 148-50 n° 13, 231-33 n° 66, 262-64 n° 86). It is prefaced by *In hunc modum plures Romani pontifices a tempore beati Gregorii scripserunt* in *Cott.* (*om.* In); *Pet.*; *App.*; *Bamb.* 47. 2; *Cass.*; *Tann.* 6. 7. 2; *1 Rot.* 30. 8; cf. G. Foliot *Gilberti ... Londoniensis epistolae*, II, ed. J.A. Giles, Oxford 1846 (Patres Ecclesiae Anglicanae), 75 n° 351; Ralph de Diceto, *Radulfi de Diceto decani Lundoniensis opera historica*, I, ed. W. Stubbs, London 1876 (Rolls Series 68), 406. The item is addressed « Universis suffraganeis Cantuariensis ecclesie » in *Cott.*; *Tann.*; *Sang.* 7. 142; *1 Abr.* 7. 14. 2; and is attributed to « Celestinus » in *Alan. app.* 72. See *WH* 1 above.

98. (a) *Audivimus et audientes admirati sumus quod cum fratribus monasterii de Rufforde ... inviolabiliter observari.* (b) *Ad hec presentium vobis auctoritate ... conspectui representent.* To (Roger) archbishop of York, and the bishops of Lincoln and Chester.

The pope affirms the total exemption of Cistercians from payment of tithes on lands worked by their labour or at their own expense. Certain subjects of the recipients wickedly misconstrue the papal privilege «de laboribus», as meaning «de novalibus»; if he had meant new works, he would have written new works, as he had in privileges to others. The recipients are ordered to ensure with censures that all in their jurisdiction refrain from extorting tithes from the monks of Rufford or of other Cistercian houses in their dioceses, in respect of lands, new or otherwise, worked by their labour or at their expense, and of animal fodder. Moreover, if any persons lay violent hands on the monks of those houses, the recipients must publicly excommunicate them, and ensure their avoidance until they make suitable satisfaction, and journey to the papal presence with letters from their diocesan bishop.

JL —, 1 May 1166. *Bridl.* 176; *Claustr.* 110-111; *Trin.* 2. 21; *Wig.* 2. 21; *Chelt.* 10. 11; *Cott.* 4. 14; *Pet.* 3. 1; *Tann.* 3. 14. 20 (a), 2. 8. 16 (b); *Sang.* 4. 10. 21 (a), 2. 8. 17 (b). Original: British Library, ms. Harley charter 111 A 3: see *PU England* 1. 434-35 n° 160; C.J. HOLDSWORTH, *Rufford Charters,* II, Nottingham 1974 (Thoroton Society: Record series, XXX), 368-69, n° 705. Pd also in *Claustr.*, *Sang.* (b).
The inscription and date of the decretal require comment. The letter survives in the chancery original, addressed to the archbishop of York, and the bishops of Lincoln and Chester, given at the Lateran on 1 May. Alexander's itinerary fixes the date in either 1166-67 or 1178-79. But there was no bishop of Lincoln in 1167 or 1178-79; Robert of Lincoln died c. 27 Dec. 1166, and Geoffrey Plantagenet was bishop-elect in the later period. Roger of York and Richard of Chester were in office throughout the relevant period, and therefore the titles and order of precedence in the chancery original point to Roger, Robert and Richard as the recipients, and to 1166 as the date of issue. The tenor of the pope's insistence on the total exemption of Cistercians from tithe payment has led most scholars to reject this conclusion, and to place the decretal in 1178-79, or imprecisely in the period 1166-79. But it is quite untrue to assert (pace *Decretals to Lincoln* 27) that the liberation of Cistercians from tithe payment began late in Alexander's pontificate, since the complete exemption was restored within fifteen months of his election in September 1159. A privilege to Pontigny on 19 Feb. 1160 retained the restricting «Sane novalium» clause of Adrian IV's pontificate (*JL* 10624; J.-P. MIGNE, *Patrologia Latina cursus completus,* CC, Paris 1855, 85-87, n° 17); but on a single day at Anagni, 20 Nov. 1160, letters to three English Cistercian houses restored the «Sane laborum» version conferring full immunity (for Rievaulx, J. DUGDALE, *Monasticon Anglicanum,* V, London 1846, 283-84 n° 9; for Rufford, *PU England* 1. 340-42 n° 80; for Sibton, *PU England* 1. 342-43 n° 81). The original chancery letter to Rufford survives (British Library, ms. Harley charter 111 A 5). The intention of *Audivimus et audientes* is therefore consistent with the earlier date. So too is the language of the letter, whose precise formulation « si de novalibus voluissemus tantum intelligi, ubi ponimus de laboribus, de novalibus poneremus, sicut in privilegiis quorundam apponimus aliorum » is commonly judged to date in its first appearance c. 1174 (G. SCHREIBER, *Kurie und Kloster im 12. Jahrhundert,* I, Stuttgart 1910 [Kirchenrechtliche Abhandlungen, LXV], 265-69, *et alii*), since it is cited from one letter of 1168 at the latest (J.-B. MAHN, *L'Ordre cistercien et son gouvernement,* Paris 1951, 108-09 and n. 3). Moreover, the decretal *Non videtur ulla* (*WH* 675a below), to Roger of York, Robert of Lincoln, and Richard of Chester, dated at Sens on 30 Sept. 1164, distinguished between the narrower privilege « de novalibus » for religious in general and the complete exemption « de laboribus » for Cistercians, in the context of resistance to Alexander's policy, affecting the houses of Rufford and Roche (*PU England* 3. 293-94 n° 151; the WH edition is misleading where the addition of « novalium » has been printed in the main text, from a later copy, 294 n. *l*). The parallel details of

inscription, subject-matter and location in *Non videtur* and *Audivimus et audientes* strengthen the proposal that the date of the latter is 1166, with important implications for the study of the category of letters to which it belongs.

130. *Certum vobis esse credimus et liquido manifestum ... firmiter observari. Datum Beneventi* (ms. *Bonev.*) *x. kal. Decembris.* To (Roger) archbishop of York and (Hugh) bishop of Durham.

The recipients are aware of the Cistercian exemption from tithe payment on their works, cultivated by themselves or at their own expense, and on the fodder of their animals. The pope commends the monks of Fountains to them, and orders them to ensure that no one in their dioceses molests the monks in this matter. But if the monks have freely made a composition, for the sake of peace, the recipients must ensure its observance.

JL —, 22 Nov. 1167-69. *Font.* 2. 7 only. Pd *PU England* 3. 298-99 n° 156.

179. *Constitutus in presentia nostra magister Thomas Barre diaconus ... ad ecclesiam de Ripelei a nobili viro Willelmo Trussebut ... appellatione remota imponas, et ecclesiam ... in pace dimitti, non obstantibus ... impetraverit. Porro si de prescripta ecclesia vel de possessionibus ipsius aliqua permutatio vel alienatio facta est, postquam sepedictus T. suam interposuit appellationem, omnia in eum statum reducas quo tempore appellationis fuisse noscuntur.* To (Roger) archbishop of York.

The deacon Thomas Barre claimed that the *dominus fundi* William Trussebut presented him to the archbishop for the church of Ripley, and that he was placed in nominal possession at the request of the English queen, and for a time received its incomes. But Bernard, nephew of the immediately preceding possessor, claimed that he had been presented to the church by his uncle, and appealed to the pope without fixing a term. The archbishop sequestered the incomes, and Thomas in turn appealed to the pope. Since Bernard already has several churches and is seeking this church as if by hereditary right, the recipient is ordered to impose silence on him, and ensure the restoration of the church to Thomas, together with its incomes from the time of sequestration, if Bernard has one or more churches with an income of twenty marks.

JL —, 1159-81. *1 Alc.* 115; *Flor.* 115; *Duac.* 50; *Cus.* 135; *Font.* 2. 36; *Bridl.* 80; *Claud.* 62; *Claustr.* 340; *Chelt.* 4. 32; *Cott.* 6. 70; and five systematic collections.

Pd to « dimitti »: *Claustr., Brug.* 45. 4; « non obstantibus ... impetraverit (*ms.* impetravit) »: *Sang.* 6. 8. 11; *Porro si ... noscuntur,* not previously printed: *1 Alc., Bridl., Claud.*

The decretal is found in full only in *1 Alc., Bridl., Claud.*; it is drastically abbreviated and ends at «imponas» in *Flor., Duac., Cus., Frcf.* 51. 29; the letter ends at «dimitti» in *Font., Claustr., Chelt., Cott.*; at «impetratis» in *Tann.* 5. 7. 9, and «impetravit» in *Sang., 1 Abr.* 6. 8. 5. The *dominus fundi* William Trussebut also appears as patron of the church of Ulceby in *Constitutus in presentia nostra G., WH* 171, *JL* 14193, 1159-77/8 (*Decretals to Lincoln,* 22-23 n° 9).

231. *Cum dubia semper in meliorem partem sint convertenda, et nos credamus R. archidiaconum de necessitate ... irritum revocetur.* To (Roger) archbishop of York, on behalf of the archdeacon of Chester.

The pope believes that the archdeacon R. remained so long in the curia from necessity, after the bishop of St Asaph's departure, not from malice. If the archdeacon's rights have been prejudiced by papal letters secured in the meanwhile, that is to be quashed without objection or appeal.

JL —, 1159-81 (? 1179-81). *Wig.* 7. 23; *Claustr.* 222; *Chelt.* 18. 12; *Cott.* 7. 49; *Brug.* 48. 2; *Frcf.* 51. 30; *Sang.* 10. 65. Pd *Claustr.*; *Brug.*

The beneficiary of the mandate is identified as the archdeacon of Chester by a comment in *Wig., Chelt., Cott.*: « pro archidiacono de Cestre (*Cott.* Cestria) ». Bishop Godfrey of St Asaph was present in the curia for the council of Tours in 1163, and bishop Adam for the Lateran council in 1179. The first appearance of the decretal in collections c. 1181 suggests that it dates from after Adam's departure in 1179, within the limits 1179-81.

235. *Cum essent in nostra presentia constituti R. clericus de Pontefracto et nobilis vir W. filius Godrici ... nulla ratione permittas.* To (Roger) archbishop of York.

On leaving the papal curia, the nobleman W. FitzGodric appointed the recipient's messenger Milo to act for him, but the clerk R. of Pontefract alleged to the cardinal commissioners that W. had promised him a certain disputed church if he would help to advance in the curia a matter of concern to W. As this promise smacked of simony, the pope imposed silence on R. in respect of the church. The recipient is ordered not to permit W. to be troubled by R. or by others in connexion with it.

JL 13883, 5 May-25 Aug. 1175. *Cantab.* 50; *1 Vict.* 52; *Cus.* 35; *Chelt.* 2. 3; *Cott.* 5. 4; *Pet.* 4. 6; and eleven systematic collections. Pd *App.* 2. 14; *X* 5. 3. 12. The nobleman involved in this case was William FitzGodric, and the matter of concern to him was almost certainly his disputed marriage (see *WH* 11 above, 420 below; *Decretales ineditae,* 123-25 n° 71). The date is fixed by the identity of Vivian, cardinal deacon of San Nicola in carcere Tulliano (J.M. BRIXIUS, *Die Mitglieder des Kardinalkollegiums von 1130-81,* Berlin 1912, 66), one of the papal commissioners named in the letter.

250. *Cum iam pridem quidam canonicus ecclesie de Bridelington ... pro correctione subiecerit. Ceterum si iam dictus prior ... molestare. Verum si idem prior ... faciatis exhiberi. Si vero his exequendis ... nihilominus exequantur.* To (Roger) archbishop of York, (Bartholomew) bishop of Exeter, and the abbot of Ford (or Rufford).

Charges against the prior of Bridlington, for his immoral character and uncanonical election, had been commissioned to the bishop of Durham and the abbot of Fountains, who had exonerated him. But the charges were repeated by the canon Walter, who also criticized the judges' procedure. The pope now commissions the recipients to investigate the matter and reach an appropriate verdict. But if the prior succeeds in the litigation he must be prevented from exploiting the opportunity to oppress Walter or any of the brethren. If he refuses to answer, the judges must suspend him; and if he wishes to appeal, they must hear the charges and the witnesses, send the sealed testimonies to the pope, and fix a term for both parties to appear before him.

JL 13891, 1161-81 (? 1174-80). *Claud.* 210; *Wig.* 7. 14; *Claustr.* 205; *Chelt.* 13. 3; *Cott.* 3. 64; *Pet.* 2. 23. 21; *2 Dun.* 93; *Tann.* 4. 5. 9; *Sang.* 5. 4. 8; *1 Abr.* 5. 5. 5; *Alan.* 2. 15. 2; *2 Comp.* 2. 18. 2. Pd *Claustr.*; *2 Comp.* (to «subiecerit»); W. ULLMANN, *A forgotten dispute at Bridlington and its canonistic setting,* in « Yorkshire Archaeological Journal », 148 (1951), 469-73.

The letter begins *Quoniam quidem* in *2 Comp.,* and breaks off at « subiecerit »; it begins at « Verum si idem » in *Claud.* The decretal *De priore quidem* (*WH* 338 below) may deal with the same case. Whether the abbot commissioner of the present case was of Ford (*Claud., Wig., 2 Dun., Tann., Sang., 1 Abr.*) or Rufford (*Chelt., Cott.*; Sufford, *Pet.*) is uncertain. Holtzmann assigned the case to Rufford in his decretal index, but to Ford elsewhere (cf. MOREY, *Bartholomew of Exeter* ..., 55). The abbot of Ford seems more probable. If Baldwin of Ford, a frequent colleague of Exeter, was the commissioner (which seems most likely), the dating limits are 1174-80. A date in the early 1160s is preferred in ULLMANN, *A forgotten dispute* ..., 466.

253. *Cum in apostolice sedis speculo et infra. fraternitati tue auctoritate apostolica indulgemus ut ecclesias ... capituli revocare.* To (Roger) archbishop of York.

The pope grants that the archbishop may, with the assent of the York chapter or its « maior et sanior pars », revoke alienations made by his predecessors and their ministers without the chapter's agreement, or that of its « maior et sanior pars ».

JL —, 1159-81. *Tann.* 3. 5. 13; *Sang.* 4. 1. 22; *1 Abr.* 4. 1. 4. Pd *Sang.*
The abbreviated text is presumably an excerpt from a York privilege.

338. *De priore quidem qui non deferens protectioni nostre ... audeant perpetrare.* To (Roger) archbishop of York.

Concerning that prior who did not defer to papal protection or appeal, but despoiled a certain canon of his garments «usque ad camisiam», and compelled him to abandon his appeal and the charges he had made against the prior and some of his brethren, the pope commissions the case to the recipient. If the canon's appeal was made to avoid discipline, no penalty is to be imposed on the prior; but if the appeal related to evident enormities and the prior disdained to defer to it, the recipient must compel him to come to the pope to make satisfaction, and impose a deterrent penalty on his accomplices.

JL 13875, 1159-81 (? 1174-80). *Wig.* 2. 9; *Claustr.* 96; *Cott.* 3. 8; *Pet.* 2. 9. 2; and ten systematic collections. Pd *App.* 10. 25; *X* 2. 28. 31.
The decretal may relate to the appeal of the canon Walter against the prior of Bridlington (*WH* 250 above).

341. *Decet nos pravas consuetudines penitus abolere et successiones, quas sacri canones detestantur quia perniciose sunt, omnimodis extirpare. Accepimus quod quedam ecclesie clericis ... vanas esse decernas.* To (Roger) archbishop of York.

The recipient must prohibit those detestable and uncanonical concessions by which churches are granted to clerks on the condition that, after their deaths, other named persons succeed them.

JL 13880, 1159-81. *Bridl.* 145; *Claud.* 202; *Chelt.* 16. 13; *Cott.* 6. 22 = 6. 66; and eleven systematic collections. Pd *App.* 28. 4; *X* 1. 35. 5.
The opening sentence is found in *Bridl.* only; elsewhere the decretal begins *Accepimus*. It is addressed to the bishop of Durham in *App. Cr.*

378. *Ea que honestatis decorem deformant ... vanas esse decernas.* To Roger archbishop of York.

Churches should not be conferred on others while their parsons are still alive. If it is established that such concessions have been made in the recipient's diocese, and the matter has been brought to judgment, he must revoke them and declare them worthless.

JL 15171, 1159-81. *1 Alc.* 88; *Cantab.* 63a; *1 Vict.* 93. I; *1 Par.* 16; *1 Berol.* 111; *Flor.* 105; *Cus.* 121; *3 Cant.* 2; *1 Dun.* 2. 3; *Font.* 3. 31; *Bridl.* 72c; *Trin.* 4. 1; *Wig.* 4. 1; *Claustr.* 142; *Chelt.* 11. 1; *Cott.* 6. 65; and twelve systematic collections. Pd *Claustr.*; *App.* 15. 11; *1 Comp.* 3. 8. 3.
Roger is named as recipient in *1 Par.* and *Frcf. Rot.* 35. 11. The decretal was formerly attributed to Lucius III (see LOHMANN, *Die Collectio Wigorniensis ...*, 78-79).

395. *Ex conquestione dilectorum filiorum nostrorum fratrum de Fontibus ... temeritatibus cohercere. Dat' Tusculani ii. idus Decembris.* To (Roger) archbishop of York and (Hugh) bishop of Durham.

The monks of Fountains have complained that certain priests in the recipients' dioceses refuse penance, communion and other ecclesiastical graces to the monks' servants and hired men, to induce them to pay tithes. The recipients know that the Cistercian order is immune by apostolic privilege from tithe payment; and even if they were bound to such payments, their servants should in no way be coerced in respect of the sacraments for that reason. They are ordered to forbid all priests and clerks in their dioceses to withhold the sacraments from the monks' servants and hired men, except for sin. If this practice continues, the pope will be gravely moved against the recipients, since they should restrain their subjects with pastoral correction.

JL —, 12 Dec. 1170-80. *Font.* 2. 11 only. Pd *PU England* 3. 400 n° 271.

404. [*R. Eboracensis archiepiscopus et H. Dunelmensis (episcopus) R. Wigorniensi episcopo. Litteras domini pape in hanc formam recepimus:*] *Ex constanti relatione dilecti filii nostri H. sancti Angeli diaconi cardinalis ... quod magister H. de Suellis ... penitentie emendare.* [*Apostolicam itaque ... annuente completuri.*] To Roger archbishop of York and Hugh bishop of Durham.

The cardinal deacon of Sant'Angelo, Hugo Pierleoni, informed the pope that Hugh of Southwell had placed forged letters before the archbishop. His attempt to deny this was disproved by sufficient witnesses, and the cardinal wished to condemn him as a forger; but he deferred to Hugh's appeal, influenced by the intervention of powerful people. The pope orders the recipients to despoil Hugh of the churches of Epperstone and Shelford, impose perpetual silence on him in respect of those churches, and confine him to a monastery for penance.

JL —, *post* April 1177. *Bridl.* 152 only. Pd G.V. SCAMMELL, *Hugh du Puiset, bishop of Durham,* 251-52; *Decretales ineditae,* 130-32, n° 76.
On the form of the letter's entry in *Bridl.*, see *Decretales ineditae,* 131-32; M. CHENEY, *Roger, bishop of Worcester ...,* 340 n° 47A.

420. *Ex litteris fraternitatis tue ad nos directis intelleximus quod N. quandam puellam infra annos nubiles ... sepedictus W. ... non differas innodare.* To (Roger) archbishop of York.

The man W. took as wife the mother of a girl to whom he had been betrothed with the consent of both her parents. The girl had been under age at the time of betrothal and declined her assent on reaching lawful age, and her father had meanwhile died. The archbishop bound both parties by oath not to come together without his licence. The pope commends his prudence, and orders him to forbid such a marriage, and inform the parties that they can marry others of their choice. He must bind them with anathema if they come together, contrary to their oath.

JL —, 1169 - early 1170s. *1 Rot.* 1. 4 only. Pd *Decretales ineditae,* 123-25 n° 71.
The decretal records an early stage in the marriage dispute involving William Fitz Godric and Aubrey de Lisours (cf. *WH* 12 and 235 above). William's initial appears correctly within the main text of the present decretal, despite the scribal rendering N. in the opening sentence.

432a. *Ex litteris tue fraternitatis et ex confessione Galteri latoris presentium ... maculam contraxisse.* To (Roger) archbishop of York.

Walter confessed to illicit relations with the mother of a girl to whom he had been betrothed, but he had not known the girl herself, since she was not yet ten years old at that time, as he alleged. Not wishing to judge the secret matters of men's hearts, the pope orders the recipient to forbid Walter to marry either woman, but to allow him after penance to marry another. The girl is blameless, and can therefore marry any other person of her choice.

JL —, 1159-81. *Cott.* 2. 21; *Pet.* 1. 24. Pd *Decretales ineditae,* 126 n° 72.

443. *Ex litteris vestre fraternitatis accepimus quod, cum olim inter R. et A. clericos super ecclesia de Rameston. et capella de Cortistocha ... duximus absolvendum.* To Roger archbishop of York, apostolic legate, and Roger bishop of Worcester.

The bishop of Worcester was previously commissioned to deal with a dispute between the clerks R. and A. over the church of Rempstone and the chapel of Costock, and an agreement was made between them. But G., who had acted in that case for A., later secured papal letters to the bishop of Durham and the dean of York on the same church and chapel, concealing the fact of the agreement and falsely presenting himself as a clerk, when he was not yet tonsured. When G. and the representative of R. were in the papal presence, the pope learned the truth of the matter from the recipients' letters. He imposes perpetual silence on G. with respect to the church and chapel, and releases R. from his claims.

JL 13159, 1165-79. *1 Alc.* 53; *Claustr.* 331; *Chelt.* 4. 15; *Cott.* 7. 10; *2 Dun.* 120; and eleven systematic collections. Pd *X* 1. 36. 6.
The full address is in *1 Alc.* Rempstone and Costock are within two miles of one another, south of Nottingham, then in the diocese of York. Cf. M. CHENEY, *Roger, bishop of Worcester* ..., 343 n° 50. The canonical comment 'Si quis tonsoratus... istud non retineat' (*Claud.* 116) is apparently based on this letter (see *Decretales ineditae,* 129-30 n° 75).

447. *Ex parte abbatis et canonicorum de Wellebech auribus nostris innotuit quod R. Mustel parrochianus tuus ... cautius evitari.* To (Roger) archbishop of York.

The abbot and canons of Welbeck complained that R. Mustel, a subject of the archbishop, had violently removed certain goods from the cemetery of their church. Since the wickedness of secular persons in laying violent hands on ecclesiastical possessions must be restrained, the recipient is ordered to compel R. to restore the property, if the charges are proven. If he disdains to obey, he is to be excommunicated and avoided until he makes satisfaction.

JL —, 1159-81. *Trin.* 4. 5; *Wig.* 4. 5; *Claustr.* 146; *Chelt.* 8. 8; *Cott.* 5. 34; *Pet.* 4. 50. Pd *Wig.*; *Claustr.* Roger Mustel occurs as tenant of William Paynel, of Hooton Pagnell, in 1172: C.T. CLAY, *Early Yorkshire charters,* VI ..., 1939 (Yorkshire Archaeological Society: Extra Series, 3), 79, 249-55, 257-58, 262.

458. *Ex parte fraternitatis tue a nobis fuit quesitum utrum, cum causam aliquam sub certa forma committimus ... admitti, quod nec nos nec aliquem predecessorum nostrorum umquam credimus expressisse.* To (Roger) archbishop of York.

In reply to the archbishop's enquiry concerning the admission of reasonable exceptions when a case is commissioned « sub certa forma », the pope replies that it is expedient for the judge to keep to the form laid down. But reasonable exceptions should be admitted, and he should proceed according to equity, unless it is stated in the commission that no exceptions should be allowed, which the pope does not believe was ever expressed by himself or any of his predecessors.

JL 13877, 1159-81. *Aur.* 64 = 114; *Bridl.* 149; *Wig.* 7. 10; *Claustr.* 201; *Chelt.* 16. 4; *Cott.* 3. 57; *Pet.* 2. 23. 14; and thirteen systematic collections. Pd *App.* 42. 1; *X* 1. 29. 13.

The incipit above is found in *Bridl., Wig., Claustr., Chelt., Cott., Pet.*; elsewhere it is « Ex parte tua », « Ex tua parte », or « Ex parte tue ». The text stops at « admitti » in *Bamb. B.* 33. 22. On commissions « sub certa forma », see M. CHENEY, *Roger, bishop of Worcester ...,* 122-24.

461. *Ex parte N. capellani nobis innotuit quod, cum ad te, frater Coventrensis, nostras litteras impetrasset ... tacita veritate impetrate.* To (Roger) archbishop of York and (Richard) bishop of Coventry.

The chaplain N. obtained papal letters to the recipient bishop of Coventry, to the effect that the first archdeaconry to become available in his church would be assigned to N. But his adversary R. secured letters to the recipient archbishop of York, to assign to R. the archdeaconry which his uncle held in the same church, if the uncle wishes to resign it. If the pope had remembered his letters in N.'s favour, he would not have written on behalf of his rival. If the archdeaconry is vacant, it must be assigned to N., notwithstanding the later letters obtained by concealment of the truth.

JL 13890, 1160-81. *Cus.* 198; *Roff.* 122; *Chelt.* 18. 23; *Pet.* 3. 64; and thirteen systematic collections. Pd *App.* 7. 21; *X* 1. 29. 12.

The letter is ascribed to Urban III in *Pet.,* and is addressed « Herefordensi episcopo et abbati Hereford. » in *Cus.* The text is corrupt in *Cus.,* and the formation of the mandatory clause is ambiguous elsewhere. The plaintiff N. appears as E. in *Cus.,* and R. in *Frcf. Max.* 38. 16α.

490. *Ex tenore litterarum (tuarum) nuper accepimus quod quidam parochianus fecit votum se Ierosolimam profecturum ... sibi iter remittas.* To (Roger) archbishop of York.

A certain subject of the recipient, falling gravely ill, sought release from a vow of pilgrimage to Jerusalem. Since a vow to God should be fulfilled and advanced with all one's strength, the recipient should seek to induce the man to keep his vow if at all possible. If he is so gravely ill that he cannot make the journey, he must give in alms to the poor or to a certain monastery the equivalent of the cost of the journey, or compensation from his possessions, and add something extra for the labour which would have been involved. If he firmly promises to do this, the recipient shall absolve him from his vow and remit the journey.

JL —, 1159-81. *Font.* 2. 41 only. Pd *Decretales ineditae,* 127-28 n° 73.

510. *Ex tua nobis parte est propositum quod, cum olim ad tuam consultationem super filiis sacerdotum ... apostolica prohibemus.* To (Roger) archbishop of York, apostolic legate.

In response to the archbishop's previous enquiry, the pope had given him leave to permit priests' sons to remain in their fathers' churches, no other person intervening, if he judged them to be of good life and character. But others obtained papal instructions to judges to impose silence on clerks who are known to be sons of the immediately preceding possessors, and to assign the churches to others, even if these cannot show that they were instituted to those churches by a bishop. The pope does not wish any dispensation granted on the basis of his earlier letters to be disturbed by the later instructions, and orders such dispensation to stand. But clerks must not be instituted to churches by lay gift, without pontifical authority, within the jurisdiction of a bishop. If any have been instituted in this way, they may not remain there.

JL 13881, 1164-81. *Chelt.* 19. 17; and ten systematic collections. Pd *App.* 19. 10; *X* 1. 17. 9. *Chelt.* has the false inscription « R. Wigorñsi ».

518. *Fraternitatem tuam scire volumus et firmiter tenere quod te ex caritatis fervore, ob multiplica tue gratissime devotionis obsequia ... fieri postulares.* To Roger archbishop of York.

Because of the many signs of the recipient's devotion to him, the pope expresses his love and his unwillingness to deny him anything. But he cannot listen favourably to his request to compel monks and canons to pay tithes for the hired lands which they hold for a period or for rent, since that would clearly conflict with justice and the decisions of his predecessors, and would seem to oppress religion. It is expressed in the writings of his predecessors that religious are exempt from tithes on their works, lands cultivated by their own hands or at their expense, or on their animal fodder. But pope Adrian changed the exemption from « works » to « new works », by a personal decision. The pope does not recall reading in the Old Testament that Levites paid tithes to Levites; and it is clear from the New Testament that people pay tithes to those churches from which they receive the sacraments. The archbishop must not take it amiss if the pope cannot accede to his petition; he will not be rebuffed in anything he may ask in harmony with God's will and justice.

JL 13873, ?1160 (– 63/64). *1 Dert.* 20a; *Eber.* 13. 1; *1 Alc.* 29; *1 Vict.* 122a; *Amb.* 16; *1 Par.* 8; *Aur.* 20; *1 Berol.* 100; *Flor.* 97; *Cus.* 108; *Wig. alt.* 8ab; *Belv.* 11. I; *Font.* 1. 9 = 3. 14a; *Bridl.* 174a; *Claud.* 32a; *Wig.* 2. 13ab; *Claustr.* 101. I; *Chelt.* 10. 4ab; *Cott.* 4. 12; and thirteen systematic collections. Pd *Belv.*; *Claustr.*; *App.* 13. 3; *1 Comp.* 3. 26. 8; E. MARTÈNE and U. DURAND, *Thesaurus novus anecdotorum,* I, Paris 1717, 599-600; J.C. ATKINSON, *Cartularium Rievallense,* London 1887 (Surtees Society, 83), 195 n° 263; J. LECLERCQ, *Études sur saint Bernard et le texte de ses écrits,* Rome 1953 (Analecta sacri ordinis Cisterciensis, IX. 1-2), 199. The decretal is found in many collections, including the earliest primitive collections, and also in archival records (for canonical sources: S. KUTTNER, *Repertorium der Kanonistik, 1140-1234*, Vatican City 1937 [Studi e Testi, 71], 276, 284-85; C. DUGGAN, *Decretal collections,* 154, 156; discussed in G. CONSTABLE, *Monastic tithes,* Cambridge 1964, 297-98; WH noted copies in British Library, mss. Cotton Julius D.I., f. 183r; Harley 3013, f. 96v; Lansdowne 415, f. 22r: *PU England* 1. 68, 129, 145. In twelve older collections (*1 Dert., Eber., 1 Alc., 1 Vict., 1 Par., Wig. alt., Belv., Font., Claud., Wig., Claustr., Chelt.*) the letter is found with an appendix of seven texts relating to tithes; six appear as an appendix in *Bridl.*, the seventh appearing separately as *Bridl.* 181; and a few of the texts are found in other collections (*Ambr.* 48. II, 49, 50; *Aur.* 21, 100; *Cott.* 4. 16ab; *Tann.* 3. 14. 18-19; *Sang.* 4. 10. 19-20; *1 Abr.* 4. 9. 3-4). See J. JUNCKER, *Die Collectio Berolinensis,* in *ZRG, Kan. Abt.,* 13 (1924), 296-97.

The decretal dates from a very early phase in Alexander III's pontificate. Though listed in *JL* and *WH* under the pope's pontifical years, 1159-81, it was well established in decretal collections by 1175 at the latest, and was possibly issued as early as 1160. The expression of gratitude to Roger of York for services rendered to the pope seems to respond to Roger's support for Alexander in the period of crisis following his election on 7 September 1159; the acceptance of Alexander as lawful pope by the English Church was secured in July 1160. His later letters to Roger on the same problem as that dealt with in *Fraternitatem tuam* are not couched in terms of comparable affection. On the other hand, Leclercq's suggestion that the letter was possibly issued before 1160 is not easily reconciled with the date of Alexander's election. The tenor of the letter agrees with the emergence of Alexander's views on tithe payment in the course of 1160 (see comment for *Audivimus et audientes, WH* 98 above). The decretal may date from 1160, and was almost certainly issued within the limits 1160-63/64. The language of the letter, except for the comments personal to Roger, was used again later in *Licet te et universos,* to bishop Didier of Thérouanne (see *PU Frankreich,* 3. 394-95 n° 240, 1169-81); and abbot Gerard of Clairvaux included a full transcript of *Fraternitatem tuam,* with its inscription to York, in a letter to the same bishop (MARTÈNE and DURAND, *Thesaurus* ..., 599-600, 1169-81).

Alexander's dictum that he did not recall reading in the Old Testament that Levites paid tithes to Levites excited some reaction among the glossators. A dissenting comment that the pope erred in this matter occurs in at least five collections, the variant versions in the manuscripts revealing a common ancestry. The most complete version appears as follows: « Hic secundum theologos erravit Alexander, cum in Levitico legatur quod levite de decimis summo sacerdoti decimas persolvebant. Sed respondent quidam quod solvebant ei decimas in partem suarum decimarum, vel solvebant summo sacerdoti sed non levitis » (*App. Ln.* 13. 3; *Frcf. Max.* 20. 9: the latter reads « decimas de decimis solvebant summo pontifici »; *App. Lp.* omits the final « sed non levitis »; *App. Cr.* has « Hic secundum quosdam erravit Alexander, cum levite summo sacerdoti, quod et ipse levita fuit, decimas dare in Levitico iuberentur »; *Chelt.* reads « Hic secundum Stephanum erravit Alexander, cum in Levitico legatur quod levite decimas summo pontifici solvebant. Solutio: non tamen levitis »). Three manuscripts of the 'Frankfurt' group have a further comment: « Hoc superficialiter allegatur, cum levite possessionem ad excolendam in terra promissionis non haberent, et decimas decimarum summo tenerentur sacerdoti persolvere » (*Frcf. Rot. Trec. Max.*; *Rot.* and *Max.* read « tenentur »; *Rot.* omits « ad excolendam »; *Trec.* ends « reddere creatori »). Both glosses appear in *Frcf. Max.,* but are the work of two separate scribes. Later, at *Ex parte tue fraternitatis* (*WH* 470, *JL* 14117, to the bishop of Troyes), *App. Ln.* 13. 5 has « Hic obviat vel corrigit Alexander id cuius sit mentio in capitulo Fraternitatem ... ».

519. (a) *Fraternitati tue duximus indulgendum ut si clerici qui in ecclesiis tue jurisdictionis ... non debeant.* (b) *Preterea clericos alterius diocesis ... nec etiam debes recipere.* To (Roger) archbishop of York.

If beneficed clerks in the archbishop's jurisdiction have gone without his consent to another diocese, intending to stay there, and have not returned when lawfully summoned by him, he can despoil them of benefices which he granted, unless they are intent on study, or can show him good reason why they should not return. Likewise, he should not keep or even receive clerks from another diocese without letters of commendation from their own bishop, or at the request or order of the apostolic see.

JL 13879, 1159-81. *Trin.* 3. 26; *Wig.* 3. 25; *Claustr.* 141; *Chelt.* 12. 7; *Cott.* 7. 32; and ten systematic collections. Pd *App.* 30. 6; *X* 3. 4. 5.
Parts (a) and (b) are marked in *Wig.* and *Chelt.*; *Frcf. Max.* 36. 4α omits (b) and ends « non possint ».

552. (a) *In eminenti specula ecclesie licet immeriti ... enodare. Consuluisti autem si causa ... unus procedat. Prime igitur questioni ... apostolicam veniendi. Quod autem quesivisti ... in eo casu debet appellationi deferri. Ab uno vero ... exprimatur.* (b) *De cetero noveris quod si sententiam ... apostolicam oportebit.* To (Roger) archbishop of York, apostolic legate.

The pope responds to three questions concerning cases commissioned without leave of appeal: if one of the parties has appealed before or after citation, or before or after sentence, the appeal is not allowed unless the appellant had set out for the apostolic see before citation; if one of the litigants has appealed because the judge refuses to hear proofs of forgery, such an appeal should be respected; if a case has been commissioned to two judges and one entrusts his function to the other, the latter may not proceed in the case without leave of appeal, unless this is expressly stated in the commission. The pope adds that, if he has mandated execution of his own sentence to another and some deception has occurred, cognizance of the whole matter does not devolve on the executor; questions arising should be referred to the apostolic see.

JL 14350, 1164-81. *Cus.* 188; *Roff.* 45; *Bridl.* 118; *Claud.* 106; *Wig.* 5. 12; *Chelt.* 15. 18; *Cott.* 3. 6; *Pet.* 2. 13. 1; and integrally or dissected in fifteen systematic collections. Pd *1 Comp.* 2. 20. 40 (ab); *App.* 49. 13 (a); 49. 12 (b); *Brug.* 47. 22 (from *Consuluisti*); *X* 2. 27. 5 (b).
Some collections and *JL* wrongly associate this decretal with *Proposuit nobis G.* and *Relatum est nobis* (see *WH* 749 and 873 below; LOHMANN, *Collectio Wigorniensis* ..., 77-78). It begins at *Consuluisti* in *Wig.*, *Chelt.*, *Cott.*, *2 Par.* 33. 5, *Brug.* 47. 22. The text is defective in *Cus.*, which omits everything from « Ab uno vero », except for the closing words « questiones que inciderint ad sedem apostolicam oportebit »; *Frcf.* 51. 3 excerpts « Dubitas si causa ... unus procedat » from the opening part of the letter, and links it with « Ab uno ... exprimatur ».

590. (a) *Inter ceteras consultationes tuas id fuit propositum ... idem in similibus.* (b) *Sane si a nobis super aliqua causa ... valeant impediri.* (c) *Item cum aliqua causa ... continet iniquitatem.* (d) *Ad hec cum laici episcopis ... propria ordinare. Dat' Anagnie iiii. kal. Maii.* To Roger archbishop of York.

The pope responds to a series of queries raised by the recipient: if a mandate is issued containing alternative propositions, of which one is false and the other true — for instance, that a church is held by one who was born in the priesthood, his father having ministered in the church immediately preceding him, or that he obtained the church illegally — the judge should decide the matter according to whichever proposition is proven to him; if letters are obtained from the pope, then others secured without mention of the first, execution of the commissions should be entirely suspended until the pope has been consulted; if a case is commissioned without leave of appeal and an unjust sentence is pronounced, this is devoid of force and should not stand if it contains an obvious injustice; when lay patrons grant churches to clerks without the bishops' knowledge or consent and then, induced by penance, present others to the same churches, and these are instituted by the bishops, the former presentations are devoid of force and the latter should stand; it is unlawful for laymen to appoint clerks to churches by their own presumption.

JL 13878 (abc), 14346 (d), 28 April 1160-76. *1 Berol.* 40; *Flor.* 89; *Duac.* 41; *Cus.* 10; *1 Cant.* 38; *Roff.* 40; *1 Dun.* 2. 30; dissected parts in thirteen primitive and thirteen systematic collections, and one fragment. Pd *App.* 41. 1 (a), 7. 3 = 41. 7 (b), 7. 4 = 36. 5 (c), 15. 3 (d); *X* 1. 3. 4 (a), 1. 29. 2 (b), 2. 27. 9 (c), 3. 38. 10 (d).

JL 14346 links (d) with *Relatum est nobis* (*WH* 880 below; see LOHMANN, *Collectio Wigorniensis* ..., 72, 77). The date is found in *Cus.*; *1 Vict.* 97. II; *Frcf.* 21. 3 (the *Frcf.* mss. have « Dat' agañ. iiii. kal. maii [iii. kal. *Trec.*; mart. *Frcf.*] »). *X* 1. 29. 2 has the wrong address: « Bonomiensi episcopo ».

618. *Licet nobis commendabiles et grati in pluribus existatis ... infestationis hora decurrat, et creditor veniens nos conveniat de reddenda ratione.* [*Dat' Ferentini xvi. kal. Octobris.*] To Roger archbishop of York and Hugh bishop of Durham.

The pope rebukes the recipients for their compliance with the English king's policies in diminishing the freedom of the Church, and records the frustration of legates whom he sent in response to archbishop Thomas's requests. Specifically, in the coronation of the young king, the king's son, the recipient archbishop performed the ceremony without mention of the Church's freedom; but the preservation of the ancient customs which endanger the Church was confirmed. The archbishop's offence was all the greater being committed in the province of another, and of one suffering exile for justice. The recipients are suspended from all episcopal office.

JL 11836, 16 Sept. 1170. *Sang.* 3. 13. 8; *1 Abr.* 3. 9. 1; *2 Dun.* 4. Pd *Materials TB* 7. 364-68 n° 701 (with the date); *et alibi.*
The letter begins « Licet nobis grati in pluribus » in *1 Abr.*; and « Licet commendabiles nobis » in *Materials TB.* It ends at « decurrat » in *Sang.* and *2 Dun.* The Durham ms. omits mention of the bishop of Durham in the address of this papal rebuke. On the coronation of the Young King, see comment at *Quanto per carissimum, WH* 772 below.

674. *Non sine multa necessitate et discrimine sui corporis A. presbiter presentium lator ... in ecclesia sancti Wilfridi de Calvertuna per manum R. archidiaconi de Sudewella ... illius iuramenti absolvant ... illius iuramenti nostra auctoritate ... compellant. Hominem vero ... satisfacturus accedat.* To (Roger) archbishop of York.

The priest A. complained of harassment in respect of the church of St Wilfrid at Calverton. He was instituted as chaplain by the archdeacon R., canon of Southwell and parson of the church, and was reappointed after R.'s death by his nephew and successor M.; and in their time he held the office for more than thirty years. He was then subjected to exactions and violence, and M. deceitfully tried to induce him to resign in return for a promise of five marks of silver yearly. At last he was suspended from office and benefice, and after many troubles restored to office only. Exiled by the archbishop, and unable to secure justice, he was constrained to swear to accept the arbitration of three of the archbishop's clerks. These, following the archbishop's will and favouring M., ordered the priest to accept five marks and relinquish his claim. The recipient should not permit this. He is ordered to require the clerks to correct whatever they may have wrongly awarded (which in the ordinary course of law they could not do). The pope has ordered the abbot of Rievaulx and the dean of Lincoln to deal with the matter, if the clerks fail to do so. If anything needs correction, the judges shall amend it and absolve the priest from his oath; but if the award is found to rest on justice and equity, they shall compel both parties to observe it without appeal. If it is shown that a certain man of M.'s laid violent hands on the priest, the recipient must denounce him as an excommunicate, and have him shunned as such until he makes amends to the victim and comes to the pope to make satisfaction.

JL 13888, 1164-81. *Wig.* 7. 18; *Claustr.* 209; *Chelt.* 6. 4; *Cott.* 6. 81; and eight systematic collections. Pd parts: *Wig.*; *Sang.* 4. 6. 4; *X* 1. 43. 2; complete: *Decretals to Lincoln,* 36-39 n° 15.

The address in *1 Rot.* 22. 16 wrongly adds « et Exoniensi episcopo et abbati de Forde ». The complete decretal is found only in *Wig.*; all collections thereafter lack « absolvant ... iuramenti » through homoioteleuton (cf. LOHMANN, *Collectio Wigorniensis* ..., 128). « Hominem ... accedat » (pd from *Sang.*: SINGER, *Neue Beiträge,* 193-94) is lacking in *Alan.* 1. 20. 1; *Fuld.* 1. 26. 3; *2 Comp.* 1. 20. 1; *X.* The affair concerns the church of Calverton, close to Southwell in Nottinghamshire; it was part of the endowment of the prebends Oxton I and II in the collegiate church of Southwell (see *Decretals to Lincoln,* 39 n.).

675a. *Non videtur ulla ratione mirandum, si laici in clericos et maxime Anglicos incandescunt ... minime displicebit. Nos enim non hoc eis de novo indulsimus,* [*sed quod*] *a predecessoribus nostris ab antiquo indultum est, sibi ullatenus confirmamus. Porro illos qui in fratres ... incommodum sustinere. Dat' Senon. ii. kal. Octobris.* To Roger archbishop of York, apostolic legate, [Robert bishop of Lincoln], and (Richard) bishop of Chester.

The pope has heard of insolent clerks in the recipients' dioceses, who do not hesitate to lay violent hands on the property of religious, and exact tithes from them on new works and animal fodder. They also seek to pervert the pope's good intentions, and describe as unjust his privilege to Cistercians that no one may exact any tithes from them on their works and animal fodder, as granted to them of old by the holy fathers and the pope's own predecessors. In response to a complaint by the monks of Rufford and Roche, the pope now orders the recipients to compel their clerks to restore whatever they may have taken from the monks, and to desist from molesting them in future. He orders them also to issue a general prohibition to their clerks and laymen, to exact no tithes whatever from Cistercians on their works and animal fodder; and if any presume to do this, the recipients must punish them with a deterrent penalty. But he will not disapprove of any composition which the monks may freely make, for the sake of peace. Moreover, those who lay violent hands on the monks or their *conversi* shall be excommunicated, as laid down in the Lateran council, and shall be avoided as such until they come to the pope with the prelates' letters. The recipients must also prevent others from erecting buildings which may be a source of disturbance to the monks' religious life, or cause them loss and inconvenience.

JL --, 30 Sept. 1164. *Font.* 2. 5; Oxford, Bodleian Library, ms. Bodl. e Mus. 195 (S.C. 3608), f. 120. Pd *PU England,* 3. 293-94 n° 151.

The bishop of Lincoln is omitted from the address in *Font.*, which also lacks the sentence « Nos enim ... confirmamus ». But the text of *Font.* is sometimes better, most importantly where the Bodl. copy adds « novalium » to « decimas » in mid-decretal, and so loses the purpose of the pope's assertion of total Cistercian exemption. The decretal is placed in a wider context in the comment on *Audivimus et audientes* (*WH* 98 above). Its internal conciliar allusion is to the Second Lateran council (1139), c. 15, *Si quis suadente diabolo* = *Decretum Gratiani* C. 17 q. 4 c. 29.

749. *Proposuit nobis G. clericus tuus quod sepe contingit ... foret dampnandus.* To (Roger) archbishop of York.

In response to a report by the archbishop's clerk G., concerning a frequent occurrence, the pope replies that an appeal in one case does not make the appellant less answerable in other cases, in which an appeal has not been made; but, since the judge seems altogether suspect to the appellant, he should not compel him to answer in other suits while that case is pending, except for a crime so grave and manifest that he may be held *ipso actu* guilty, and rightly to be condemned.

JL 14350, 1159-81. *Wig.* 7. 1; *Claustr.* 192; *Chelt.* 15. 20; *Cott.* 3. 11; and twelve systematic collections. Pd *X* 2. 28. 24.
JL wrongly lists this letter with *In eminenti* and *Relatum est nobis* (see *WH* 552 above, and 873 below).

765. *Quanto Cisterciensis ordo maiori religione preminet et ampliori redolet odore ... invitare. Accepimus autem unde si verum ... contraire statutis. Dat' Anag'. viii. kal. Decembris.* To (Roger) archbishop of York and (Hugh) bishop of Durham.

By papal privilege, Cistercian monks are exempt from payment of tithes or first fruits on works cultivated by themselves or at their own expense, but some persons by a malicious misreading allege that by « labores » the privilege intends « novales ». The pope does not wish them to be harassed in this way; if he had meant new works, he would have written new works, as he does in privileges to other religious. He strictly orders the recipients not to pervert the chapter in this way, nor to permit their subjects to oppress the monks by such an interpretation. If they or their subjects act against this prohibition, he will impose such a sentence that they will know what a perilous thing it is to resist apostolic decisions.

JL —, 24 Nov. 1160-81. *Font.* 2. 10 only. Pd *PU England*, 3. 385 n° 251.
For the formulation of this doctrine of Cistercian tithe exemption, see *Audivimus et audientes* (*WH* 98 and comment, above).

772. *Quanto per carissimum filium nostrum H. illustrem regem Anglorum ... commoneas exhibere. Dat' Rome apud sanctam Mariam novam xv.* (vel *xii.*) *kal. Julii.* To (Roger) archbishop of York.

Since king Henry helped God's Church in its extreme necessity, and also for his constant devotion, the pope wishes to increase his honour, and exalt the king and his people. Therefore, at Henry's request and after consulting his brethren, the pope grants that the king's eldest son Henry shall be crowned in England. He mandates the archbishop, since it pertains to his office, to place the crown by apostolic authority on the head of the king's firstborn son, when required by the king to do so. The pope confirms what the archbishop will do. The archbishop will also show the son due reverence and subjection, saving his father's mandate, and will admonish others to do likewise.

JL 11353, 17 or 20 June 1161. *Pet.* 3. 31; and eight systematic collections. Pd *Cass.* 55. 4; *Materials TB* 6. 206-07 n° 310; A. DUGGAN (HESLIN), *The coronation of the Young King*, London/Edinburgh 1965 (Studies in Church History, 2), 177-78. The date of the decretal appears variously as 17 June (*Bamb.* 47. 4; *Cass.; Frcf. Max.* 10. 5α), or 20 June (*Pet.*; *Tann.* 6. 7. 4; *1 Abr.* 7. 14. 4). It was formerly placed in the year 1167 (*JL, Materials TB,* etc.), but is correctly dated 1161 (A. DUGGAN, *The coronation* ..., 165-78). Alexander III's response to Henry II's services and devotion suit the circumstances of his own early troubled years, but not those of the crisis years of the Becket dispute. The commission to York was appropriate in June 1161, with Canterbury vacant; it is inconceivable for 1167, with Becket in exile. It seems that Becket had the present mandate in mind when writing to the pope after his reconciliation with Henry II at Fréteval in 1170 (see *Miserationis oculo, Materials TB* 7. 326-38 n° 684, at 331: « Constabat enim eas (litteras), quando Cantuariensis ecclesia vacabat, eo proposito fuisse impetratas »).

773. *Quanto personam tuam sicut carissimi fratris nostri ... districte compellant. Si autem illi tres ... firmiter observes. Dat' Tusculani xviii. kal. Februarii.* To (Roger) archbishop of York.

The pope is disturbed by the numerous complaints which have reached him concerning the recipient's oppression of religious. He writes in particular about a certain grange disputed between the archbishop and the abbot and monks of Fountains. The latter had held the grange by the concession of the archbishop's predecessors, but he had seduced the abbot with promises, and the abbot committed it to him, without consulting the brothers and hoping for a merciful verdict. But the archbishop retained it, and closed his ears to entreaties. The pope is further concerned by the archbishop's failure to observe a mandate issued by pope Adrian on this issue. He therefore orders the recipient to restore the grange, if the abbot conceded it to him without the brethren's consent or later confirmation. If he wishes to raise this or any other quarrel with the monks, he should then meet them in a friendly way, or do justice to them in the presence of the dean of Chester, the archdeacon of Oxford, and the prior of Guisborough, when summoned by them. The pope has mandated these judges to induce him to give effect to this order, or if necessary compel him.

JL —, 15 Jan. 1173. *Font.* 2. 14 only. Pd *PU England,* 3. 330-31 n° 194.
The letter records one stage in a protracted dispute over the grange of Warsill in Yorkshire; a newly edited mandate to the bishops of Chichester and Hereford, the abbot of Ford and the dean of Chichester deals with another aspect of the same dispute (see *Causam que inter Eboracensem, JL* —, c. 1175: *Decretales ineditae,* 87-88 n° 47, with a discussion of the case).

840. *Quotiens a viris ecclesiasticis et infra. fraternitati tue per apostolica scripta ... Romani pontificis absolvas.* To (Roger) archbishop of York.

The archbishop must order all monks, canons and other ecclesiastics in his province, under threat of the loss of office and benefice, to presume for no reason to draw one another to a secular judge in any dispute they may have, or to compel one another to answer in a secular court. If anyone rashly attempts to do so after the archbishop's prohibition, the latter must suspend him from office, without leave of appeal, and must not absolve him without papal authority.

JL —, 1159-81. *Asl.* 13; *Tann.* 4. 6. 2; *Sang.* 5. 5. 2; *1 Abr.* 5. 6. 2. Pd *Sang.*
This item preserves only the incipit and mandatory clause of a decretal not otherwise identified.

854. *Referente nobis dilecto filio nostro magistro G. clerico tuo ad nostram noveris audientiam pervenisse ... nullatenus est admittendus.* To (Roger) archbishop of York.

The archbishop's clerk Master G. reported to the pope the case of a certain girl, daughter of Hugh, who was betrothed to G., with the parents' consent and mutual promises. But after they had lived in the parental home, G. put off the marriage and was clandestinely united with the girl's sister in another district. These two lived together more than a year, and a child was born to them. At length, the marriage was challenged before the archbishop, in the presence of both parties. But the man died, and a dispute arose between the relations concerning certain estates: the woman's side claimed inheritance for the child, as if born of lawful wedlock; the brothers of the man claimed inheritance, as if he had died without children, the union being unlawful. The archbishop did not wish to decide the matter, and asked the pope if such a marriage should be judged legitimate, so that the issue could succeed to the parental property. The pope replies that the justice of public honour prevented such a marriage, and if contracted it should have been dissolved. Since the son can be excused neither by permission of the church nor by his parents' ignorance, he cannot be admitted to succession.

JL 17623, 1159-81. (*Bridl.* 162); *Pet.* 1. 31; *Cott.* 2. 11; *Tann.* 7. 13. 8; *Sang.* 9. 34; *1 Abr.* 8. 11. 2; *Alan.* 4. 12. 1; *Fuld.* 4. 12. 3; *2 Comp.* 4. 11. 1; *X* 4. 17. 10. Pd *Sang.*; *X.*

The *pars historica* is pd from *Sang.*, but is omitted in *Alan., Fuld., 2 Comp., X,* which have only « Referente nobis et infra. Fraternitati tue ... admittendi ». The decretal is attributed to Celestine III in *JL* (from *Alan., Fuld., 2 Comp., X*); its correct assignment to Alexander III is fixed by its presence in an abbreviated form in the early collection *Bridl.* (« De eo qui ex sorore sponse sue ... admittenda »), and by identification in several collections (*Cott., Pet.*; « Idem » = Alexander III, *Bridl., Tann., Sang., 1 Abr.*). In the opening sentence, Master G. appears as T. in *Tann.*, and O. in *Sang.* The location of the clandestine union is given as « extra archiepiscopatum » in *Pet.*, and « extra archidiaconatum » in *Tann., Sang., 1 Abr.*

863. *Relatum est auribus nostris* (vel *ad audientiam nostram*) *quod frater noster R. Cestrensis episcopus Johannem de Blisfelde ... studiosius exequaris.* To (Roger) archbishop of York

The pope has heard that bishop Richard of Chester bound John of Blithfield with anathema, because he would not consent to the appointment of a priest's son to the church in which his father had ministered; and the bishop did not hesitate to institute the son to that church against the wishes of John, on whose estate the church lies. The agreement of patrons must be preserved in appointments to churches, and no one should be instituted in them against their will, unless their objections are malicious, and especially the sons of priests should not be so appointed. The recipient must investigate the case and, if the charge is established, strictly enjoin the bishop to release John from excommunication, and remove the priest's son without delay. If the bishop is unwilling to do this, the recipient must execute the pope's instructions within two months of their receipt.

JL —, 1161-81. *Font.* 1. 4a; *Claustr.* 341; *Chelt.* 4. 12; *Cott.* 6. 45; *Tann.* 6. 3. 25; *Sang.* 7. 49; *1 Abr.* 7. 3. 3. Pd *Claustr.*; *Sang.*
The address is omitted in *Font.*, and the decretal is addressed to the bishop of Exeter in *Tann.*, *Sang.*, *1 Abr.*; the address to York in *Cott.* is better, and suits the context of the letter. The incipit is found in several variants: « Relatum (Perlatum, *Chelt.*) est ad audientiam nostram », *Font.*, *Claustr.*, *Chelt.*; « ... ad nostram audientiam », *Sang.*; « ... auribus nostris », *Cott.*; « Perlatum est ad aures nostras », *Tann.*, *1 Abr.*; again the *Cott.* version seems the better. The bishop of Chester involved in the case was Richard, and the lay patron John was perhaps the lord of Blithfield (mss.: Bliffelde, Blisfelde, Blifeld, etc.) in Staffordshire.
The chapter « Si infra certum terminum » of the decretal *Meminimus nos* (*WH* 649, *JL* 13162), to Roger bishop of Worcester, is wrongly appended to *Relatum est* in *Font.* = 1. 4 (b).

870. *Relatum est auribus nostris quod Nicolaus archidiaconus de Bedeford' canonicus Beverlacensis ... hoc possit inquirere, fraternitati tue ... ipsius ecclesie requirere audeat ... voluerit deservire.* To (Roger) archbishop of York, apostolic legate.

Nicholas, archdeacon of Bedford and canon of Beverley, claims his share of the common income of Beverley, equally with those who strive night and day to serve it, and claims that he has the pope's letters to support him in this. It is unworthy and absurd for him to make such a claim, unless it is the custom of the church, so the recipient is ordered to admonish him not to use the pretext of papal letters to require an income contrary to the custom and institution of the church, unless he wishes to serve there assiduously in his own person, or for half the year.

JL 13885, 1164-81. *1 Berol.* 71; *Bridl.* 166; *Claud.* 194; and eleven systematic collections. Pd *App.* 30. 1; *1 Comp.* 3. 5. 7; and Mansi, 22. 535 (from *1 Comp.*; wrongly attributed by Mansi to Gregory VIII).
The *Bridl.* text lacks « inquirere, fraternitati tue ... ipsius ecclesie » (per homoioteleuton « inquirere/requirere »).

873. *Relatum est auribus nostris quod quidam clerici in beneficiis ecclesiasticis ... idoneis ordinentur.* To (Roger) archbishop of York.

It is reported that certain clerks with 100 or 200 marks income in ecclesiastical benefices claim that they have been promised the first churches to fall vacant, by monks or canons or others who have the patronage; and, lest others be instituted to those churches when they fall vacant, they appeal, so that they can by some artifice give effect to their purpose in the meanwhile. The pope is asked if the diocesan bishop should defer to such an appeal, and replies that the Lateran council ruled that promises relating to churches not yet vacant are void; and therefore, when churches fall vacant, there should be no neglect in ordaining suitable persons to them, on the pretext of such promises.

JL 14350, 1179-81. *Wig.* 5. 13; *Claustr.* 333; *Chelt.* 15. 19; *Cott.* 3. 4; *Pet.* 2. 16. 2; and fourteen systematic collections. Pd *App.* 47. 7; *X* 3. 8. 3.

The address in *Cott.* adds « et Lundonensi episcopo »; *Pet.* adds « vel Londonensi episcopo ». The conclusion is defective in *Tann.* 6. 4. 3, stopping short at « nituntur »; a later hand has added in the margin: « episcopus officium suum nihilominus adimpletur ».

For the faulty association of this decretal with *In eminenti* and *Proposuit nobis G.*, see *WH* 552 and 749 above. The internal reference to a Lateran council ruling is to Alexander's own canon *Nulla ecclesiastica,* from the 1179 council (MANSI, 22. 222, cap. 8).

874. *Relatum est auribus nostris quod quidam in episcopatu tuo constituti, ut iurisdictionem tuam ... prosequi non possint.* To (Roger) archbishop of York.

Certain people in the archbishop's diocese appeal when they have no cause, with the purpose of avoiding his jurisdiction. The remedy of appeal was invented to relieve oppression; and therefore, if any of his subjects think they should appeal on any matter, he should compel them by papal authority, without leave of appeal, to prosecute their appeal within a year, either in person or through a suitable representative, or to stand to his judgment, unless they can show manifest and reasonable cause why they cannot do so.

JL —, 1159-81. *Wig.* 7. 3; *Claustr.* 194; *Chelt.* 15. 22; *Cott.* 3. 42; *Pet.* 2. 1. 2; *1 Rot.* 31. 5; *Tann.* 5. 12. 12; *Sang.* 6. 13. 13. Pd *Claustr.*

The address in *Chelt.* is: « Ad abbatem ». In *1 Rot.* the decretal begins « Relatum est audientie nostre quod quidam in archiepiscopatu tuo », and ends « non possunt ».

880. (a) *Relatum est nobis ex parte tua quod, cum in Lateranensi concilio ... fuerit interiectum.* (b) *Quod autem consulis ... fuerit inchoatum.* (c) *De cetero tue prudentie ... non potest de iure conferri.* To Roger archbishop of York.

The pope responds to questions raised by the archbishop. The Lateran council ruled that a church or ecclesiastical benefice should be conferred on a person who can reside there, and exercise the cure of souls in person, but some persons presented on these conditions refuse to keep their promise. The recipient can reject such persons when presented, and remove them if they have been instituted, unless they are absent with their prelates' leave, as for study or other honest cause. Appeal against the intention of the decree is indefensible. Further, if a suitable person is presented to a vacant church but not admitted by the diocesan, and a second presentee is instituted by the bishop and holds corporal possession, the latter is to be preferred — « in hoc casu melior sit conditio possidentis », since the patron's initiative is not ratified until approved by the bishop. Moreover, if laymen draw up instruments of grant or gift to clerks or colleges, with such words as « concessi vel dedi ecclesiam, et presenti carta confirmavi », it is clear that nothing is given unless the bishop's agreement is added, for a church cannot be granted by a layman. Patronage can lawfully be conferred on a church by a layman, with the authority and assent of the bishop.

JL 14346, 1179-81. *Roff.* 45. V-VII; *Bridl.* 118. f-h; *Claud.* 106. f-h; *Wig.* 4. 31+32; *Chelt.* 8. 3; *Cott.* 3. 23+6. 43; *Pet.* 2. 10. 2 (a); and (whole or part in) fourteen systematic collections. Pd *App.* 15. 1+2; *X* 3. 4. 4+3. 38. 5.
The decretal is frequently associated with *In eminenti* (see *WH* 552 above). It appears in its true form in *Chelt.*; and as a unit, but marked as part of *In eminenti,* in five systematic collections (*Bamb. A, D, O* = *Oriel. 1* 44. 1; *Lips.* 52. 1; *Cass.* 53. 1; *Tann.* 6. 3. 1; *Bamb. C* breaks off at 44. 1, with the inscription and reference to *In eminenti,* but lacks the text). It occurs with its three chapters in sequence but as the closing sections of *In eminenti* in *Roff., Bridl., Claud.*; it is divided but in adjacent chapters in *Wig., Cott., App.* Six further systematic collections contain one or more of its dismembered chapters.
The Lateran decree cited in the opening sentence is Alexander's canon *Quia nonnulli* of the 1179 council (MANSI, 22. 225, cap. 13).

914. *Si quis obiciat suggestionem falsi et eam probare voluerit, si dicat probationes suas esse in transmarinis partibus ... super principali causa.* To (Roger) archbishop of York.

If someone alleges forgery and is prepared to prove it, but claims that his proofs are overseas, he should be granted deferment; and if such deferment is refused, he can appeal, even if appeal was forbidden on the principal issue.

JL —, 1164-81. *Chelt.* 17. 23 only. Pd *Decretales ineditae,* 128-29 n° 74.
This short item seems a canonist's re-working of the chapter *Quod autem quesivisti*

from the decretal *In eminenti* (*WH* 552 above), as indicated by a marginal comment adjacent to it in the *Chelt.* ms. (f. 90va): « Supra. De appellationibus. Consuluisti. Quod autem. » (refers back to f. 81ra). But *Quod autem quesivisti* makes no reference to proofs overseas.

916. *Si quis tonsoratus tacita veritate quod non sit clericus ... istud non retineat.* To Roger archbishop of York and Roger bishop of Worcester.

If a tonsured person who is not a clerk has obtained a benefice by concealing the fact that he is not a clerk, he may not retain it, even if he becomes a clerk later.

JL —, 1165-79. *Claud.* 116 only. Pd *Decretales ineditae,* 129-30 n° 75.
This brief item is almost certainly a canonist's maxim based on a passage in the decretal *Ex litteris vestre fraternitatis*, to the same recipients, concerning a dispute between the clerks R. and A. over the church of Rempstone and the chapel of Costock (*WH* 443 above). In that letter the pope referred to the proctor G. « se clericum mentiens cum nondum esset tonsoratus ». For the present item, the *Claud.* rubricator wrote: « De laico tonsorato qui hoc pretextu adipiscitur ecclesiam ». See *Decretales ineditae,* 129-30; M. Cheney, *Roger, bishop of Worcester* ..., 343 n° 50, 359 n° 81A.

990. *Solet frequenter sicut audivimus evenire ut super clandestinis coniugiis ... possint questione pulsari.* To (Roger) archbishop of York.

The pope has heard that clandestine marriages are contracted very frequently in the recipient's province, and that he is assailed by the questions of litigating parties — the one asserting, the other denying that a marriage took place. Lest the absence of witnesses makes worthless what should be strengthened by the Church's authority if contracted in public, the pope orders the recipient to issue a general prohibition, under pain of perpetual anathema, that marriages do not take place secretly in future, but publicly in the presence of suitable witnesses, so that the marriage shall gain fitting validity, and the parties may not be beset by so ambiguous a question.

JL 14162, 1159-81. *Chelt.* 9. 75; *Tann.* 7. 10. 6; *Sang.* 9. 6; *1 Abr.* 8. 9. 3; *Brug.* 52. 1; *Frfc.* 4. 9; *1 Comp.* 4. 4. (4). Pd *1 Comp.*
The decretal is wrongly addressed to Palermo in *Chelt.*, through a scribal transfer from the preceding letter.

998. *Suggestum est auribus nostris quod, cum ecclesie de Masham, de Malesart et de Landeford de assensu domini fundi ... episcopi auctoritate fulcitur.* (*Dat' Venetiis in Rivo alto vii. kal. Julii.*) To Roger archbishop of York and the (dean and) chapter of York.

The pope has heard that, whereas the churches of Masham, Malzeard and Langford were granted and assigned to St Peter's church at York as a prebend, with the assent of the lord of the estate and the archbishop of York's authority, the canons of Newburgh challenge that concession and seek to void it, on the grounds of a grant made previously to themselves. The pope asserts that the assent of patrons must be sought and awaited in the granting of churches, but they cannot be canonically conferred without the bishop's authority. He therefore rules that the earlier concession should be preferred if it was made with the assent of the patron and the bishop's authority, or if the latter's agreement followed. But whichever was based on these two requirements should be preferred, even if it was the later concession.

JL 13882, 25 June 1177. *Claud.* 173; *Wig.* 4. 28; *Chelt.* 8. 1; *Cott.* 6. 42; eleven systematic collections; and York Cathedral Library, *Registrum magnum album,* part III, f. 93r. Pd *X* 3. 38. 20.
The York archival copy preserves the full address and date, and confirms the place-names as Masham and Kirkby Malzeard in Yorkshire, and Langford in Nottinghamshire (the decretal mss. omit the dean from the address, and wrongly transmit Masham as Ockham). The churches were on the estates of the Mowbray family, and the circumstances of the dispute between the canons of Newburgh and St Peter's church in York are recorded in the Mowbray charters, which parallel with unusual clarity the successive stages of the affair as summarized in Alexander's decretal. The churches were three in a group of seven granted to Newburgh by Samson d'Aubigny and Roger de Mowbray c. 1145; archbishop Henry Murdac's confirmation was sought, 1147-53, but there is no record that it was conceded. The three churches were among a group of six granted by Roger de Mowbray to St Peter's church in York in the years 1154-57, in the early years of Roger of York's archiepiscopate, and he witnessed the award. Subsequently, within the years 1163-69, the three churches were granted by Roger de Mowbray to St Peter's, to form a prebend in the church of York. The charters therefore attest the canons' claim that the grant to them was earlier; but the later grant to St Peter's church was confirmed by archbishop Roger's assent. These details match exactly those rehearsed by Alexander in his decretal of June 1177, but the outcome of the dispute needs further study. The copy of a Mowbray charter of 1186-90 (Oxford, Bodleian Library, ms. Dodsworth 94, f. 75v) records Nigel de Mowbray's confirmation of all his father's gifts to Newburgh, including the churches of Masham, Malzeard and Langford, but its authenticity has been queried. Later medieval lists of York jurisdictions include Masham and Kirkby Malzeard in the prebend of Masham. (For the Mowbray evidence, see D.E. Greenway, *Charters of the Honour of Mowbray, 1107-1191,* London 1972

[Oxford University Press for The British Academy], 138-41, 143-44, 151, 210-211: n[i] 196, 197, 199, 203, 214, 325, 326; see also W. PAGE, *Victoria history of the county of Yorkshire,* III, London 1913 [repr. Folkestone 1974], 88).

1009. *Super eo quod a nobis requisivit tua fraternitas utrum appellationi, quam quis metu litterarum ... fuisse interpositam.* To (Roger) archbishop of York.

The archbishop asked if full deference should be paid to an appeal launched by one of the parties through fear of letters which he heard his adversary had obtained from the pope, and whether the judge to whom the adversary secured papal letters has any powers. The pope replies that no deference should be paid to such an appeal, which it seems was launched to frustrate the legal process.

JL 14163, 1159-81. *Bridl.* 113; *Claud.* 101; *Chelt.* 17. 27; *Cott.* 3. 6d; *Pet.* 2. 13. 1d; *1 Rot.* 31. 10; *Gilb.* 2. 19. 3; *Fuld.* 2. 24. 3; *2 Comp.* 2. 19. 4. Pd *2 Comp.*; (and from *2 Comp.*): MANSI, 21. 1097.
The letter may well be part of a longer decretal not otherwise identified. Its address to York was unknown to *JL* (= « episcopo cuidam ») and *2 Comp.*; it is found in *Bridl., Claud.*; *1 Rot.* has « eidem » = « Eboracensi archiepiscopo »; and *Cott., Pet.* include the letter as the final chapter of *In eminenti ... Consuluisti,* to York (*WH* 552 above).

1058. *Veniens ad apostolice sedis clementiam W. clericus nobis proposuit quod, cum a R. patrono ecclesie de Wad. ... conferas et assignes.* To (Roger) archbishop of York.

The clerk W. alleged to the pope that he was presented to the archbishop for the church of Wath-upon-Dearne by the patron R., when the church was already vacant for three years, but the archbishop declined to put him in possession, although he was suitable, on the grounds that the right of patronage was disputed by the knight J. But the latter came to the church in the same week, and gave his assent to W., and conferred the church on him, as far as he had the right to do so. However, he later changed his mind, and consented to another clerk already well endowed with prebends and churches, so that by this action he could acquire the patronage. The clerk W. therefore appealed to the pope, and placed himself, the church and all its possessions under papal protection. The pope orders the recipient to confer the church on W., without leave of appeal, if he is suitable and was presented to the church by R. when it was vacant, and if J. later consented to him.

JL —, 1164-81 (? 1175-81). *Wig.* 4. 12; *Claustr.* 153; *Chelt.* 4. 28; *Cott.* 6. 54; *Tann.* 6. 3. 27; *Sang.* 7. 51; *1 Abr.* 7. 3. 4; *1 Rot.* 12. 13; *2 Dun.* 4. 54. Pd *Claustr.*; *Sang.*

The incipit « Veniens ad nos W. clericus » appears in *Wig.*, *Claustr.*, *Cott.*

This decretal must be read with *Proposuit nobis* (*WH* 748, *JL* —, 1164-81: pd *Claustr.* 150, *App.* 49. 11), which deals with the same case. The latter, to the bishop of Durham and the monks of Revesby, begins « Proposuit nobis dilectus filius noster Willelmus clericus presentium lator quod, cum ipse ad ecclesiam de Wad. (*varr.* Wadher, Walda) a Reinero Flandrensi venerabili fratri nostro Eboracensi archiepiscopo, apostolice sedis legato, presentatus fuisset ... », and so identifies the plaintiff clerk William and the patron Reiner the Fleming, and dates the case from Roger of York's appointment as legate in 1164, at the earliest. It mandates the recipients to investigate the case, if the archbishop does not promptly institute William in accordance with the papal mandate, on their instructions, to accept him for the church on the same terms as those expressed in *Veniens ad apostolice,* and to remove any other. If another has been intruded after William's presentation or appeal, the latter must be restored and receive the fruits from the time of the first presentation (cf. SCAMMELL, *Hugh du Puiset* ..., 83-84). The letters were apparently issued at the same time, the commission to Durham and Revesby as a precaution against the archbishop's non-compliance. Their most evident association in the collections is in the Durham ms. *2 Dun.* 53 and 54, where they appear together as marginal additions in a later hand. Reiner II the Fleming is well known in archival sources, and appears as a tenant of William Percy in the latter's feudal return in 1166 (H. HALL, *Liber Rubeus de Scaccario,* I, London 1896 [Rolls Series, 99], 426; for the Fleming family, see C.T. CLAY, *Early Yorkshire families* ..., 1973 [Yorkshire Archaeological Society: Record Series, 135], 33). Holtzmann suggested that Walden Stubbs (= Stubbs, Stubbis, Stubbeswalding; cf. *varr.* in collections: Wald. *Wig.*, Waldene *Claustr.*, Wall. *Chelt.*) in the Yorkshire West Riding as the location of the dispute. A more probable solution is Wath-upon-Dearne (= Wade, Wat[e], Wad., Waht.: A.H. SMITH, *The Place-names of the West Riding of Yorkshire*, I, Cambridge 1961 [English Place-name Society, 30], 118-20; cf. *varr.* in collections: Wad. *Tann.*, *Sang.* (before adjustment), *1 Abr.*, *1 Rot.*; and for *Proposuit nobis*: Wad., *Font.* 1. 35, Wadher, *App.* 49. 11). The Fleming family held lands in Wath-upon-Dearne, also in the West Riding (see A. HAMILTON THOMPSON and C.T. CLAY, *Fasti parochiales,* II ... 1943 [Yorkshire Arch. Soc.: Record Series, 107], 105). The Percy barony was divided between the earl of Warwick and Jocelin of Louvain in 1175, as a result of which Reiner the Fleming's Percy fee was thereafter held of Jocelin (see C.T. CLAY, *Early Yorkshire Charters* ..., 1963 [Yorkshire Arch. Soc.: Record Series, Extra Series, 9], 85-88). It is possible that Jocelin was the knight J. in dispute with Reiner over the patronage of the church of Wath-upon-Dearne, and that their rival claims resulted from the division of the Percy barony in 1175.

Abbreviations

Canones-Sammlungen = E. Friedberg, *Die Canones-Sammlungen zwischen Gratian und Bernhard von Pavia,* Leipzig 1897 (repr. Graz 1956).

Decretales ineditae = S. Chodorow and C. Duggan, from the papers of W. Holtzmann, *Decretales ineditae saeculi XII,* Città del Vaticano 1982 (*MIC,* 4).

Decretals to Lincoln = W. Holtzmann and E.W. Kemp, *Papal decretals relating to the diocese of Lincoln,* Hereford 1954 (Lincoln Record Society Publications, 47).

Duggan, *Decretal Collections* = C. Duggan, *Twelfth-century decretal collections and their importance in English history,* London 1963 (University of London Historical Studies, 12).

Holtzmann-Cheney = C.R. Cheney and M.G. Cheney, from the papers of W. Holtzmann, *Studies in the collections of twelfth-century decretals,* Città del Vaticano 1979 (*MIC,* 3).

JL = P. Jaffe, S. Loewenfeld, et al., *Regesta pontificum romanorum,* Leipzig 1885-1888.

Mansi = J.D. Mansi, *Sanctorum conciliorum nova et amplissima collectio,* Firenze 1759 — Venezia 1798.

Materials TB = J.C. Robertson and J.B. Sheppard, *Materials for the history of Thomas Becket, archbishop of Canterbury,* London 1875-85 (Rolls Series, 67).

MIC = *Monumenta Iuris Canonici, Series B: Corpus Collectionum,* Città del Vaticano.

Pd = printed in:

PU England = W. Holtzmann, *Papsturkunden in England,* I-III, Berlin 1930-31, 1935-36, Göttingen 1952 (Abhandlungen der Akademie der Wissenschaften in Göttingen, NF 25, Dritte F. 14-15, 33).

PU Frankreich = J. Ramackers, *Papsturkunden in Frankreich,* IV, Göttingen 1942 (Abh. Akad. Göttingen, Dritte F. 27).

PU Portugal = C. Erdmann, *Papsturkunden in Portugal,* Berlin 1927 (Abh. Akad. Göttingen, NF 22).

RW Calendar = M. CHENEY, *Roger, bishop of Worcester, 1164-79*, Cambridge 1980, *Appendix II: Calendar of papal letters*, 317-73.

RY Calendar = *Calendar of decretals to Roger of York*, Part II (b) of this paper.

SG = *Studia Gratiana.*

SINGER, *Neue Beiträge* = H. SINGER, *Neue Beiträge über die Dekretalensammlungen vor und nach Bernhard von Pavia*, Wien 1914 (Sitzungsberichte der Kais. Akademie der Wissenschaften in Wien, philos.-histor. Klasse, 171).

WH = WALTHER HOLTZMANN, *Regesta decretalium saeculi XII.*

ZRG Kan. Abt. = «Zeitschrift der Savigny-Stiftung für Rechtsgeschichte», Kanonistische Abteilung.

Sigla of decretal collections

The complete list of all known decretal collections of the twelfth-century, with full bibliographical details of editions, analyses and secondary literature, is provided in Holtzmann-Cheney, xx-xxxi, and *Decretales ineditae*, xix-xxxi.

1 Abr.	= *Abrincensis prima*: Singer, *Neue Beiträge*, 355-400.
Alan.	= *Coll. Alani*: R. Von Heckel, in *ZRG Kan. Abt.*, 29 (1940), 226-334.
Alan. app.	= Cf. above: *Alan.*, 309-334.
1 Alc.	= *Alcobacensis prima*: Holtzmann-Cheney, 8-25; Duggan, in *SG* 14 (1967), 51-71.
Ambr.	= *Ambrosiana*: Holtzmann-Cheney, 35-42.
App.	= *Appendix Concilii Lateranensis.*
— *Cr.*	= *editio princeps*: P. Crabbe, *Concilia omnia tam generalia quam particularia* (2nd edn. Cologne 1551), 2, 820-944; Mansi, 22, 248-453.
— *Lp.*	= Leipzig, Universitätsbibliothek, ms. 1242, ff. 73v-110v.
— *Ln.*	= Lincoln, Cathedral Chapter Library, ms. 121, ff. 1r-61r: Holtzmann-Cheney, 124-27.
Asl.	= *Fragm. Asloense*: Oslo, Staatsarchiv, 4 folios used as binding material (photocopies in W. Holtzmann files; present location unknown).
Aur.	= *Aureavallensis*: W. Holtzmann, in *ZRG Kan. Abt.*, 16 (1927), 77-115.
Bamb.	= *Bambergensis*: W. Deeters, *Die Bambergensis-gruppe der Dekretalensammlungen des 12. Jhdts.*, Bonn 1956 (Inaugural Dissertation ... der Philos. Fakultät die Rheinischen Friedrich Wilhelms-Universität).
— *A*	= Bamberg, Staatsbibl., ms. Can. 17 (P. 1. 11), ff. 1v-47r.
— *B*	= Amiens, Bibliothèque de la Ville, ms. 377, ff. 83r-133r.
— *C*	= Paris, Bibliothèque Nationale, ms. lat. 17971, ff. 153-184: as *Compendiensis*, Singer, *Neue Beiträge*, 8-67.
— *D*	= Tortosa, Biblioteca del Cabildo, ms. 40, ff. 1-91.
— *O*	= Oxford, Oriel College ms. **53**, ff. 340-49v (*olim* 240-49).

Belv.	= *Belverensis*: DUGGAN, *Decretal Collections*, 71-73, 154-62, (numerical concordance with *WH*: 212).
1 Berol.	= *Berolinensis prima*: J. JUNCKER, in *ZRG Kan. Abt.*, 13 (1942), 284-426.
Bridl.	= *Bridlingtonensis*: Oxford, Bodleian Library, ms. Bodley 357 (S.C. 2452), ff. 80r-133v.
Brug.	= *Brugensis*: *Canones-Sammlungen*, 136-70.
1, 3 Cant.	= *Cantuariensis prima, tertia*: DUGGAN, *Decretal Collections*, 73-76, 162-71, and pl. III, (numerical concordance with *WH*: 212).
Cantab.	= *Cantabrigiensis*: *Canones-Sammlungen*, 5-21.
Cass.	= *Casselana*: J.H. BOEHMER, *Corpus iuris canonici*, II (Halle 1747). DEETERS, *Bambergensisgruppe* ..., 7-9.
Chelt.	= *Cheltenhamensis*: London, British Library, ms. Egerton 2819, ff. 11r-102r.
Claud.	= *Claudiana*: London, British Library, ms. Cotton Claudius A. iv, ff. 189r-216r; HOLTZMANN-CHENEY, 132-34.
Claustr.	= *Claustroneoburgensis*: F. SCHÖNSTEINER, in « Jahrbuch des Stiftes Klosterneuburg », 2 (1909), 1-154.
1, 2 Comp.	= *Compilatio prima, secunda*: ANTONIO AGUSTÍN, *Antiquae collectiones decretalium*, Lérida 1576; reissued in *Opera omnia*, IV, Lucca 1769; E. FRIEDBERG, *Quinque compilationes antiquae necnon collectio canonum Lipsiensis*, Leipzig 1882 (repr. Graz 1956).
Cott.	= *Cottoniana*: London, British Library, ms. Cotton Vitellius E. xiii, ff. 204r-288r.
Cus.	= *Cusana*: HOLTZMANN-CHENEY, 66-74.
1 Dert.	= *Dertusensis prima*: W. HOLTZMANN, in *ZRG Kan. Abt.*, 16 (1927), 39-77.
Duac.	= *Duacensis*: HOLTZMANN-CHENEY, 64-65.
1 Dun.	= *Dunelmensis prima*: HOLTZMANN-CHENEY, 75-99; DUGGAN, *A Durham canonical manuscript of the late-twelfth century*, London/Edinburgh 1965 (Studies in Church History, 2), 179-85.
2 Dun.	= *Dunelmensis secunda*: HOLTZMANN-CHENEY, 300-18.
Eber.	= *Eberbacensis*: W. HOLTZMANN, in *ZRG Kan. Abt.*, 17 (1928), 548-55.
Erl.	= *Erlangensis*: Erlangen, Universitätsbibliothek, ms. 342, ff. 291r-306v; DEETERS, *Bambergensisgruppe* ..., 9-10.
Flor.	= *Florianensis*: HOLTZMANN-CHENEY, 43-63.
Font.	= *Fontanensis*: HOLTZMANN-CHENEY, 100-15.

Frcf.	= *Francofortana*:
— *Frcf.*	= Frankfurt, Stadt- und Universitätsbibliothek, ms. Barth. 60, ff. 2r-85r: S. KUTTNER, in *ZRG Kan. Abt.*, 22 (1933), 370-80.
— *Rot.*	= Paris, Bibliothèque Nationale, ms. lat. 3922A, ff. 173r-209r: HOLTZMANN-CHENEY, 160-68.
— *Trec.*	= Troyes, Bibliothèque de la Ville, ms. 961, ff. 1r-96v.
— *Max.*	= London, British Library, ms. Egerton 2901, ff. 1r-97v.
Fuld.	= *Fuldensis*: HECKEL, in *ZRG Kan. Abt.*, 29 (1940), 165-70 and 335-39.
Gilb.	= *Coll. Gilberti*: HECKEL, in *ZRG Kan. Abt.*, 29 (1940), 180-225.
Lips.	= *Lipsiensis*: E. FRIEDBERG, *Quinque compilationes antiquae* ..., 189-208; DEETERS, *Bambergensisgruppe* ..., 10-11.
Oriel.	= *Orielensis*: HOLTZMANN-CHENEY, 127-31.
1 Par.	= *Parisiensis prima*: *Canones-Sammlungen*, 45-63.
2 Par.	= *Parisiensis secunda*: *Canones-Sammlungen*, 21-45.
Pet.	= *Petrihusensis*: Cambridge, Peterhouse, mss. 193, final quire; 114, first and final quires; 193, first quire; 203, final quire; 180, first and final quires.
Reg.	= *Regalis*: London, British Library, ms. Royal 15. B. iv, ff. 107v-118v.
Roff.	= *Roffensis*: DUGGAN, *Decretal Collections*, 173-87, (numerical concordance with *WH*: 212).
1 Rot.	= *Rotomagensis prima*: HOLTZMANN-CHENEY, 160-207.
Sang.	= *Sangermanensis*: SINGER, *Neue Beiträge*, 68-354.
Tann.	= *Coll. Tanneri*: W. HOLTZMANN, in *Festschrift zur Feier des 200jähr. Bestehens der Akad. der Wissenschaften in Göttingen*, Göttingen 1951, 83-145.
Trin.	= *Trinitatis*: DUGGAN, in *Traditio*, 17 (1961), 506-26.
1 Vict.	= *Victorina prima*: HOLTZMANN-CHENEY, 26-34.
Wig.	= *Wigorniensis*: H.E. LOHMANN, *Collectio Wigorniensis*, in *ZRG Kan. Abt.*, 22 (1933), 36-187.
Wig. alt.	= *Wigorniensis altera*: DUGGAN, *Decretal Collections*, 152-54 and pl. I.
X	= *Decretales Gregorii IX*: E. FRIEDBERG, *Corpus iuris canonici*, II, Leipzig 1881.

IV

English secular magnates in the decretal collections

Almost a century ago, Maitland showed that more than a third of the permanently important decretals of Alexander III (1159-81) had English cases for their subject matter;[1] and the work of later scholars has revealed still more strikingly the English element in decretal collections of the later-twelfth century. In fact, almost forty per cent of all decretals in the collections had English recipients—reflecting the formative role of English collectors—and it is therefore not surprising that the collections shed more light on facets of English society than on those of any other part of Western Christendom.[2] The limited theme of the present paper is the role of English secular magnates, their interests and activities, as reflected in the collections. The treatment is merely selective, based on a small proportion of the relevant letters, preparatory to a more comprehensive survey. Yet this brief review lifts the veil on an exceedingly rich canvas of English political and social history. It is focused in turn on royal policies and purposes, patronage rights, marriage litigation, and a range of miscellaneous topics.[3]

---

[1] F.W. Maitland, *Roman canon law in the Church of England* (London 1898) 123-24.

[2] Cf. W. Holtzmann, 'Über eine Ausgabe der päpstlichen Dekretalen des 12. Jahrhunderts', *Nachrichten Akad. Göttingen* (1945) 15-36, esp. 34, Anhang 1; Z.N. Brooke, 'The effect of Becket's murder on papal authority in England', *Cambridge Historical Journal* 2 (1928) 213-28; idem, *The English Church and the papacy* (Cambridge 1931) 212-14; C. Duggan, *Twelfth-century decretal collections and their importance in English history* (London 1963) 140-51; idem, *Canon law in medieval England: the Becket dispute and decretal collections* (Variorum CS 151; London 1982) III and 'Addenda et corrigenda' 1-5; idem, 'Decretals of Alexander III to England', *Miscellanea Rolando Bandinelli papa Alessandro III*, ed. F. Liotta (Siena 1986) 85-151 (hereafter 'Decretals of Alexander III'); idem, '*Improba pestis falsitatis*: Forgeries and the problem of forgery in twelfth-century decretal collections (with special reference to English cases)', *Fälschungen im Mittelalter* (MGH Schriften 33; Hanover 1988) 2.319-61; M.G. Cheney, *Roger, bishop of Worcester, 1164-1179* (Oxford 1980: hereafter *Roger of Worcester*) esp. 193-212.

[3] On patronage rights, cf. P. Landau, *Ius patronatus: Studien zur Entwicklung des Patronats im Dekretalenrecht und der Kanonistik des 12. und 13. Jahrhunderts* (Cologne/Vienna 1975). On marriage questions, cf. C. Donahue, 'The dating of Alexander the Third's marriage decretals: Dauvillier revisited after fifty years', ZRG Kan. Abt. 69 (1982) 70-124 (hereafter 'Alexander III's marriage decretals'); C. Duggan, 'Equity and compassion in papal marriage decretals to England', *Love and marriage in the twelfth century*, edd. W. van Hoecke and A. Welkenhuysen (Leuven 1981) 59-87 (hereafter 'Equity and compassion'); and Cheney, *Roger of Worcester* passim.

Such categories are not mutually exclusive—royal interests sometimes include the patronage of churches, or involvement in dynastic marriages; marriage disputes, inheritance and property conflicts, and patronage rights are at times interwoven within a single case.[4]

I. Royal interests and policies

The English king Henry II figures very prominently in the collections. He was the recipient of three decretals of sufficient importance to be recorded in the collections, is named in others, and cited by un-named reference or implication in many. It is a reflection of the regional provenance of the collections that some of these letters were of interest primarily to English and Anglo-Norman collectors, and were not more generally recorded. Political interests provide the context of some, but many defined important canonical principles and were widely received.

A. Dynastic and political issues

The king's concern with the security of his dynasty and the succession was reflected at an early date in his reign. In *Quanto per carissimum* (17 or 20 June 1161), to archbishop Roger of York, Alexander III granted Henry the right to have his first-born son crowned by York, Canterbury then being vacant.[5] The pope acknowledged the king's devotion to him (in that time of schism and crisis), and wished to increase his honour: 'quanto nos eum propter sue devotionis constantiam maiori affectione diligimus, et cariorem in nostris visceribus retinemus, tanto ad ea que ad honorem et incrementum et exultationem ipsius et suorum cognoscimus pertinere, libentius et promptius aspiramus'. The coronation was in

---

[4] See passim below, esp. sections I.C, II.B at n.36, and III.B and C. Studies on English bishops as papal judges delegate include numerous cases involving English secular magnates: see esp. A. Morey, *Bartholomew of Exeter, bishop and canonist* (Cambridge 1937) 44-78; idem and C.N.L. Brooke, *Gilbert Foliot and his letters* (Cambridge 1965) 230-44; Cheney, *Roger of Worcester* 113-65 and Appendices; cf. also Duggan, *artt. citt.* nn. 2 and 3 supra, and 5 infra. The volume of *Decretales ineditae saeculi XII* is especially rich in English cases not previously printed: cf. nn. 17, 33-35, 42, 46 and 47 infra.

[5] WH 772, JL 11353, 17 or 20 June 1161; Printed in *Materials for the history of Thomas Becket, archbishop of Canterbury*, edd. J.C. Robertson and J.B. Sheppard (RS 67; London 1881; hereafter *Materials TB*), 6.206-07 no. 310: cf. A. Duggan (Heslin), 'The coronation of the Young King', *Studies in Church History* 2 (1965) 177-78; C. Duggan, 'Decretals of Alexander III' 137; idem, 'St Thomas of Canterbury and aspects of the Becket dispute in the decretal collections', *Mediaevalia Christiana, XIe-XIIIe siècles: Hommage à Raymonde Foreville* ed. C.E. Viola (Paris 1989) 87-138 (hereafter 'St Thomas of Canterbury') 97 no. 6.

the event deferred until 14 June 1170, in the dramatically altered circumstances of the closing phase of Becket's exile, in defiance of both Canterbury's rights and papal prohibition. This later crisis also left its record in the collections, in the letters *Licet nobis*,[6] to York and Durham, and *Oportuerat vos*,[7] to London, Salisbury, Exeter, Chester, Rochester and St Asaph (both 16 September 1170), recording the papal sentences on prelates who had officiated or were present at the ceremony. These were the censures whose publication by Thomas provoked the reaction which led to his death on 29 December 1170. They are very familiar from non-canonical sources, but are also found in a few English or Anglo-Norman collections, one of which (*Abrincensis prima*, from Mont-Saint-Michel) uniquely preserves, as a marginal addition, the king's self-exculpatory letter *Ob reuerentiam*, to the pope on hearing of Thomas's death.[8]

Political factors likewise provide the setting of *Non est vobis* (*ex* 1173), to the prelates and clergy of England and the English king's continental lands.[9] In view of its condemnation of Henry II's actions, it is perhaps significant that no English primitive collection includes this letter, but it was received by the early Italian collections *Cusana* and *Berolinensis prima*[10] and transmitted through various systematic collections to the *Decretales* of 1234. The context of the letter is the revolt of Henry's sons against him in 1173-74 and the consequent general hostility of his external foes and disaffected subjects in the island and on the continent. As the mandate records, Henry detained his sons' wives, the French king's daughters (Margaret and Alice), and Louis VII sought papal intervention to secure their release.[11] The pope commissioned the archbishop of Tarentaise, the bishop of Clermont, and the prior of Chartreuse (or the prior of Mont-Dieu) to admonish the English king to restore the wives within forty days of receipt of the mandate, failing which all divine office should be suspended in the province in which they were detained or to which transferred, except for infant baptism and

---

[6] WH 618, JL 11836, 16 Sept. 1170; Printed in *Materials TB* 7.364-68 no. 701: cf. Duggan, 'Decretals of Alexander III' 133-34; idem, 'St Thomas of Canterbury' 106 no. 17.

[7] WH 692, JL 11835, 16 Sept. 1170; Printed in *Materials TB* 7.360-64 no. 700; *Radulfi de Diceto decani Lundonensis opera historica*, ed. W. Stubbs (RS 68: hereafter *Diceto*): cf. 1.340; Duggan, 'St Thomas of Canterbury' 105-06 no. 16.

[8] *Abrincensis prima*: Avranches, bibl. de la Ville 149, fol. 87v, lower margin, (? January) 1171; Printed in *Materials TB* 7.440 no. 739 (from E. Martène and U. Durand, *Thesaurus novus anecdotorum* 1 [Paris 1717] 559): cf. Duggan, 'St Thomas of Canterbury' 106-07 no. 18.

[9] WH 669, JL 12248, *ex* 1173; Printed (abbrev.): X 4.1.11; (complete): A. Duchesne, *Historiae Francorum scriptores* (Parisiis 1641) 769, Bouquet, *Recueil des historiens des Gaules et de la France* 15.940, Mansi, 21.1032, PL 200.965.

[10] *1 Berol.* 46, *Cus.* 42.

[11] Margaret was married to the young king Henry; Alice was betrothed to Richard, but they were never in fact married.

penance for the dying. The recipients of *Non est vobis* were ordered to induce Henry II to comply with the mandate and to make the interdict effective, if he did not do so. The precise outcome of the mandate is not clear, but Henry evidently circumvented its provisions, since the French king's daughters were still in his company when he returned to England in 1174.[12] The decretal proved of interest to the glossators for the penalty of interdict of a whole province prescribed in this situation, the *Tanner* collection noting in a marginal comment—'Ecce quod pro delicto unius tota terra interdicitur'.[13]

B. Jurisdictional conflicts

The importance of the decretal collections in the context of the Becket dispute remains a controversial subject, but there is no doubt that numerous decretals issued in the course of the quarrel and its aftermath dealt explicitly with royal interests, and those of secular magnates more generally.[14] The dispute was essentially a jurisdictional conflict, in which the crisis and Thomas's exile afforded a more favourable opportunity for secular encroachments in areas of jurisdiction claimed by the Church. Thus, in *Ad audientiam nostram* (19 May 1168), to all the bishops of England, the pope condemned an evil custom which had arisen in that time of strife between king and archbishop, whereby laymen widely throughout England conferred churches and benefices by their own authority:[15]

> quod post instantem turbationem que inter karissimum in Christo filium nostrum Henricum, illustrem Anglorum regem, et venerabilem fratrem nostrum Thomam Cantuariensem archiepiscopum exigentibus peccatis emersit, quedam prava consuetudo in partibus vestris inolevit, scilicet quod laici ecclesias et ecclesiastica beneficia soleant passim in regno Anglorum quibus vellent conferre, et auctoritate sua clericos investire.

He utterly quashed such grants by laymen and ordered the bishops to set aside all fear, favour and prohibition—'cuiuslibet timore, gratia et prohibitione postposita' —and compel the clerks involved to surrender whatever they had received. Doubtless perceiving the reality of power in England at that time, the pope de-

---

[12] Cf. *Diceto*, 1.382: 'se cum tota domo sua praeparavit ad redditum, reginam Alienor, reginam Margaritam, filium et filiam, Johannem et Johannam, et uxores filiorum suorum, intra paucos dies secum adducens'; and *Gesta regis Henrici secundi Benedicti abbatis*, ed. W. Stubbs (London 1867) 1.72: 'Et adduxit secum utramque reginam...'

[13] *Tann.* 7.5.20, p. 698.

[14] Cf. now Duggan, 'St Thomas of Canterbury' passim.

[15] WH 20, JL 11398, 19 May 1168; Printed in *Materials TB* 6.419-20 no. 413: cf. Duggan, 'St Thomas of Canterbury' 104 no. 14.

clared the clerks excommunicate, if the bishops themselves were remiss in this. Only a single English manuscript preserves this letter.[16]

Three decretals addressed to the king have a special importance in the context of jurisdictional conflicts. At some uncertain date, conceivably during the controversy and almost certainly not later than the agreement between Henry II and the legate Pierleoni in 1175-76, the king was himself the recipient of *Quanto superni*, in which the pope asserted the principle of clerical immunity in an actual case, where the subdeacon I. was suspected of murder.[17] The king's bailiffs or ministers must not seize him or draw him to secular judgment, even if guilty, which the pope does not think is evident. The letter is of interest, not only for its clear enunciation of a famous canonical doctrine, but also for the pope's reminder to the king of his responsibilities in respect of churches and ecclesiastics:

> Nihil enim est in quo omnipotentem Deum magis valeas offendere, quam si ecclesias et ecclesiasticos viros per te et per tuos indebite molestare presumpseris, quibus teneris ex commissa tibi potestate regie tuitionis presidium exhibere.

In similar vein, the pope again addressed the king in *Quanto te superna* (? *c.* 1179), on the patronage of churches.[18] Following an admonitory *arenga*, he affirmed the Church's superior jurisdiction in patronage disputes, in a sentence which became the classical definition: 'Causa patronatus ecclesiarum ita coniuncta est et connexa ecclesiasticis causis quod non nisi ecclesiastico iudice diffiniri valet'. And in *Magnificentie tue* (1159-81), in response to a notable instance of royal petition on behalf of an individual magnate, the pope declined to accede to Henry II's request that the knight R. could remove a clerk from the church of 'Bliburg.', which he had canonically acquired.[19]

---

[16] *Belverensis* 21: Oxford Bodl. MS e Mus. 249 (a codex of Gilbert Foliot materials), fol. 129va-130ra.

[17] WH 774, JL —, 1159-75/76; found only in the Cottonian and Peterhouse collections, *Cott.* 5.27 and *Pet.* 4.38; Printed in *Decretales ineditae saeculi XII*, from the papers of W. Holtzmann, ed. and revised by S. Chodorow and C. Duggan (MIC Series B, 4; Città del Vaticano 1982; hereafter *Decretales ineditae*) 59-60 no. 35: cf. Duggan, 'St Thomas of Canterbury' 99-100 no. 9.

[18] WH 775, JL 13727, ? *c.* 1179; Printed in *App.* 47.4; (abbrev.) X 2.1.3: cf. Duggan, 'St Thomas of Canterbury', 125-26 no. 38. The decretal was cited in the commentary *De iure naturali*: K.W. Nörr, 'Die Summen *De iure naturali* und *De multiplici iuris divisione*', ZRG Kan. Abt. 48 (1962) 145 no. 7. Cf. Landau, *Ius patronatus* 124, 127 and 206-10. For the English context of the letter, cf. M.G. Cheney, 'The compromise of Avranches of 1172 and the spread of canon law in England', EHR 56 (1941) 190-95; J.W. Gray, 'The *ius presentandi* in England from the Constitutions of Clarendon to Bracton', ibid. 67 (1952) 481-509, esp. 481-90; and W.L. Warren, *Henry II* (London 1973) 542-46.

[19] WH 639, JL 13726, 1159-81. Printed in *App.* 50.32, *1 Comp.* 3.33.26: cf. Duggan, 'St Thomas of Canterbury' 124-25 no. 37.

C. Royal influence in the acquisition of churches

Many decretals concerned with the acquisition of benefices and with showing favour to laymen or religious refer to Henry II by name. Royal pressure, even to the extent of fear—'metu regio cooperante'—is sometimes expressly cited. The intervention of Queen Eleanor is recorded in one letter, and that of King William of Scotland in others. The decretal *Constitutus in presentia* (1159-81), to the archbishop of York, records the complaint of Thomas Barre that, after presentation to the church of Ripley by the patron William Trussebut, he was inducted at the prayers of the English queen—'ad preces carissime in Christo filie nostre Anglorum regine in imaginariam possessionem', but his right was challenged by Bernard, nephew of the preceding possessor.[20] The king of Scotland's territorial interests in England are attested in the well-known decretal *Audita querela* (1165-78), to the bishop of Worcester and the archdeacon of Ely, involving the churches of Sandy and Potton, in Bedfordshire: the Scottish king's clerk Thomas de Paraviso had acquired the church of Potton at his presentation, but was challenged by the parson of Sandy.[21] And in a comparable context, *Dilectus filius* (1174-80), to the bishop of Bath, responded to Earl Simon of Northampton's complaint that the Scottish king, while in occupation of his patrimony, had disposed of churches within his patronage, without consulting him.[22] Both the complaint and the decretal postdate the capture of the Scottish king by Henry II's forces at Alnwick in 1174.

II. Secular magnates and church patronage

The rights of secular magnates are touched upon more frequently in patronage disputes than in any other topic in the collections.[23] The patron of a church might be an ecclesiastic, a religious community, or a layman, and in the decretals

---

[20] WH 179, JL —, 1159-81; Printed (incomplete) in *Claustr.* 340, *Brug.* 45.4; final passage: Duggan, 'Decretals of Alexander III' 121-22.

[21] WH 97, JL 14143, 1165-78; Printed in *App.* 22.4, X 2.13.4: cf. Cheney, *Roger of Worcester* 153, 278-79, App. I.47, and 322-23, App. II.12. The letter also appears in abbreviated form, beginning *Licet nuntius Hugonis*. The identification of Sandy and Potton was made by Maitland in a famous passage: 'Anyone who for his sins has endured the railway journey between Oxford and Cambridge will guess that the one village is Sandy, and the other Potton; but to the decretists the whereabouts of these places was less than nothing': *Roman canon law* 123.

[22] WH 364, JL 13764, 1174-81; Printed in *App.* 47.2, *2 Comp.* 3.24.1: cf. Landau, *Ius patronatus* 200-02.

[23] All aspects of church patronage, with copious citation of the decretals, are authoritatively treated in Landau, *Ius patronatus*, passim: cf. notes 18 and 22 supra, and 24, 25, 27-29 and 31 infra.

he was frequently a secular lord, often referred to as the *patronus*, or the *dominus fundi*, the lord of the land forming the church's endowment. He was perhaps the founder or the founder's heir, or the husband of the heiress; but the right of patronage could be transferred from one to another. Of the large number of decretals which relate in some way to patronage rights and disputes arising over them, some record the pope's advice to bishops on principles of general application, but most respond to specific enquiries, in which the churches and their patrons were named. Despite the decretal copyists' well-known propensity to disregard or abbreviate historical details, many identities are still clearly preserved or can be deduced.

A. General principles

Decretal statements of doctrine on the relative functions of bishops and lay patrons most commonly assert the Church's rights, though those of lay patrons are scrupulously safeguarded in individual cases. Two decretals of Alexander III to Roger of York assert the essential authority of the bishop, without which the lay presentation has no validity. In *Inter ceteras* (1160-76), the pope speaks of lay patrons who grant churches without episcopal consent, but then (induced by penitence) present others to the bishops, who institute them.[24] In such a case, the later presentation must stand—'concessione priori, que nulla est, omnino evacuata. Non enim licet laicis clericos in ecclesiis presumptione propria ordinare'. The problem of successive presentations occurred again in *Relatum est nobis* (1179-81), relating apparently to an actual case.[25] In this instance, though both nominees were suitable, the bishop did not institute the first, but accepted the second, who then held corporal possession. The pope ruled in favour of the latter, citing incidently a Roman law dictum, because of the necessary role of the bishop—'in casu isto melior sit conditio possidentis, quoniam antequam presentatio per diocesianum episcopum adprobetur, ratam non est quod a patrono fuerit inchoatum'; and he proceeded to reject the validity of instruments drawn up by lay patrons, recording concessions or grants with such words as 'concessi vel dedi ecclesiam et presenti carta firmavi', since nothing is given unless the bishop's consent is added 'nihil datum videtur; a laico enim ecclesia non potest de iure conferri'.

---

[24] WH 590 a-d, JL 13878(abc), 14346(d), 28 April 1160-76; Printed in *App.* 41.1, 41.7 = 7.3, 36.5 = 7.4, 15.3; X 1.3.4, 1.29.2, 2.27.9, 3.38.10: Duggan, 'Decretals of Alexander III' 132-33; and Landau, *Ius patronatus* 164 nn.577-78.

[25] WH 880, JL 14346, 1179-81; Printed in *App.* 15.1+2, X 3.4.4 + 3.38.5: Landau, *Ius patronatus* 70-71, 77-79, 83-84, 89-90, 155-56, 159-60, 165 n.579, 179 n.633; and Duggan, 'Decretals of Alexander III' 141-42.

The pope's prudence was revealed in a letter concerned mainly with frustratory tactics. In *Ex tenore litterarum* (1159-74), to William of Norwich, Alexander dealt among other matters with the wearisome litigation which the bishop endured on the death of parsons or patrons, and replied that the bishop should furnish the parsons with his own legal instruments and those of the patrons, so that, on the death of the parson, neither his son nor a vicar nor anyone else might hinder the bishop's right of conferring the church on a suitable person.[26] And in a letter of much historical interest, *Consultationibus singulorum* (1173-76), to Simon of St Albans, Alexander ruled on the problem arising where there was doubt concerning a patron's right at the time of presentation.[27] If a clerk was instituted by the ordinary at the presentation of one who was then thought to be the patron, but the right of patronage was by judicial decision later acquired by another, he should not be removed, if the presenter had possession at the time. If, in contrast, hwas not in fact the patron or possessor of the patronage, but was merely thought to be so, by English custom the clerk could be removed—'secundum consuetudinem Anglie poterit ab ecclesia removeri'.

The problem was treated later by Lucius III from a different aspect. In *Tua nos fraternitas* (1181-85), to John of Norwich, he drew a significant distinction between lay and religious patrons: if a patron presents a suitable clerk to the bishop, but then requests acceptance of another, although the first was not refused, the issue can be left to the bishop's discretion, if the patron is a layman, whereas the first has the better right if the presentation belongs to a college or religious person.[28] The letter also condemns the settlement of patronage disputes between laymen and religious, whereby the layman secures free right of presentment, but the religious obtain a new or larger portion in the church. Such an agreement is simoniacal and illegal, and the religious should have no advantage from it. As for the appropriation of churches by religious communities, by the grant of lay patrons, Alexander III had written to the religious and clergy of the York province, in *Cura pastorali* (1160-76): religious cannot acquire churches in this way without the bishop's consent, nor retain them except by long prescription or the bishop's later consent:[29]

> nisi longa fuerit prescriptione munitus aut postea diocesiani episcopi habuerit forte consensum. Nos enim, cum laici non possint in alios, nisi ius quod habent, trans-

---

[26] WH 488 a-d, JL 12253(abc), 14146(d), 1159-March/April 1174; Printed in *Claustr.* 132, *App.* 10.5, 26.3, X 2.28.4, 2.20.20: cf. Duggan, '*Improba pestis falsitatis*' 331-33 no. 5, with text.

[27] WH 184 abc, JL 12636.II, 8 April 1173-76; Printed in *App.* 7.17, 15.20, X 1.29.10, 3.38.19, 3.24.4: cf. Landau, *Ius patronatus* 70, 74-76, 80-82, 89-90, 153-54 and nn.547, 550 and 552, 195, 197-98, 200-05.

[28] WH 1039 abc, JL 14029(ac), 15186(b), 1181-85; Printed in *App.* 17.4, 15.8, *1 Abr.* app. 18, X 2.24.11, 1.36.9, 3.38.24: cf. Landau, *Ius patronatus* 156-59, 170-71 n.597.

[29] WH 329, JL 13893, 23 January 1160-76; Printed in *App.* 15.9, X 3.38.11: cf. Landau, *Ius patronatus* 70, 72.

ferre, huiusmodi concessiones viribus carere decernimus et irritas penitus esse sancimus.

B. Individual cases

Numerous decretals dealing with specific patronage disputes—with named persons, churches and religious communities—fix the enquiry more securely in English society. Among the English magnates so identified are Hugh de Lacy and earl Roger of Hereford, together with William of Poitou and Walter of Mayenne, Simon of Northampton, Hugh of Norfolk, William de Lucy, Bertram de Bulmer, Rainer the Fleming and Jocelin of Louvain, Richard de Lucy, William Trussebut, Richard Grammaticus, Hugh de Moreton, Johel and Reginald de Valletort, Arnold de Percy, Philip de Colombières and Ralph Brito.[30] Various knights are recorded simply by their initials, some of whom will doubtless be identified by further study.

Several decretals show lay patrons in conflict with religious houses over appointments to churches. The respective roles of bishops and lay patrons in this context were defined by the pope in *Dilecti filii nostri* (1170-73), to the dean and archdeacon of Lincoln and the abbot of Rievaulx.[31] In a dispute between the canons of Guisborough and the clerk Robert over the church of Crathorne in Yorkshire, previously commissioned to the dean of York and the prior of Newburgh, the canons had argued their claim by the grant of the *dominus fundi*, but the clerk maintained his by the gift of the archbishop of York. The pope had instructed the earlier judges that the archbishop's gift should prevail over the lay grant, since it was the function of bishops to confer ecclesiastical benefices and of lay patrons to give assent—'episcoporum est ecclesiastica beneficia conferre, laicorum vero, qui habent in ecclesia ius patronatus, assensum prebere, quibus in concessionibus ecclesiarum illud est observandum quod sancti patres reservare noscuntur'. But the canons' messenger had meanwhile informed the pope that, with the consent and authority of the former archbishop Thurstan of York, Arnold de Perci had granted them the church of Crathorne and other churches built on his land, 'secundum consuetudinem terre', to hold in full and free possession after the deaths of the parsons in them at that time. Uncertain of the truth of the matter, the pope commissioned the new judges to investigate and resolve the

[30] Cf. *sub nominibus*: *Decretales ineditae*; Duggan, 'Decretals of Alexander III'; Cheney, *Roger of Worcester*; et infra, passim.

[31] WH 354, JL 14085, 1170-73; Printed in *App.* 15.22, *1 Comp.* 3.33.24, W. Holtzmann and E.W. Kemp, *Papal Decretals relating to the diocese of Lincoln in the twelfth century* (Lincoln Record Society 47; Lincoln 1954; hereafter *Decretals to Lincoln*) 6-9 no. 4: cf. Landau, *Ius patronatus* 75, 150-55, 192 n.682, 212 n.746.

case. In the event, a contract was agreed, whereby the canons gave the church to Robert for a yearly pension of half a mark.[32]

Almost certainly at an early date in his pontificate, Alexander III condemned the improper grant of the patronage of the church of Sheriff Hutton in the North Riding, which the former abbot Geoffrey of York transferred to Bertram de Bulmer and his heirs—'de voluntate potius quam de iure'. In *Ad aures nostras*, to Roger of York, Alexander asserted that the patronage of churches should be transferred from laymen to churches, not from churches to laymen—'cum patronatus ecclesiarum non ab ecclesiis ad laicos sed a laicis ad ecclesias sint transferendi'.[33] He ordered the archbishop to revoke the grant, though it seems from cartulary evidence that the mandate was not effective. The decretal marks one stage in a long-protracted dispute between the monks of St Mary's abbey in York and the Bulmer family.

In *Causam que inter* (1164-79), a letter of outstanding political interest, Alexander commissioned the bishops of Exeter and Worcester to resolve a patronage dispute between two *nobiles viri* over the church of Walton.[34] With evident concern for conflicting jurisdictions, he affirmed his unwillingness to write on such a matter, but nevertheless preferred the issue to be resolved by ecclesiastics rather than by secular judges—'Licet autem super huiusmodi inviti scribamus, maluimus tamen ea coram ecclesiasticis personis tractari quam ad examen secularium personarum tractanda perferri'. The letter survives only in the mutilated Cottonian collection, with its historical details almost undecipherable, but the rival claimants were almost certainly Richard Grammaticus, the feudal tenant of Bickerton, and a member of the de Arches family, lords of Thorp Arch. All three locations—Walton, Bickerton, and Thorp Arch—are close neighbors in the Yorkshire West Riding.

Not infrequently, disputes over patronage were ended by composition. An alleged abuse by a lay patron is recorded in *Ex conquestione prioris* (1173-78), to the bishops of Exeter and Worcester.[35] The canons of Huntingdon complained that R. Pyel had granted them the *ius patronatus* of the church of Isham in Northamptonshire, but later secured the institution of a certain clerk in the church, without consulting them. The pope ordered the judges to remove the clerk, if the charges were established, and to allow no one to be instituted there

---

[32] Holtzmann-Kemp, *Decretals to Lincoln* 9 n.

[33] WH 53, JL —, 1159-81 (? 1159-60); Printed in *Decretales ineditae* 121-23 no. 70: cf. Duggan, 'Decretals of Alexander III' 118.

[34] WH 118, JL —, 1164-79; Printed in *Decretales ineditae* 98-99 no. 55: cf. Cheney, *Roger of Worcester* 324, App. II.16.

[35] WH 401, JL —, 1164-79 (?1173-78); Printed in *Decretales ineditae* 96-97 no. 54: cf. Cheney, *Roger of Worcester* 339-40, App. II.47.

except at the community's presentation. The outcome of the dispute was evidently a compromise, with the patronage divided, since a moiety of the patronage of Isham was held by Huntingdon Priory in the early thirteenth century, the other half being in lay hands.

A complex interplay of patronage and marriage interests is strikingly illustrated in *Querimoniam prioris* (? c. 1176), to Roger of Worcester.[36] The church of Painsick had formerly been granted by Hugh de Lacy to the canons of Llanthony in Gloucestershire. Earl Roger of Hereford, husband of Hugh's granddaughter and heiress Cecilia, later recognized the concession, and the *quondam* bishop John of Worcester invested the brethren, who then held peaceful possession. But Roger and Cecilia were separated, and Cecilia married William of Poitou; and, when William died, she married Walter of Mayenne. Walter withdrew the fruits of the church from Llanthony and assigned them to the priest Roger, claiming that the bishop's institution was of no effect, since Cecilia was at the relevant time in the power of the man from whom she was later separated, and that her patrimony was not fully restored unless she was able to do as she wished with the church, which was in her patronage. The pope declared it absurd that the ordination of churches should be changed with each such change of patron—'absurdum videtur omnino et ab ecclesia Dei penitus eliminandum ut ad singulas patronorum secundum humanam conditionem mutationes ecclesiarum debeant ordinationes mutari'. The dispute was resolved in the presence of the bishops of Exeter and Worcester, with the agreement of Walter and Cecilia. The priest Roger resigned the church, and its concession to Llanthony was confirmed by the judges. Roger was then admitted as perpetual vicar by the bishop of Worcester, at the presentation of the prior and brethren of Llanthony.

The *nobilis vir* William Trussebut appears in two decretals: as the *dominus fundi* of the church of Ripley, recording the English queen's intervention (*Constitutus in presentia*, to the archbishop of York, 1159-81);[37] and as patron of the church of 'Blesebia', most probably Ulceby in Lincolnshire. The clerk G. complained that he had bought half the tithes and oblations of the church for one year from the parson, but the patron William Trussebut took them away, took the church also from the clerk's brother, and gave it to the king's chaplain Geoffrey, who gave it in turn to the canons of Thornton. In an interesting ruling in *Constitutus in presentia G. clericus* (1159-81), to unknown recipients, the pope declared that it was not fitting to sell tithes and oblations, but it was not forbid-

---

[36] WH 790, JL 14141, ? c. 1176; Printed in *App.* 15.7, X 3.38.9: cf. Cheney, *Roger of Worcester* 354, App. II.72; and ibid. 144 and 264-65, App. I.31 and 32.

[37] Cf. n. 20 supra.

den to sell them for one year, so the judges should restore them to the complainant, with compensation for injuries.[38]

Rainer the Fleming also appears in two decretals, issued simultaneously in a single case. The clerk W. alleged that the patron Rainer presented him to the church of Wath-upon-Dearne in Yorkshire, but the archbishop of York declined to put him into possession because the *ius patronatus* was disputed by the knight Jocelin. The latter also conferred the church on W., but later agreed to another. In *Veniens ad apostolice* (? 1175-81), to the archbishop of York, the pope ordered the archbishop to confer the church on W., if he was presented by Rainer when the church was vacant, and if Jocelin later consented to him.[39] The second mandate, *Proposuit nobis*, ordered the bishop of Durham and the monks of Revesby to give effect to the pope's instructions, if the archbishop did not promptly do so. The background of these letters was almost certainly the division of the Percy barony in 1175, between the earl of Warwick and Jocelin of Louvain, which resulted in Jocelin holding Rainer's Percy fee.[40]

In a dispute with the bishop of Hereford, over the *ius patronatus* of the churches of Moreton Valence and Whaddon in Gloucestershire, Hugh de Moreton appealed to the pope, but later conceded the bishop of Hereford's claim. The bishop had drawn him to the archbishop's court by papal commission, but Hugh had appealed, feeling himself oppressed—'sentiens se gravari'. The archbishop thereupon placed him under excommunication, and the churches under interdict, because appeal had been prohibited. The decretal *Significavit nobis* (1174-77), to the archbishop of Canterbury and the bishop of Exeter, responded to Hugh's complaint to the pope.[41] Alexander III affirmed his duty to look to the welfare of all—'ad nostrum spectat officium universorum saluti consulere', ordered the judges to take assurances from Hugh, lift the sentence, and proceed to a conclusion. In the subsequent hearing, Hugh confirmed the churches to Hereford, reserving the rights of Worcester, and recognized his father Roger's gift of the churches to form a prebend of Hereford.

---

[38] WH 171, JL 14193, 1159-1177/78; Printed in *2 Comp.* 3.11.1; Holtzmann-Kemp, *Decretals to Lincoln* 22-23, no. 9. The king's chaplain Geoffrey became provost of Beverley after Becket's elevation; he became chancellor to the Young King, and was drowned in 1177.

[39] WH 1058, JL —, 1164-81 (?1175-81); Printed in *Claustr.* 153, *Sang.* 7.51: cf. Duggan, 'Decretals of Alexander III' 145-46.

[40] WH 748, JL —, 1164-81 (?1175-81); Printed in *Claustr.* 150, *App.* 49.11 cf. Duggan, 'Decretals of Alexander III' 146.

[41] WH 971, JL 13812, 1174-77; Printed in *Claustr.* 195, *Lips.* 52.11: cf. Cheney, *Roger of Worcester* 363, App. II.90A; and ibid. 260-62, App. I.28 and 28A, c. 19 March 1177.

III. Secular magnates in marriage disputes

In recording the interests of English secular magnates, marriage decretals are numerically second only to those relating to patronage disputes. The status of the parties is sometimes uncertain; but even in such cases it is frequently evident that secular magnates and their interests were involved, and their substantial social standing can be inferred, even where no rank is stated. In some decretals the identity of the parties is now recorded by their initial letters only—the knight R., the noble lady R., and so forth. But powerful lords are often named in the letters—including Hugh de Lacy and Roger of Hereford, William FitzGodric, Francus de Bohun and Ralph de Arderne, Gilbert of St Leger and Hugh of Polstead, Hugh de Ralegh, Robert of Manston, Walter of Woodhill (Wahull/Odell), and Edwin of Balsall, to name but a few.[42] Even where no evidence of identity is recorded, a phase in otherwise well-known litigation is sometimes found at times in the collections, notably that of Richard of Anstey and Mabel de Francheville over the inheritance of William de Sackville's estate, the issue turning on the legitimacy of Mabel's mother.[43]

A. Litigants in the curia

A surprisingly large number of lay litigants presented their cases in person in the curia and brought back the pope's commissions. Their status is not always mentioned, but they can scarcely have been of small material means. A typical example is recorded in Alexander III's decretal *Lator presentium R.* (1175-80), to the bishop of Exeter and the abbot of Ford.[44] The commission deals with a property claim of R. against his uncle Hugh, concerning 40 acres of land. Their

---

[42] Cf. Duggan, 'Equity and compassion' 59-87, esp. 68-85; Donahue, 'Alexander III's marriage decretals' 74-79: WH 12, 439, 723. Most of the lords listed here occur in the present paper. Additionally, for William I and William III de Roumare, cf. Holtzmann-Kemp, *Decretals to Lincoln* 20-21 no. 8 and 56-57 no. 23; Duggan, 'Equity and compassion' 71-72 and nn.32 (*Significavit nobis*, WH 973, JL 13937, 30 June 1177) and 33 (*Comes Willelmus*, WH 133, JL 16611, 15 April-25 October 1191); for Walter of Woodhill, see *Decretales ineditae* 108-10 no. 63: *Ex parte mulieris*, to the prior and brethren of Dunstaple, WH 466, JL —, 1162-81; and for Edwin of Balsall, see *Pervenit ad nos*, to the bishops of Hereford and Worcester, WH 723, JL 13901, 1159-81, and Donahue, 'Alexander III's marriage decretals' 79, WH 723.

[43] *Super eo quod*, Innocent II to Henry of Winchester, WH 1016, JL 8274, 1139-41; Duggan, 'Equity and compassion' 69 and n.28. A version of Innocent II's mandate is included in a letter of archbishop Theobald to Alexander III: *The letters of John of Salisbury*, 1, *The early letters* (1153-1161) edd. W.J. Millor and H.E. Butler, revised C.N.L. Brooke (Nelson's Medieval Texts; London 1955) 227-37 no. 131, at 228-29; see also 267-71.

[44] WH 604, JL 14218, 1175-80; Printed in X 4.17.5: cf. Duggan, 'Equity and compassion' 75.

grandfather had had two wives, of one of whom R.'s father was born, his uncle Hugh of the other. But Hugh was unwilling to allow R. his share of the inheritance; and in the presence of a secular judge, he challenged the legitimacy of R.'s father and therefore also his inheritance. The question of birth was then debated before the bishop of Norwich. In the face of Hugh's alleged delaying tactics, R. appealed to the pope, and appeared in person before him, despite physical danger—'non sine multo discrimine sui corporis'. The pope ordered the judges to decide the truth of the matter within two months of receiving the letter, and to signify (*significetis*) their decision to the secular lord, so that the question of inheritance could be decided under his jurisdiction—'extunc seculari domino sub cuius iudicio causam de hereditate intrarunt significetis, ut pro questione nativitatis non dimittat, quin causam super hereditate audiat et decidat'.

It may be assumed that a union between persons of substance was at issue in *Cum haberet uxorem* (1192), of Celestine III to the bishop of Lincoln.[45] The man in this case, John, is described as advanced in years, and his adultery with Maxilla and their perjury have gravely scandalized the church—'presertim cum in dies suos ambo processerint, et tam diu in publico adulterio et periurio ex certa scientia perdurantes ecclesiam gravi scandalo perturbarent'. But John appeared in person in the curia, and was the bearer of the pope's commission to the judges. He had lawfully married Alice, but committed adultery with Maxilla; though he confessed and publicly abjured the latter, he broke his oath and went though a form of marriage with Maxilla, while Alice was still alive, and continued to live with her after Alice's death. The pope ruled that they should be separated, do penance and accept perpetual continence, and provide for their ten children, as far as their means allowed.

B. The FitzGodric case[46]

But if the social standing of some litigants is uncertain, there is no doubt of the powerful status of others. Three decretals of Alexander III to Roger of York reflect in a single case the dynastic and territorial interests which often underlay disputed marriages and protracted litigation. In *Ex litteris fraternitatis* (c.1169-early 1170s), the pope ordered Roger to forbid the marriage of W. and the mother of a certain girl, to whom he had been previously betrothed while she was under age, and to excommunicate them if they broke their oath to him.[47] The

---

[45] WH 243, JL 17678, 28 June-25 December 1192; Printed in X 4.7.5; Holtzmann-Kemp, *Decretals to Lincoln* 60-61 no. 25: cf. Duggan, 'Equity and compassion' 74-75.

[46] The case is fully discussed in *Decretales ineditae* 123-25, for no. 71; cf. Donahue, 'Alexander III's marriage decretals' 74-75, for WH 12.

[47] Printed in *Decretales ineditae* 123-25 no. 71: WH 420, JL —, 1168-75 (1169-early 1170s), found only in *1 Rot.* 1.4; cf. Duggan, 'Equity and compassion' 69-70; idem, 'Decretals of Alexander III' 126.

parties were in fact the nobleman William FitzGodric and Aubrey de Lisours, of the Lacy of Pontefract family. When William undertook to refer the matter to the pope and accept his judgment, the archbishop absolved him and sent him to the curia. It was presumably a visit for that purpose and others which was recorded in *Cum essent in nostra* (1175), in which Alexander informed the archbishop that the clerk R. of Pontefract and the *nobilis vir* William FitzGodric had been in his presence in a dispute over a certain church, but William had appointed Roger's messenger Milo to act for him, on his own departure.[48] In the presence of cardinal commissioners, R. claimed that William had promised him the disputed church, if he could promote 'a certain business' of his in the curia—'si quoddam negotium ipsius militis posset in curia nostra promovere'. Since the promise smacked of simony, the pope imposed silence on R., and ordered Roger not to allow the knight to be troubled by R. or others in respect of the church on the pretext of that promise.

It is a fair conjecture that William's *quoddam negotium* was his marriage to Aubrey de Lisours. In *Accessit ad presentiam* (1175 or soon after), Alexander rehearsed the course of the dispute and reached a reluctant conclusion.[49] William had explained how, after the passing of several years and the death of the girl's father, the English king had given her mother to him in marriage, and he had accepted her to quieten the discord that had arisen between the families:

> karissimus in Christo filius noster Anglie rex matrem sepedicte puelle memorato W. tradidit in uxorem, quam idem W., ut discordia inter consanguineos suos et consanguineos mulieris sopiretur, accepit, solempniter desponsavit et sine contradictione ecclesie duxit.

The pope carefully expounded the canonical implications of the case, but allowed that the union of William and the mother could be tolerated, lest the discord be re-awakened—'Verum, si tibi visum fuerit, ut cum matre ipsius puelle remaneat, ne discordia inter utriusque consanguineos olim exorta, nunc autem sopita, denuo suscitetur, id dissimulare poteris et equanimiter tolerare'. The union being tolerated by the church, the children of the union could not be debarred from the inheritance of either party.

The political implications of the case are self-evident, in the dynastic interests of the parties and the decisive role of the king. Aubrey had been previously married twice, first to Robert FitzEustace, probably the father of the girl in question, and of John, who became constable of Chester; and second to William of Clairfait. In due course, the whole Lacy of Pontefract inheritance passed to

---

[48] WH 235, JL 13883, 1175; Printed in *App.* 2.14, X 5.3.12: cf. Duggan, 'Equity and compassion' 69-70; idem, 'Decretals of Alexander III' 122-23.

[49] WH 12, JL 13887, 1175+; Printed in *App.* 6.7, X 4.2.5: cf. Duggan, 'Equity and compassion' 69-70; idem, 'Decretals of Alexander III', 115; Donahue, 'Alexander III's marriage decretals' 74-75.

Aubrey and was transmitted to her grandson Roger in 1194; her Lisours inheritance passed to her son William, whose father was William FitzGodric.

C. The Bohun-Arderne dispute[50]

The inheritance dispute between Francus de Bohun and Ralph de Arderne, reminiscent of the Anstey case in some respects, turned on the legitimacy of Ralph's mother Agatha, and elicited two decretals of exceptional interest, not only for their canonical doctrine, but also in their context of jurisdictional conflict. The decretals record an early stage in the Bohun *v.* Arderne dispute, a settlement of which was finally reached in 1199. Agatha was born of Avelina (Ralph's grandmother), apparently through her illicit union with Ralph FitzSavaric, who died without legitimate heir; Francus was the son of Ralph FitzSavaric's brother Geldwin. An earlier commission of Alexander III on this dispute is now lost, but in *Causam que inter* (October 1178) he commissioned the bishops of London and Winchester to restore to Ralph everything he had possessed when his grandfather set out for Jerusalem, and of which he had been violently dispossessed.[51] They were to do this before proceeding to the principal question of right. And in a ruling which attracted wider interest in the period, the pope affirmed that it pertained to the king to judge such matters of possession. The king had been disturbed by what the pope had previously written concerning possessions, and the judges should leave that question to the king. They should resolve the principal matter, whether Agatha was born of lawful marriage:

> ne videamur iuri et dignitati karissimi in Christo filii nostri Henrici illustris Anglorum regis detrahere, qui sicut accepimus commotus est et turbatus quod de possessionibus scripsimus ... de causa principali videlicet utrum Agatha mater predicti R. de legitimo fuerit matrimonio nata plenius cognoscatis.

But the matter was later recommissioned to the bishops of Exeter (since Francus objected to the bishop of London as Ralph's lord) and Winchester and the abbot of Ford, in *Causam que vertitur* (1179-80).[52] The judges were ordered to examine most carefully the circumstances of Agatha's birth, including the question of notoriety. Even if born in fact of Ralph FitzSavaric, she was not his

---

[50] The case is discussed in Morey, *Bartholomew of Exeter* 68-70; C. Duggan and A. Duggan, 'Ralph de Diceto, Henry II and Becket, with an appendix on decretal letters', *Authority and power: studies on medieval law and government presented to Walter Ullmann*, edd. B. Tierney and P. Linehan (Cambridge 1980) 75-76; and C. Duggan, 'Equity and compassion' 76.

[51] WH 120, JL 14002, 1 October 1178; Printed in App. 33.4, X 4.17.7; draft collation C. Duggan-A. Duggan, 'Ralph de Diceto' 78-80, App. III; cf. C. Duggan 'Equity and compassion' 76.

[52] WH 123, JL 13932, *ex* 1178-81; Printed in X 1.29.7, 4.17.4, 2.14.3.

lawful daughter, if born while Avelina was living with her first husband Alan, or if she had public relations with Ralph in the lifetime of her second husband R. de Windsor. In the face of alleged frustratory tactics, the pope now ordered the judges to reach a conclusion within three months, notwithstanding his previous letter on the restoration of possessions to Ralph, and leaving the judgment of possessions to the king (an evident allusion to *Causam que inter*), or any other letters—'Nullis obstantibus litteris sive que de restitutione possessionis R. de Ardena facienda, sive que de possessionis iudicio regi relinquendo fecerint mentionem'.

D. Mary of St Leger and Matilda of Polstead

In the FitzGodric and Arderne disputes cited above, dynastic marriages and contested inheritances, as well as political and jurisdictional implications, are clear enough. In other instances, such material factors are less explicit, yet sometimes underlie the ostensible human preferences which the decretals record. Such an example is that of the respective unions of Mary, daughter of Gilbert of St Leger, and Matilda, daughter of Hugh of Polstead, the women being in fact related. In *Ex litteris venerabilis* (1175-81), Alexander III commissioned the bishops of Winchester, Bath and Hereford (a significantly weighty panel) to resolve this complex case.[53] Mary had been betrothed in her absence to R., and later a contract of marriage was drawn up in her presence, on the intervention of certain of her relations. When the suspicion that R. wished to marry another was conveyed to the archbishop of Canterbury, the latter forbad him to do so before the earlier vows were examined. He nevertheless married Matilda, but then confessed that he had contracted marriage with Mary and had married Matilda on base advice—'prava quorundam suggestione seductus'. For her part, Mary claimed that her father's objection had not been raised at her wish and that no obligation had been incurred by her and R., except the promise. She appealed to the pope, but meanwhile married W., against the archbishop's order. The pope advised the commissioners that the second marriage should be observed, if there was no impediment except the promise of Mary and R. The various pressures and interventions, which the decretal records, leave little doubt that material motives lay behind these manoeuvres, but it is probable that authentic human sentiments were also involved.

[53] WH 439, JL 14311, 5 February 1175-81; Printed in *App.* 6.28; X 4.16.2. The commission was cited in *Ex litteras quas*, to the archbishop of Canterbury, who had reported the case to the pope, WH 426a, JL 13793, same date; printed in *App.* 6.20, X 4.1.7. Cf. Duggan, 'Equity and compassion' 70-71; Donahue, 'Alexander III's marriage decretals' 77-78.

In many cases where the validity of a marriage or its offspring was called into question, it is clear that the property interests of the two families were motivating factors, or could be conjectured. In such a dispute, the man G. had clandestinely married the sister of his betrothed and they had had a child; but when G. died, his brothers claimed the estate, as if he had died without legitimate heir, whereas the woman's relations claimed lawful succession of the child. In *Referente nobis* (1159-81), to the archbishop of York, the pope ruled against the claims made on behalf of the child.[54] In another dispute, Robert of Manston sought to disinherit his neice, on the grounds that she was born before her mother's marriage, though her father was said to have married her later. In *Conquestus est nobis* (5 July 1177), the pope ordered the bishops of Exeter and Worcester to declare the daughter legitimate if the facts were so.[55] And in a similar case, the knight P. brought a case in the name of his wife Sibilla against R.; in this instance, in *Meminimus nos* (1161-81), the pope instructed the bishop of Exeter to declare R. legitimate if his parents were married after his birth, but *spurius* if he was begotten in adultery.[56] In such disputes, the material interests of the contestants were evident, but they may also be inferred in such a case as that of Hugh de Ralegh, sometime sheriff of Devon. Late in his life, his long-standing marriage to Muriel was called in question on grounds of consanguinity. With prudence and caution, the pope commissioned the case to the bishop of Exeter, in *Pervenit ad audientiam* (1161-70), and the Exchequer records show that Hugh was succeeded by his brother.[57]

IV. Miscellaneous topics

A. Abuse of clerks and churches by laymen

Many decretals record complaints of violence to clerks and abuse of church property by laymen, as frequently instanced in patronage disputes. A general condemnation of such violence was expressed by Alexander III in *Non sine dolore* (1159-81), to the archbishop of Canterbury and his suffragans: laymen have grown accustomed to usurp control of church appointments and do not fear to use violence against canonically instituted clerks, even to the extent of mur-

---

[54] WH 854, JL 17623 (wrongly ascribed to Celestine III), 1159-81; Printed in *Sang.* 9.34, X 4.17.10: cf. Duggan, 'Decretals of Alexander III' 138-39.

[55] WH 150, JL 14167 [13929], 5 July 1177; Printed in *App.* 33.3, X 4.17.1: cf. Cheney, *Roger of Worcester* 327, App. II.22 (cf. ibid. 337, App. II.43B, a reworked part of WH 150).

[56] WH 650, JL 13917, 1162-81; Printed in *App.* 33.1: cf. Duggan, 'Equity and compassion' 77.

[57] WH 701, JL 14214, 1162-1169/70; Printed in *App.* 8.23, *1 Comp.* 4.19.3: cf. Morey, *Bartholomew of Exeter* 67-68; Duggan, 'Equity and compassion' 70; idem, 'Decretals of Alexander III' 90 and 105-06 no. 83.

der—'ecclesiasticos viros canonice in ipsis ecclesiis ordinatos iniuriis multis afficiunt, aliquando eos verberibus affligunt, et interdum etiam, quod est auditu terribile, occidere non verentur'.[58] The physical constraint of an individual clerk is exemplified in *Si vobis constiterit* (1159-81), to the archdeacon and dean of Derby: the deacon R. was captured and imprisoned until he abjured the church of 'Heneifra'—'captus et carceri mancipatus ecclesiam de Heneifra abjuraverit, et per tantam violentiam ab eo fuerit iuramentum extortum'.[59] The seizure of church property is recorded in *Ex parte abbatis* (1159-81), to the archbishop of York.[60] The canons of Welbeck in Nottinghamshire complained of the seizure of certain chattels from the cemetary of their church in Welbeck by R. Mustel. The pope's response widened his censure to the wickedness of laymen more generally in this respect—'compescenda est laicorum improbitas si quando ad ecclesiastica bona manus extendunt violentas'.

In *Ex parte Ade* (1175-80), to the bishop of Hereford and the abbot of Ford, the pope recommissioned a curious case for investigation: the priest Adam complained that the knight H. had challenged his occupancy of the church of 'Culinton' or 'Culmiton', though he had held it for more than thirty years.[61] Concealing the fact that he was a layman, the knight secured a papal commission and, acting through an intermediary, obtained a judgment against Adam; and the son of the knight's dapifer obtained possession:

> Miles cuidam H. nomine ipsum exinde gravibus molestiis et iniuriis lacessivit et tandem tacito quod laicus esset ... litteras impetravit ... Tandem vero cum idem miles per interpositam personam prefatum A. presbiterum coram predictis iudicibus traxisset in causam ... [iudices] prescriptam abiudicaverunt ecclesiam, quam nunc prescripti militis dapiferi filius detinet occupatam.

The new commissioners were mandated to make a careful enquiry and reach a canonical judgment.

B. Tithes and financial transactions

Incomes and financial transactions, sometimes involving tithes, gave rise to disputes and resulting papal commissions. Thus, Gerard of 'Calest.' (possibly Calstock in Cornwall) made an agreement with the clerk William, whereby he

---

[58] WH 671, JL 13818, 1159-81; Printed in *App.* 14.5, *1 Comp.* 5.34.12.

[59] WH 925, JL —, 1159-81; Printed in *Wig.* 7.74; found in *Wig.* and *Claud.* 213 only.

[60] WH 447, JL —, 1159-81; Printed in *Wig.* 4.5, *Claustr.* 146: cf. Duggan, 'Decretals of Alexander III' 127.

[61] WH 448, JL 13955, 1175-80; Printed in *App.* 8.22, X 2.20.7. The historical context of this letter will be examined in a separate paper. The church in question has been proposed as Cullompton in the county of Devon, in the diocese of Exeter, but Collington in Herefordshire is a more probable identification.

would receive his own tithes and those of his villeins in the parish—'decimas proprias et rusticorum suorum quos in parochia de Calest. habere dinoscitur', in return for an annual payment of five shillings to William, whose sister he had married. In *Pervenit ad nos* (1161-70), to Bartholomew of Exeter, Alexander III ordered that the tithes must be left untouched.[62] And in *Querelam prioris* (1159-81), to the archdeacon of Bedford, he replied to a complaint of the prior and canons of Harrold that they had been despoiled of lands and tithes, and that John of Bidon kept for himself the tithes from a park which he had constructed in their parish—'et Johannes de Bidun parcum in parochia sua construxit, unde decimas queritur sibi subtractas esse'.[63] The pope ordered the restoration of the canons' rights.

Towards the close of the century, Celestine III (1191-98) sent two commissions to the abbot of Ramsey and the archdeacon of Ely, to protect certain tithe incomes of Burchard, archdeacon of Durham (and treasurer of York), in the church of N., of which he was rector. In *Ex transmissa querela*, the pope ruled that the knight M. must pay tithes to Burchard in respect of a windmill constructed on his land, within the confines of Burchard's parish—'molendinum quoddam ad ventum in terra quadam infra fines parochie sue'.[64] And in *Pervenit ad audientiam*, he ordered that the lords of land left fallow for grazing be compelled to pay tithe in respect of the hay produced—'ecclesie de qua premisimus feni decimas quod de terra provenit memoratis earum dominis per ecclesiasticam districtionem exsolvi sublato appellationis obstaculo compellatis'.[65]

But it would be misleading to instance only those decretals which protected the rights of clerks against lay encroachments. In *Ex transmissa conquestione* (1161-1166x81), to Bartholomew of Exeter, the pope condemned the crime of usury as more grave when committed by clerks and religious—'tanto gravius in ecclesiasticis et religiosis personis'. The father of Thibaut Scalers had pledged lands in Dullingham in Cambridgeshire to the monks of Warden, in return for a loan, but Thibaut and his widowed mother now complained that the monks of Warden refused to return the land, although more than the loaned sum had been repaid.[66] And in a similar situation, R. Buger reported in person to the pope

---

[62] WH 720, JL 13918, 1162-81 (?1162-70); Printed in *Brug.* 17.9, X 1.43.3: cf. Duggan, 'Decretals of Alexander III' 90 and 98-99 no. 73. The alternative reading *quas* is found in some collections.

[63] WH 786, JL —, 1159-81; Printed in *Wig.* 7.5, *Claustr.* 196.

[64] WH 508, JL 17620, 1191-early 1197; Printed in *2 Comp.* 3.17.7, X 3.30.23. Cf. M.G. Cheney, 'The decretal of pope Celestine III on tithes of windmills, JL 17620', BMCL 1 (1971) 63-66; from Friedberg's edition of X, the archdeacon in question was thought to be Bertrand of Dol, but was in fact Burchard of Durham, who held the church of Heighington in Durham and other northern benefices (ibid. 66).

[65] WH 699, JL 17621, 1191-early 1197; Printed in *2 Comp.* 3.17.6 (with the reading *a memoratis*).

[66] WH 500 (*olim* 501), JL 13998, 1162-81 (?1162-66x81); printed in *App.* 16.10, *1 Comp.* 5.15.7: cf. Duggan, 'Decretals of Alexander III' 90 and 103-04 no. 80.

that he had loaned the clerk Alan FitzWalter the large sum of one hundred pounds sterling for the pledge of certain churches and a lay fee —'quasdam ecclesias et quoddam laicale feudum in Blyton'. Although the loan was not repaid, R. had been despoiled of the pledges, so Alexander III, in *Ex relatione dilecti* (1159-81), ordered the archbishop of Canterbury to ensure the restoration of the lay fee and incomes to R.—'cum nobis fidelis sit et devotus'.[67]

C. Lay benefactions and pastoral care

A pre-occupation with the many individual clashes of interests and moments of crisis perhaps obscures the vital role of the magnates in the fabric of Christian society in the period—as founders of churches and benefactors of religious communities, and in numerous other ways. These themes are well known from general history, but are also constantly implied in the decretals. A lay lord's concern with the specific spiritual needs of his lowly subjects is, not surprisingly, less frequently mentioned, but a striking instance is recorded in Alexander III's *Significavit nobis* (1164-79x81), to the bishop of Worcester.[68] The knight Henry 'Bram' informed the pope that the chapel of the village of 'Bram' was so far distant from its mother church, and the journey so difficult that children died un-baptized, and parishoners died without the last sacraments:

> tantum distat a matrice ecclesia quod propter loci distantiam et vie difficultatem aliquando pueri sine baptismate et habitatores loci sine penitentia et perceptione dominici corporis moriuntur. Unde nobis humiliter supplicavit ut habitatoribus predicte ville in hac parte consuleremus.

The pope therefore ordered the bishop to assign a chaplain to celebrate in the chapel and provide for these needs, without loss to the mother church.[69] In this instance, Alexander readily acceded to the knight's apparent concern for the pastoral care of his subjects. Conversely, if need arose, he did not hesitate to remind the clergy of their duty to give a good example to the laity, as when instructing them to refrain from avaricious exactions of payment *pro scolis regendis*:

> Viris ecclesiasticis plurimum expedire dinoscitur ut in cunctis actibus suis modum et honestatem observent, et que de radice avaricie vel cupiditatis procedunt ita

[67] WH 481, JL —, 1159-81; Printed in *Brug.* 25.2.

[68] WH 970, JL —, 1164-81; Printed in *Wig.* 4.45, unknown elsewhere; cf. Cheney, *Roger of Worcester* 97 and 363, App. II.90.

[69] Cf. *Ad audientiam nostram noveris*, WH 25, JL 13884, 1159-81x82, Lucius III or Alexander III to Roger of York, mandating the provision of a chapel for villagers too far distant from their parish church in adverse winter weather: Duggan, 'Decretals of Alexander III' 116 no. 25.

satagant abdicare quod laicos ad perfectionem morum atque virtutum bonis informare possint exemplis.[70]

ALPHABETICAL INDEX OF LETTERS

	WH	JL	fn
Accessit ad presentiam	12	13887	49
Ad audientiam nostram communi fama	20	11398	15
Ad audientiam nostram noveris	25	13884	69
Ad aures nostras pervenit	53	——	33
Ad hec, cum laici: cf. Inter ceteras			
Audita (olim) querela	97	14143	21
Causam que inter nobiles	118	——	34
Causam que inter R. et F.	120	14002 (13106)	51
Causam que vertitur	123	13932	52
Comes Willelmus	133	16611	42
Conquestus est nobis Herbertus	150	14167 (13929)	55
Constitutus in presentia nostra G.	171	14193	38
Constitutus in presentia nostra magister	179	——	20,37
Consultationibus singulorum	184	12636.II	27
Cum essent in nostra	235	13883	48
Cum haberet uxorem	243	17678	45
Cura pastorali	329	13893	29
Dilecti filii nostri decanus	354	14085	31
Dilectus filius noster nobilis	364	13764	22
Ex conquestione prioris	401	——	35
Ex litteris fraternitatis	420	——	47
Ex litteris quas super causa	426	13793	53
Ex litteris venerabilis fratris	439	14311	53
Ex parte abbatis	447	——	60
Ex parte Ade	448	13955	61
Ex parte mulieris S.	466	——	42
Ex relatione dilecti	481	——	67
Ex tenore litterarum	488	12253+14146	26
Ex transmissa conquestione T. Escalers	500	13998	66
Ex transmissa querela B.	508	17620	64

[70] WH 1087, JL —, 1174-79, to archbishop Richard of Canterbury and his suffragans; Printed in *1 Dert.* 25 and *1 Par.* 1; the extract printed here is based on *1 Alc.* 101 and *1 Cant.* 9.

	WH	JL	fn
Inter ceteras consultationes	590	13878+14346	24
Lator presentium R.	604	14218	44
Licet nobis commendabiles	618	11836	6
Magnificentie tue	639	13726	19
Meminimus nos	650	13917	56
Non est vobis	669	12248	9
Non sine dolore	671	13818	58
Oportuerat vos	692	11835	7
Pervenit ad audientiam nostram ex conquestione B.	699	17621	65
Pervenit ad audientiam nostram quod Hugo de Ralega	701	14214	57
Pervenit ad nos quod cum Willelmus	720	13918	62
Pervenit ad nos quod quidem miles R.	723	13901	42
Preterea quando inter: cf. Tua nos			
Proposuit nobis	748	——	40
Quanto per carissimum	772	11353	5
Quanto superni dextera	774	——	17
Quanto te superna	775	13727	18
Querelam prioris	786	——	63
Querimoniam prioris	790	14141	36
Referente nobis	854	17623	54
Relatum est nobis	880	14346	25
Si vobis constiterit	925	——	59
Significavit nobis Henricus Bram	970	——	68
Significavit nobis Hugo de Morton	971	13812	41
Significavit nobis O. Andegavensis	973	13937	42
Super eo quod	1016	8274	43
Tua nos fraternitas	1039	14029+15186	28
Veniens ad apostolice sedis	1058	——	39
Viris ecclesiasticis	1087	——	70

Errata:

p. 600, line 14, hwas *should read* he was
p. 600, line 18, 181l *should read* 1811
p. 603, line 7, Painsick *should read* Painswick
p. 605, line 14, is sometimes *should read* can also be
p. 611, line 9, cuidam *should read* quidam

V

DECRETAL LETTERS TO HUNGARY*

The post-Gratian decretal collections contain almost 1100 letters, of which decretals to England form by far the most numerous regional element, followed in turn by those to Italy, and the French and Spanish decretals. Comparatively few were sent to Scandinavia or Hungary, very few indeed to Germany, eastern Europe and other regions, and only two were sent to Ireland, both within fourteen days of one another.[1] These proportions do not accurately reflect the proportion of letters dispatched, but they reflect to some extent the areas of most frequent appellate relations with the curia, and also in which the greater initiative was shown in collecting and codifying decretals received. The decretals to Hungary provide the focus of the present study, which deals with sixteen letters, including two to the king of Hungary, six to the archbishop of Esztergom and two to the archbishop of Kalocsa (one of them jointly to both archbishops) and one to the suffragans, clergy and nobles of both provinces, one each to the bishops of Győr and Vác, suffragan sees of Esztergom, and one to recipients in the diocese of Nitra, subject to Esztergom, but now in Czechoslovakia. Broadening the perspective to the historical sphere of Hungarian interests in the south, to Croatia and Dalmatia, decretals to the bishops of Arbe and Osor, in the province of Zara, and to the archbishop of Split are included.

---

* The present study is a development of a lecture on „Hungarian decretals in English collections", given in the Theological Seminary in Budapest in May 1990. A list of abbreviations used for the names of collections is given at the end of this chapter.

1 W. HOLTZMANN, „Über eine Ausgabe der päpstlichen Dekretalen des 12.Jahrhunderts", *Akad. Göttingen* (1945) 34, Anh. 1. In an overall total of 1055 decretals for all regions, Holtzmanns table records 12 items for Hungary and Dalmatia: one before Eugenius III, 8 for Alexander III and one each for Lucius III, Clement III and Celestine III. The present study includes 16 decretals, from Alexander III and his successors, to Celestine III. The two Irish decretals are *Cum in dandis*, Clement III to the archbishop of Dublin, 3 March 1190: WH 257, JL 16567; and *Cum ad sedem*, Clement III to the archbishop of Cashel, 17 March (!) 1190, WH 213, JL 16564; ed. in M. P. Sheehy, *Pontificia Hibernica*, Dublin 1962, 1. 63-4 no. 19, and 66-7, no. 21; the full texts appear together in the register derivative *Seg*. 17 and 18.

The indispensable starting-point for a study of these letters is the work of Walther Holtzmann, notably in his essays on „Alexander III and Hungary" in 1926, his critical edition of nine Hungarian decretals in 1959,[2] and his materials preparatory to a *regesta* of all decretals in the collections.[3] With the publication of the *Decretales ineditae saeculi XII* in 1982, the age-long process of printing the decretals was brought up to date, including certainly one and probably two previously unprinted letters to Esztergom.[4] The purpose of the present paper is to re-consider the corpus of Hungarian decretals in the collections, noting especially their first appearance in the collections and later transmission. A striking feature is the extent to which the Hungarian letters appeared first in English or Anglo-Norman collections, or preserve better texts in them, or were significantly transmitted through them. This feature is above all remarkable in the English Cottonian and Peterhouse collections (which in fact provide about half of all the new texts in the *Decretales ineditae*). Three Hungarian decretals are discovered only in *Cott.* and *Pet.*, a further letter is found only in *Tanner*, *Sangermanensis* and *Abrincensis prima*, and a fifth only in *Cheltenhamensis*, *Tann.*, *Sang.* and *1 Abr.* The integrity of a sixth Hungarian decretal is established in *Cott.*, *Pet.*, *Tann.* and *Sang.*[5] In some letters the historical details or editorial emendations are better in these works, especially in the English and Rouen manuscripts. The trans-channel links between the canonists of Lincoln (and Oxford) and Rouen were doubtless a factor after the translation of Walter of Coutances from Lincoln to Rouen in 1184-85 (conf. 17 November 1184, received in Rouen, March 1185).

The letters assembled here are of interest, not only for their immediate contexts, but also for the light thrown on the state of the Hungarian

2 W. HOLTZMANN, „Papst Alexander III. und Ungarn", *Ungarische Jahrbücher* 6 (1926) 397-426; idem, „XII. századi pápai levelek kánoni gyűjteményekből", *Századok* 93 (1959) 404-17.

3 In preparation by S. CHODOROW and C. DUGGAN, for the *MIC series*.

4 Respectively, *Decretales ineditae* 1603 no. 91: *Porro licet*, and 169-71: *Amara nimis;* see part III, below.

5 Cf. below, parts III, *Amara nimis* and *Porro licet*, and IX, *Licet litteras:* in *Cott.* and *Pet.* only; part I, *Nuntios*, in *Tann.*, *Sang.* and *1 Abr.* only; part VII, *Volentes vos*, in *Chelt.*, *Tann.*, *Sang.* and *1 Abr.* only; part V, *Ad apostolice sedis* (abcde), sections in many collections, but the integrity of the letter (previously WH 14 + 309, JL 15196 + 15213) is established in *Cott.*, *Pet.*, *Tann.* and *Sang.*

kingdom, Church and society at that time, a feature which Holtzmann noted also for Norway in his edition of Norwegian decretals through the same period.[6] The letters of papal advice to Hungarian prelates on judicial procedures and juristic principles are also noteworthy — the Romano-canonical principle *actor forum rei sequatur*, for instance, appears in phraseological variants in two decretals.[7] In the following survey of Hungarian decretals, the letters are arranged in the following sequence:

Kingdom of Hungary:

I. Alexander III to the king of Hungary (See also IV):

Provinces of Esztergom and Kalocsa:

II. Alexander III to the archbishops of Esztergom and Kalocsa

Province of Esztergom:

III. Alexander III to the archbishop of Esztergom (3 letters)

IV. Alexander III, concerning the archbishop of Esztergom (3 letters: to the archbishop of Esztergom; to the king of Hungary; to the suffragans, provosts, abbots, magnates, clergy and people)

V. Lucius III to the archbishop of Esztergom

VI. Alexander III to the bishop of Győr

VII. Alexander III to recipients in the diocese of Nitra

VIII. Celestine III to the bishop of Vác

Province of Kalocsa:

IX. Alexander III to the archbishop of Kalocsa

Province of Split:

X. Alexander III to the archbishop of Split/Spalato

Province of Zara:

XI. Clement III to the bishop of Osor/Ossero

XII. Celestine III to the bishop of Arbe

6 W. HOLTZMANN, „Krone und Kirche in Norwegen im 12. Jahrhundert", *Deutsches Archiv für Erforschung des Mittelalters* 2 (1938) 341-400.

7 See at nn. 17 and 19 below.

I. To the king of Hungary

Nuntios infra. De cetero notum

Alexander III congratulates the king of Hungary on the baptism of his first-born son

The passage *De cetero notum* is found only in *Tann.*, *Sang.* and *1 Abr.*[8] It is noted in all three collections as an excerpt from an otherwise unknown letter *Nuntios*, of Alexander III to the king of Hungary *(ingurinorum, Tann.; ingernorum, Sang.; unguriorum, 1 Abr.)*[9] The pope conveys to the king his joy on learning of the baptism of his first-born son — *aqua est et Spiritu sancto renatus et perceptione ecclesie sacramentorum christianorum meruit collegio sociari*. Presumably in response to a comment made by the king, the pope assures him that the validity of baptism does not depend on the merits of the officiating priest, and proceeds to cite texts from St Paul, which are also found in Gratian — *non est enim baptismus eius qui baptizat, sed illius in cuius nomine baptizatur.*[10] When this letter was first edited, from *Sang.* and *1 Abr.*, Singer questioned its authenticity, thinking it more probably a paraphrase of the chapters in Gratian, but Holtzmann accepted it, and noted that the death of king Stephen III without an heir pointed to Béla III (from 1172) as its recipient, giving the dating limits 1172-81. If, as seems probable, Gratian was the source of the texts in question, the letter affords an example of the chancery use of the *Decretum* in Alexander III's pontificate.[11]

* * *

WH 690, JL — , 1172-81. *Tann.* 3.19.3, *Sang.* 4.14.3, *1 Abr.* 5.1.2. Pd Sang.; HOLTZMANN, Századok 415 no. 7.

---

8 WH 690, JL – , 1172-81. *Tann.* 3.19.3, *Sang.* 4.14.3, *1 Abr.* 5.1.2. Pd *Sang.;* HOLTZMANN, *Századok* 415 no. 7.

9 *Pars capituli Nuntios: Tann., Sang., 1 Abr.; infra* add. *Sang.*

10 St Paul, 1 Cor. 3.67; Gratian, De consecr. D.4 caps 39 and 47.

11 Cf. n. 12 below.

II. To the archbishops of Esztergom and Kalocsa

Coniugatus in monasterium

Alexander III to the archbishops of Esztergom and Kalocsa, concerning the reception of married men in monasteries, and their ordination to the priesthood or episcopate

Coniugatus in monasterium (1159-79), addresssed jointly to the archbishops of Esztergom and Kalocsa, is one of the very few decretals of Alexander III to Hungary to be found widely in the collections — in the primitive Roman/Spanish, Italian, English and French collections, and in the great systematic collections from the seminal *Appendix* through to the *Decretales* of 1234. It ruled firstly (a) that a husband may not be received into a monastery, unless his wife had been similarly converted — *nec recipiatur apud Deum illius viri conversio, cuius sequitur coniugalis federis prostitutio;* and since the clerical order excels the monastic, no married man may be advanced to holy orders, unless released by his wife who also professed continence — *ut fiat deinceps de carnali spirituale coniugium.* And secondly (b), since all the greater care should be taken to avoid error in the promotion of one who is set above all ranks, the recipients must not ordain a married man as bishop, unless his wife first professes continence, and assumes the veil and dress appropriate to religion. The pope does not wish the husband's promotion to be the occasion of perdition to his wife left in the world.

* * *

WH 136, JL 14104, 1159-79: (a) *Coniugatus in monasterium* + (b) *Sane si coniugati. Pd Századok* 411-12 no. 3. Complete: *1 Dert.* 14, *Eber.* 7.1, *1 Par.* 145, *Aur.* 43ab + 47c, *Flor.* 166, *Roff.* 106, *Wig.* 1.10, *Claustr.* 36, *Cott.* 2.39, *Pet.* 1.45. Sections: *Claud.* 123 A (a[ii-iii]) + 123 B (b[ii-iii]), *App.* 5.6+7, *Bamb.* 49.6+7, *Lips.* 58.6+7, *Cass.* 57.7+8, *Tann.* 7.2.5+6, *Sang.* 8.13+14, *Frcf.Max.a* 4.3 + 3.5, *1 Rot.* 1.7(a), *1 Comp.* 3.28.5+6, *X* 3.32.5(a[ii-iii]) + 6(b[ii-iii]). Kalocsa's designation was especially unfamiliar to the scribes, and frequently appears in the address as *Coloniensi, Colonensi or Colon.* (instead of *Colocensi*), presumably through greater familiarity with the archbishopric of Cologne. [The complex transmission of this letter will be made clear in the *Regesta decretalium,* and a study of the four Frankfurt collections is in an advanced state of preparation by Peter Landau.]

III. To the archbishop of Esztergom

Porro licet, *Amara nimis* and *Etsi questiones*
The scruples of archbishop Lucas of Esztergom

Of the sixteen decretals considered in this paper, at least two and very probably three record the excessive conscientiousness of archbishop Lucas of Esztergom. And of these, *Porro licet* and *Amara nimis* are known only from the Cottonian and Peterhouse collections of the mid-1190s, and were printed for the first time in the *Decretales ineditae* in 1982, whereas *Etsi questiones* is known from seven collections, and was partly transmitted to the *Decretales* of 1234.

Porro licet survives only in a damaged and partly illegible condition in *Cott.*, and in a clean and legible text in *Pet.* Both transcriptions are imperfect and present textual problems, but the letter clearly replies to the archbishop of Esztergoms pangs of conscience concerning the mutilation he had imposed, before his ordination, on a self-confessed thief. The language of the letter implies that the sin of avarice was also in some way involved — *ex quo de cupiditatis delicto penitens et contritus fuisti*. Since the mutilation of the thiefs nose would not normally have resulted in death, the pope declared that, since there was no intention of killing, the matter was not an impediment to the archbishop's election, ordination or promotion, and he re-glossed in this sense a passage wrongly attributed to St Augustine, which the archbishop had evidently cited against himself, and a text from Innocent I, both found in Gratian's *Decretum* — presumably a further example of the chancery use of the *Decretum* in Alexander's pontificate.[12]

An edition of this letter is provided in the *Decretales ineditae*, with a discussion of the textual and historical issues involved. The conclusions proposed there are that the letter dated in all probability in or from 1181, in the closing year of Alexander III's pontificate, or conceivably at the outset of that of Lucius III, and that its recipient was unlikely to have been archbishop Lucas, who survived into that year, but was more probably Nicholas (1181-83), soon after his elevation. The arguments marshalled

12 *Decretales ineditae* 160 nn. 1 and 2 and 162-63; cf. Gratian C.23 q.8 c.33 and q.5 c. 29 (correctly attributed to St Jerome), and D.50 c.1; cf. n. 11 above.

against the identification of Lucas are that *Etsi questiones* (1167-68), a well-known letter of Alexander III to Lucas, dealt with a series of scruples which Lucas had raised with Alexander in respect of his elevation and other matters, and that it is improbable that he would have raised such doubts seriatim, in different letters, or that Alexander would have failed to allude to the fact, hadhe done so. The evidence carefully presented in the *Decretales ineditae* cannot be lightly set aside, but further reflection suggests the reverse conclusion, especially in conjunction with the discovery of *Amara* nimis, also in *Cott.* and *Pet.*, with an address to the archbishop of Canterbury. The recipient archbishop had raised with the pope the problem of offences he had unwittingly committed, in handling a consecrated host, while in the hands of his enemies, where he still remained, and that of drunken rustics who had crucified another of their kind. The pope, in reply, prescribed appropriate penances. The attribution to Canterbury in these English manuscripts cannot be reconciled with any known evidence, and no more probable recipient of the decretal can be proposed than Lucas, who is independently recorded as the recipient of papal letters while imprisoned during the rule of the anti-king Ladislas, between May 1162 and January 1163.[13]

The long admonitory decretal *Etsi questiones* was certainly sent by Alexander III to Lucas in the period 1167-68, in response to various scruples of conscience raised by the archbishop concerning his election and promotion — his brothers gift of a horse to the papal legate who brought his * pallium, the indemnity promised to his church, his earlier election to Eger and translation to Esztergom. The pope dealt painstakingly with each problem in turn, repeatedly insisting that Lucas had no cause for anxiety, citing human laws and scriptural authority — „trepidaverunt timore, ubi non erat timor... super hoc in conscientia tua nullus unquam debet scrupulum dubitationis emergere... cum nos nec minimum conscientie scrupulus ex hoc suboriri noscamus." But finally, concerning a drunken monk, the pope declined to answer the archbishop's question — he had written enough already, and could not deal with every syllable of the archbishop's questions — „nec nos questionibus tuis sillabatim per omnia possumus

13 *Decretales ineditae* 169-71; to the apparatus and notes given there, add G. GYŐRFFY, „Thomas à Becket and Hungary", *Hungarian Studies in English*, 4 (1969), 47-9: GYŐRFFY notes two periods of imprisonment in 1162.

respondere." The archbishop is not a man of mediocre worth, but versed in the scriptures and learned in sacred and profane letters, a doctor of the Church — „ecclesie doctor." He must set aside all doubts, and devote all his efforts to his pontifical office, so that he will in the end receive the commendation of Christ, the chief shepherd.

The evidence of the three letters is coherent. The prelate who evoked the papal response of mingled praise and reproach in *Etsi questiones* was * clearly a man of exceptional scrupulosity, who finally exhausted the popes patience. The nature of the queries in *Amara nimis* and *Porro licet* is entirely consistent with his character. Moreover, as the pope acknowledged, Lucas was a learned man, respected in the schools of France and the Rhineland for his character and learning. He was precisely the sort of prelate to have cited scriptural and canonical authorities in a letter to the pope, in respect of his scruples, as had the recipient of Alexander's reply in *Porro licet*. It is much more probable that Lucas received in sequence *Amara nimis* (1162), *Porro licet* (1167-68) and *Etsi questiones* (20 Sep. 1167-19 Sept. 1168), than that he was immediately followed in 1181 by an archbishop who exemplified identical traits of character. But it is unlikely that he raised similar questions with Alexander after receiving the pope's reply in 1167-68.

* * *

Amara nimis: WH 87, JL – , 1159-81; *conieci* 1162. Cott. 4.82, Pet. 3.86. Pd *Decretales ineditae* 169-71 no. 96.

Porro licet: WH 730, JL – , 1159-81; *conieci* 1167-68. Cott. 5.26, Pet. 4.36. Pd *Decretales ineditae* 160-63 no. 91. ?1181.

Etsi questiones: WH 387, JL 11308, Benevento 20 Sept. 1167-19 Sept. 1168. *App.Cr.* 50.1(i-vii), *Pet.* 4.5(i-ix), *Bamb.O* 57.7 (iii-ix), *1 Rot.* 14.3(i-vi, ix), *1 Comp.* 5.2.20 (i-v), *Sang.* 4.2.2(i) + 2.1.6(ii-v), X 5.3.18(i-iii,v; cf. *QF* 30 (1941) 21-3 and 38-9. Pd App.Cr.; crit. edit. HOLTZMANN, *Századok* 93 (1959) 408-9 no. 1, with scriptural allusions: Ps. 13.5, Isai. 33.15 and Matth. 25.23.

IV. Concerning the archbishop of Esztergom

Si velis, Gravat nos and *Totiens iam*
Alexander III on the recalcitrance of archbishop Lucas of Esztergom

Three decretals of Alexander III, relating to a crisis at the highest political and ecclesiastical levels in Hungary, are found exclusively in a manuscript in the cathedral library at Tortosa. They are addressed respectively to archbishop Lucas of Esztergom, the king of Hungary, and the suffragans of Esztergom and Kalocsa, together with the prelates, nobles, and all the clergy and people throughout the Hungarian kingdom. Their immediate context was the archbishop's failure to obey papal instructions to lift the sentences of excommunication which Lucas had imposed on archbishop Andreas of Kalocsa. The provenance of the completed collection is certainly Spanish, but its archetypal material is closely parallel with that in two Cistercian manuscripts, from Alcobaça and Eberbach, now in Lisbon and the British Library respectively.[14] No item in the Tortosa collection has been dated later than 1179, which is also the date of these three decretals.

The Hungarian background is clear from Alexander's letter to Lucas, *Si velis*, a long and sharp rebuke to the archbishop for failing to obey his orders to lift the sentence which Lucas had laid on Andreas. The pope recalled a series of comparable problems involving Lucas, reaching back as far as a blessing of king Stephen and his mother, the election of Andreas to Gyõr, the blessing of king Béla, and a dispute over the provostship of *Albensis regalis* — the royal chapel at Székesfehérvár. If Lucas now persists in rejecting his authority, the pope will treat him as excommunicate, and release his subjects from obedience to him. In *Gravat nos*, to the king of Hungary, the pope records that Andreas has reported his loss of royal favour through falsehoods and jealousy; he has claimed in the pope's presence — „in nostra presentia constitutus" — that he has intentionally offended the king in nothing.[15] The pope urges the king to accept this

14 *1 Alc.* and *Eber.*

15 Andreas was the only Hungarian prelate present at the Third Lateran Council in 1179 (where he is recorded last in the list: cf. appendix to *1 Vict.*, fol. 266v[a], „De ungaria. andreas bahasisensis archiepiscopus"). He presumably secured these letters at that time.

verbal satisfaction, and promises still greater papal favour in the future, if he does so. Otherwise, the pope will withdraw favour from him, and prohibit divine service „in Albensi ecclesia, ubi sedes regalis est." And in *Totiens iam*, to the Hungarian suffragans, the provosts, abbots and magnates, and all the clergy and people „per regnum Ungarie constituto", the pope laments their failure to act on previous papal letters. Having fully
* heard Lucas's charges against Andreas, including violence against Lucas's clerks, the pope declared Andreas immune or absolved. He has deferred to Lucas more than is proper, and now orders under pain of anathema any of the recipients who continue to avoid Andreas to be themselves avoided as excommunicates; and if Lucas continues his charges against Andreas, he is to be deprived of the obedience of his own subjects.[16]

* * *

Si velis: WH 919, JL – , c. March 1179. *1 Dert.* 63: crit. ed. HOLTZMANN,
* *Ungarische Jahrbücher* 4013 no. 3, and *Századok* 413-14 no. 5.

Gravat nos: WH 531, JL – , c. March 1179. *1 Dert.* 64: crit. ed. HOLTZMANN, *Ungarische Jahrbücher* 403 no. 4, and *Századok* 414-15 no. 6.

Totiens iam: WH 1029, JL – , c. March 1179. *1 Dert.* 62: crit. ed. HOLTZMANN, *Ungarische Jahrbücher* 401 no. 2, and *Századok* 412 no. 4.

V. To the archbishop of Esztergom

Ad apostolice sedis

Lucius III to the archbishop of Esztergom, on tithes, delegated jurisdiction, appeals and clerical immunity

Ad apostolice sedis, to the archbishop of Esztergom, is the only decretal of Lucius III (1181-85) to Hungary in the collections, and in it the pope replies to a series of questions raised by the archbishop. It deals firstly with a custom which has grown up in Hungary (wrongly transcribed as *Anglia* in *Tann.* and *Sang.*), whereby people move from one diocese to another, but are required by both bishops to pay tithes, even after residing there a long time. The pope declares that, in respect of manufacture, trade or agriculture, tithe should be paid to the church in which divine service is heard and the sacraments received throughout the year. As for the tithes

16 On the series of crises involving Lucas, see GYŐRFFY, „Thomas à Becket and Hungary", 47-8.

of the harvest or the fruits of trees, a definite answer cannot be given if they are produced in a parish in which the payers do not reside, since custom varies on this point, and the archbishop should choose whichever gives rise to least scandal. Other sections deal with delegated jurisdiction and frustratory appeals. The jurisdiction of a delegate does not lapse with the death of the delegator, if the litigation has already begun; and in the case of frustratory appeals, an appropriate term should be set, and the appellant must submit to the judge from whom he appeals, if he fails to pursue the appeal within the term. Further, a clerk can be tried only by an ecclesiastical judge, above all in criminal matters, even if the custom of the realm holds that thieves are subject to secular judges. The imperial law follows the canons in this, and no custom should be prejudicial to them. Finally, following the maxim *actor forum rei sequatur*,[17] it is more appropriate that thieves should be brought first before secular judges, but if these fail to do justice or are negligent, the accused can be judged by the church.

The closing section of the letter, *Cum sit generaliter traditum... convenire*, was earlier thought to be a separate item, and the component parts therefore have two numbers in JL and even in Holtzmann's register, and the final passage is therefore not included in his printed critical edition. But the evidence of the manuscripts, especially *Cott.*, *Pet.*, *Tann.* and *Sang.* is conclusive. All the relevant collections preceding the famous thirteenth-century works are English or Anglo-Norman, except for the Oriel manuscript of the *Bamberg* collection *(Bamb.O)*, which has evident English associations; and part (a) appears as an addition in a different hand, at the end of Book II in the Worcester collection (*Wig.* 2.⁺38), though it does not appear in Lohmann's printed analysis through photographic error.

Lucius III Strigoniensi archiepiscopo.

(a) Ad apostolice sedis regimen licet immeriti dignatione vocati divina omnibus sumus ecclesie filiis debitores et pro scientie nostre modo respondere cogimur consultationibus singulorum. Intelleximus autem ex litteris tuis quod quedam consuetudo in Ungaria inolevit, ut multitudo populi plerumque de parochia unius episcopi in alterius diocesim transferant, in qua licet per multa tempora moram habuerint uterque tamen episcoporum,

17 *Cf. Ideo inter alios*, Alexander III to the bishop of Győr, VI below.

tam is cuius parochiam dimiserint, quam ille cuius parochiani facti sunt, decimationem requirunt. Unde invidie et contentiones oriuntur. Ideoque tua nos duxit fraternitas consulendos, cui potius decime sunt reddende. Noveris igitur, quod si de artificio vel negotiatione vel agricultura, quam infra terminos parochie in qua morantur exercent, aut de aliis huiusmodi decime persolvantur, equum est ut ecclesie illi reddantur, in qua ille qui reddit per totum anni circulum audit divina et percipit ecclesiastica sacramenta. Apostolus enim dicit: Si seminavimus vobis spiritualia, magnum est, si colunt temporalia vestra metimus? Super decimis vero messium vel fructibus arborum, si colunt in alia parochia quam in ea in qua habitant, quoniam a diversis diversa consuetudo tenetur, certum aliquid non duximus respondendum. Tu vero hoc eligas in hoc casu ex quo nullum vel minus noveris scandalum solet generari. Quod autem de prediis dicimus, id volumus de vineis et arborum fructibus observari. (b) Sane quoniam rescripto nostro postulas edoceri, si in obitu delegantis iurisdictio delegatorum expiret, tibi breviter respondemus quod, si ante obitum mandatoris lis fuerit contestata, non expirabit mandatum, alioquin procedere illius commissionis intuitu non valebunt. (c) De illis autem qui ante vel post litis ingressum causa frustratorie dilationis appellant, hoc convenit observari, ut pro qualitate negotii, temporis et persone, distantia quoque loci perspecta ad prosequendam appellationem congruus appellanti terminus assignetur, infra quem si forte appellationem prosequi contempserit, eius a quo appellavit, iudicio stare sublato appellationis diffugio compellatur. (d) Clerici vero maxime in criminalibus in nullo casu possunt ab alio quam ab ecclesiastico iudice condempnari, etiam si consuetudo regni habeat ut fures a iudicibus tamen secularibus iudicentur, cum imperatores etiam dicant quod leges eorum sacros non dedignantur canones imitari, in quibus generaliter traditur, ut de omni crimine clericus coram ecclesiastico iudice debeat conveniri, non debet in hac parte canonibus ex aliqua consuetudine preiudicium generari. (e[i]) Postremo quia dubitas apud quem illi qui homines, agros, vineas, seu quaslibet ecclesie possessiones invadere, vastare vel auferre presumpserint, debeant conveniri, presenti significatione mandamus, quod cum generaliter traditum sit etc. (e[ii]) Cum sit generaliter traditum, ut actor forum rei sequatur, convenientius tamen videtur, ut prius raptores apud iudices seculares conveniantur, sed si iusticiam exhibere contempserint, aut iudices ex quacumque causa fuerint negligentes, qui sacrilegi iudicandi sunt ab ecclesia, de crimine illo censuram in illos ecclesiasticam poteris exercere. Verum quoniam iudices seculares in exhibenda iusticia personis ecclesiasticis sepe in iudicio sunt remissi, iam per consuetudinem est favore ecclesie introductum ut malefactores suos venerabilium locorum rectores possunt sub quo maluerint iudicio convenire.

* * *

WH 14 + 309, JL 15196 + 15213, ed. *Századok* 93 (1959) 415-17 no. 8, 1181-85. *Wig*. 2.⁺38(a), *Cott*. 4.5 (a-e[i])+ 5.36 (e[ii]), *Pet*. 4.52 (e[ii]), *Bamb.O* (olim *Oriel 1*) 57.39 (a) + 40 (bcd), *App.Cr*. 50.39 (a), *Tann*. 4.6.4-5 (abde[ii]), *1 Comp*. 3.26.29 (a) + 2.1.8 (d), *1 Comp.Rot*. 2.20.45 (c), *Sang*. 4.9.13 (a) + 5.5.8-9 (abde[ii]), *1 Abr*. 5.6.3 (e[ii]), *Alan*. 2.1.4 (e[ii]), *2 Dun*. 99 (e[ii]), *Fuld*. 2.2.5. (e[ii]), *2 Comp*. 2.2.4 (e[ii]), *Ricc*. (Fragm H) 37(d), X 3.20.45(a) + 2.1.8 (d) + 2.2.8(e[ii]).

VI. To the bishop of Győr

Ideo inter alios

Advice to the bishop of Győr on the administration of justice

Adecretal of Alexander III, dealing with juridical and procedural questions, is found in whole or parts in numerous collections. It occurs with various incipits — *Nos inter alios, Nos qui inter alios, Cum nos inter alios* and *Ideo inter alios*, of which the last is now accepted as the most probable form. Of its four component sections, three are listed in JL, addressed to the bishop *(sic)* of Genoa, and one to the archbishop of Canterbury.[18] The widespread attribution to Genoa is problematical, since the recipient is described as bishop throughout the decretal's transmission, until its editorial emendation to archbishop in the *Decretales*. In the course of its transmission through the collections, the address underwent a bewildering variety of forms, of which the most frequent was *Genuensi* or *Januensi*, for Genoa, but they also include *Exoniensi* and *Bononiensi*, for Exeter and Bologna, and many undecipherable forms — *Dinnen, Luminensi, Lennensi, Geminiensi, Gemietisi, Geriensi, Giriensi* and others.

In reply to the recipient's questions, the pope first speaks in familiar chancery form of the pre-eminence of the Roman Church and its consequent duty to respond to consultations, and deals in turn with a series of juridical questions. Firstly, if the subject of a diocesan bishop is publicly

18 JL 13970 and 12411 respectively.

defamed, but accuser and witnesses are lacking, the bishop should submit him to purgation, unless he appeals to a superior judge, whose ruling he must then obey. Secondly, in the case of a manifest fact, the depositions of witnesses are unnecessary; but if the matter is not manifest and the accused denies it, the witnesses should, by the custom of the Roman Church, be advised, though not compelled, to bear witness, unless it is clear to the judge that they are restrained from bearing witness through fear of the adverse party — though by secular law they may be compelled in some areas to do so. Thirdly, if a priest or clerk brings a property claim against a layman, who asserts that the possessions at stake are his own, the issue should be brought to the secular court, following the maxim *actor semper forum rei debeat sequi,*[19] though in many places the custom is otherwise. Fourthly, the subject of a bishop can be freed from his jurisdiction on grounds of enmity, or opposition, or any evident grounds for suspension — *nullus a suspecto iudice debeat iudicari.*

The letter was listed by Holtzmann among the decretals to Genoa in his „Kanonistische Ergänzungen zur Italia Pontificia" in 1958, but by the time of its publication he had decided against that attribution — „Genua ist sie jedenfalls zu streichen."[20] Having considered Chur, Gurk, Evora, Orense, Genf, Cracow and Győr as possible interpretations of the various manuscript readings, he decided at that time for Cracow or Győr, and his final unpublished preference was apparently for Győr, though with a mark of interrogation. The assignment to Győr is almost certainly correct, on the basis of two early Italian collections: the primitive collection at San Ambrogio has the address *G. euricen. epo.* (*legi: Ambr.* 45-47, but cf. Holtzmann and Holtzmann/Cheney: *G. curicensi episcopo,* the basis for the Cracow proposal);[21] and Bernard of Pavia's early systematic collection *Parisiensis secunda* (Bologna, 1177-78) reads *G. eurien. episcopo* (2 *Par.* * 29.7). Additionally, a fragment of Bernards *1 Comp* in Paris MS nouv. acq. 2622 reads *G. erure epo.*, and three manuscripts of the Frankfurt collection have the corrupt derivations *Geriensi* (wrongly altered to *Genuensi in Frcf.Rot.*) and *Giriensi* for the recipient bishop. The probable ancestry of the many variations in *Gueriensis/ Jauriensis* (Győr) is persuasive.

19 Cf. Ad *apostolice sedis,* to Esztergom, V above.
20 *QF* 39 (1958) 101-03 no. 115.
21 HOLTZMANN/CHENEY, 41 nos 45-7.

* * *

WH 514a (olim 276), JL 13970 (abc) + 12411 (d), Ferentino, 25 October 1174-10 October 1175. For the complex transmission of the letter in whole or sections, see „Kan. Erg.", *QF* 38 (1958), 101-03 no. 115.

VII. To recipients in the diocese of Nitra

Volentes vos reddere

Alexander III to recipients in the diocese of Nitra, on the presentation and institution of chaplains within the diocese

The mandate *Volentes vos reddere* survives only in four English and Anglo-Norman collections — *Chelt.*, *Tann.*, *Sang.* and *1 Abr.*, and its transmission raises many problems. No manuscript names the pope who sent the letter, but *Tann.*, *Sang.* and *1 Abr.* have the single word *Idem*, which refers back to Alexander III, while *Chelt.* omits the sender's name and has the problematical heading *Niterinensi ecclesie pertinentibus*, which had evidently caused the scribe some difficulty. The more recent re-binding of the volume in the British Library confirms the problem, in revealing the same hesitant transcription in a scribal guide-line down the edge of the inner margin — *NiteRinesi (? Niterinensi) ecclesie pertinentibus.*[22] Holtzmann recognized the possible corruption of *Nitriensis* in this reading, identifying Nitra/Neutra, a suffragan of Esztergom, now in Czechoslovakia. But although he would not base an identification on this single dubious reading, the suggestion of Nitra remains a most probable working hypothesis.

The letter appears in *Sang.* within the title *De acquirenda et retinenda possessione ecclesiarum et de collusione possessorum punienda.* In this letter the pope orders the recipients to show due obedience and reverence to their diocesan bishop; they must not institute chaplains in their churches in his diocese, unless the appointees are first presented to him; and they must answer to him *de spiritualibus*, and to them *de temporalibus.* They must observe his interdicts, attend his synods, and answer other lawful

22 A similar scribal uncertainty is seen in the corrections and variations in the incipit — the large coloured initial of *Volentes* has been corrected from *Nolentes* in *Chelt.*, and the initial *N* is left uncorrected in *Sang.;* and *nos* appears as *vos* in *1 Abr.*

summonses. If they contravene this ruling, the pope will ratify any sentence the bishop canonically lays on them. The letter in fact follows the familiar formulae of papal letters to religious houses, concerning their relations with their diocesan bishop, and is presumably a section of a longer letter to such a house or filiation in the Nitra diocese.

[Alexander III] Niterinensi ecclesie pertinentibus.

Volentes vos reddere apostolicis monitis ad virtutem obedientie promptiores, vobis per apostolica scripta precipiendo mandamus quatinus venerabili fratri nostro episcopo vestro debitam in omnibus obedientiam et reverentiam impendatis et devote parere curatis, nec aliqui vestrum in ecclesiis suis que sunt infra episcopatum eius presumant instituere capellanos, nisi prius eidem episcopo presententur, ut ab eo curam animarum recipiant, ita quidem quod sibi de spiritualibus et vobis quorum ecclesie sunt de temporalibus debeant respondere.

* * *

WH 1088, JL — , 1159-81. *Chelt.* 4.24, *Tann.* 2.6.10, *Sang.* 2.6.10, *1 Abr.* 2.4.3. Pd *Sang.*

VIII. To the bishop of Vác[23]

Ea noscitur

Celestine III to the bishop of Vác, on the absolution of those who do violence to clerks

The decretal *Ea noscitur* was issued by Celestine III, within the dating limits 5 November 1191 and 4 June 1192[24], as recorded in an excerpt from the the registers of Clement III and Celestine III in the Siguënza manuscript (*Seg.* 52). In response to the recipient bishop's consultation, the pope dealt with various aspects of the canonical requirements of those who lay violent hands on clerks, but lack the capacity to travel to the apostolic

23 Celestine III's decretal *Ex parte Bartholomei* (WH 450, JL 16604), occurs with various addresses (*Aurelian., Varm.* or *Varin., Variensi, Varien.*). Following Theiner, it is addressed to Séez (Sagiensi) in JL, and Friedberg noted the conjecture by Gonzalez that the reading was Vaciensi, Vác. But on his reading of *Cauriensi* in *Seg.* 52, Holtzmann decided for Coria, 21 Jan.-12 March 1193.

24 Corrected from 9 January by Pfaff, *HJb* 78 (1959) 116 and 137.

see for absolution, as the general law demands.[25] The fragility of their sex does not permit women to make the journey, and the old, sick or disabled cannot do so. But they can be counselled by their bishops, and by their authority restored to the community of the faithful, after appropriate satisfaction. It is necessary for others, whether poor or rich, to appear in person before the pope or his legate for absolution. Those who are granted absolution, when in fear of death, must first swear to approach the Roman Church or its legate when restored to health, and accept its mandate.

The letter is found in ten collections, including the Rouen supplement to the Frankfurt collection (*1 Rot.*), several primitive collections (mostly post *1 Comp.*), the Sigüenza manuscript, the famous systematic collection of Gilbertus Anglicus (1202), *Fuldensis* (largely derived from Gilbert and Alan), the Este manuscript at Modena, Johannes Gallensis's *2 Comp.* (1210-12), and the *Decretales* of 1234. The later collections assign the letter to Clement III (1187-March 1191), and lack the recipient's name, but the earlier collections correctly identify Celestine III as sender, explicitly or by inference, though some omit the recipient. He is corruptly named *coarienent. episcopo* in *Mon.* 83, and *vanenen. episcopo* in *Seg.* 52. Only the Rouen canonists preserve a complete and unambiguous version — *Celestinus III Waciensi episcopo. libro 1 R(egistri)*, that is Celestine III to the bishop of Vác (Vaciensis, Vácz), a suffragan of Esztergom, in the first register of Celestine III.

* * *

Ea noscitur: WH 374: (i) *Ea noscitur* + (ii) *Quod utique* + (iii) *Super quo tibi*, JL 16623, 5 November 1191-4 January 1192, *1 Rot.* 25.9, *Hal.* 27, *Mon.* 83, *Gilb.* 5.14.1 (ii-iii), *Est.* 5.18.1 (ii-iii), *Fuld.* 5.21.1. *Crac.* 85, *Seg.* 52, *2 Comp.* 5.18.1 (ii-iii), *X* 5.39.13 (iii); crit.ed. *Századok* 93 (1959) 417 no. 9.

25 *Si quis suadente*, 2nd Lateran Council, 1139.

IX. To the archbishop of Kalocsa

Licet litteras

Alexander III to the archbishop of Kalocsa, concerning the translation of bishop Prodanus to the see of Zagreb.

* *Litteras vestras*, to the archbishop of Kalocsa, is known only in the Cottonian and Peterhouse collections. The pope appears simply as *Idem* in the manuscripts, but was certainly Alexander III, within the period 1163-72. The decretal records his receipt of letters from the king of Hungary, the king's mother, the archbishop and others, in support of the translation of bishop Prodanus to a see whose name is corrupt in the extant texts. From these letters and from the king's messengers, the pope has learned of no necessity or usefulness to justify his consent to the request, and asserts that translation should not be made without good reason. Nevertheless, in consideration of the king's devotion and the bishop's character and learning, he grants the request with clement dispensation. But he does not wish to be petitioned frequently about similar translations, and the archbishop must induce the king to refrain from them.

The internal references point to Stephen III as the petitioner, within the years 1163-72,[26] since his brother and successor Béla III imprisoned Euphrosyne, the queen mother, whose support for the translation the decretal records. But the English scribes of the only surviving copies had evident difficulty in deciphering the name of the diocese in question. The earlier transcription, in the badly mutilated Cottonian manuscript, records the petition *pro uen. fr. n. prodan. [...]* o *in culpa uen. ecca. transferendo*, while the slightly later Peterhouse manuscript has the still more garbled version *pro uen. fri. nostro prodan. epo. in cupa uen.fr.ecca. transferendo* (presumably repeating *uen.fri....uen.fr.* in scribal confusion). On the advice of Schünemann, Holtzmann proposed the emended solution *pro venerabili fratri nostro Prodano episcopo in Culpanensem ecclesiam transferendo* (that is, *in culpa uen. ecca. = in culpanensem ecclesiam*). The *ecclesia Culpanensis*, taking its name from the river Culpa/Cupa or Kulpa/Kupa (cf. *cupa* in *Pet.*), identifies the church of Zagreb or Agram, then a suffgragan of Kalocsa, now itself an archbishopric; and bishop

26 GYŐRFFY, „Saint Thomas à Becket", 47-8.

Prodanus in fact occurs in the list of bishops of Zagreb in the relevant period.

* * *

WH 616, JL — , *Cott.* 4.61, Pet. 3.65. *Ungarische Jahr.* 141-42 no. 1; *Századok* 7 410-11 no. 2, 1163/4-72.

X. To the bishop of Split/Spalato

Super eo quod a nobis

Alexander III to the archbishop of Split/Spalato concerning bigamists and simoniacs in ordinations, and uncanonical marriages

The decretal *Super eo quod,* a letter of Alexander III in response to questions raised by the archbishop of Split/Spalato, was treated in three sections in its transmission through the collections. The first and second dealt respectively with bigamists and simoniacs involved in ordinations. In the case of the former, those who ordain them must be deprived of their power and office of ordination, and bigamists receiving orders must be deprived of them, but dispensation is possible in the case of the ordainer. As for simoniacs, the pope replies that he cannot give a certain answer to the recipient, unless he is more surely informed of the circumstances. Some may be ordained simoniacally, without themselves being aware of the fact, and these can remain in their orders, since they are not simoniacs. The third part of the letter, which was not transmitted to the *Decretales,* throws light on uncanonical marriages in the fourth and fifth degrees of consanguinity. Because of the hardness of the people's hearts — *propter duritiam populi* — the archbishop can overlook such uncanonical marriages in silent discretion.

The full text of the letter, which perhaps throws light on the state of religious observance in the society of the region at that time, is known from archival sources only, but a slightly truncated version appears integrally in *Cass.* and *1 Rot.*, and in component chapters (abc) in *Sang.* (c), *1 Comp.* (abc) and the *Decretales* (ab). On the evidence of the Kassel and Rouen manuscripts, the decretal apparently first found its way into the collections from the papal registers, or from an archival source derived from them, since the former preserves the inscription *Idem* (= Alexander III) *in registro spalaten. archiepiscopo,* and the latter originally read

Alexander in Registro Spalaten. episcopo, later emended with the superscript variant *alias Lucius* for the pope's name, and the correction *archiepiscopo* for the recipient's office. The incorrect attribution to Lucius III was transmitted to *Sang., 1 Comp.* and *X,* with the variants *Spolet., Spoletano, Spaloton., Spal.* and others, for the recipient. In his study of the register of Alexander III in the hands of the canonists, Holtzmann noted the archival transmission of the letter, edited by Farlati, with the address *venerabili fratri G(erardo) Salonitano archiepiscopo apostolice sedis legato,* and the date Datum *Beneventi ii kal. februarii,* that is Benevento, 31 January 1168-70. The archival and canonical transmission of the letter are separately registered in JL 11690 and 14100, but relate to one and the same letter.

Alexander III in Registro Spalatensi archiepiscopo.

(a) Super eo quod a nobis tua fraternitas requisivit quid videlicet faciendum sit de bigamis, inquisitioni tue taliter respondemus, quod ordinatores eorum potestate et officio ordinandi, et ordinati, si ad sacros ordines fuerint promoti, eisdem debent ordinibus omnino privari, cum bigami iuxta apostolum non ad sacros ordines debeant promoveri, vel in eis si promoti fuerint aliquatenus permanere. In ordinatore autem potest dispensatio adhiberi, ut ordinandi potestate et officio non privetur. (b) De simoniace vero ordinatis, iuxta postulationem tuam certam tibi non possumus dare responsum, nisi plenius nosceremus qualiter fuerint ordinati, cum quidam licet secundum quandam speciem, utpote ignorantibus ordinatis, simoniace ordinentur, in suis tamen possunt ordinibus remanere, quia simoniaci non sunt. (c) Verum super eo quod quarto vel quinto gradu consanguinitatis in provincia tua dicuntur esse coniuncti, propter duritiam populi talia matrimonia, licet sint contra sacrorum canonum institutionem contracta, sub silentio et dissimulatione poteris preterire.

* * *

WH 1008, JL 14100=11690, Benevento, 31 Jan. 1168-70. *Cass.* 21.21, *1 Rot.* 5.2, *Sang.* 9.16(c), *1 Comp.* 1.13.3 (a), 5.2.18 (b), 4.14.1(c), X 1.21.2(a), 5.3.22(b). *Pd 1 Comp.* (abc), *X* (ab), Farlati, *Illyria sacra* 3.191, Smičiklas, *Cod. dipl. Croatiae, Dalmatiae et Slavoniae* 2.122 no. 117. Cf. W. Holtzmann, „Die Register Papst Alexanders III. in den Händen der Kanonisten", *QF* 30 (1940) 58 no. 30.

XI. To the bishop of Osor

Ad audientiam apostolatus

Clement III to the bishop of Osor and the abot of St Andrew of [?...], on the priest who inadvertantly wounded a member of his household, who later died

Ad audientiam apostolatus is listed in JL among the letters of Clement III (1187-91), with the address *Episcopo Abserenti (Absorensi ?) et abbati sancti Andreae de Bergis*, suggesting as recipients the bishop of Osor/ Oser/Ossero on the Dalmatian island of Kres/Cres/Cherso, a suffragan of Zara, and the head of an abbey of uncertain location. This reading was derived from the Lucca collection *(Luc. 3): abseren. episcopo et abbati sancti andree de b'gis*. Otherwise, of the nine collections known to transmit the letter, only the Siguænza manuscript *(Seg. 11)* provides a territorial designation for the bishop, but it omits the name of the co-recipient abbot's house — *abseren. episcopo et abbati sancti andree de [...];* and the Reims collection (*Rem.* 30) has the garbled reading *episcopo et abbati* sancti andree. Holtzmann considered the possibility that the place-name spellings were corruptions of Oslo and Bergen in Norway, but noted the absence of an abbey of St Andrew in the latter; and in his analysis of *Seg.*, he accepted the identification of Osor as the recipient bishop, and suggested the emendation *abbati sancti Andree de Pelago.* for his colleague. There seems little doubt that Osor was the recipient bishop *(Absarensis/Absorensis)*, and the more precise date 3 July — 16 September 1189 is provided by the register derivative in *Seg.*

The recipients had sought the pope's advice in the case of a priest who, when correcting a member of his household, struck him with his belt, from which a knife accidentally slipped from its sheath, and wounded him. But when the man survived for some time and recovered from his wound, he was stricken by a more grave infirmity and died. Since doubt arose whether the wound was the cause of death, the priest was suspended from office and benefice, and the recipients consulted the pope. The pope replied that, since the safer course should be followed in doubtful matters — *cum in dubiis semitam debeamus eligere tutiorem*, they should enjoin the priest not to minister in holy orders in the future, but they can allow him to minister in minor orders after appropriate penance. On the other hand, if they establish that the man died from some other infirmity, the priest can celebrate divine office, as in the past, with their licence.

Idem [Clemens III] Abseren. episcopo et abbati sancti Andree de [? Pelago]. In eodem libro.

Ad audientiam apostolatus nostri ex parte vestra pervenit quod quidam presbiter, volens corrigere quendam de familia sua, eo cingulo quo cingi solebat illum verberare temptavit, et contigit quod cultellus de vagina que cingulo adherebat elapsus eum in dorso aliquantulum vulneravit. Postmodum vero cum ille vulneratus aliquamdiu vixisset et iam convaluisset a vulnere, alia graviori ut dicitur infirmitate percussus, cum sana mente ac devotione debita viam est universe carnis ingressus. Quia vero utrum occasione vulneris decessisset dubium habebatur, eodem presbitero ab omni officio beneficioque suspenso, quid super hoc vobis esset agendum apostolicam sedem consulere voluisti. Nunc itaque vestre discretionis industrie duximus respondendum quod, cum in dubiis semitam debeamus eligere tutiorem vos convenit iniungere presbitero memorato ne de cetero in sacris ordinibus ad ministrandum accedat. Iniuncta tamen ei penitentia congruenti, poteris ei concedere ut sit contentus in minoribus ordinibus ministrare. Si vero vobis legitime constiterit quod ille ex alia infirmitate obierit, de vestra licentia poterit, sicut erat solitus, divina officia celebrare. Dat. Lat.

* * *

WH 15: JL 16546, 3 July – 16 September 1189. *Seg.* 11, *Luc.* 3, Mon 79, *Rem.* 30, *Gilb.Br.* 5.5.1, *Fuld.* 5.5.1, *Est.* 5.5.1, 2 *Comp.* 5.6.1, *X* 5.12.12 ; *Pd Luc.*, *2 Comp.A*, *X*. Date in *Seg.* and *Luc.*

XII. To the bishop of Arbe

Ex tue fraternitatis consulto

Celestine III to the bishop of Arbe, on clerical transgressions

The decretal *Ex tue fraternitatis consulto* is registered in JL among the letters of Clement III (1187-91), as a response to an unknown bishop, on priests or other clerks in holy orders who are guilty of moral transgressions, perjury, false witness or murder. The question is: can they officiate in their orders after due penance, or be advanced to higher orders in consideration of other merits? The pope declared, on the basis of the sacred canons, that they can neither be promoted nor even retain their previous rank, even after penance, if their offences are notorious or can be judicially proven. On the other hand, if their offences are neither notorious nor proven, they should be admonished, in the interests of their own salvation, not to minister in their orders. But in this situation, since the sin is secret, the recipient cannot debar them from ministry or promotion.

Until the discovery of the Sigüenza collection by Fransen, *Ex tue fraternitatis consulto* was known only in the collection of Gilbertus Anglicus, *Fuld.* and *Comp.*, assigned to Clement III, without identification of its recipient. The Sigüenza manuscript records the decretal among the letters of Celestine III, within the limits 15 April — 25 October 1191, with the address *Arben. episcopo,* that is Arbenensi episcopo, to the bishop of Arbe or Rab, in the province of Zara. It also uniquely preserves the final sentence.

Celestinus III Arbensi episcopo

[i] Ex tue fraternitatis consulto percepimus, te velle apostolice sedis certitudinem[a] edoceri, utrum sacerdotes, vel alii in sacro ordine constituti, qui per lapsum carnis reatum adulterii incurrerunt, vel fornicationis, vel incestus, vel periurii, vel alii falsi testimonii, vel homicidii crimine irretiti., bonum recte conscientie perdiderunt, si peracta condigna penitencia de commisso, in prioribus ordinibus tolerari, vel aliis suffragantibus meritis provehi valeant ad maiora. Super quo fraternitatem tuam presenti responsione reddimus certiorem quatinus si notoria sint[b] crimina, que prediximus, vel ordine iudiciario comprobata, tales reos censura sacrorum canonum, etiam post peractam penitenciam, non tantum ad altiora progredi non permittit, verum etiam iubet gradum pristinum non tenere. Porro si proposita crimina contra aliquem notoria non fuerint, vel ordine iudiciario comprobata, monende sunt persone tales, que eis retinentur obnoxie[c] et terrore iudicii divini obtestande, ut in testimonium dampnationis sue in suscepto ordine non ministrarent. [ii] Verumtamen hoc in casu ultimo, cum peccatum occultum sit, si promoveri vel ministrare desiderant, non potes nec debes ratione aliqua prohibere. Datum Rome.

* * *

WH 515: JL 16617: Clement III, *episcopo cuidam*, 1187-91. Part [i] only: *Gilb.* 1.9.2, *Fuld.* 1.11.1, *2 Comp.* 1.8.3; complete text only in *Seg.* 45: *Idem arben. episcopo, in eodem libro* = Celestine III arbensi episcopo, 15 April—25 October

1191. *Pd* part [i] *2 Comp.*, MANSI 22.550, *PL* 204.1479 no. 4; part [ii] *Seg.* in *RHE* 50 (1955) 432.

[a]certitudine *Gilb.* [b]sunt *2 Comp.* [c]qui eisdem tenentur obnoxii *2 Comp.*

Abbreviations

Canones-Sammlungen = Emil FRIEDBERG, *Die Canones-Sammlungen zwischen Gratian und Bernhard von Pavia* (1897; repr. 1956).

Decretales ineditae = Stanley CHODOROW and Charles DUGGAN, from the papers of W. HOLTZMANN, *Decretales ineditae saeculi XII*, MIC 4 (1982).

HOLTZMANN-CHENEY = Christopher R. CHENEY and Mary G. CHENEY, from the papers of W. HOLTZMANN, *Studies in the collections of twelfth-century decretals*, MIC 3 (1979).

JL = *Regesta pontificum romanorum ... ad annum 1198*, ed. P. JAFFÉ; 2nd ed. S. LOEWENFELD *at al.*, 2 vols. Leipzig (1885-8).

MANSI = *Sanctorum conciliorum nova et amplissima collectio*, ed. J. D. MANSI (1759-98).

MIC = *Monumenta Iuris Canonici, Series B: Corpus Collectionum*, Città del Vaticano.

Pd = *printed in*

PL = *Patrologiae cursus completus, series latina*, ed. J. P. MIGNE, Paris 1844-64.

QF = *Quellen und Forschungen aus italienischen Archiven und Bibliotheken.*

RHE = *Revue d'Histoire Ecclésiastique*

SINGER, *Neue Beiträge* = H. SINGER, *Neue Beiträge über die Dekretalen-sammlungen vor und nach Bernhard von Pavia*, Sitzungsberichte der Kais. Akademie der Wissenschaften in Wien, philos.-histor. Klasse 171 (1914).

WH = Walther HOLTZMANN, *Regesta decretalium saeculi XII.*

ZRG Kan. Abt = *Zeitschrift der Savigny-Stiftung für Rechtsgeschichte, Kanonistische Abteilung.*

Sigla of decretal collections

The complete list of all known decretals collections of the twelfth century, with full bibliographical details of editions, analyses and secondary literature, is provided in HOLTZMANN-CHENEY, xx-xxxi, and Decretales ineditae , xix-xxxi.

1 Abr.	=	*Abrincensis Prima: Singer, Neue Beiträge*, 355-400.
Alan.	=	*Coll. Alani:* R. von Heckel, in *ZRG Kan.Abt.* 29 (1940) 226-334.
1 Alc.	=	*Alcobacensis prima:* Holtzmann-Cheney, 8-25; Duggan, in *Studia Gratiana* 14 (1967) 51-71; idem, *Decretals of Alexander III* 87-106.
* *Ambr.*	=	*Amrosiana:* Holtzmann-Cheney, 35-42.
App.	=	*Appendix Concilii Lateranensis:*
Cr.	=	*editio princeps: Concilia omnia tam generalia quam particularia*, ed. P. Crabbe (1551), 2. 820-944; Mansi, 22. 248-453.
Aur.	=	*Aureavallensis:* W. Holtzmann, in *ZRG Kan. Abt.* 16 (1927) 77-115.
Bamb.	=	*Bambergensis:* W. Deeters, *Die Bambergensisgruppe der Dekretalen-sammlungen des 12. Jhdts.*(1956): Inaugural Dissertation ... der Philos. Fakultät die Rheinischen Friedrich Wilhelms-Universität.
* *O*	=	Oxford, Oriel College 53, fols. 34049v (*olim* 240-49)
Cass.	=	*Casselana:* J. H. Boehmer, *Corpus iuris canonici 2* (1747); Deeters, *Bambergensisgruppe* 7-9.
Chelt.	=	*Cheltenhamensis:* London, British Library Egerton 2819, fols. 11r-102r.
Claud.	=	*Claudiana:* London British Library Cotton Claudius A.iv, fols. 193r-220r (*olim* 189r-216r); Holtzmann-Cheney, 132-4.
Claustr.	=	*Claustroneoburgensis:* F.Schönsteiner, in *Jahrbuch des Stiftes Klosterneuburg 2* (1909) 1-154.
1, 2 Comp.	=	*Compilatio prima, secunda:*
A.	=	*Antiquae collectiones decretalium*, ed. Antonio Agustín (1576); reissued in *Opera omnia 4* (1769).
F.	=	E. Friedberg, *Quinque compilationes antiquae necnon*

V

		collectio canonum Lipsiensis (1882; repr. 1956).
1.Comp.Rot.	=	*Compilatio prima*, abbreviation with additions in Paris, Bibliothèque Nationale lat. 3922A, fols. 211r-227v: StephanKuttner, *Repertorium der Kanonistik: Prodromus corporis glossarum* 1, Studi e Testi 71 (1937) 313-4; Holtzmann-Cheney 138-9.
Cott.	=	*Cottoniana:* London, British Library Cotton Vitellius E.xiii, fols. 204r-288r.
Crac.	=	*Cracoviensis:* Cracow, Kapit. Katedr. 89, 129-47, 150-1; analyzed A. Vetulani, in *Studia 'zródloznawcze/Commentationes 8* (1963) 49-80.
1 Dert.	=	*Dertusensis prima:* WH in ZRG *Kan. Abt.* 16 (1927) 39-77.
2 Dun.	=	*Dunelmensis secunda:* Holtzmann-Cheney 300-18.
Eber.	=	*Eberbacensis:* WH in ZRG *Kan. Abt.* 17 (1928) 548-55.
Est. *	=	*Estensis:* Modena, Bibl. Esten. R.4.16 (Lat. 968, *olim* XII.L.8), fol. 78r-117v.
Flor.	=	*Florianensis:* Holtzmann-Cheney, 43-63.
* *Frcf.*	=	*Francofortana:* Frankfurt, Stadt- und Universitatsbibliothek, Barth. 60, fols. 2r-85r: S. Kuttner, *in ZRG Kan. Abt.* 22 (1933) 370-80.
Max.	=	London, B.L. Egerton 2901, fols. 1r-97r.
Fuld.	=	*Fuldensis:* Heckel, in ZRG *Kan. Abt.* 29 (1940) 165-70 and 353-9.
Gilb.	=	*Coll. Gilberti:* Heckel, in *ZRG Kan. Abt.* 29 (1940) 180-225.
Br.	=	Brussels. Bibliothèque Royale 1407-9 (Cat. 2560), fols. 93-148v.
Hal.	=	*Hallensis:* Holtzmann-Cheney, 233-42.
Lips.	=	*Lipsiensis:* Friedberg, Quinque compilationes antiquae 189-208; Deeters, *Bambergensis-gruppe* 10-11.
Luc.	=	*Lucensis:* Holtzmann-Cheney, 243-71.
Mon.	=	*Monacensis:* Holtzmann-Cheney, 221-32.
Oriel. I	=	*Bamb (O).*
1Par.	=	*Parisiensis prima: Canones-Sammlungen*, 45-63.
2 Par.	=	*Parisiensis secunda: Canones-Sammlungen*, 21-45.
Pet.	=	*Petrihusensis: Cambridge, Peterhouse* 193, final quire; 114, first and final quires; 193,first quire; 203, final

		quire; 180, first and final quires.
Rem.	=	*Remensis:* Reims, Bibl. de la Ville 692, fols. 32r-35v
Ricc.	=	*Fragm. H. (= Fragm. Riccardianum):* Florence, Bibl. Riccardi 338, fols. 215v-223v. WH used the abbreviation „Ricc."
Roff.	=	*Roffensis:* Duggan, *Decretal Collections* 173-87 (numerical concordance with WH 212).
1 Rot.	=	*Rotomagensis prima:* Holtzmann-Cheney 160-207.
Sang	=	*Sangermanensis:* Singer, *Neue Beiträge* 68-354.
Seg.	=	*Coll. Seguntina:* Sigüenza, Bilb. del cabildo, 10, fols. 137-176v. Analyzed by WH in RHE 50 (1955) 400-53.
Tann.	=	*Coll. Tanneri:* W. Holtzmann, in *Festschrift zur Feier des 200 jahr. Bestehens der Akad. der Wissenschaften in Güttingen* (1951) 83-145.
1 Vict.	=	*Victorina prima:* Holtzmann-Cheney, 26-34.
Wig.	=	Wigorniensis: H. E. Lohmann, „Die Collectio Wigorniensis", in ZRG *Kan. Abt.* 22 (1933) 36-187.
X	=	*Decretales Gregorii IX:* Friedberg, *Corpus iuris canonici* 2 (1881).

Errata:
The following should read as 's:
p. 5 note 1, Holtzmans
p. 10, lines 17&21, Esztergoms & thiefs
p. 11, line 23, brothers
p. 12, line 9, popes
p. 18, line 30, Bernards

p. 14, line 7, Lucas's should read Lucas'
p. 14, line 15, 4013 should read 403
p. 22, line, 7, *Litteras vestras* should read *Licet litteras*
p. 29, line 14, *Amrosiana* should read *Ambrosiana*
p. 29, line 25, 34049 should read 340–49
p. 30, line 16, fol. 78r-117v. should read fols. 78r-117v.
p. 30, line 18, Universitatsbibliothek should read Universitätsbibliothek

VI

ITALIAN MARRIAGE DECRETALS IN ENGLISH COLLECTIONS: WITH SPECIAL REFERENCE TO THE PETERHOUSE COLLECTION

Dauvillier rightly observed that the most important work in the elaboration of the classical law of marriage was that of Alexander III (1159-81)[1]. From an historical viewpoint, it is no less true that a clear majority of Alexander's permanently important rulings on marriage questions are found in English or Italian decretals. Indeed, in a recent re-examination of Dauvillier's seminal work, focused on 49 letters (all but one being decretals of Alexander III), 20 are Italian, 18 English, ten French and one German[2]. The proportions are not altogether surprising, since roughly three quarters of all Alexander's decretals in the collections were sent to English or Italian recipients-about 400 to England or the Angevin territories on the continent, and more than 120 to Italian prelates, in a total of over 700 letters[3]. But an even more remarkable feature is the high proportion of Italian marriage decretals in English collections, some indeed otherwise unknown, others appearing for the first time in English and Anglo-Norman collections.

An early stage in the process by which a coherent body of marriage decretals was achieved is seen in the 'French' collections *Cantabrigiensis* (now in the library of Trinity College, Cambridge) and *Victorina prima* (from

* A list of abbreviations, including the sigla of decretal collections, is given at the end of this paper. Numbers printed throughout the paper in brackets and bold type refer to the select analysis of the Peterhouse collection in Part 1.

1. J. DAUVILLIER, *Le mariage dans le droit classique de l'Église depuis le Décret de Gratien (1140) jusqu'à la mort de Clément V (1314)*, Paris 1933, p. 473.

2. C. DONAHUE, *The dating of Alexander the Third's marriage decretals: Dauvillier revisited after fifty years*, «Zeitschrift der Savigny - Stiftung für Rechtsgeschichte, Kanonistische Abteilung (hereafter ZRG Kan. Abt.)», LXIX, p. 74 - 81; on Alexander's marriage decretals to England, cf. C. DUGGAN, *Equity and compassion in papal marriage decretals to England*, in *Love and marriage in the twelfth century*, edd. W. VAN HOECKE and A. WELKNHUYSEN, Leuven 1981, p. 59-87.

3. W. HOLTZMANN, *Über eine Ausgabe der päpstlichen Dekretalen des 12. Jahrhunderts*, «Nachrichten Akad. Göttingen», 1945, 34, Anh. 1. On Italian decretals in general, see especially *KE* (1957), p. 67 - 73 = (1959), p. 13 - 19, *et passim*.

St-Victor in Paris). The Cambridge collection was once assumed to be of English provenance, but is classified as French by Holtzmann, and is certainly related to the St-Victor collection, which in some respects preserves an earlier arrangement, and the Paris and Orval collections (*Parisiensis prima* and *Aureavallensis*), which make up the 'French' family. But there are undoubted links between the 'French' collections and English sources[4]. The marriage decretals in *1 Vict.* are found scattered in small groups among the other letters, but the inscriptions and incipits of 25 of them are also gathered together under the heading *De coniugiis*, as its 110th item. In precisely the same order as in this list in *1 Vict.*, with a few additions, the letters appear in an unbroken sequence in *Cantab.* (nos. 75-96), as a clearly distinct and separately transcribed section of marriage decretals[5]. For present purposes, it may be noted that eleven of these letters were sent to Italian recipients, respectively to Cassino (75), Termoli (78), Brescia (81), Anglona (84), Palermo (87), Trani (89), Bari (90), Pisa (91), Fondi (92A), Salerno (94), and Bisceglie (95), and a further decretal to Bisceglie (97) appears as the first of a group of four additions[6]. The commission to the bishop of Anglona is addressed in *Cantab.* and *1 Vict.* in an unusually accurate form (which was later lost in the letter's transmission through the collections), and that to the bishop of Fondi is found only in these two collections[7]. Neither has letters later than Alexander III.

In the closing months of Alexander's pontificate, or shortly after, the archetype of the 'Worcester' family opened its seven-fold division with a book of marriage decretals, entitled *de statu et iure coniugii sive contracti sive contrahendi*[8]. This work of clearly English authorship was linked with Exeter and Worcester, and was destined to leave its imprint, through the systematic *Appendix Concilii Lateranensis* (from 1184), on many great collections in the succeeding decades, and through them on the official corpus of canon law in the next century[9]. The 'Worcester' archetype has not survived, but can be

4. *Victorina prima*: HOLTZMANN-CHENEY, p. 26-34; *Cantabrigiensis*: E. FRIEDBERG, *Die Canones - Summlungen zwischen Gratian und Bernhard von Pavia* (hereafter *Canones - Sammlungen*), Leipzig 1897 (repr. Graz 1958), p. 5 - 21; *Parisiensis prima*: *ibid.*, p. 45 - 63; *Aureavallensis* (Orval): HOLTZMANN, «ZRG Kan. Abt.», XVI (1927), p. 77-115.

5. HOLTZMANN-CHENEY, p. 28; *Cantab.* 75-100: Cambridge, Trinity College MS R. 9. 17, fols 98r-107v; *Canones-Sammlungen*, p. 18-21.

6. Appendix 1, below: Comparative Table: *Cantabrigiensis*, 75 - 97.

7. *Cantab.* 84 and 92A: pd *Canones-Sammlungen*, p. 19-20.

8. H. E. LOHMANN, *Die Collectio Wigorniensis*, «ZRG Kan. Abt.», XXII (1933) p. 39-40, 79-89 and 164-68; the *terminus a quo* of the «Worcester» archetype is fixed by its inclusion of *Recepimus* (Wig. 7.59), to the bishop of Durham and the abbots of Bury St Edmunds (who had meanwhile died) and St Albans: *WH* 846, *JL* 14365, Tusculum 23 January 1181.

9. C. DUGGAN, *English canonists and the* Appendix Concilii Lateranensis, *with an analysis of the St John's College, Cambridge, MS 148'*, «Traditio», XVIII (1962) p. 459 - 68; repr. in *Canon Law in medieval England: The Becket dispute and decretal collections*, Variorum reprints, London

deduced from its descendants. Its book of marriage decretals comprised 44 letters, of which 12 were sent to Italian recipients-to Trani (3), Asti (15), Termoli (18), Brescia (22), Palermo (23), Civita Castellana (24), Pisa (25), Salerno (28), Cassino (36), Padua (38 and 40) and Lucca (41)[10]. Seven of these letters had previously appeared within the sequence 75-94 in *Cantab.* (though the 'Worcester' archetype was not directly dependent on it), and ten in the Italian primitive collection *Cusana* [11]. A further letter is addressed to Cassino in the 'Worcester' archetype and its descendants, but elsewhere to the archbishop of Ravenna, Genoa or York; and the assignment to York seems most likely[12]. The first addition to the archetype in the 'Worcester' collection *Wigorniensis* is the commission to Anglona noted in *Cantab.* and *1 Vict.* above, but it appears in *Wig.* with the dubious address *Meldelsi*, discussed below[13]. Again, neither the archetype nor *Wig.* has letters later than Alexander III, though decretals of Lucius III and Urban III were added by later hands in *Wig*[14].

The final extant members of the 'Worcester' family are the Cottonian and Peterhouse collections, dating from the mid-late 1190s[15]. Like their 'Worcester' ancestors, they are arranged in seven books on a subject-matter basis, and leave some of the longer decretals undissected, but they carry the organization of topics further within the component books, and are influenced by other major lines of transmission. By an unfortunate coincidence, each manuscript has suffered substantial loss through damage or dismemberment. The Cottonian collection was severely damaged by the fire in the Cotton Library in 1731, and the Peterhouse collection was dismantled and some of its quires used as binding material in four Dyngley volumes in the Peterhouse Library, with the loss of several quires[16]. They are carefully presented manuscripts, transcribed in double columns, without marginal glossing. They are closely

1982, VIII; P. LANDAU, *Die Entstehung der systematischen Dekretalensammlungen und die europäische Kanonistik des 12. Jahrhunderts*, « ZRG Kan. Abt.», LXVI (1979), p. 124-32 *et passim*; HOLTZMANN-CHENEY, p. 132 -134.

10. Appendix 2, below: Analysis and Comparative Table: *Wigorniensis* 1.3 - 45.

11. *Ibid.*

12. *Wig.* 1.42: *WH* 43, *JL* 14164, 1159-81; DUGGAN, *Decretals of Alexander III to England*, in *Miscellanea Rolando Bandinelli Papa Alessandro III*, ed F. LIOTTA, Siena 1986, p. 117-118.

13. *Wig.* 1.45: LOHMANN, *Collectio Wigorniensis*, p. 88; cf. Part 3, below: *Decretals to Ascoli Piceno, Asti and Anglona.*

14. C. DUGGAN, *The Trinity collection of decretals and the early Worcester family*, «Traditio», XVII (1961), p. 516; repr. in *Canon Law in medieval England*, VII.

15. *Cottoniana*: London, BL Cotton MS Vitellius E. xiii, fols. 204r-288r; *Petrihusensis*: Cambridge, Peterhouse MSS 193 final quire, 114 first and final quires, 193 first quire, 203 final quire, 180 first and final quires Cf. C. DUGGAN, *Twelfth-Century decretal collections and their importance in English history* (hereafter *Decretal collections*), London 1963, p. 95, 103-09; 187-92: tables V-VII.

16. *Ibid.*, p. 103-04.

related to one another in subject-matter, organization, format and palaeographical detail, and there is nothing inconsistent with their being the products of a single scriptorium. The Peterhouse collection (*post* 1195) is later in contents and organization, and more finished in presentation: it distributes more appropriately decretals found in the closing folios of the Cottonian collection (where they were presumably late acquisitions), inserts the rubrics for titles within the books, and at times assembles titles by simply listing cross references to decretals transcribed in other sections[17].

From a broader historical viewpoint, the most valuable feature of the Cottonian and Peterhouse collections is the extraordinary number of rare or otherwise-unknown decretals which they contain, as clearly shown in the *Decretales ineditae saeculi XII*, published in 1982. Of the 108 letters printed in that volume, mostly for the first time, 45 are found in either *Cott.* or *Pet.*, or in both[18]. They include letters to recipients in the provinces of Sens, Reims, Bordeaux, Canterbury and York, and to Scotland, Norway, Hungary and Jerusalem. The number of such discoveries would have been far greater, if Holtzmann had not already published the Norwegian and Italian decretals, many of them from the Cottonian and Peterhouse manuscripts[19].

There is no doubt of the English provenance of these collections. Their basic derivation from the 'Worcester' tradition and inclusion of many English decretals unknown elsewhere, with unusually accurate names of persons and places, their palaeographical character and archival location - all such features confirm their English origin. Moreover, the Cottonian-Peterhouse scribes reveal a rare familiarity with old English place-names, transcribed in forms unlikely to have emanated in such literation from the Roman curia, with the Old English runic characters thorn, the suffix -th, and wen[20]. A further notable feature is that this rich store of rare decretals, appearing for the first time in collections made in England in or after the mid-1190s, were almost all issued

17. E.g., *Pet.* MS 203, final quire, fol. 1va.

18. *Decretales ineditae saeculi XII*, ed. et rev. S. CHODOROW and C. DUGGAN, from the papers of W. HOLTZMANN, *Monumenta Iuris Canonici, Series B: Corpus Collectionum* (hereafter *Decretales ineditae*), 4, Città del Vaticano 1982, epp. 1,6,9,10, 13-16, 21, 22, 24, 25, 32, 35-38, 40 (38 and 40 in *Chelt.* and *Cott.* only), 44, 48, 55, 57, 58, 62-64, 68, 70, 72, 80, 83 (in *Pet.* and *Bridl.* only), 86-89, 91, 92, 96, 98, 100, 105-07; sections of 14, 32, 64 and 89 are found also in a small number of other collections. Additionally, the most complete version of 30 (a) is in *Pet.*, and sections of 43 are in *Cott.* and *Pet.*

19. W. HOLTZMANN, *Krone und Kirche in Norwegen im 12. Jahrhundert*, «Deutsches Archiv» II (1938), p. 383-395, nos. 1-11; cf. V. SKÅNLAND, *Supplarende og kritiske bemerkningen til Eirik Vandrik: Latinske dokument til Norsk historie fram til ar 1204*, «Historisk Tidsskrift», XLI (1961-62), p. 136-138, no. 11; HOLTZMANN, *KE*.

20. E.g., *priori sancte fritheswithe* (Fritheswthe/Frideswide): *Cott.* 6.21, fol. 266rb; *Referentibus canonicis de Kinelworthe* (Kenilworth): *Pet.* 2.18.2, cod. 193, first quire, fol. 2r[a]. The scribes also reveal a knowledge of arabic as well as roman numerals.

by Alexander III, who had died at least fourteen years earlier. The wider technical context of the Cottonian and Peterhouse collections, their varied sources and probable provenance, are fully discussed in a forthcoming study[21]. The theme of the present paper is their reception of Italian marriage decretals, the Peterhouse collection being chosen as the basis of reference, because of its more developed form and less mutilated physical condition.

1. Italian marriage decretals in the Peterhouse collection

Thirty-two of the 34 decretals listed below, from a total of 95 items in Book I of the Peterhouse collection, were sent to recipients in the following dioceses or provinces: Agrigento (**63**), Anagni (**64**), Anglona (**88**: MS: Mainz), Ascoli Piceno (**25**), Asti (**66**; MS: St Albans), ? Bari (**38**; MS: *Belarensi)*, Bisceglie (34), Brescia (39), ? Capua (**69**), Cassino (29), Civita Castellana (40), Conza (**23**), Cosenza (**95**), Fermo (**68**), Florence (11 and 91), Genoa (4), Grado (33), Lucca (42), Mottola (**86**), Padua (2 and 54), Palermo (41), Pavia (32), Pisa (47), Rapolla (7), Salerno (3), Salpi (56), Termoli (78), Tivoli (**44**), Trani (18) and Veroli (59); additionally, one letter was sent to cardinal Laborans (27), and one to unidentified recipients (R. hospitalario et R.) in the region of Cassino (**61**). The decretals assigned here to Ascoli Piceno, Asti and Anglona were either not accepted or not recognized as such by Holtzmann, and therefore are not listed in his *Kanonistische Ergänzungen* (*KE*). Nor are they so addressed in the Cottonian and Peterhouse collections, but their Italian provenance is argued below[22].

Many of the 34 decretals are widely found in the collections generally, and are familiar to historians of canon law. Of the 20 Italian decretals included in Charles Donahue's study on Dauvillier's classic work, eleven are found in *Cott.* and Pet., addressed to Padua (2), Salerno (3), Genoa (4), Rapolla (7), Trani (18), Cassino (29), Pavia (32), Grado (33), Brescia (39), Padua (54), and Anglona (**88**; MS: Mainz)[23]. Some of the 34 letters are rescripts on various principles of law, each letter dealing with a series of questions raised by the recipient, and are comparable with well-known letters sent to prelates in England, France and other regions. They are occasionally left undissected in *Cott.* and *Pet.*, reflecting the unsystematic conventions of their earliest

21. An analysis of the Royal, Bridlington, Claudian, Cheltenham, Cottonian and Peterhouse collections is in an advanced state of preparation for publication in the *Monumenta Iuris Canonici* series (Biblioteca Apostolica Vaticana).

22. Part. 3, below: *Decretals to Ascoli Piceno, Asti and Anglona.*

23. DONAHUE, *The dating of Alexander III's marriage decretals*, p. 75-81, WH, sub numeris 41, 204, 436, 476, 610, 620, 635, 798 (abbrev. of 885), 985 (assigned to Meaux; *recte* Anglona), 991 and 1033.

ancestors, though component parts of some have been detached and transposed to other sections[24].

A few of the letters require brief comment. The attribution of *Si quando fratres* (**38**) to Bari is hypothetical. The letter is not included in Holtzmann's *KE*, but Bari (*Barensis*) has been proposed in the *Decretales ineditae*, from a consideration of its subject-matter and address (*Belarensi*) in *Pet.*[25]. The identification of Salpi as the recipient of *Continebatur in litteris* (56) rests on Holtzmann's recognition of *Salpen.* in the Leipzig and Vienna copies of the *Appendix*; the decretal is found integrally only in the Italian primitive collection *Cusana*, but with the false attribution *Alpenen. concilio*, and both Uppsala and Spalato had been conjectured from the variant manuscript readings[26]. The decretal *Requisivit a nobis* (7) lacks an address in both *Cott.* and *Pet.*, but is a mandate of Lucius III to the bishop of Rapolla. It is of special interest in the study of English collections, as one of the earliest letters of Lucius III added by later hands to those of Alexander III in the Durham and Worcester collections, and it appears also in a supplement to the 'Worcester' archetype in the Klosterneuburg collection[27].

All but five or six of the 34 decretals are letters of Alexander III, the exceptions being of Lucius III (**7**), Celestine II (11), Eugenius III (**25** and possibly **66**), Benedict VIII (33) and Urban III (91), though (33) and (91) are wrongly assigned to Alexander III in *Pet.*, as is (33) in *Cott.*, which lacks (91). *Ad aures nostras* (55) is addressed to the abbot of Cassino in both *Cott.* and *Pet.*, as a result of the doubtful 'Worcester' transmission mentioned above, and was probably sent to York[28]. The latest item among the marriage decretals in *Pet.* is *Si matrimonii causa* (1193-98), of Celestine III to archbishop Hubert Walter of Canterbury, but a further letter of Celestine to Hubert, *Appellationis inhibitio* (7 September 1195), is found in *Pet.* 2[29]. Neither of these letters was known to *Cott.*

Peterhouse Collection Book I

(Peterhouse cod. 193, final quire, fols 7rb-8vb + cod. 114, first quire, fols 1ra-8vb + final quire, fols 1va-3rb; cf. Cottonian Collection: BL Cotton MS

24. *KE*, sub numeris.

25. *Decretales ineditae*, p. 173-74, no. 98; cf. n. 45, below.

26. *KE* 190abc; *Cott.* 2.51 and *Pet.* 1.56 = part (a) only; both *Cott.* 4.67 and *Pet.* 3.70 (Ypsalensi episcopo) assign part (c) to Lucius III.

27. Part 4, below: *Decretals to cardinal Laborans, Acerno, Cosenza and Rapolla*; *1 Dun.* 3.68: fol. 18ra, Lucius III Rapulensi (R.Apulensi^{ac}) episcopo; Wig. add. 2: fol. 63v^{a-b} (letters of Lucius III), margin: Rapullensi episcopo; *Claustr.* 319 *sine inscript.*

28. Cf. n. 12, above.

29. *Pet.* 1.83, *WH* 908, *JL* 17165, 1193-98; *Pet.* 2.17.3 + 2.15.2, *WH* 91, *JL* 17679 + 17614.

Vitellius E.XIII, fols 210va-225rb.) The list provides for each item the corresponding location in *Cott.* (which does not include nos 27, 32 or 91), the **WH**, **KE** and **JL** references, and the date. Square brackets indicate omissions from the manuscript; angle brackets supply passages lost or illegible through damage; and round brackets note faulty readings. Letters numbered in bold type (**7**, **23**, **25**, **27**, **38**, **44**, **61**, **63**, **64**, **66**, **68**, **69**, **86**, **88** and **95**) are the subject of special consideration in the present study.

2. Alexander III [G.] Paduano episcopo. *Sollicitudini sedis...stare.*
   Cott. 2.2: *WH* 991, *KE* 132, *JL* 14235, 1168-81.

3. Alexander III Salernitano archiepiscopo. *Licet preter...incurrit.*
   Cott. 2.3: *WH* 620, *KE* 176, *JL* 14091, Autumn 1176.

4. Alexander III Januensi [archi]episcopo. *Quia tua fraternitas... adimplevit.*
   Cott. 2.4: *WH* 1033, *KE* 116, *JL* 13969, 1159-81.

7. **[Lucius III Rapullensi episcopo.]** *Requisivit a nobis...debebit.*
   Cott. 2.7: *WH* 885, *KE* 207, *JL* 15165, 1181-85.

11. Celestinus [II] papa Florentine ecclesie episcopo.
    Videtur nobis...assumere.
    Cott. 2.81: *WH* 1084(a), *KE* 22 (a), *JK* +384, 1143-44.

18. <Alexander III Tranensi archiepiscopo.>
    Continebatur in litteris...separetur.
    Cott. 2.16 (ab): *WH* 204 (ab), *KE* 191(ab), *JL* 14032 (a),
    Anagni 9 Sept. 1173-76.

23. **<Idem [= Alexander III] Con>sano electo**. *De muliere...deponas.*
    Cott. 2.20: *WH* 335a, *KE* 204, *JL* —, c. 1169.

25. **Eugenius papa III Presbitero Esculano episcopo** (MS: pħo esculapio).
    Iuvenis (MS: [ ]Eniens) *ille...dividas*. *Cott.* 2.22: *WH* 596, *KE*--,
    JL 9655, 1145-53.

27. **Alexander III [Laboranti sancte] Marie (MS: Marito) in porticu cardinali (MS ma**[ac]) **[apostolice sedis legato]**. *Super eo quod...dissolvi.*
    Cott. —: *WH* 1010, *KE* 2, *JL* 14161, 1178.

29. Alexander III Cassinensi (MS: Casian.) abbati. *Ex litteris tuis...ignorent.*
    Cott. 2.25:*WH* 436, *KE* 167, *JL* 13838, 1159-81.

32. Idem [= Alexander III] Papiensi electo.
    Ad audientiam nostram...compellas.
    Cott. —: *WH* 41(a), *KE* 95(a), *JL* 13137, *post* 21 May 1180.

33. Benedictus VIII Gradensi (MS: Alexander III Grandensi) patriarche (atque Dominico eius suffraganeo). *Affatus est...voluntati.* *Cott.* 2.12: (from *Lex divine*), *WH* 610, *KE* 145, *JL* 3773, *c.* 1012.

34. Alexander III Vigiliensi episcopo. *Super eo quod...assumi.* *Cott.* 2.27: *WH* 1012, *KE* 199, *JL* 14133, Benevento 15 Oct. 1167-69.

38. Alexander III ? Barensi (MS: Belarensi) episcopo. *Si quando fratres...habere.* *Cott.* 2.32: *WH* 911a, *KE*--, *JL*--, 1159-81. [Cf. Part 2, below.]

39. Alexander III [W.] Brixiensi (MS: Brisiensi) episcopo. *Ex publico...transire.* *Cott.* 2.33: *WH* 476, *KE* 105, *JL* 13787, 1159-79.

40. Alexander III Magistro Fidantie canonico Civitatensi. *Ad audientiam nostram...denunties.* *Cott.* 2.34: *WH* 75, *KE* 21, *JL* 13854, Capua 21 Dec. 1176.

41. Alexander III Panormitano archiepiscopo. *Veniens ad presentiam... postponas.* *Cott.* 2.35: *WH* 1074, *KE* 218, *JL* 14165, 1159-81.

42. Alexander III Lucensi episcopo. *Consuluit nos...promovendus.* *Cott.* 2.36: *WH* 187(ab), *KE* 40(ab), *JL* 14005, 1159-81.

44. Alexander III Tiburiensi (MS: triburiensi) episcopo. *Casum quem...iniungas.* *Cott.* 2.38: *WH* 106, *KE* 9, *JL*--, 1159-81.

47. Alexander III Pisano archiepiscopo. *Quidam intravit...corporis.* *Cott.* 2.41: *WH* 814, *KE* 35, *JL* 14061, 1159-81.

54. Alexander III Paduano episcopo. *Littere quas...permittas.* *Cott.* 2.48: *WH* 635, *KE* 133, *JL* 14055, 1166-81.

56. Alexander III [Salpensi episcopo]. *Continebatur in litteris...postponas.* *Cott.* 2.51: *WH* 202(a), *KE* 190(a), *JL* 14101, 1159-81.

59. Alexander III Verulano episcopo .viii. libro registrum. *Ex relatione J.... videaris. Cott.*--: *WH* 483, *KE* 16, *JL* 10641, Benevento 20 Sept. 1167-19 Sept. 1168.

61. Alexander III R. hospitalario [et] R. *Non semel...terminetis.* *Cott.* 2.55: *WH* 670, *KE* 166, *JL*--, 1171-74.

63. Alexander III Agrigentino (MS: Agrigrantino) episcopo. *Latrix presentium A....redire. Cott.* 2.57: *WH* 608, *KE* 221, *JL*--, 1159-81.

64. Alexander III Anagnino (MS: Anaguino) episcopo. *Notum sit... probatur.* *Cott.* 2.58: *WH* 681, *KE* 13, *JL*--, October 1170.

66. [Eugenius III *vel* Alexander III] Asteni electo (MS: Alexander III abbati sancti Albani). *Singulorum consultationibus... reportare.* *Cott.* 2.65: *WH* 989, *KE*--, *JL* 12636, late 1145-early 1146, or August1172-July 1173.

68. Alexander III Firmano episcopo. *In litteris quas...imponas.* *Cott.* 2.61: *WH* 556, *KE* 49, *JL* 13935, 1159-81.

69. Alexander III archiepiscopo [Capuano et I. archidiacono sancti Germani]. *Cum in ecclesia...honoret.* *Cott..* 2.62: *WH* 258, *KE* 170, *JL*--, 1168-81.

78. Alexander III episcopo et dilectis filiis canonicis et omni clero et populo Termulano (MS: transmulanensi). *Cum inter I. veterem...inferri.* *Cott.* 2.67: *WH* 266, *KE* 186, *JL* 14194, Benevento 26 Sept. 1167-69.

86. Alexander [III] episcopo de Motulo. *Conquerente nobis I....astringas.* *Cott.* 2.75: *WH* 142, *KE* 203, *JL*--, 1159-81.

88. Alexander III Anglonensi episcopo (MS: Maguntino archiepiscopo). *Significavit nobis...decidas.* *Cott.* 2.76: *WH* 985, *KE*--, *JL* 13746, 1159-81.

91. Urbanus III (MS: Alexander III) Florentino episcopo. *Litteras fraternitatis...relinquendum.* *Cott.*--: *WH* 627, *KE* 24, *JL* 15734, 1185-87.

95. [Alexander III Cusentino archiepiscopo.] *Viduis vero...adhiberi.* *Cott.* 5.11: *WH* 1085, *KE* 211, *JL*--, 1159-81.

2. Italian marriage decretals found only in the Cottonian and Peterhouse collections (Anagni, Cassino region, Capua, Mottola, Conza, Cosenza, possibly Bari, and Larino or Lesina), or otherwise rarely known (Fermo, Tivoli and Agrigento)

The inclusion of rare decretals in the Cottonian and Peterhouse collections has been mentioned above. The compilers of these large collections drew on a range of well-known lines of transmission, but also on a geographically broad spread of otherwise-unknown letters of Alexander III. The intricate web of their possible sources will be discussed elsewhere. To cite a single example, the presence in *Cott.* and *Pet.* of decretals of Alexander III to archbishop Eystein of Trondheim and his suffragans may be explained by his presence in England in the early 1180s. An exile from the Norwegian kingdom, he stayed in the abbey of Bury St Edmunds from August 1181 to February 1182, and his help at that time in securing a free election of the new abbot and his report in the presence of king Henry II are recorded by Jocelin of Brakelond[30].

The Italian decretals rediscovered in *Cott.* and *Pet.* relate by no means only to marriage questions. Three such letters of Alexander III to Italian recipients are known only in the Cottonian collection, but were perhaps also in the lost quires of the Peterhouse collection. With careful discrimination, a letter to the bishop of Pavia dealt with schismatic clergy in the city[31]. Another, to the decumans and college of priests at Milan, concerned the election of the primicerius there[32]. A third, to the archbishop of Capua, ruled on the resistance of the abbess-elect of S. Maria in Capua to the archbishop's requirement of her profession of obedience. The matter was brought to the pope by the bishop of Aquino and the abbot of S. Vicenzo, and the pope's response included the precise form of profession required from the elect and possible sanctions in the event of her resistance[33]. A fourth decretal in *Cott.* and *Pet.*, but otherwise known only in the Anglo-Norman *Sangermanensis* and *Abrincensis prima*, records the count of Fondi's pious desire to build a church on his estate at *castellum Scrofule*; in acceding to his proposal, the pope sent an autographed stone for incorporation in the building, and confirmed the direct subjection of the estate and church to the Roman see[34]. But the marriage decretals are the focus of interest here.

The close and constant relations between the English church and the Roman curia, as also between the English kingdom and the Regno, are too familiar to require further explanation. Likewise, many reciprocal influences are evident in the early English and Italian decretal collections—the presence of Italian decretals in the primitive Durham collection, the unique survival of a cluster of English decretals, concerning the church of Bungay and a clerk of earl Hugh of Norfolk, in the Italian *St Florian* collection, and the reception of the early English *Wigorniensis altera* (*c.* 1175) by the 'Italian' family of collections— these are but a few characteristic examples[35]. The inclusion of nine rare Italian marriage decretals in *Cott.* and *Pet.* (mostly in both) suggests the accessibility of a collection of such letters to the archetype's compiler, and

30. DUGGAN, *Decretal collections*, p. 116-17.

31. *In litteris quas* (1177), *KE* 93, *JL* —, *Cott.* 5.22 only.

32. *Conquerebamini vos* (1172-73), *KE* 86, *JL* —, *Cott.* 6.82 only.

33. *Venerabilem fratrem* (1166-69), *KE* 171, *JL* —, *Cott.* 6.88 only.

34. Alexander III to the count of Fondi (*nobili viro de Aquila, Fundano comiti*): *Dilectus filius P.* (1173), *KE* 161, *JL* —, *Cott.* 4.80, *Pet.* 3.84, *Sang.* 7.127, *1 Abr.* 7.11.

35. For the Durham collection, cf. HOLTZMANN-CHENEY: p. 35-42, *Collectio Ambrosiana*, esp. p. 36; and p. 75-99, *Collectio Dunelmensis prima*, esp. p. 76-77. For the Norfolk/Bungay decretals, cf. *Decretales ineditae*, p. 81-86, no 46; p. 92-96, nos. 51-53, and p. 112 no. 65 (all *sub annis* 1174-75/76). For *Wigorniensis altera*, cf. DUGGAN, *Decretal collections*, p. 69-70 and p. 152-54; and MARY G. CHENEY, *Roger, bishop of Worcester, 1164-1179*, Oxford 1980, p. 200-202.

their occasional juxtaposition in the manuscripts lends colour to such a suggestion. The letters were sent respectively to Conza (**23**), Tivoli (**44**), recipients in the Cassino region (**61**), Agrigento (**63**), Anagni (**64**), Fermo (**68**), the province of Capua (**69**), Mottola (**86**) and Cosenza (**95**). Among the numerous channels of English influence and presence in the Regno, Henry II's daughter Joanna was married to William II of Sicily in 1177, her escort on the journey being the bishop of Norwich, John of Oxford. Among the prelates of English origin in sees of the Regno were Herbert of Middlesex, archbishop of Conza[36]; Richard Palmer, successively bishop of Syracuse and archbishop of Messina; Walter Offamil, archbishop of Palermo, and his brother Bartholomew, successively bishop of Agrigento and archbishop of Palermo[37]. A high point of English contact with Sicily was reached in the course of the Third Crusade, but it is unlikely that a collection of marriage decretals issued exclusively by Alexander III would have been acquired there at that late date.

A feature of these rare Italian decretals in *Cott.* and *Pet.* is that they deal mostly with specific cases, and reveal the pope's discretion and insight in dealing with the moral and human problems involved. They therefore nicely complement the more familiar letters, many of which objectively define doctrinal principles, without reference to individuals. The new letters likewise clearly assert the canonical doctrines at issue. Indeed they proclaim the sanctity and permanence of Christian marriage, but they also reflect the humanity and common-sense of Alexander III, his recognition of human vulnerability, as well as culpability-the equity and compassion which have been discussed elsewhere in his treatment of English cases[38]. Several letters protect the status or well-being of the women involved, others record the presence of one or more of the parties in person in the curia, doubtless reflecting the relatively easy access for Italian litigants.

Three decretals relate to marriage disputes in dioceses of the Roman province, addressed respectively to the bishops of Fermo (**68**), Anagni (**64**) and Tivoli (**44**), and in each case the status of the woman involved is the primary interest[39]. The indissolubility of lawfully contracted marriage and the

36. Herbert was the recipient of *De muliere*; Pet. 1.23, above.

37. E. JAMISON, *The Sicilian Norman kingdom in the mind of Anglo-Norman contemporaries*, «Proceedings of the British Academy», XXIV (1938), p. 237-285, esp. from p. 250 *passim*; A. L. POOLE, *From Domesday Book to Magna Carta, 1087-1216*, Oxford 1951, p.330-332; M. PACAUT, *Papauté, Royauté et épiscopat dans le Royaume de Sicile (deuxième moitié du xiième siècle)*, in *Potere, società e popolo nell'età dei due Guglielmi*, Bari 1981, (Centro di studi normanno-svevi. Atti, 4), p. 37-61, esp. p. 43 and 51-52; Pacaut comments (p. 51) on the small number of papal letters to the Sicilian-Norman kingdom, in comparison with those to England and France, in *JL. IP.*, and the *Papsturkunden*.

38. DUGGAN, *Equity and compassion, passim*.

39. The decretal to Anagni is in Cott. and Pet. only; that to Fermo is in *Cott.*, *Pet.*, 2 *Comp.* 2.12.5 and *X* 2.20.24; and that to Tivoli is in *Roff.* 104, *Claustr.* 301, *Chelt.* 9.57, *Cott.* and *Pet.*

admissibility of evidence against it were defined by the pope in *In litteris quas*, to the bishop of Fermo. The bishop had reported that a nobleman in his diocese had lived with his wife for seven years after their marriage, but then alleged that he had previously known her father's cousin, and adduced three relations to support his claim. The pope declared the immunity of lawful marriage from malicious accusations. Since caution and circumspection are necessary in matrimonial cases, the bishop must not allow a separation on such testimony. Only witnesses of proven life and reputation, who would be unlikely to perjure themselves for anything, could be admitted-*nisi essent probate vite et opinionis, de quibus verisimile non esset quod deberent pro aliquo deierare*. Even so, penance must be imposed on the husband for the sin which he confessed.

The rights and reputation of a woman who had been violently abused were defined by the pope in *Notum sit fraternitati*, to the bishop of Anagni. The woman had been seized by force and outraged by evil men, when she journeyed to Veroli to gain a papal indulgence on the occasion of the dedication of a church for the sick in the leprosaria there. Despite her public acknowledgement of the violence done to her against her will, she was repudiated by her husband, and came to the pope for help. He therefore now sends her back to the bishop, with his mandate to compel her husband to receive her with marital affection, and to do her no harm on account of this matter. If he declines to obey the bishop's orders, the latter must excommunicate him and anyone who impedes her reception. He must forbid all-*tam clericis quam laicis et mulieribus*-to reproach her in any way, and in a striking concluding sentence the pope declares the immunity from punishment of one who is blameless, and the innocence of one whose mind is pure-*nec corpus eius corrumpitur, qui sanam habere mentem probatur*.

In contrast, the decretal *Casum quem*, to the bishop of Tivoli, dealt with the impulsive and erratic behaviour, and human frailty, of a certain woman. Although betrothed, she was suborned by the advice of certain relatives, and took a vow of chastity before the bishop-*votum in manu tua promisit castitatis*, but later changed her mind, married the man without the Church's knowledge, and was now close to childbirth. Having regard for her human weakness-*fragilitatem sexus sicut convenit attendentes*, the pope instructs the bishop to let them live together, unless the woman had bound herself to the religious life-*vinculo professionis* (vel *promissionis*) *astricta se religioni reddiderit*, and if there is no other reasonable hindrance. But she must do penance for the vow she took in anger.

Five decretals deal with specific cases or principles, addressed respectively to recipients in the province of Capua (**69**), the region of Cassino (**61**), Mottola (**86**), Conza (**23**) and Cosenza (**95**)[40]. Nowhere did Alexander III state more

40. All five decretals are in *Cott.* and *Pet.* only.

clearly the sacramental nature of the marriage bond, and his duty to strive by every means to defend it, than when dealing with discreditable allegations against a woman within the jurisdiction of Capua-*Cum in ecclesia Dei magnum sit matrimonii sacramentum, ad ipsum conservandum debemus studio totius attentionis intendere, ne quos Deus coniunxit videamur, quod absit, minus provide dividere.* In this letter, most probably to the archbishop of Capua and archdeacon John of San Germano, the pope recalled that the woman had recently complained to him about her husband Marsilius, but others had now informed him that her husband's uncle (also named Marsilius) had laid charges against her, to the effect that he had himself known her before her marriage, and had adduced witnesses to the fact at the time. He also brought forward two witnesses to her alleged act of adultery with a certain man, whom they observed in her company enter the grounds of a certain knight, one witness claiming that he actually saw the disgraceful act-*addidit se vidisse, quando vir ille cum ea sub ficu rem nefandam commisit.* With prudent care, the pope declared that the parties must not be separated on this testimony, which was unacceptable-the witnesses were not under oath, and were moreover altogether suspect, since witnesses are not usually adduced for acts of this kind. Unless there is some other impediment, the recipients must compel the man to take back the woman, and love and honour her as his wife-*ut mulierem ipsam recipiat et eam tanquam uxorem suam diligat propensius et honoret.*

The human rights and weaknesses involved in such disputes are treated with circumspection in *Non semel sed secundo*, to unidentified commissioners (*R. hospitalario et R*) in the region of Cassino. The plaintiff C. has three times told the pope that he found his wife with a certain Nicholas in his chamber, and that she took to flight when he seized the adulterer. When she alleged that she was unjustly ejected, the dean of Cassino wished to compel her husband to take her back, but changed his mind on learning the truth. But now the abbot of Cassino, acting on a papal commission secured on the wife's behalf, intends to force him to accept her. The pope therefore now rules by apostolic authority that the husband must not be compelled to take back his wife, if it is manifest and attested that he found her basely compromised with the aforesaid Nicholas. But since he should be reconciled with her, or remain continent while she lives, the judges should strictly advise him how difficult, if not impossible, this would be: *ipsum monere curetis attentius et hortari, ut considerans et attendens quomodo vix aut nunquam poterit continere, ipsam sibi reconciliet, ne forte adulterii crimen incurrat.* If he is unwilling to be reconciled with her, they must compel him with ecclesiastical censures to remain continent in her lifetime. If the facts are otherwise, they should nevertheless reach a canonical judgment.

In a complementary ruling, in *Conquerente nobis* to the bishop of Mottola, the pope succinctly repeated in familiar scriptural language the inadmissibility of a wife putting aside her husband, except for adultery, and the necessary reconciliation or vow of continence even in that situation. In this case, the plaintiff husband had reported in person to the pope that his wife had left him, and fled to the bishop of Mottola's diocese. The pope ordered the bishop to compel the woman, under pain of excommunication, to return to her husband, with his possessions which she had taken away with her- *ut ad predictum virum suum cum rebus suis, quas asportavit, mora et occasione postposita redeat.*

The decretal *De muliere* (**23**), to the archbishop of Conza, throws light on social and psychological aspects of contemporary society, and perhaps also on arranged and dynastic marriages. It deals with the delicate case of a 'woman' in her eleventh year-*nunc in anno xi. constitutam,* who seeks a separation from a man, to whom she was married when under age-*infra x. annum*, and by whom she was known. Although such separation is contrary to nature-*licet contra naturam hoc esse noscatur*, the pope orders the archbishop to make a careful enquiry, to discover if the man apparently pleased her, or if she consented, after their physical union in her tenth year, or at the beginning of the eleventh-*in x. anno vel in principio xi^{mi}*, and to discover also the measure of her discretion, and whether malice was involved in the affair. If all these factors or most of them concur, the two cannot be separated, though she is said to object in her eleventh or twelfth year. But if he subdued her by force, and she did not consent at that time, and at once objected in her eleventh year, the archbishop-elect must not delay a sentence of separation.

The single sentence *Viduis vero...adhiberi* (95) is found as the final item, without inscription, in the first book of the Peterhouse collection, and is otherwise known only in the fifth book of the Cottonian collection (5.11), addressed to the (arch)bishop of Cosenza. The ruling states that, by custom and law, blessing is to be denied to widows who re-marry, since almost everywhere in the world that blessing is usually given only to virgins *propter eminentiam sacramenti.*

Because of the supposed improbability of its concluding sentence, the authenticity of *Latrix presentium A.* (**63**), to the bishop of Agrigento, was doubted by Singer. But the letter was later accepted by Holtzmann in the light of the absence of the relevant passage in the Norman *Rotomagensis prima* (where, however, the letter is written over an erasure)[41]. The woman A. confessed to the pope that she had lived a dishonourable life, when deserted by her husband, but now wished to be reconciled with him and expiate her sin. The pope expressed his concern to look to her salvation, lest worse befall-

41. *Sang.* 8.66: H. SINGER, *Neue Beiträge über die Dekretalensammlungen vor und nach Bernhard von Pavia*, «Sitzungsberichte der Kais. Akad. der Wissenschaften in Wien, phil. - hist. Kl», CLXXI (1) (1913), p. 323-24, n. 70: *WH* 608, *KE* 221. In addition to *Cott.*, *Pet.* and *Sang.*, the letter is in *Claustr.* 321, *Tann.* 7.7.3, *I Abr.* 8.5.2, *I Rot.* 1.15 and *Gilb.Brux.* 4.14.1b.

Verum quia nostra interest saluti eius consulere et, ne labatur in deterius, providere, and ordered the bishop to strive to reconcile her with her husband, if he is alive and can be found, and to compel him to take her back, because his desertion of her created the circumstances of her sin-*Ex eo enim, quod eam dereliquit, visus est ei dedisse materiam et occasionem peccandi.* If he cannot be found, the bishop should let her be joined in marital affection with the man who wished to accept her, provided that she returns to the first man, if he is found-*ita quod ad priorem virum debeat, cum fuerit inventus, redire.*

The doubts expressed concerning this letter's authenticity are perhaps resolved by consideration of comparable rulings in English cases. In *Ex litteris fraternitatis*, to archbishop Richard of Canterbury, Alexander III dealt with a quarrel between the clerks H. and Adam over the church of Great Leighs in Essex[42]. Although H. had been appointed parson of the church, Adam was later instituted to it, on the report of the magnate Richard de Lucy that H. was dead, which was untrue. The pope therefore ordered the church to be restored to H., despite the fact that the bishop of London had instituted Adam, thinking H. was dead, just as a wife who has married a second time, thinking her husband is dead, should be restored to the first when the truth is known-*sicut mulier, que putans virum suum mortuum nupsisset secundo, redderetur priori, cum de facto* (vel *defuncto*) *constaret.* And in the mandate *Suggestum fuit nobis,* to bishop John of Chichester, Alexander dealt with the case of a man who went to Jerusalem, when he was alienated from his young wife, but had not returned, though several years had passed, and no certain news could be secured about him[43]. Since the wife, unwilling to wait longer, now wished to marry another, the pope instructed the bishop to try to persuade her to wait, and to make diligent enquiries about the man, but to allow her to marry whom she wishes, if all else fails, lest worse befall-*ne in deterius labatur*[44]. But should the man ever return, the dispute concerning the alleged consanguinity between them must be resolved-*Verumtamen, si vir aliquo tempore redierit, inter ipsum et virginem causam consanguinitatis que inter eos proponitur audire poteris et fine canonico terminare*, which clearly implies that they should then be reunited, if there are no impediments on that account. By a curious coincidence this final phrase is omitted in the English and Norman collections *Tanner*, *Sang.* and *1 Abr.*, just as the corresponding phrase is omitted from *Latrix presentium A.* in *1 Rot.*

42. WH 421, *JL* —, 1179-81: *Cott.* 6.55, *Tann.* 5.1.12, *Sang.* 6.1.15, *1 Abr.* 6.1.7 and *2 Dun.* 102. Cf. M. CHENEY, *Roger, bishop of Worcester*, p. 340, no 48.

43. *WH* 1006, *JL* —, 1174-81: *Fragm. Salmantinum* 8, *Chelt.* 9.60, *Cott.* 2.74, *Pet.* 1.85, *Tann.* 7.10.10, *Sang.* 9. 13 and *1 Abr.* 8.10.2. The dating limits of the letter are narrowed by the identification of John as bishop of Chichester in the Salamanca fragment; cf. DUGGAN, *Equity and compassion*, p. 81-82.

44 Cf. *ne labatur in deterius* in *Latrix presentium A.* (preceding paragraph).

The Italian provenance of two further decretals is conjectural. *Si quando fratres* (**38**) is found only in *Cott.* and *Pet.*, with its address lost through mutilation in the former, and the ambiguous reading *Belarensi* in the latter. Holtzmann's suggestion that the letter was sent to Beauvais (*Belvacensi*) is perhaps weakened by the immediately-preceding letter in very similar terms, clearly addressed to the bishop of Beauvais in both collections. Among the possible emendations is *Barensi*, for Bari[45]. In response to the recipient's enquiry about clandestine marriages, the pope ruled that, if the contracting parties later wished such a marriage to be publicly celebrated, according to custom-*et in facie ecclesie ea celebriter, prout moris est, publicare voluerint*, the published marriage and children subsequently born of it are to be judged legitimate, unless there is clear and reasonable impediment.

Lator presentium A. is known only in the fifth book of *Cott.*, but was presumably also in the lost quires of *Pet.* Its uncertain form of address, *lernien./lerinen. episcopo*, cannot refer to Lerins, which was the site of a famous abbey, not a bishopric; and the mandatory clause (*fraternitati tue*) within the letter confirms that the recipient was a bishop. Larino (*larinen.*), or possibly Lesina (*lesinen.*), both in the province of Benevento, have been proposed by Holtzmann as the bishopric in question[46]. The letter reflects both the pope's prudence in dealing with delicate sexual transgressions and his concern with the seal of confession. A penitent man had disclosed in person to him that, following illicit relations with a certain woman, he had married another, related to her in the third or fourth degree. Then, moved to repentence, he confessed his sin to a priest living with the Hospitallers, but the priest disclosed his sin, unmindful of his office and God's precept-*officii et dignitatis oblitus et dominici precepti, quo prohibetur fratris turpitudinem revelare.* Such a shameful punishment can drive men to the depths of despair, and must be suitably punished-*tam piaculare flagitium, quo facile possent homines in desperationis laqueum cadere, digna est animadversione plectendum.* If the facts are so, the bishop must suspend the priest, and send him to the pope without delay. As for the man, if his offence and the consanguinity are public, he must be separated from the woman forthwith; but, if his offence is secret, he is to be permitted to remain with his wife, penance being imposed upon him-*si publicum est crimen et consanguinitas, a muliere non differas separare. Si autem occultum est delictum. eum cum uxore sua iniuncta sibi penitentia permanere permittas.*

45. Cf. n. 25, above, and DUGGAN, *Equity and compassion*, p. 82-83 and nn.62-63.

46. *Cott.* 5.56: *WH* 599, *KE* 187, *JL* —, 1159-81. Reference to a bishop of Lesina in the province of Benevento is extremely unlikely in the period (IP 9 161), and the bishop of Lesina in Dalmatia is an improbable identification.

3. Decretals to Ascoli Piceno, Asti and Anglona

Three decretals appear in the Cottonian and Peterhouse collections, addressed respectively *presbitero esculapio*, to the abbot of St Albans, and to the archbishop of Mainz. The recipient of *Iuvenis ille* (**25**), a decretal of Eugenius III, has not until now been identified, and in Holtzmann's judgment its provenance cannot be determined[47]. The decretal *Singulorum* (**66**) is at present everywhere assigned to Alexander III, and its recipient accepted as the abbot of St Albans, to whom it is addressed in almost every systematic collection containing it, and in the Jaffé-Loewenfeld *Regesta*. *Significavit nobis* (**88**) was attributed by Friedberg and Kehr to Alexander III and the bishop of Anglona, but Lohmann's later proposal of the bishop of Meaux as its recipient has been generally accepted. The solutions proposed here are that *Iuvenis ille* was sent by Eugenius III to bishop Presbiterus of Ascoli Piceno, that *Singulorum* was sent by Alexander III or Eugenius to a bishop elect of Asti, and that *Significavit nobis* was indeed addressed to the bishop of Anglona, as previously supposed, though Alexander III is explicitly named as its sender only in two late copies.

ASCOLI PICENO

The decretal *Iuvenis ille* of Eugenius III appears in *JL* 9655 with the address *Aesculapio presbytero*, under the pope's pontifical years (1145-53)[48]. It was transmitted though numerous collections from *c.* 1179 to the *Decretales* of 1234. The letter concerns a certain young man who married a girl not yet seven years old, and sought through human frailty to consummate the marriage, but failed. For the Church's honour, because she was called his wife, and because of the doubtful matter, the pope ruled that the man should be separated from the girl's relation, whom he had subsequently married.

The letter is found in at least 29 manuscripts, as well as printed editions, most frequently with the inscription *Esculapio presbitero*, occasionally *presbitero Esculapio*, and more rarely *Esculapio episcopo*: other less common variants include *Esculiano, Esculatio, Estulapio, Exculapio* and *Asclepio*. Holtzmann retained the version *presbitero Esculapio* in his records. But the decretal was clearly sent to a bishop, not a simple priest, and was presumably addressed to bishop Presbiterus (Prete) of Ascoli Piceno, who occupied the see

47. *WH* 596: 'Das Stück ist vorläufig nicht zu lokalisieren'. The location of Ascoli might be deduced from Friedberg's analysis of *Compilatio prima*: E. FRIEDBERG, *Quinque compilationes antiquae nec non collectio canonum Lipsiensis*, Leipzig 1882 (repr. Graz 1956), 45: *1 Comp.* 4.1.18: Eugenius III presbit. Aesculano. *Iuvenis ille*.

48. Appendix 4, below: Text and apparatus of *Iuvenis ille*.

throughout Eugenius III's pontificate, and the correct form of address is therefore *Eugenius III Presbitero Esculano episcopo*. This identification is supported by the primitive Durham collection (a careful collection, with early Italian connexions), which preserves the inscription: *Eugenius papa presbitero Esculiano*[49], and it is perhaps also significant that *Presbiterus* appears with a capital initial in the Cottonian collection. The letter is not included in Holtzmann's *Kanonistische Ergänzungen*, which has no decretals to Ascoli Piceno, nor in Kehr's *Italia Pontificia*.

ASTI

Two quite separate decretals of Alexander III are conflated in *JL* 12636 as a single letter to Simon, abbot of St Albans, in response to questions submitted by him, and dated Anagni, 8 April 1173-76. The error doubtless arose from their very similar incipits-*Singulorum consultationibus* and *Consultationibus singulorum* (neither found elsewhere in the collections or *JL*), the parallel themes of their introductions, defining the pope's responsibility in resolving doubtful questions put to him, and the fact that both letters are frequently found addressed to St Albans in the collections. The longer letter, *Consultationibus*, deals in three parts with the spoliation of churches, presentation to churches, and the granting of churches. No problem arises in connexion with this much-discussed decretal, which was certainly sent to St Albans on 8 April 1173-76.

The shorter letter, *Singulorum*, concerns a specific and highly-interesting marriage case[50]. The man O., though married, took another woman who was unaware of his existing marriage, and had children by her. But on the death of his wife, he sought to leave the second woman, on the pretext that he could not be united with her while his wife was living. The pope affirmed the canonical law that a man cannot marry a woman with whom he had previously committed adultery, especially if he had made her a promise while his wife was still alive, or if she was involved in his wife's death. He neverthless ruled in the present case that, since the second woman was unaware of the marriage, it would be improper for the man to gain advantage from his deliberate contravention of the canons. Unless she seeks a separation, they must not be parted, lest he should seem to profit from his sin. The case has been assumed to have an English context, since the decretal is printed in all the standard editions with an address to St Albans[51]. Indeed, every systematic collection from *Appendix* (from 1184) onwards includes the letter in an abbreviated

49. *1 Dun.* 1.47, fol. 7 rb.

50. Appendix 5, below: Text and apparatus of *Singulorum*.

51. Cf. DUGGAN, *Equity and compassion*, p. 73.

version, omitting the *arenga* and beginning *Propositum est nobis*, with the St Albans address. The shorter version and address to St Albans are also found in primitive collections, among the earliest copies, but far less consistently.

The problem of the two 'St Albans' decretals was noted by Juncker in his analysis of *Berolinensis prima*, and later discussed by Lohmann in his study of *Wigorniensis*, and by Holtzmann in *WH*, leading to the acceptance of the St Albans address for both letters[52]. But a reconsideration of the transmission of *Singulorum* and its abbreviated version through the early and so-called primitive collections suggests a different conclusion. The relevant details of addresses and incipits are set out in the table below, the collections being arranged in their regional or family groups. It should be noted that six of the early collections (*Parisiensis prima*, *Cusana*, *Cantuariensis tertia*, *Dunelmensis prima*, *Fontanensis* and *Regalis*) and the archetype of the 'Worcester' family have no letters later than the death of Alexander III, and that only two of these collections, *Cus.* and *Reg.*, have the shorter text. The only early collection with both the complete text and an unambiguous address to St Albans is the 'French' *1 Par.*, which begins *Consultationibus*. The related Orval collection (*Aur.*), which was completed after the accession of Lucius III (1181-85), has two copies of the letter, each with the faulty reading *Albini* for *Albani* in the address, and the shortened text[53].

French collections

1 Par. 107. Alex. III abbati sancti Albani. *Consultationibus.*
Aur. 66 = 117. Idem S. (sancti) Albini abbati. *Propositum.*

Italian collection

Cus. 197. (*sine inscript.*) *Propositum.*

English collections

English family

3 Cant. 9. (*sine inscript.*) *Singulorum.*
Roff. 98. Idem abbati sancti Albani. *Propositum.*
1 Dun. 3.9. Astinensi electo. *Singulorum.*
Font. 1.45. (*sine inscript.*) *Singulorum.*
Reg. 79. Ad remse. (? Remensem). *Propositum.*

52. Cf. J. Juncker, *Die Collectio Berolinensis*, «ZRG Kan. Abt.» XIII (1924), 403-404, *1Berol.* 120; Lohmann, *Collectio Wigorniensis*, p. 69 (*JL* 12636) and 82, *Wig.* 1.15, *WH* 989.

53. Cf. *Lucius III Albino* (? *Albano*; recte *Ambianensi*) *episcopo*, for *Quod sedem apostolicam* (*Pet* 1.90; *WH* 822a, *JL* 11866).

Bridlington family

Bridl. 150. Aman. Electo. *Insinuatum.*

Claud. 128. Alex. III Simoni abbati sancti Albani. *Propositum.*

Worcester family

Wig. 1.15. Astionensi electo. *Singulorum.*

Claustr. 42. (*sine inscript.*) *Singulorum.*

Chelt. 9.16. Astiniensi electo. *Singulorum.*

Cott. 2.65 ///abbati sancti Alban///. Singulorum.

Pet. 1.66. Alex. III abbati sancti Albani. *Singulorum.*

Although, at first sight, the clearest support for assigning *Singulorum* to St Albans appears in *1 Par.*, the letter's inaccurate incipit in that collection has been noted above, and the collection's occasional unreliability in such details has been proven elsewhere in other contexts[54]. And in fact, both 'St Albans' decretals are found within a sequence of eleven items in *1 Par.* (nos. 97-107), which are in reality only six letters, at least three of which have false inscriptions[55]: 97 appears as a decretal of Alexander III to the bishop of *Salebur.*, but is an excerpt from a letter of Adrian IV to the archbishop of Salzburg; 98 is listed as a letter of Alexander III to bishop John of Norwich, but is part of a decretal to archbishop Roger of York; 101-05 appear with two inscriptions (at 101 and 102) to the abbot of St Albans, but comprise a single letter to archbishop William of Sens; 106 is correctly assigned to Eugenius III, but omits the recipients Ardicio and Omnebene; 99-100 and 107 are both addressed to St Albans, and are the two 'St Albans' letters in question, each with the incipit *Consultationibus* in this collection.

Among the early Italian collections, only *Cusana* includes the decretal, in its shortened version and without an address. The three early English collections *3 Cant.*, *Font.* and *Claustr.* likewise omit the address, but they preserve the full text. Four further English collections-*Roff.*, *Claud.*, *Cott.* and *Pet.*-received the St Albans address, but are later compilations: Roff. is a handsome Rochester manuscript, including letters of Lucius III (1181-85), and an appended item of Celestine III (1191-98) in a different hand[56]; *Claud.* incorporates letters of Urban III (1185-87), and drew on a late recension of the the systematic *Appendix* (from 1184), which was certainly the source of its version of the letter (which was not in the Bridlington archetype)[57]; *Cott.* and *Pet.* are works from the closing years of the century, in which the 'Worcester'

54. Duggan, *Decretals of Alexander III to England*, p. 109-110, and nn. 50-51.

55. Appendix 3, below: *Analysis of Parisiensis prima*, 97-107.

56. Duggan, *Decretal collections*, p. 76-78 (esp. p. 77 and n. 3; and p. 78 and n. 5) and pp. 173-87: Appendix IV.

57. *Ibid.*, p. 84-95, esp. p. 89, n. 1 and p. 91-2; Holtzmann-Cheney, p. 132-34.

stock was greatly expanded from other sources, and influenced by them; and their St Albans address for the letter differs from that in their earlier 'Worcester' and 'Cheltenham' relations (*Astionensi/Astiniensi electo*). The forms of address *Ad remse.* and *Aman.* in Reg. and Bridl. are problematical.

The four English collections *1 Dun.*, *Bridl.*, *Wig.* and *Chelt.* describe the recipient as bishop-elect, as *Astinensi*, *Astionensi* and *Astiniensi* in *1 Dun.*, *Wig.* and *Chelt.* respectively, suggesting the bishop-elect of Asti (*Astensis*) in the province of Milan. Neither Lohmann nor Holtzmann accepted this solution. After careful reflection on the complex and contradictory evidence, Holtzmann decided on balance for the St Albans identification, noting its appearance in the early collections *1 Par.* and *Aur.* (the latter including the personal initial of Simon, abbot of St Albans), and in the generally reliable *Cott*[58]. But, for reasons adduced above, neither of these factors is conclusive. The attribution to Asti therefore runs counter to the judgment of scholars hitherto, but seems nevertheless more convincing.

The solution to this problem is perhaps provided by the third component of the Durham collection *Dunelmensis prima* (*1 Dun.* 3), which reveals both correspondence and contrast with *1 Par.*, in respect of the letters in question[59]. Four decretals in *1 Par.* 99-107 (99-100, 101-05, 106 and 107) are also included in *1 Dun.* 3, chapters 10, 22, 13 and 9 respectively. Two of the four are addressed *in situ* to St Albans in the Durham collection: *1 Dun.* 3.13 (= *1 Par.* 106) is correctly though incompletely addressed *Eugenius papa Omnibono*; in a striking parallel error with that in *1 Par.* 101-05, *1 Dun.* 3.22 is addressed *in situ* to St Albans, but the correct address to archbishop William of Sens is inserted in the margin- *Willelmo Senonensi archiepiscopo*; *1 Dun.* 3.10 (= *1 Par.* 99-100) is correctly addressed to St Albans; and its immediate neighbour *1 Dun.* 3.9 (= *1 Par.* 107) is addressed *Astinensi electo*. The decretals *Singulorum* and *Consultationibus* appear together in the Durham collection (*1 Dun.* 3.9 and 10), as the first two letters, following the canons of the council of Tours (1163). Each has a clear address (with the full initial protocol for *Consultationibus*), its correct incipit, arenga and complete text. There is no reason to question the almost-exact address to Asti (*Astinensi*) in a collection which preserves the most accurate extant form of an address to Ascoli (*Esculiano*: *1 Dun.* 1.47), as shown above. Nevertheless, the origin of a false transmission of the address and even the incipit of *Singulorum* may be retraceable in some way to the juxtaposition of the two

58. Lohmann, *Collectio Wigorniensis*, p. 69: *JL* 12636, and 82: *Wig.* 1.15; *WH* 989. The misreading *Albini* for *Albani* re-appears in some later collections (cf. *Lips.* 59. 1 and *Cass.* 58.1), as does Simon's initial or name as abbot (cf. *Lips.* and *Claud.* 128).

59. Cf. Holtzmann-Cheney p. 91-93; and Appendix 3, below: *Analysis of Parisiensis prima*, 97-107.

letters with such similar *arengae* in the Durham collection, or more probably a related source.

The identification of Asti is also supported on grounds of probability. No other decretal to Asti is found in the collections, though its bishop appears within other commissions of Alexander III, notably as co-judge with the bishop of Tortona in *Causam matrimonii*, to the bishop of Pavia, concerning a marriage dispute between the Siderios and Canes in the city of Pavia, and in *Proposuit nobis*, to the provost and prior of Mortara[60]. It is difficult to see how a unique and false address to an elect of Asti could have originated, above all in English collections exclusively. There are, moreover, grounds for dating the letter not later than the early-mid 1170s, which would match the election of William to Asti between August 1172 and July 1173[61]. As bishop-elect of Asti, William was commissioned by Alexander III in that period, to deal with a difficult case in the diocese of Vercelli, between the nuns of S. Maria della Rocca and the monks of S. Benigno di Fruttuaria, and was later recommissioned in the same case when bishop[62]. There is no intrinsic reason to question his commission as bishop-elect in *Singulorum*, but it is also possible that the letter was sent by Eugenius III to Anselm, William's predecessor, when bishop-elect of Asti in the opening months of 1146[63], since none of the collections with the Asti address names the sender, and its first appearance is in the Durham collection, which has other decretals of Eugenius III.

ANGLONA

The decretal *Significavit nobis* (**88**) is at present accepted as a mandate of Alexander III to the bishop of Meaux, arising from a dispute referred to the pope by the bishop of Troyes in the province of Sens[64]. It concerns a dispute

60. *Causam matrimonii*: *WH* 109, *KE* 92, *JL* 14332, Anagni 12 November 1173-76; *Cum locum non habeat*: *WH* 270, *KE* 94, *JL* 14333, 1169-78, also to the bishop of Pavia, deals with the same case; *Proposuit nobis*: *WH* 750, *KE* 99, *IP* 6^1. 232 n. 15, *JL* 14021, 11 May 1166-78.

61. Appendix 3, below: *Analysis of Parisiensis prima*, 97-107; none of the letters in this sequence can be dated after 1176, and one is firmly dated June 1173-74. The dating limits of the Asti vacancy are based on documents listed in F. Savio, *Gli antichi vescovi d'Italia dalle origini al 1300*, repr. Turin 1899 (Biblioteca della antica e nuova Italia 139), p. 150-51.

62. *IP* 6^2 48 nos. 4 and 5.

63. In a letter to bishop Gisolfo of Vercelli (*A tua non credimus*, 17 April 1146), Eugenius III refers to an earlier commission to archbishop Robert of Milan (who had meanwhile died) and the bishops Anselmo of Asti and Guido of Ivrea *(controversiam que inter te et Vercellensis aecclesie canonicos agitatur, R. bone memorie Mediolanensi archiepiscopo et. A. Astensi atque G. Yporiensi episcopis cognoscendam terminandamque commisimus)*: *Papsturkunden in Italien*, 3, p. 118-19 no. 4.

64. Appendix 6, below: Text and apparatus of *Significavit nobis*. Only the late copies in *Cott.* and *Pet.* name Alexander III as the sender; *Cantab.*, *1 Vict.*, *Wig.*, *Chelt.* and *1 Abr.* all omit the pope's name, and *Tann.* has Idem.

between a man and a woman who had lawfully contracted marriage, but were alienated and living apart. In the presence of his diocesan bishop, who has reported the matter to the pope, the man sought to have his wife restored to him, to have her with him in his home. But the woman objected, alleging that he had done shameful things to her; that the marriage was never consummated, although she had lived with him for seven years; and that she could clearly prove with documents that he had confessed to this, and had consulted sorceresses and sought a remedy from doctors. When the bishop was reportedly unwilling to set an appropriate term to decide the case, the man appealed to the pope, setting a term at the next *Letare Jerusalem* Sunday. But he neither appeared nor sent his representative, though the woman's messenger arrived. The pope therefore commissions the recipient bishop to summon the parties and resolve the matter within thirty days of receiving the mandate.

The decretal first appears, in a much truncated version, in the 'French' collections *Cantab.* and *1 Vict.*, with the inscription *Anglonensi episcopo*, in response to a report from the diocesan bishop, identified as *Catanen.* It was registered in *JL* 13746 from *Cantab.*, in the summary form *Anglonensi episcopo scribit ex relatione episcopi Catanensis de muliere* etc., and was printed by Friedberg in his analysis of the collection[65]. The letter was clearly then accepted as a mandate to the bishop of Anglona in the Basilicate, in response to a report from the bishop of Catania in Sicily. A complete text of the letter was later printed by Singer, from the Avranches collection *Abrincensis prima* (from 1198), where it appears in an appendix[66]. The address is omitted in *1 Abr.*, but the reporting bishop appears there as *Ra.cenensis.* On this accumulated evidence, Kehr accepted the address to Anglona, and identified the diocesan bishop as Robert of Catania, dating the letter 1171-81[67]. Twenty years later, Lohmann proposed an entirely different but coherent solution, from evidence in the 'Worcester' collection *Wigorniensis* (*post* 1181). In this English collection, in the earliest extant transcription of the full letter, he found the somewhat garbled address *Meldelsi episcopo* and the internal reading *trecensis episcopus*, which in conjunction naturally suggested to him the bishops of Meaux and Troyes (*Meldensis* and *Trecensis*)[68]. This solution was accepted by Holtzmann, and stands in the projected *Regesta decretalium*. But neither the earlier solution in its entirety nor the later is convincing. It is inherently improbable that so delicate and circumstantial a matter was transferred from Catania to Anglona, across the straits of Messina

65. *Canones-Sammlungen*, p. 19: *Cantab.* 84.

66. SINGER, *Neue Beiträge*, p. 394-395: *1 Abr.* ap. 13.

67. *IP* 9.470 no. 2.

68. LOHMANN, *Collectio Wigorniensis*, p. 88: *Wig.* 1. 45.

and in a different province. On the other hand, the alternative identification of Meaux and Troyes depends almost certainly on scribal errors.

The letter is known altogether in eight collections: in *Cantab.*, *1 Vict.* and *1 Abr.*; in four members of the 'Worcester' family (*Wig.*, *Chelt.*, *Cott.*, *Pet.*); and in *Tanner*. Though earliest in transcription, *Cantab.* and *1 Vict.* cannot be the sources of the later versions, since the latter have full texts and variant readings. Nevertheless, their uncorrupted address to Anglona (otherwise unknown in the collections) is persuasive evidence, strengthened by the letter's inclusion in a sequence of marriage decretals in *Cantab.*, eleven of which have unambiguous Italian addresses[69]. The attribution to Meaux rests solely on the readings *Meldelsi* and *trecensis* in *Wig.* The letter was not in the 'Worcester' archetype, nor in its early derivative *Claustr.* (Klosterneuburg). Its first complete transcription is as an addition to Book 1 in *Wig.*, in a hesitant and much corrected text. It is clear that the *Wig.* scribe was uncertain of the place-names[70]. Later members of the family have the addresses *Magolonensi* (? *Magalonensi*: Maguelonne) in *Chelt.*, and *Maguntino archiepiscopo* (Mainz) in *Cott.* and *Pet.*; all transmit the internal reading *trecensis*, even where the recipient is named archbishop of Mainz; but they are the only collections to do so. Elsewhere, the reporting diocesan appears as *Catanen.* in *Cantab.* and *1 Vict.*, *N.cestrensis* (? Chester) in *Tann.*, and *Ra.cenensis* in *1 Abr.* On palaeographical grounds, it can easily be seen how *Anglonensi* might be transliterated to *Magolonensi*, and further altered to the more familiar *Maguntino archiepiscopo*. (*Anglon./ Magolon./Maguntin.*). By a similar but converse process, *Ra.cenensis*, *N.cestrensis* and *trecensis* might be retraced to the rarely encountered *tricaricensis* (*ra.cenen. / n.cestren. / trecen. / tricaricen.*), that is to the bishop of Tricarico, the immediate neighbour of Anglona in the province of Acerenza. The bishop of Anglona was a most appropriate recipient of a papal mandate, to settle a problem reported to the pope by the bishop of Tricarico.

4. Decretals to cardinal Laborans, Acerno, Cosenza and Rapolla

Among other letters of unusual interest in the Peterhouse collection, but lacking in *Cott.*, the decretal *Super eo quod* (**27**), on the admissibility of evidence in marriage disputes, appears with the perplexing inscription

69. *Cassinen.* (75), *Termulan.* (78), *Brixiensi* (81), *Anglonen.* (84), *Panormitano* (87), *Tranen.* (89), *Pisano* (91), *Fundan.* (92A), *Salernitano* (94), and *Vigilien.* (95 and 97). It is also possible that *Barenen.* (90) is a corrupt transcription of *Barensi* (Bari); cf. n. 45, above.

70. *Wig.* 1. 45, fol. 12va-b; it is clear from an inspection of the manuscript that the scribe was uncertain of several readings, including the address.

Alexander III Marito in porticu cardinali. It is registered in *JL* 14161 with the versions *Marco cardinali* and *Matthaeo cardinali* (from *2 Comp.* and *X*). The decretal was sent in fact to the distinguished canonist Laborans, almost certainly when he was papal legate in north Italy in 1178. He is accurately identified in the earliest known transcription of the letter, in the French collection *Brugensis* (Reims, *c.* 1187): *L(aboranti) sancte Marie in porticu cardinali*. It occurs otherwise only in the Durham collection *2 Dun.*, the Anglo-Norman *Sang.* and *1 Abr.*, and the early thirteenth-century *Alan.*, *Fuld.*, *2 Comp.* and *X*. No Italian collection of the twelfth century includes the letter, though *Brugensis* was partly dependent on English and Italian sources (including the 'Worcester' and *Cusana* traditions), under the authorship of Ralph of Sarre, dean of Reims and a native of Kent[71]. The decretal concerns the claim of a certain woman that a man had promised to marry her, which he denies. On the question of the admissibility of her mother's testimony, the pope replies that it is suspect, since she is seen to desire too much (*nimis diligere*) the betterment and honour of her daughter, if the man is superior in riches, power and noble status. On the other hand, if the mother of either party admits consanguinity, there is a substantial presumption (*presumptio est non modica*) that her claim is true. In this situation, the two should not be united, unless the marriage is already confirmed (*firmatum*); if it is sworn and confirmed (*iuratum est et firmatum*), it cannot be dissolved except on the oath of many.

The decretal *Venientes ad nos*, to the bishop of Acerno, is found only in the English collection *Tanner* and its Norman descendants *Sang.* and *1 Abr.*, and is indeed the only letter to Acerno in the collections, or in the *Italia pontificia*, where it is attributed with reservations to Eugenius III, presumably from the address *Idem Acerno episcopo*, which refers back misleadingly to *Eugenius papa Esculapio episcopo, Iuvenis ille* (*Sang.* 8.79), with letters of Alexander III intervening[72]. The decretal concerns a complex marriage dispute, and has an evident importance in the development of Alexander's doctrine[73]. Two men and two women had brought a report to the pope from the bishop of Acerno. They stated unanimously, under examination, that one of the men gave one of the women an undertaking that he would take her as his wlfe, and she affirmed that she would receive him as her husband. But the second man, whom she had previously deeply loved, approached and so enticed her that he

71. Cf. L. FALKENSTEIN, *Zu Entstehungsort und Redaktor der Collectio Brugensis*, in *Proceedings of the Eighth Congress of Medieval Canon Law, San Diego, August 1988*, Città del Vaticano 1992 (Monumenta Iuris Canonici, Series C: Subsidia, IX), p. 117-162.

72. *IP* 8.379 'Documenta Romanorum pontificum Acernensi ecclesiae eiusque episcopis data non pervenerunt ad nos. Utrum rescriptum Eugenii III (*n. 1*) ad Acernensem ep. directum fuerit annon, in dubio remanet; 1. [Eugenius III] Acern. ep.: respondet eius litteris de matrimonio duarum mulierum. - Venientes ad nos'. Cf. DONAHUE, *The dating of Alexander III's marriage decretals'*, p. 81, *WH* 1077.

73. Appendix 7, below.

betrothed and married her. The first man, seeing himself deceived, thereupon married her sister. The pope ruled that, if the first man did not proceed further than his public oath to take the woman as his wife, then she should be allowed to remain with the second man, who married her, with penance for her breach of faith. But, if the betrothal between the first man and woman progressed to mutual consent in accepting one another, then neither man could have her—the first because he knew and married her sister, the second because he could not marry another's wife. Nor can the first man canonically have the sister of the woman he had previously sworn to marry. The bishop must separate them, and grant them permission to contract lawful marriages after appropriate penance.

The collections preserve only three decretals to the archbishop of Cosenza, all being letters of Alexander III. *Continebatur in litteris* was widely received, but *Viduis vero* and *Inter alia* are known only in English collections—*Viduis vero* in *Cott.* and *Pet.* (**95**), and *Inter alia* in the Bridlington collection[74]. Moreover, the latter is the only collection to include both *Continebatur* and *Inter alia*, and indeed makes a marginal cross-reference between them, where Alexander altered an earlier ruling[75]. The first three parts of *Inter alia* deal with questions raised by the archbishop concerning the wives or concubines which priests had had before their ordination. The pope's ruling on the first question, concerning a priest who had then married a woman corrupted by another, is incomplete through defective transcription, but clearly hinged on the question of notoriety. On the second question, the pope rules that no faith should be placed in the claims of a priest who retracted his earlier admission that he had been married to such a woman, but now (so that he might fulfil his priestly office—*ut uti valeat sacerdotio*) claims that she had been his concubine. Thirdly, concerning a priest who had two wives before his ordination, but had not consummated the marriage with one of them, he cannot be judged a bigamist or debarred from his priestly functions, if his claim is true. The fourth section deals with an entirely different problem: in the course of a playful diversion to while away the tedium of a journey, a certain layman leapt onto the back of a deacon, and was mortally wounded by the pruning sickle attached to the deacon's belt. Although the pope had previously decided otherwise on this question (in *Continebatur in litteris*), he now rules that the matter does not justify the deacon's being debarred from promotion if he is otherwise suitable, as the archbishop of Cosenza claimed.

74. *Continebatur*: *WH* 203, *KE* 209, *JL* 13856; Appendix 8, below: *Inter alia*: *WH* 586, *KE* 210, *JL* —, *Bridl.* 163: pd. *KE*; *Viduis vero* (95), Part 2, above: *Italian marriage decretals*, *WH* 1085, *KE* 211, *JL* —, *Cott.* 5.11 and *Pet.* 1.95: pd. *KE*.

75. Oxford, Bodleian Library, MS Bodl. 357 (S.C. 2452): *Bridl.* 158 (MS: clix.), *Continebatur*, fol. 125 r^b-v^a, *marg.*: infra clxiiii. contra; *Bridl.* 163 (MS: clxiiii), fols. 126r^b-v^a.

Requisivit a nobis, a decretal of Lucius III (1181-85) to the bishop of Rapolla (**7**), was transmitted through many well-known collections to *1 Comp.* and *X*[76]. It appeared in the *Appendix* collections (from 1184), with an accurate address (*Rapuln.*) in the Lincoln codex, but also in supplements to three English primitive collections, which had no letters later than Alexander III in their archetypal material—among later entries by a different hand in the *Wig.* codex, among additions on the final folio of *1 Dun.* 3, and as one of two decretals of Lucius III among the post-archetypal letters in *Claustr.*, where it lacks the address and opening sentence, and begins *Quesivit*[77]. In his reply to the bishop, the pope declared that the woman who had sworn to marry a man, but now refuses, should be admonished rather than compelled to do so, since marriages should be free—*cum libera debeant esse matrimonia*, and the outcome of such compulsion is often difficult; and the wife, whose husband committed adultery with her mother, cannot have further relations with him, or marry another while he is still alive.

Conclusion and Prospectus

The crucial importance of Alexander III in the evolution of the canon law of marriage was recalled at the outset of this paper, together with the dominant share of English and Italian marriage cases in decretal records. From these rich and complex sources, the limited aspect selected here was the reception of Italian letters in English collections, focused primarily on the Cottonian and Peterhouse collections, with brief allusion to other sources. In further and complementary essays, the range of enquiry will be widened to embrace all English and Italian collections. The additional focal points of interest will include the reception of widely-known Italian decretals which appear for the first time in English or Anglo-Norman collections, or in English archives, and (as a corollary to the present enquiry) the evaluation of Italian cases unknown to English collectors, some involving identifiable members of famous Italian families. These are among the lines of enquiry to be pursued in the later studies.

76. Cf. Appendix 9, below.

77. Cf. n. 27, above; see also DONAHUE, *The dating of Alexander III's marriage decretals*, p. 79, *WH* 798.

APPENDICES

For reasons of space, the decretals printed in Appendices 4-9, below, are not edited texts, but all the relevant manuscripts have been consulted in their presentation.

Appendix 1: Comparative Table: Cantabrigiensis 75-97

Italian marriage decretals in the 'Cambridge' collection (Trinity College MS R.9.7): *Cantab.*, 75-97, fols. 98r-107r; *Canones-Sammlungen*, 18-20; collated with *1 Vict. Wig.*, *Cott. Pet.* and *Cus.*

	Cantab.	*1 Vict.*	*Wig.*	*Cott.* 2	*Pet.* 1	*Cus.*	*KE*
Cassino	75	29	36	25	29	-	167
Termoli	78	33	18	67	78	18	186
Brescia	81	37	22	33	39	159	105
Anglona	84	61	45*	76	88	-	-
Palermo	87	7	23	35	41	204	218
Trani	89(ab)	10(ab)	3	16(ab)	18	180(c)	191(abc)
Bari	90	11	-	-	2.7.2	-	188
Pisa	91	16	25	41	47	203	35
Fondi	92A	69	-	-	-	-	162
Salerno	94(a-d)	22(a-d)	28	3	3	165	176(a-1)
Bisceglie	95	23	-	27	34	-	199
Bisceglie	97(bcd)	75	4.14	5.12	4.14	175	198(a-e)

* *Wig.* 1.45 not in archetype.

Appendix 2: Analysis and Comparative Table: Wigorniensis 1.3-45

Italian marriage decretals in the 'Worcester' Collection (BL Royal MS 10 A.II): *Wig.* 1.3-45, fols 5ra-13r; 'Collectio Wigorniensis', 79-88; collated with *Cott.*, *Pet.*, *1 Vict.*, *Cantab.*, *1 Par.* and *Cus.*

3. Tranensi archiepiscopo (MS: Trevorensi episcopo). *Continebatur in litteris.*
   Pet. 1.18: *WH* 204(ab), *KE* 191, *JL* 14032, Anagni 9 Sept. 1173-76.

15. Astionensi electo. *Singulorum consultationibus.*
   Pet. 1.61 (abbati sancti Albani): *WH* 989, *KE*--, *JL* 12636.

18. [Episcopo et dilectis filiis] canonicis et universo clero et populo Termulano (MS: Tremulano). *Cum inter l.*
   Pet. 1.78: *WH* 266, *KE* 186, *JL* 14194, Benevento 26 Sept. 1167-69.

22. Brixiensi episcopo. *Ex publico instrumento.*
Pet. 1.39: *WH* 476, *KE* 105, *JL* 13787, 1159-79.

23. Panormitano archiepiscopo. *Veniens ad presentiam.*
Pet. 1.41: *WH* 1074, *KE* 218, *JL* 14165, 1159-81.

24. Magistro Fidantie [canonico] Civitatensi. *Ad nostram noveris.*
Pet. 1.40: *WH* 75, *KE* 21, *JL* 13854, Capua 21 Dec. 1176.

25. Pisano archiepiscopo. *Quidam intravit.*
Pet. 1.47: *WH* 814, *KE* 35, *JL* 14061, 1159-81.

28. Salernitano archiepiscopo (MS: episcopo). *Licet preter.*
Pet. 1.3: *WH* 620, *KE* 176, *JL* 14091, Autumn 1176.

36. Cassinensi (MS: Cassiano) abbati. *Ex litteris tuis.*
Pet. 1.29: *WH* 436, *KE* 167, *JL* 13838, 1159-81.

38. Eborardo Paduano (MS: Parduano) episcopo. *Sollicitudini apostolice.*
Pet. 1.2: *WH* 991(abc), *KE* 132, *JL* 14235, 1168-81.

40. Paduano episcopo. *Littere quas.*
Pet. 1.54: *WH* 635, *KE* 133, *JL* 14055, 1166-81.

41. Lucensi episcopo. *Consuluit nos.*
Pet. 1.42: *WH* 87(ab), *KE* 40(ab), *JL* 14005, 1159-81.

45. Anglonensi (MS: Meldelsi) episcopo. *Significavit nobis.*
Pet. 1.88 (Maguntino archiepiscopo): *WH* 985, *KE*--, *JL* 13746, 1159-81.

Comparative Table

Wig.	*Cott.* 1	*Pet.* 1	*1 Vict.*	*Cantab.*	*1 Par*	*Cus.*	*KE*
3	16(ab)	18(ab)	10(ab)	89(ab)	180-1	180(c)	*191(abc)
15	65	66	-	-	107	197	-
18	67	78	33	78	137	18	186
22	33	39	37	81	138	159	105
23	35	41	7	87	-	204	218
24	34	40	66	46	133	122	21
25	41	47	101;16	91	-	203	35
28	3	3	*22+68	94+48	21-9	165	176
36	25	29	*29=100	75	168	-	167
38	2	2	-	-	-	133	132
40	48	54	-	-	-	63	133
41(ab)	36(ab)	42(ab)	-	-	-	-	40(abc)
45	76	88	61	84	-	-	-

* 191(c) = *Cott.* 5.51; *1 Vict.* 22 = 115; *1 Vict.* 29 = 100.

Appendix 3: Analysis of *Parisiensis prima*, 97-107

Paris, Bibl. nat. MS lat. 1596, fols. 28v-30v; *Canones-Sammlungen* 57-58.
1 Par. 99-100 and 101-05 comprise two decretals only; nos. 99, 101, 102 and 107 all have the address *Alexander III abbati sancti Albani*, at least two (101-102) erroneously.

97 Alexander III Salebur. episcopo. *Tua fraternitas...exhibenda.*
Excerpt from: Hadrianus IV Ebrardo Salzeburgensi archiepiscopo. *Dignum est. WH* 344, *JL* 10445, 1154-59.

98 Alexander III Johanni Norwicensi episcopo. *Sane si a nobis...impediri.*
Excerpt from: Alexander III R. Eboracensi archiepiscopo. *Inter ceteras. WH* 590, *JL* 13878, 28 April 1160-76.

99 Alexander III abbati sancti Albani. *Consultationibus...prorogare.*

100 *De cetero. Si aliquis...spoliari.*
99-100: *WH* 184, *JL* 12636, Anagni 8 April 1173-76.

101 Alexander III abbati sancti Albani. *Quesitum est...generali.*

102 Alexander III abbati sancti Albani. *Super eo vero...recepisse.*

103 *Preterea super hoc...potestatem.*

104 Item. *Si vero aliquis...ministrare.*

105 Item eidem in eadem consultatione. *Si vir et mulier...uxorem.*
101-05: *recte* Alexander III Willelmo Senonensi archiepiscopo, *Sicut Romana. WH* 944, *JL* 12293 + 13874, Anagni 2 June 1173-74.

106 Eugenius papa III (Arditioni sancte Romane ecclesie subdiacono et magistro Omnibono). *Litteras dilectionis...procedat. WH* 625, *JL* 9654, 1 August 1151-52.

107 Alexander III abbati sancti Albani. *Consultationibus...reportare. WH* 989, *JL* 12636, 8 April 1173-76; *proposui*: Eugenius III *vel* Alexander III Astensi episcopo. *Singulorum*, late 1145-early 1146 or August 1172-July 1173.

Appendix 4: Text and apparatus of *Iuvenis ille*

Eugenius III Presbitero Esculano episcopo.

Iuvenis ille qui puellam nondum septennem duxit, quamvis etas repugnaret, ex humana tamen fragilitate forsitan temptavit quod complere non potuit. Quia igitur in his que dubia sunt, quod certius estimamus tenere debemus, tum propter honestatem ecclesie, quia ipsa coniux ipsius fuisse dicitur, tum propter predictam dubietatem mandamus tibi ut consobrinam ipsius puelle, quam postmodum duxit, ab eo dividas.

1 Berol. 54, *Flor.* 51, *Cus.* 142, *1 Dun.* 1.47, *Bridl.* 43, *Claud.* 113, *Chelt.* 9.50, *Cott.* 2.22, *Pet.* 1.25, *2 Par.* 81.3, *App.* 12.8, *Bamb.* 51.7, *Erl.* 51.9, *Lips.* 60.8, *Cass.* 59.7, *Tann.* 7.8.7, *Sang.* 8.79, *Brug.* 48.3, *Frcf.* 1.4, *1 Comp.*

4.1.18, *X* 4.1.3. Pd. *App.*, *Cass.*, *1 Comp. A*, *X*. *Bridl.* has no inscription, and the pope's name is omitted in *Claud.*; otherwise the letter is ascribed to Eugenius III in all collections, except *Flor.* (*Alexander papa III*) and *Cass.B* (Aug., *propter rubricatorem*). The recipient's name is omitted in *Flor.*, *Bridl.*, *App.Cr.* (which has the corrupt form *Sed presbytero*) and *X*; elsewhere it appears as *Esculapio*, except in *1 Dun.* (*Esculiano*), *App.Ln* (*Siculapio*), *Bamb.DT* (*Esculatio* and *Esculacio*), *Erl.* (*Estulapio*), *Cass.* (*Exculapio*), *Brug.* (*Asclepio*), and in *1 Comp.* (Friedberg's ed.: *Aesculano*; Agustín's ed.: *Aesculapio*; Friedberg's ed. of *X* omits the inscription, but has *Esculapio* in n. 3). *Presbitero* appears as *episcopo* in *App.LpV*, *Sang.* and *Frcf.FTM*; it precedes the diocesan title in *Cus.*, *1 Dun.*, *Cott.* (with a capital initial *Psbro.*), *Pet.* (p̃ho), *Brug.* and *1 Comp.*; otherwise it follows.

Appendix 5: Text and apparatus of *Singulorum*

[Eugenius III Anselmo *vel* Alexander III Gulielmo] Astensi electo.

Singulorum consultationibus quantum nobis deus ministravit ex officii nostri debito respondere compellimur, ut dubia sub examine apostolice sedis plenius elucescant et questiones a Romana ecclesia valeant enodari, que disponente domino inter alias ecclesias optinet primatum. Propositum quidem nobis est ex parte tua quod vir quidam O. nomine dum uxorem haberet sibi aliam huius rei insciam copulavit, de qua plures filios sustulit. Sed prima mortua nititur a secunda discedere, asserens quod uxore sua vivente eam sibi non licuerit copulare. Licet autem in canonibus expressum habeatur ut nullus sibi copulet matrimonio quam prius polluit adulterio, et illam maxime cui fidem dederat uxore sua vivente, vel que machinata est in mortem uxoris. Quia tamen prefata mulier erat inscia quod ille aliam uxorem haberet viventem, et indignum esset ut predictus vir, qui scienter contra canones venerat, lucrum de suo dolo reportaret, consultationi tue taliter respondemus quod, nisi predicta mulier divortium petat, ad petitionem viri non sunt ab invicem separandi, cum ex suo delicto videretur commodum reportare.

1 Par. 107, *Aur.* 66=117, *Cus.* 197, *3 Cant.* 9, *Roff.* 98, *1 Dun.* 3.9, *Font.* 1.45, *Reg.* 79, *Bridl.* 150, *Claud.* 128, *Wig.* 1.15, *Claustr.* 42, *Chelt.* 9.16, *Cott.* 2.65, *Pet.* 1.66, *App.* 6.1, *Bamb.* 50.1, *Lips.* 59.1, *Cass.* 58.1 *Tann.* 7.5.1, *Sang.* 8.35, *Brug.* 49.14, *Frcf.* 4.13, *1 Comp.* 4.7.1, *X* 4.7.1. Pd. *App.*, *Cass.*, *1 Comp. A.*, *X*.

Appendix 6: Text and apparatus of *Significavit nobis*

Alexander III Anglonensi episcopo.

Significavit nobis venerabilis frater noster Tricaricensis episcopus quod, cum inter quendam parrochianum suum et mulierem quandam legitimum matrimonium fuisset contractum, uxor negabat se cum eodem viro carnale commercium habuisse, asserens quod ipse vir esset impotens ad carnale debitum reddendum. Cum idem vir in presentia eiusdem constitutus quereret uxorem sibi restitui, ut ipsam in propria domo haberet, et ea sibi utendi libera daretur facultas. Mulier autem asserebat se ei restitui non debere, quia cum semper fuisset in domo matris sue et potius ipsa virum traduxit quam a viro traducta fuisset, et in eam quedam horrenda commiserat que pro pudore exprimere supersedit. Asserebat etiam eadem mulier se cum eo per septennium permanisse et intercedentibus ieiuniis et orationibus nunquam pertulisse carnalis commixtionis amplexum, licet ei sui corporis liberam fecisset potestatem. Asserebat preterea liquidis documentis posse probare eundem virum confessum fuisse quod nunquam eam cognovisset, et ad sublevandam impotentiam coeundi consulisset incantatrices mulierculas et a medicis remedium postulasset. Episcopo vero eodem iamdicte cause debitum sicut asserit nolente finem imponere, prefatus vir ad audientiam nostram appellavit, et dominicam proxime preteritam qua cantatur *Letare Ierusalem* terminum sue appellationi prefixit, sed altera parte per suum nuntium veniente ipse nec venit nec responsalem misit. Confidentes itaque de tue discretionis prudentia causam ipsam experientie tue committimus, presentium auctoritate mandantes quatinus partibus coram te convocatis causam ipsam diligentius audias, et eam infra .xxx. dies post harum susceptionem litterarum sublato appellationis remedio debito fine decidas.

Cantab. 84, *1 Vict.* 61, *Wig.* 1.45, *Chelt.* 9.43, *Cott.* 2.76, *Pet.* 1.88, *Tann.* 7.10.7, *1 Abr.* ap. 13. Pd. *Cantab.* (incomplete), *1 Abr.*

The early truncated version in *Cantab.* and *1 Vict.* has significant textual agreements with that in *1 Abr.* (e.g., *Asseverabat* where the other collections have *Asserebat*). The full mandatory clause, printed above, occurs in *1 Abr.* only; elsewhere the letter ends: 'partibus convocatis causam diligentius audias, et eam infra .xxx. dies post harum susceptionem decidas'.

Appendix 7: *Venientes ad nos*, to the bishop of Acerno

Alexander III Acernensi (MSS and *WH*: Acerno) episcopo[78].

Venientes ad nos latores et latrices presentium litteras tue fraternitatis nobis presentaverunt quibus nos movisti. Ipsi vero, auditis excessibus eorum et super his sollicite requisiti, unanimi et consona voce dixerunt quod, cum unus ex ipsis quandam ex predictis mulieribus usque ad tres septimanas se in uxorem ducturum prestita fide firmasset, et mulier ipsa se eundum virum in coniugem recepturam iurasset, alter predictorum virorum, quem prius ipsa mulier adamaverat, interim accessit ad eam et usque adeo sibi ipsam allexit, quod eius

78. Cf. n. 72, above.

et trium consanguineorum ipsius mulieris precedentibus iuramentis eam desponsavit atque traduxit. Cum autem vir predictus, qui prius ipsam mulierem [se in uxorem ducturum] iuraverat, se videret in hac parte delusum, sororem eiusdem mulieris sibi matrimonio copulavit. Auditis itaque hiis, que unanimiter et concorditer nobis proposuerant, secundum ea, que ex ipsorum confessione cognovimus, tue discretioni mandamus quatinus, si vir ipse, qui unam ex mulieribus ipsis publice iuraverat se habiturum in matrimonio, amplius non processit, nisi quod ipsam tantum iuravit, ita quod nec ipse mulierem in suam nec ipsa eum in suum receperit, eandem mulierem cum secundo viro, qui eam traduxit, sine contradictione et molestia qualibet esse permittas, iniuncta sibi penitentia de fidei lesione. Si vero usque adeo inter primum virum et mulierem ipsam in desponsatione fuerit processum, quod uterque alterum mutuo consensu in suum recepit, neuter virorum ipsorum eam vel potest vel debet habere: primus, quia sororem eius cognovit et eam sibi matrimonio copulavit; et secundus, quia uxorem alterius sibi non poterat copulare. Utrum autem primus vir sororem eiusdem mulieris, quam postea desponsavit atque traduxit, habere debeat, non est tue fraternitati, sicut arbitramur, incognitum, cum secundum censuram canonum puella alicui desponsata nemini de cognatione ipsius nubere possit. Unde a te non est aliquatenus sustinendum ut vir ipse sororem mulieris, quam prius iuraverat, debeat aliqua ratione tenere, sed eis abinvicem separatis utrique eorum [penitentia iniuncta] post peractam penitentiam, vel congruam partem penitentie, facultatem et licenciam habeant alia legittima matrimonia contrahendi.

WH 1077, *KE* 180, *IP* 8.379 no. 1, *JL*--, 1159-81: *Tann.* 7.8.13 (*acerno*); *Sang.* 8.84 (*acerno*); *1 Abr.* 8.6.8 (*aceno*). Pd *Sang.* The printing from *Sang.* and *1 Abr.* is defective, and is corrected here from the earlier and amended reading in *Tann.* The letter is wrongly attributed to Eugenius III in *IP*.

Appendix 8: *Inter alia*, to the archbishop of Cosenza

Alexander III Cusentino archiepiscopo.

(a) Inter alia de quibus nos consulere voluisti, id a nobis te meminimus quesivisse, utrum presbiter, qui uxorem ante sacros ordines duxerit corruptam ab alio, debeat in presbiteratus ordine ministrare. Super quo utique consultationi tue taliter duximus respondendum, quod non fuit tibi super hoc [...] si non erat notorium. (b) De altero vero presbitero, quem asseris olim coram capitulo tuo super eo, quod domi mulierem ab alio corruptam habebat, tractum in causam dixissse se mulierem ipsam ante sacros ordines duxisse uxorem, nunc eam, ut uti valeat sacerdotio, suam asserit concubinam, hoc tibi de iure credimus respondendum, quod si tractus in causam coram capitulo eam uxorem publice recognovit, nunc autem contradicit, assertioni sue non debet fides aliquatenus adhiberi. (c) De presbitero vero, qui duas uxores ante sacros ordines duxit, sed alteram non cognovit, respondemus quod non potest bigamus reputari nec ei, quominus uti valeat sacerdotio, debet interdici, si alteram virginem habuerit. (d) De diacono vero, qui putatoriam falcem accinctam habebat ad renes et ludebat cum aliis pro labore itineris mitigando, in cuius dorsum insiliens alius, volens sicut moris est equitare, ipsius falce vulneratus est et mortuus sicut asseris, licet olim scripserimus aliter, si alias idoneus est, ut proponis, non est, quantum ad hunc articulum pertinet, quod eius promotioni de canonicis obviet institutis

WH 586, *KE* 210, *JL*--, 1159-81: *Bridl.* 163 only. Pd *KE*; cf. n. 73, above.

Appendix 9: *Requisivit a nobis*, to the bishop of Rapolla

Lucius III Rapullensi episcopo.

Requisivit a nobis tua fraternitas qua censura debeat compelli mulier que iurisiurandi religione nubere renuit, cui se nupturam interposito iuramento firmavit. Quesivisti etiam utrum ea cuius vir matris thorum polluit ad alia vota cum mater fieri desideret viro possit vivente transire. Ad que tibi breviter duximus respondendum quod mulier que se nupturam iuravit, cum libera debeant matrimonia, monenda est potius quam cogenda, maxime cum coactiones huiusmodi difficiles exitus soleant frequenter habere. Illa sane cuius vir cum matre adulterium et incestum commisit, nec viro suo coniungi carnaliter nec eo vivente cum alio matrimonium inire debebit.

WH 885, *KE* 207, *JL* 15165, 1181-85. Pd *App.* 45.6, *Cass.* 58.32, *1 Comp.* 4.1.12, *X* 4.1.17; cf. nn. 75 and 76, above.

ADDITIONAL NOTE. Among prelates of English origin listed in the present essay (at n. 37) are Walter and Bartholomew 'Offamil', accepted as such by many scholars. But this interpretation has been challenged by L. J. A. LOEWENTHAL, *For the biography of Walter Ophamil, archbishop of Palermo*, «English Historical Review», LXXXVII (1972), p. 75-82, and Norbert KAMP, *Kirche und Monarchie im staufischen Königreich Sizilien*, München 1975 (Münstersche Mittelalter-Schriften, X, 1: 3), p. 1112, n. 14, where it is argued that this form of the name results from a false Latin rendering of a Greek title.

POSTSCRIPT. While the present paper was in the press, the Ninth International Congress of Medieval Canon Law assembled in Munich, for the period 13-18 July, 1992. Among the musical compositions presented by *Die Gruppe für Alte Musik München*, on the evening of 14 July, was the song *Juvenis qui puellam*, of Guillaume Dufay (c. 1400-1474), its text being derived from Eugenius III's decretal *Iuvenis ille qui puellam*, transmitted through the collections to the *Decretales Gregorii IX*, 4.1.3. The significance of the text for Dufay's own career is explored in Professor Ernest Trumble's *Autobiographical implications in Dufay's song-motet* Juvenis qui puellam, in «Revue Belge de Musicologie», XLII (1988), p. 31-82. The localization of the original case has hitherto been considered indeterminable, but the solution proposed here is that the letter was sent by Eugenius III to bishop Prete (Presbiterus) of Ascoli Piceno (1145-53: *vide supra* Ascoli Piceno, part 3 and nn. 47 and 48, and Appendix 4).

ABBREVIATIONS

KE = W. Holtzmann, *Kanonistische Ergänzungen zur Italia Pontificia*, «Quellen und Forschungen aus italienischen Archiven und Bibliotheken» XXXVII (1957), p. 55-102, and XXXVIII (1958), p.67-175; and separately, Tübingen 1959, p. 1-157.

JL = P. Jaffé, *Regesta pontificum Romanorum*, ed. secundam curaverunt S. Loewenfeld, F. Kaltenbrunner and P. Ewald, Leipzig 1885-1888.

IP = P. F. Kehr, *et al.*, *Italia pontificia sive Repertorium privilegiorum et litterarum*, 10 vols, Berlin 1906-76.

WH = W. Holtzmann, *Regesta decretalium saeculi XII*, rev. et ed. in preparation by S. Chodorow and C. Duggan.

Sigla of Decretal Collections

For full details of manuscripts and literature, see *Decretales ineditae saeculi xii* (cf. n. 18, above), xix-xxxi, *sub nominibus*.

1 Abr. = *Abrincensis prima*; *Alan.* = *Alanus*; *App.* = *Appendix Concilii Lateranensis*; *Aur.* = *Aureavallensis*; *1 Berol.* = *Berolinensis prima*; *Bridl.* = *Bridlingtonensis*; *Brug.* = *Brugensis*; *1,3 Cant.* = *Cantuariensis prima, tertia*; *Cantab* = *Cantabrigienis*; *Cass.* = *Casselana*; *Chelt.* = *Cheltenhamensis*; *Claud.* = *Claudiana*; *Claustr.* = *Claustroneoburgensis*; *1,2 Comp.* = *Compilatio prima, secunda*; *Cott.* = *Cottoniana*; *Cus.* = *Cusana*; *1 Dun.* = *Dunelmensis prima*; *Erl.* = *Erlangensis*; *Flor.* = *Florianensis*; *Font.* = *Fontanensis*; *Frcf.* = *Francofortana*; *Fuld.* = *Fuldensis*; *Lips.* = *Lipsiensis*; *1,2 Par.* = *Parisiensis prima, secunda*; *Pet.* = *Petrihusensis*; *Reg.* = *Regalis*; *Roff.* = *Roffensis*; *1 Rot.* = *Rotomagensis prima*; *Sang.* = *Sangermanensis*; *Tann.* = *Tanner*; *1 Vict.* = *Victorina prima*; *Wig.* = *Wigorniensis*; *Wig. alt.* = *Wigorniensis altera*; *X* = *Decretales Gregorii IX*.

VII

THE CASE OF BERNARD OF OSMA:* ROYAL INFLUENCE AND PAPAL AUTHORITY IN THE DIOCESE OF OSMA

THE election of Bishop Bernard of Osma, former prior of Osma, took place not later than 15 February 1174. But the validity of his election was subsequently challenged on grounds of simony, and he was deposed sometime after mid-July 1176.[1] A decretal of Alexander III to Archbishop Cerebruno of Toledo, *Consuluit nos*, dealt in its opening section with the question of appeals where manifest crimes were involved, or frustratory tactics employed, and in its second part with the charges raised against the election of Bernard, *quondam* bishop of Osma. The letter was received into the canonical collections from 1179 onwards, and ultimately into the official *Decretales* of 1234.[2] There is no ambiguity about the provenance of this letter.

In contrast, the provenance of *Quia requisistis*, a letter of Alexander III to the canons of an uncertain cathedral, has given rise to speculation.[3] It likewise deals with the deposition of a *quondam* Bishop B., the necessary election of his successor, and more specifically with the assent of the English king Henry, without which the electors fear to act. But it has proven impossible to link this letter with any known English or Angevin case, and the purpose of the present essay is to propose that *Quia requisistis*, in its uncorrupted form, also referred to Bernard of Osma's deposition, though no known text confirms this thesis.

The decretal *Quia requisistis* is listed in Jaffé's *Regesta* among the letters of Alexander III, with the problematical address—'decano et capitulo cuidam (al. Vocestem) permittit ut loco B. episcopi depositi, impetrato assensu H(enrici) Anglorum regis, alium eligant.'[4] Its earliest known appearance is in the four extant copies of the 'Frankfurt' collection (from 1183 onwards), with the rubric 'propter vitandum scandalum in electione

* For Abbreviations and Sigla of Decretal Collections, with MS details of texts edited here, see pp. 93–6 below.

[1] See nn. 42–6 below.

[2] See Text II below.

[3] See Text I below.

[4] Jaffé 13728.

regius requiritur assensus (vel consensus)'.[5] It was later received into the Compilatio prima (1190) of Bernard of Pavia, the Collectio Alani (*c.*1206), Fuldensis (*c.*1216), and the Compilatio secunda (1210–15) of John the Welshman.[6] But it is otherwise unknown in decretal collections, and was not received into the *Decretales* of 1234. The 'Frankfurt' archetype evidently lacked the complete address, since all four copies name Alexander as the sender, but originally omitted the recipients' identity. An editor or corrector later inserted 'decano et canonicis Wincestrie' interlineally in the Rouen codex, and 'decano et canonicis Wircestrie' in that from St Maximin in Trier, suggesting Winchester and possibly Worcester respectively.[7] All subsequent copies name the recipients as the dean and chapter, or dean and canons, of a certain church, unidentified except by the corrupt version 'Vocestem' in Compilatio prima, and 'Clarensi' in a Munich copy of Compilatio secunda, where in all probability it was transposed in scribal error from a nearby decretal to Clermont Ferrand.[8] The sender appears as Lucius III (1181–5) in Compilatio prima, and the printed editions in Mansi and Migne repeated this error.[9]

The English provenance of the decretal seems at first consideration indisputable. The recipients have sought the Pope's advice in a delicate situation: their bishop has been deposed, and they have asked the Pope if they should proceed to an election, which they dare not do without the royal consent. The Pope replies that, if they have no alternative, they should approach the illustrious King Henry of England, and leave him in no doubt that their former bishop B. has been permanently deposed. Then, with the King's assent, they should unanimously agree on an honourable, learned, and suitable person, and elect him as their pastor and

[5] Frcf.FRTM 10.4. The 'Frankfurt' group is named after the modern location of the first known manuscript, but other members of the group are found in Paris, Troyes, and London. The work perhaps originated in Sens or Troyes, and later developments were completed in Rouen and possibly Lincoln; see S. Kuttner, 'Collectio Francofortana', *ZSRG.K*, 22 (1933), pp. 370–80; P. Landau, 'Die Entstehung der systematischen Dekretalensammlungen und die europäische Kanonistik des 12. Jahrhunderts', ibid., 66 (1979), pp. 124ff. An analysis of the group is in an advanced stage of preparation by Professor Landau.

[6] 1 Comp. 1.4[5] and 2 Comp. 1.3.2, in *Antiquae collectiones decretalium*, ed. Antonio Agustín; analysed E. Friedberg, *Quinque compilationes antiquae*; Alan 1.6.6, Fuld. 1.6.16: see R. von Heckel, 'Die Dekretalen-sammlungen des Gilbertus und Alanus nach den Weingartener Handschriften', *ZSRG.K*, 29 (1940), pp. 116–357, at pp. 231–2 and 335.

[7] Frcf.R fol. 178va; Frcf.M fol. 19v; but cf. n. 17 below.

[8] 2 Comp. 1.2.4: *Cum te audierimus*, Jaffé 13568, WH 314, Clement III to Bishop Gilbert of Clermont, 1190.

[9] Mansi (from Agustin edn), 22.482; *PL* (from Mansi) 201, col. 1375.

bishop, so that under his prudent rule their church will prosper in spiritual and temporal matters alike. The king is styled *rex Anglie* or *rex Anglorum* in every extant version of the letter; his personal name appears in full as Henry in all four 'Frankfurt' manuscripts (*Heinricus* in Frcf.F), and abbreviated elsewhere to H.—a plausible identification, since the English king throughout the relevant period was Henry II (1154–89). The bishop who was deposed is identified by the initial B. only, without diocesan designation.

The political realities then prevailing in England were consistent with the problem which gave rise to the decretal. It is well known that royal control of episcopal elections was among the issues in the dispute (1163–70) between Henry II and Becket, and in relations between the English Church and Crown in a longer historical context. King Henry's determination that elections would take place in his chapel and with his assent, and that homage would precede consecration, was made clear in the twelfth clause of the Constitutions of Clarendon in January 1164:

> Cum vacaverit archiepiscopatus vel episcopatus vel abbatia vel prioratus de dominio regis, debet esse in manu ipsius ... Et cum ventum fuerit ad consulendum ecclesie, debet dominus rex mandare potiores personas ecclesie et in capella ipsius domini regis debet fieri electio, assensu domini regis et consilio personarum regni, quas ad hoc faciendum vocaverit. Et ibidem faciet electus homagium et fidelitatem domino regi, sicut ligio domino ... priusquam sit consecratus.[10]

In the event, the problem was not mentioned in the compromise reached between the King and the papal legates, Albert and Theodwin, at Avranches in May 1172, following Becket's death on 29 December 1170, and in practice Henry retained the decisive voice in the choice of the elect. In 1173, the Young King Henry, in revolt against his father and concerned to assert his own royal prerogatives, alleged that the several elections made to vacant English bishoprics in that year had not been free, in particular that the Winchester electors had received his father's mandate in these terms: 'I order you to hold a free election, but I wish you to choose no one save Richard my clerk, archdeacon of Poitiers', that is to say, Richard of Ilchester, perhaps the most powerful royal administrator at that time:

[10] D. Whitelock, M. Brett, and C. N. L. Brooke, eds, *Councils and Synods, with other Documents Relating to the English Church* (Oxford, 1981), I.ii (1066–1204), p. 882.

> sicut pro certo accepimus id tale patris mei mandatum ipsorum introitus fuit: Henricus rex Anglorum *etc*, fidelibus suis monachis Guintoniensis ecclesie, salutem. Mando vobis ut liberam electionem habeatis, et tamen nolo ut aliquem accipiatis, nisi Richardum clericum meum, Pictavensem archidiaconum.[11]

It is unlikely, in fact, that Henry sent a mandate precisely in these terms to the Winchester electors, but the letter attributed to the Young King may well be genuine, and certainly corresponded with the realities of the electors' choice. Giraldus Cambrensis scathingly deplored the empty and delusive nature of so-called canonical elections in the period, and the prince's intervention in them:

> Hodie, loco omnium istorum, successit canonica electio, cum scilicet, Deo auctore, magis literatum et honestum eligit ecclesia ministerio ... Hodie vero, loco canonice electionis, in plerisque partibus successit intrusio principis, sub voce tamen electionis, vana et umbratili pronunciatione, ubi vox quidem solum auditur, nec voluntas attenditur.[12]

[11] *RHGL* 16 (Paris, 1806), p. 645. Cf. *Councils and Synods*, 1.ii, pp. 948, 958–9, and nn., on the Young King's plea for free canonical elections: 'strange music from the mouth of any Angevin'. The seven elections of 1173 were those of Richard of Dover to Canterbury, Richard of Ilchester to Winchester, Geoffrey Ridel to Ely, Robert Foliot to Hereford, Reginald FitzJocelin to Bath, John Greenford to Chichester, and the King's illegitimate son Geoffrey to Lincoln. With evident justice in some cases, the Young King's letter further alleged that the persecutors of the martyr were being promoted to English bishoprics. All seven elections were challenged and examined by the Pope, but the elect were confirmed and consecrated in 1174, except for the illegitimate Geoffrey, whose confirmation was deferred on grounds of his birth and age, and in the event he was never consecrated to Lincoln; he became Archbishop of York after his father's death, in the reign of Richard I. On the elections, see R. Foreville, *L'Église et la royauté en Angleterre sous Henri II Plantagenet* (Paris, 1943), pp. 377–84; for testimonials written in support of Richard of Ilchester and other elect in 1173–4, see A. Morey and C. N. L. Brooke, eds, *The Letters and Charters of Gilbert Foliot* (Cambridge, 1967), pp. 291–302, nos 220–6 and 228, and W. J. Millor and C. N. L. Brooke, eds, *The Letters of John of Salisbury*, 2 (*1163–1180*) (Oxford, 1979), pp. 761–85, nos 311–19; for Richard of Ilchester, see C. Duggan, 'Richard of Ilchester, royal servant and bishop', *TRHS*, ser. 5, 16 (1966), pp. 1–21, esp. pp. 13–14, and 'Bishop John and archdeacon Richard of Poitiers: their roles in the Becket dispute and its aftermath', in R. Foreville, ed., *Thomas Becket: actes du colloque internationale de Sédières, 1973* (Paris, 1975), pp. 71–83, and R. V. Turner, *The English Judiciary in the Age of Glanvill and Bracton, c. 1176–1239* (Cambridge, 1985), *passim*. Somewhat implausibly, Giraldus Cambrensis later recorded that Richard of Winchester blamed Richard of Canterbury for the loss of all that St Thomas the Martyr had gained, *Giraldi Cambrensis opera*, ed. J. F. Dimock, *RS*, 21, 7 (1877), p. 70: 'totum revera, quantum in ipso fuit, martyr obtinuit. Quia si successor eius decimam partem bonitatis et probitatis eius habuisseet, nullum ecclesia de articulis illis amisisset.'

[12] Ibid., p. 59: the language of Gerald's definition: 'literatum et honestum eligit ecclesia

And in the decretal *Qua fronte* (1176–77/81) Alexander III severely rebuked Archbishop Richard of Canterbury for his compliance in the confirmation of episcopal elections in the royal chamber. In Alexander's judgement, Richard was manifestly perverting the order of law in this matter, contrary to the freedom of the Church, for which his predecessor, the glorious martyr St Thomas, had died: 'Iam enim non in ecclesia, sicut est canonicum et honestum, non in palatio, non in camera tua, sed in propria camera regis, contra debitum iuris et contra pontificalis ordinis dignitatem, episcoporum electiones diceris confirmare.'[13]

But the decretal *Quia requisistis* does not convincingly read like a letter of Alexander III to English electors on such a subject, nor is it possible (as noted above) to match its historical details with any known problem in Henry II's dominions. If its explicit and unvarying reference to the English king Henry were correct, to whom was the decretal sent, and who was the Bishop B., whose perpetual deposition gave rise to the problem? There was in fact no English bishop B. deposed in Henry II's reign, nor has one been discovered in Henry's continental lands, or in Ireland.[14]

In his edition of Compilatio prima, Antonio Agustín noted the uncertainty of the decretal's address, but nevertheless assumed an English context. From the variant *Vocestem* found in his sources, he conjectured Rochester as the place-name: 'mendosam esse hanc vocem existimo: sed quid substitutam, non habeo; forte *Rocestren*. scribendum: sic enim *Rofensis* ecclesia in Britannia appellatur.'[15] But this was an impossible solution, since Rochester was a monastic cathedral, without a dean and canons. Moreover, its bishop, Walter, Archbishop Theobald's brother, ruled securely throughout the relevant period.[16] For similar reasons, *Wincestrie* and *Wircestrie*, inserted editorially in Frcf.R and Frcf.M, cannot

---

ministerio' agrees with that of Alexander III in *Quia requisistis*: 'in personam honestam litteratam et idoneam unanimiter conveniatis, et eam in pastorem et episcopum concorditer eligatis, cuius providentia, etc.'

13 *Qua fronte*, Jaffé 14312, WH 755: pd X 2.28.25; App. 31.2–3, and 43.3. The probable date of this letter (early 1176 to mid-1177 [1176–81]) is discussed in C. Duggan, 'St Thomas of Canterbury and aspects of the Becket dispute in the decretal collections', in C. E. Viola, ed., *Mediaevalia Christiana XIe–XIIIe siècles: Hommage à Raymonde Foreville* (Paris, 1989), pp. 121–2, no. 34.

14 In his unpublished notes, Holtzmann considered the possibility of an Irish context, but the meagre records of Irish bishoprics in the period give no support for this suggestion. Many papal letters to Ireland in the thirteenth century refer to royal intervention and licence to elect: see M. P. Sheehy, *Pontificia Hibernica, 640–1261*, 2 (Dublin, 1965), *passim*.

15 Agustín, p. 19, n. b.

16 Walter was Bishop of Rochester, 1148–82.

validly identify Winchester or Worcester,[17] though *Wincestrie* is an accurate form for Winchester, and is found both correctly and incorrectly supplied for adjacent letters in the 'Frankfurt' collection.[18] The fragility of the 'Frankfurt' evidence on this point must indeed be emphasized: as mentioned above, all four copies originally lacked a complete address, and impossible versions were later inserted in two.

With such seemingly intractable problems, it is scarcely surprising that the authenticity of the letter has been questioned. The erroneous reference to the English king Henry was already present in the decretal's first known transcription in the collections, and was consistently transmitted through all the later collections which contain it. The letter first appears in the 'Frankfurt' collections, in a sequence of mostly English decretals relating to similar problems.[19] It is preceded there by *Cum de tua*, to John, bishop-elect of Chichester, concerning canonical objections to his election,[20] and by *Quod diligentia*, to the cardinal legate Ildebrando, on the return of an elect from schism to Catholic unity.[21] It is followed by *Qua fronte* (cited above), to Richard of Canterbury, on the confirmation of elections in the English king's chamber,[22] and by *Nosti sicut*, to Roger of Worcester, on administrative improprieties by Geoffrey, bishop-elect of Lincoln and illegitimate son of Henry II.[23] A later addition in Frcf.M is *Quanto per carissimum*, to Roger of York, on the projected coronation of Henry II's heir.[24] It is easy to see how an English identification could replace a less familiar form in such a setting, or could be so constructed by the compiler to suit an English context. A strikingly similar error was in fact made in the Klosterneuberg collection (*post* 1181), a member of the

[17] Both Winchester and Worcester were monastic cathedrals. Henry of Blois was Bishop of Winchester, 1129–71, followed by Richard of Ilchester 1174 (el. 1173) to 1188. Alfred was Bishop of Worcester, 1158–60, followed by Roger, 1164 (el. 1163) to 1179.

[18] Correctly: Frcf.FRM 2.5: *Super eo quod interrogasti*: Jaffé 8274, WH 1016, Innocent II to Bishop Henry of Winchester, 1139–41. Incorrectly: Frcf.FTM (*non leg. photogr.* R) 2.4: *Super eo quod asseris* = part (b) of *Consuluit nos*, Jaffé 13790, WH 191, Alexander III to the Archbishop of Bordeaux, 1159–81; by scribal error this item also appears as Innocent II to Henry of Winchester. Within two places of *Quia requisistis*, a further scribal error is found in Frcf.FR 10.6, where the recipient is named bishop of Norwich instead of Worcester: *Nosti sicut*, Jaffé 12753, WH 679, Alexander III to Roger of Worcester, 1173–5.

[19] Frcf. 10.2–6.

[20] Jaffé 12367, WH 226, summer 1174.

[21] Jaffé 12632, WH 818, 6 April 1164–5, the only non-English decretal in the sequence.

[22] Jaffé 14312, WH 755, 1176–9.

[23] Jaffé 12753, WH 679, 1173–9: wrongly addressed to the bishop of Norwich in Frcf.RM (*om.* FT).

[24] Frcf.M 10.5: Jaffé 11253, WH 772: 17 June 1161; see Anne Duggan (Heslin), 'The Coronation of the Young King in 1170', *SCH*, 2 (1965), pp. 165–78.

Worcester family of collections, in *Consuluit nos*, the decretal of Alexander III to Cerebruno of Toledo, cited above. In the Klosterneuberg codex, the king of Castile and the former Bishop Bernard of Osma appear as the king of England and a *quondam* bishop, whose diocese is transmitted in the garbled form *eximense*:

> Hec autem quod rex et princeps anglie h. quondam eximense episcopo pecuniam recepisse dicuntur, ut eius electioni prestaret assensum, et quod idem episcopus archidiacono s. beneficium certi redditus et cuidam clerico ante electionem prioratum dicitur promisisse, ut uterque eorum archidiaconus scilicet et clericus eius electioni consentirent, etc.[25]

The decretal *Consuluit nos* occurs in numerous collections, ranging from members of the primitive Tortosa, French, Italian, and English families, through most of the well-known systematic collections, to the *Decretales*.[26] In all the systematic collections which include it, from the Appendix concilii Lateranensis (*post* 1184) onwards, the letter appears as two separate items, occasionally with cross-references between them, and the two sections are registered separately in Jaffé's *Regesta*, the second beginning *De hoc autem*.[27] Occasionally, also, one part of the other is found in isolation in primitive collections, but nine primitive or technically-transitional collections preserve the complete text as an entity, and there is no doubt that it is a single letter. Likewise, there is no doubt that it was sent by Alexander III to the Archbishop of Toledo, as more than fifty manuscript readings testify.[28]

The first part of the rescript concerns appeals. The Archbishop has asked the Pope if appeals should be deferred to, if launched when manifest crimes were involved, or for frustratory motives to delay the judicial process. The Pope replies that appeals should not be deferred to, if made by those who have manifestly and notoriously committed adultery, or laid violent hands on a clerk. But many matters are described as notorious when they are not so, and therefore the Archbishop should take care not

[25] Claustr. 181, fol. 63: Jaffé 14112 and 14110, WH 193, 1176–9: it is not clear whether the initial h. was intended for the king (? Henry) or the bishop (? h. misreading for b. = Bernard).

[26] On the collections and their family relationships, see W. Holtzmann, 'Über eine Ausgabe der päpstlichen Dekretalen des 12. Jahrhunderts', *Nachrichten Akad. Göttingen* (1945), pp. 15–36. The latest lists of collections, with manuscript locations and relevant literature, are in Holtzmann–Cheney, pp. xx–xxxi,and Chodorow–Duggan, pp. xix–xxxi; see also Sigla of Decretal Collections below.

[27] Jaffé 14112 and 14110,both *sa* 1159–81.

[28] See Text II below, with apparatus of manuscript locations and select textual variants.

to treat a doubtful matter as notorious. However, those who appeal from the archbishop's court should be compelled to prosecute their appeal within a suitable term, or stand to his judgement without leave of appeal.

The second part of the decretal, *De hoc autem*, deals with the case of Bernard of Osma. The Pope responds to an accusation that the king and his magnates had accepted money from the *quondam* bishop, to assent to his election, and that before the election the Bishop had promised a benefice with a certain income to the archdeacon of Soria, and the office of prior to a certain clerk, so that they would assent to it. The Pope replies that, if it is manifest that the archdeacon and clerk had received so detestable and wicked a promise or its implementation, or if they had confessed in law or could be lawfully convicted, they should be permanently deposed from the ministry of the altar. But if the matter is not manifest,[29] and they have neither confessed nor been convicted, yet are publicly defamed on its account, they should be subjected to canonical purgation; and, if they fail in this, they should be punished as authors of so serious a crime. The Archbishop should carefully admonish the king and his magnates, and induce them to restore in full to the church of Osma whatever they may have received from the Bishop, to assent to his election. They cannot, without grave risk to their salvation, keep what they may have received.

The transmission of *De hoc autem* through the collections clearly shows how the historical details of a case, which were of less interest to the collectors than its juristic principles, sometimes became confused and distorted.[30] Only the primitive Tortosa, Eberbach, and Orval collections (Dert., Eber., Aur.) transmit an accurate identification of Osma, though it was also inserted as an alternative reading in the margin of the Lincoln codex of the Appendix. Elsewhere it appears in numerous corrupt forms, sometimes as Exeter, and in the 'Frankfurt' codex (Frcf.F) as Reims. Likewise, Soria appears accurately (or nearly so) only in the Tortosa, Orval, and St Florian (Flor.) collections, and in three copies of the 'Frankfurt' collection (Frcf.FRM); it is identified by the initial S. in six collections.[31] Otherwise it is transcribed in various distorted forms, sometimes as Exeter, and as Sens in three copies of the Appendix (LpVLn). Agustín's edition of Compilatio prima reads Exeter for both bishop and archdeacon;

[29] Many collections (including 1 Comp. and X) read this sentence also as relating to a manifest matter—*si vero id manifestum est*—a reading which is in turn discussed by some glossators. But *manifestum non est* occurs in the earliest collections, and seems the more likely form.

[30] See Text II below: passages b–b, c–c, and d–d, and relevant apparatus.

[31] Ibid., passage c–c and apparatus: Eber., 1 Alc., Claustr., Wig. 5.7, Cott., Pet.

he recognized the textual error, but emended both to Osma in his critical apparatus;[32] and Friedberg's edition of the *Decretales* correctly supplied Osma for the bishop, but omitted the archdeacon's territorial designation.[33] No printed edition has so far identified the archdeacon of Soria, but the older collections, which were unknown to Agustín and Friedberg, make his identity clear.

The misreading of Exeter for Osma (*exoniensis/oxomensis/oximensis*) is not surprising; indeed the form *Exomensis* sometimes occurs for Osma in witness-lists of Spanish royal charters in the period.[34] The name of Bishop Bartholomew of Exeter (1161–84), a frequent recipient of papal decretals, was a common source of confusion to decretal scribes.[35] His personal name in abbreviation was sometimes mistaken for Bath (*barth./bath.*); and his diocesan appellation was liable to confusion variously with Oxford, Lisieux, Osma, and Huesca (*oxon./lexou./oxom./oscen.*). Apart from *Quia requisistis*, the collections otherwise preserve only one letter to Osma, which two collections read as Exeter.[36] The collections include two decretals to Huesca, of which one occurs addressed to the bishop of Exeter and the prior of Our Lady *Augustini* (*recte*: *Caesaraugustane* = Zaragoza),[37] and the other is found with an address to the bishop of Ely (*eliensi*).[38] By a

[32] Agustín, ed., p. 279 n.(g) at *a Bernardo Exon.*: 'Ab Ernardo quondam Certomensi, concil. alias *Ceromensi*, sic in priori edit. concil. *a Bernardo*, in poster. Ego mendosa esse omnia suspicor, et scribendum: *a Bernardo Oxomen*. Est autem Exonia in Britannia, Oxoma in Hispania: *Exonensi*, unus Tarraconensis non recte; n.(k) at *Archidiacono Exonen.*: *Exon.* tres. Tarracon. *Sevien.* concil. *Exom. Archid.* vetus Gregor. *Obsom. Archid.* alter vetus. *Exonien.* Cont. et alii: scribo *Oxomensi*; n.(gg) at *sine deminutione* [sic]: *Ecclesiae Ceromensi sine*, concil. *ecclesiae Exon.* duo Tarr. et Barcin. *Exon. ecclesiae sine*, tertius Tarrac. *Exom.* vetus Gregor. *Obsom.* alter vetus. *Exonien.* Cont. et alii: scribo, *ecclesiae Oxomiensi sine*: est autem Oxoma sub Toletano Antistite, cui hoc rescriptum mittitur.'

[33] X 5.3.11: ed. p. 752: [a Bernardo quondam Oxomensi (*var.* Exoniensi) episcopo] . . . Oxomensis (*varr.* Exonensis, Seviensi) archidiacono . . . ecclesiae Oxomensi (*varr.* Exonensi, Exonien., Cremonensi).

[34] J. González, *El reino de Castilla en la época de Alfonso VIII*, 3 vols (Madrid, 1960), 2, pp. 462–3, no. 280, 23 May 1177, and 2, pp. 474–5, no. 289.

[35] The general problem was noted long ago by F. W. Maitland, *Roman Canon Law in the Church of England* (London, 1898), pp. 122–3: 'to the decretists the whereabouts of these places was less than nothing. They might be in Spain; they might be in Hungary; they might be nowhere.' See also Holtzmann, 'Über eine Ausgabe', p. 30.

[36] *Innotuit nobis*, Clement III to Bishop Martin of Osma, Jaffé 16597 + 16621, WH 566, 18 June 1190; addressed to Exeter in Monacensis 80 and Halensis 17: see Holtzmann–Cheney, pp. 230 and 236.

[37] *Relatum est*, Alexander III to the Bishop of Huesca and the Prior of Neustra Señora del Pilar in Zaragoza, Jaffé 14041, WH 862, 1167–70; cf. Sang. 8.5 fol. 85vb: *Idem exon. episcopo et priori sancte Marie Augustini*.

[38] *Super quoddam*, Clement III to the Bishop of Huesca, Jaffé 16606, WH 1019, 11 February 1188; addressed to the Bishop of Ely in Monacensis 4: see Holtzmann–Cheney, p. 225.

curious coincidence, the possibility of simony in fact arose in the vacancy which preceded Bartholomew's election to Exeter in 1161: on the one hand, Archbishop Theobald requested the King not to allow a simoniac to secure the see; on the other hand, Bartholomew was warned by John of Salisbury not to promise an archdeaconry to his rival Robert Fitz-Harding.[39] But there are obvious differences between the Osma and Exeter cases. Bartholomew was neither accused nor deposed, and was destined to become one of the most distinguished and respected English bishops, a famous judge delegate, and, with Roger of Worcester, one of the *duo magna luminaria Anglicane ecclesie*, in Alexander's judgement.[40] The Spanish provenance of the decretal *Consuluit nos* is clear.

The king involved in the accusation of simony was undoubtedly Alfonso VIII (1158–1214) of Castile, husband of the English king Henry's daughter Eleanor, and later famous victor of Las Navas de Tolosa (1212). He is not identified in any of the numerous surviving copies of the decretal; indeed, the single text with a territorial designation wrongly calls him king of England.[41] The *quondam* bishop of Osma was Bernard, former prior of Osma, elected not later than 15 February 1174,[42] consecrated before 15 August,[43] and recipient of a privilege from Alfonso VIII at Toledo on 24 September in the same year.[44] His tenure of the bishopric was secure for two years: he confirmed a royal grant in favour of the cathedral and archbishop of Toledo at San Esteban de Gormaz on 24 February 1175,[45] and another in favour of the monastery of San Miguel de Villamayor as late as July 1176.[46] He was subsequently deposed for simony, and his successor, Michael, appears as bishop-elect by 23 May 1177, confirming a royal concession to the cathedral of Sigüenza, and as bishop in a witness-list to a royal grant to Pedro Gutierrez on 23 June,

[39] A. Morey, *Bartholomew of Exeter: Bishop and Canonist* (Cambridge, 1937), pp. 8–13.
[40] Ibid., p. 45.
[41] Claustr. 181: cf. n. 25 above.
[42] González, 2, pp. 326–7, no. 197, a royal confirmation in favour of Toledo; cf. J. Loperráez Corvalán, *Descripción Histórica del Obispado de Osma con el catálogo de sus prelados*, 3 vols (Madrid, 1788: repr. Madrid, 1978): 1, p. 148 and n. 2: *Ego Bernardus Episcopus electus Oxomens. confirmo*.
[43] Ibid., pp. 148–9 and p. 149, n. 1: *Ego Bernardus Episcopus Oxomens. confirmo*.
[44] González, 2, pp. 347–9, no. 211, a royal confirmation of the possessions of the church of Osma; cf. Loperráez Corvalán, 3: *Colección Diplomática*, pp. 36–8, no. 27.
[45] F. J. Hernández, ed., *Los cartularios de Toledo: catálogo documental = Monumenta Ecclesiae Toletanae Historica, Series 1: Regesta et Inventaria Historica*, 1 (Madrid, 1985), pp. 165–6, no. 171: Alfonso and Eleanor grant the monastery of Covarrubias and all its lands and possessions to the cathedral of Toledo and Archbishop Cerebruno, in reparation for violation of the cathedral.
[46] González, 2, pp. 432–3, no. 262, at Belrod.

both documents drawn up at Sitio de Cuenca, in the presence of Archbishop Cerebruno of Toledo, who presumably consecrated Michael within that period.[47] On the evidence of the documents cited here, the maximum limits of the Osma vacancy were July 1176 to 23 May 1177. Michael's name does not appear in the *Series episcoporum*, where Bernard's dates are given as 1174–85; but this was an oversight.[48] In company with Cerebruno and his suffragans, Raimundo of Palencia, Gonzalo of Segovia, and Arderico of Sigüenza, Michael was present at the Lateran Council in March 1179,[49] was the recipient of a royal charter at Ayllon on 15 July 1180,[50] and held the diocese until his death in 1185.

The decretal *Consuluit nos* was clearly written after the *quondam* Bishop Bernard's deposition, though his sentence is not explicitly mentioned in the letter; nor is there evidence whether or not Michael had yet succeeded. The archdeacon who was allegedly promised a benefice for his compliance was the archdeacon of Soria, to the east of Osma; for him and the clerk who was promised the office of prior, the result of the papal commission has not been established. The royal *principes* involved in the case were Count Nuño Pérez de Lara and Don Pedro de Arazuri, *curadores del rey* or royal guardians. Count Nuño, who had been imperial standard-bearer to Alfonso VII as early as 1145,[51] was among the most powerful magnates of the realm during Alfonso VIII's minority, and through the

[47] Ibid., 2, pp. 462–4, nos 280 and 281.

[48] P. B. Gams, *Series episcoporum ecclesiae Catholicae* (Regensburg, 1873–86: repr. Graz, 1957), p. 56: 'Bernard OSB 1174–post 9.viii.1185'. But cf. Loperráez Corvalán, 1, p. 148: 'post hunc (scilicet Johannem) fuit Episcopus Bernardus, Prior Oxomensis tempore Regis Aldephonsi, et consecratus a d. Celebruno Toletano Archiepiscopo, et Episcopis Soscelmo Seguntino et Gonzalvo Segoviensi; iste fuit simoniacus, et ideo fuit depositus per Alexandrum Papam, et factus fuit Prior Oxomensis. Vixit autem in Episcopatu duobus annis' (cited by Holtzmann); and F. Zamora, *Diccioniario de Historia Eclesiástica de España*, 3 (Madrid, 1973), p. 1848: 'Bernardo OSB: 1174–76, depuesto accusando de simonia'. Both Loperráez Corvalán and Zamora give Michael's dates as 1177–85; but cf. citation in Loperráez Corvalán, i, p. 161: 'Post hunc (de D. Bernardo) fuit Michael Episcopus . . . Rexit Ecclesia VII. annos.'

[49] Mansi, 22.216 and 466; cf. Paris, BN, MS lat. 14938, fol. 266ra–b (text very close to Mansi, 22.466), list of prelates attending the council: 'Provinciae toletane: Celebrinus toletanus archiepiscopus. raimundus palentinus episcopus. Gonsalbus Sogobiensis. Michael olxumensis. Oderricus sequentinus.' The dates given for Gonzalo of Segovia by Gams (*Series episcoporum*, p. 70) and J. García Hernando (*Diccionario de Historia Eclesiástica de España*, 4 [1975], p. 2400) can be improved: both cite 1170 as the last known date for Guillermo, Gonzalo's predecessor, and 1177 as the earliest known date for Gonzalo, leaving a seven-year gap. But Gonzalo was already bishop by early 1173: he confirmed a concession by Alfonso VIII and Eleanor to the church of Toledo and its archbishop, Cerebruno, at Toledo on 30 March 1173, a licence for work on the completion of the building (Hernández, pp. 156–7, no. 162); and he was one of Bernard of Osma's consecrators in 1174 (Loperráez Corvalán, 1, p. 161).

[50] Loperráez Corvalán, 3, p. 3: *Coleccion Diplomática*, pp. 38–40, no. 28 (15 July).

[51] Hernández, pp. 53–4, no. 50, 1 September 1145.

period of the Osma crisis;[52] but he did not long survive the affair. At Sitio de Cuenca in July 1177, together with his wife Teresa, he endowed the altar of St Thomas of Canterbury in Toledo Cathedral, for his own memorial celebrations.[53] He had died by 30 September 1178, when Alfonso and Eleanor confirmed at Simancas the provision which the then-deceased count—*vir pie recordationis*—had made.[54] Don Pedro was present on that occasion, and later confirmed a charter of Alfonso and Eleanor, protecting that provision for St Thomas's altar and its chaplain, William, at Toledo on 5 January 1181 (which itself reaffirmed a charter of Eleanor and Alfonso, at Toledo on 30 April 1179).[55] He appeared in witness-lists to royal charters at least until 14 May 1181.[56]

But in spite of such pious benefactions, as well as the papal mandate in *Consuluit nos*, the money received in connection with Bernard's election was not then restored. Thirty years after the election, Alfonso VIII drew up his will at Fuentidueña, on 8 December 1204. Among its provisions was that reparation should be made to the church of Osma for 5,000 maravedis received from a certain person (*a quodam*) by Don Nuño and Pedro de Arazuri, for the institution of a bishop in the church vacant at that time. This happened, the King asserted, at a moment of attack by the kings of León and Navarre, and by the Saracens, the money being expended by the magnates in the defence of Calahorra; it was done without his knowledge, when he was himself a minor (*puer*), in the magnates' control and care. In recompense he now assigned to the church of Osma the castle and city of Osma and all its rights in reversion after the death of Count Gundisalvo, with whom he had agreed a life-tenure exchange.

> Sciendum est preterea quod, cum ego eram puer et a regibus Leogionis et Navarre, etiamque a Sarracenis, regnum meum acriter infestabatur, immo nitebantur ut me exheredarent, comes dompnus Nunnus et Petrus de Arazuri, in quorum potestate eram et a quibus nutriebar, pro instituendo in Oxomensi ecclesia pastore, que tunc temporis episcopo vacabat, quinque milia morabetinorum, me inconsulto et ignorante, a quodam perceperunt; quos in defensione

[52] González, 1, pp. 170–1 *et passim*.
[53] Hernández, pp. 173–4, no. 180.
[54] González, 2, pp. 505–7, no. 307; Hernández, pp. 176–7, no. 184.
[55] González, 2, pp. 542–3, no. 324, and pp. 603–4, no. 355; Hernández, pp. 178–9, no. 186, and pp. 182–3, no. 191.
[56] González, 2, pp. 635–8, no. 368, at Burgos.

> cuiusdam civitatis mee que Calagurra dicitur, que iam pro ingenti guerra pene consilio et auxilio erat destituta, expendiderunt. Ideoque, pro recompensatione dicte pecunie, prefate ecclesie Oxomensi castellum de Oxoma cum villa et cum omni iure suo post decessum comitis Gundissalvi, cui in concambium dedi diebus suis habendam pro hereditate sua quam michi dedit, integre dari precipio.[57]

The King's self-exculpatory language in 1204 was perhaps consciously deceptive: the bishop involved in the simoniacal election was not identified, the affair was not dated, and the circumstances and process of the election were imprecisely phrased. Alfonso was eighteen years old at the time of the election, had been married to Eleanor for about four years, and was experienced in the Cortes and on military campaigns.[58] Nevertheless, the power and status of the royal guardians and the military pressures were doubtless continuing and important factors. After Alfonso's death (6 October 1214), his son Enrique I confirmed the bequest which his father had made, in a royal grant to the bishop of Osma, at Talavera, on 17 February 1217: 'Dono itaque vobis et concedo villam que Oxoma dicitur, cum omnibus pertinentiis suis, quam pater meus ad mortem suam vobis reliquisse dicitur, scilicet, cum Castro et cum aldeis, etc.'[59]

The historical circumstances of the Osma election, the precise sequence of events, and the roles of the principal figures involved can doubtless be assessed more securely by Spanish scholars. The more limited purpose of the present study is to show that a close comparison of *Consuluit nos*, which manifestly relates to the Osma affair, and *Quia requisistis*, which purports to relate to a similar English problem but cannot in fact do so, supports the possibility that they have a common ancestry. Historical errors in transcription and even conscious adaptations are very familiar in the collections.[60] Alexander III's decretal *Amara nimis*, for instance, is

[57] González, 3, pp. 341–7, no. 769, at pp. 345–6; Hernández, pp. 258–61, no. 282, at p. 260.

[58] González, 1, pp. 144, 185–90, *et passim*; cf. 2, pp. 253–4, no. 148, 17 September 1170: grant by Alfonso and Eleanor to Bishop John of Osma in favour of the church of Osma. Alfonso's language in 1204 implies an earlier date than 1174, which presumably resolves a problem raised by Dr Linehan in 'The synod of Segovia (1166)', *Bulletin of Medieval Canon Law*, 10 (1980), p. 38, n. 30: 'the reference in the king's will . . . serves to highlight our ignorance of the ecclesiastical history of the 1160s since bishop Juan of Osma is thought to have ruled his diocese undisturbed from 1148 to 1173.' The will in fact refers to Bernard's election.

[59] González, 3, pp. 740–1, no. 1011.

[60] On the subject of forgeries in the collections, cf. C. Duggan, '*Improba pestis falsitatis*: Forgeries and the problem of forgery in twelfth-century decretal collections', in H. Fuhrmann, ed.,

found only in the English Cottonian and Peterhouse collections, with an impossible address to the archbishop of Canterbury, but was very probably sent to Archbishop Lucas of Esztergom.[61] Lucas was certainly the recipient of Lucius III's decretal *Ad apostolice sedis*, but it appears in the English and Anglo-Norman collections Tanner and Sangermanensis with an internal reference to English custom—*quedam consuetudo in Anglia* (recte: *Hungaria*).[62] Urban III's *Ad audientiam nostram*, to Archbishop Walter of Rouen, speaks of the forgery of the French king's seal, which the Estensis collection reads as that of King H(enry) of England.[63] Most pertinent in the present context, the Klosterneuberg collection transmits a reference to the king of Castile and his magnates as *rex et princeps* [*sic*] *Anglie*, in *Consuluit nos*, as recorded above.[64]

The decretal *Quia requisistis* seems therefore derived from a genuine letter to Osma, distorted in transmission, or even adapted to suit an English context. If this hypothesis is correct, it was sent by Alexander III to the canons of Osma within the period late 1176 to early 1177, since Michael was already bishop-elect by 23 May in the latter year.[65] *Consuluit nos* was sent by Alexander III to Cerebruno of Toledo after Bernard's deposition, but it does not explicitly antedate or postdate Michael's election. Its presence in the Tortosa (Dertusensis) collection sets the date of the Third Lateran Council in March 1179 as its latest possible limit.

King's College London

Texts

For reasons of clarity and space, only the manuscript traditions and variants in the names of persons and places are noted here. The precise manuscript details, including the folio locations of texts, are given in the Sigla of Decretal Collections below.

Fälschungen im Mittelalter: Internationaler Kongress der Monumenta Germaniae Historica, München 1986 (Hanover, 1988), 2, pp. 319–61; cf. esp. pp. 328–9, no. 3.

[61] Chororow–Duggan, pp. 169–71, no. 96.

[62] Tann. 4.6.4, p. 656a; Sang, 5.5.8, fol. 52v[a-b].

[63] Estensis 6.9.2: Duggan, '*Improba pestis falsitatis*', pp. 355–6, no. 18.

[64] See n. 25 above.

[65] See nn. 46–8 above.

Bernard of Osma

I QUIA REQUISISTIS

This decretal is printed here as transmitted through the collections, but (as explained above) its historical details cannot be reconciled with any known case.

[a]Alexander III decano et canonicis Wincestrie/Wircestrie/Vocestem/Clarensi. [? *recte*: . . . canonicis Oxomensis ecclesie].[a]
Quia requisistis a nobis utrum ad electionem faciendam procedere debeatis, proponentes quod eam facere sine assensu regio non audetis, si aliter fieri non possit, ad [b]Henricum in Christo filium nostrum illustrem regem Anglorum[b] accedentes, ei studiosius intimetis B. quondam episcopum vestrum perpetuo esse depositum, et eiusdem regis impetrato assensu in personam honestam, litteratam et idoneam unanimiter conveniatis, et eam in pastorem et episcopum concorditer eligatis, cuius providentia et gubernatione ecclesie tam in spiritualibus quam in temporalibus grata valeant incrementa provenire.

WH 810, Jaffé 13728, *post* July 1176–*ante* May 1177.
Tradition: Frcf.FRTM 10.4 (cod. Frcf. = FrF; cod. Rot. = FrR; cod. Trec. = FrT; cod. Max. = FrM; consensus codd. = Fr); 1 Comp. 1.4.5 (ed. Agustín = 1CpA; ed. Friedberg = 1CpF; consensus edd. = 1Cp); Alan. 1.6.6 (Al; cod. Vercelli = Alv); Fuld. 1.6.16; 2 Comp. 1.3.2 (ed. Agustín = 2CpA; ed. Friedberg = 2CpF; cod. Monacen. = 2 CpM; consensus edd. = 2Cp).
Printed: 1 Comp.; 2 Comp.

a–a Alexander III] Alexander FrRT(III *add. supra* R); Lucius III 1Cp   decano . . . Clarensi *om.* Fr; decano et canonicis Wincestrie *add. supra* FrR; decano et canonicis Wircestrie *add. marg.* FrM; decano et canonicis Vocestem 1Cp(Vocesten 1CpF); decano et capitulo 2Cp(*add.* Clarensi M)Al(decano et ca. Alv)   **b–b** Heinricum FrF; H. 1CpAlv2Cp   in Christo filium nostrum] dilectum filium nostrum in Christo 1CpAlv2Cp   illustrem *om.* 1CpAlv2Cp   Anglie FrF1Cp2Cp.

II CONSULUIT NOS

[a]Alexander III Toletano archiepiscopo.[a]
(a) [i] Consuluit nos tua fraternitas utrum deferendum sit appellationibus que super manifestis criminibus interponuntur, aut eorum appellationibus qui causa frustratorie dilationis appellant, nec appellationem interpositam prosequuntur. [ii] Super quo utique consultationi tue taliter respondemus quod, si quando aliqui quos manifestum sit et notorium uxorem alterius detinere aut iniecisse manus violentas in clericum

appellaverint, eorum appellationibus non est aliquatenus deferendum; sed, cum multa dicantur notoria que non sunt, providere debes ne quod dubium est pro notorio videaris habere. [iii] Illos autem qui appellant a presentia tua cogere debes infra tempus conveniens appellationem interpositam prosequi, aut iudicio tuo appellatione cessante parere. **(b)** De hoc autem quod rex et [b]principes sui a Bernardo quondam Oximensi[b] episcopo pecuniam recepisse dicuntur, ut eius electioni suum prestarent assensum, et quod [c]idem episcopus archidiacono Soriensi[c] beneficium certi redditus et cuidam clerico ante electionem suam prioratum dicitur promisisse, ut uterque eorum archdiaconus videlicet et clericus eius electioni consentirent, hoc tue prudentie duximus respondendum quod, si manifestum est eundem archdiaconum et clericum ob causam illam promissionem tam iniquam et detestabilem aut promissam rem receipisse, aut si exinde confessi fuerint in iure, vel legitime convinci potuerint, ab altaris ministerio perpetuo sunt deponendi. Si vero id manifestum non est, nec inde convicti vel confessi fuerint, et inde publica laborant infamia, eis canonica purgatio debet indici, in qua si defecerint tamquam auctores tanti sceleris sunt puniendi. Regem autem et principes suos sollicite monere debes et diligenter inducere ut si qua receperint a prefato episcopo ut eius electioni suum prestarent assensum, [d]ecclesie Oximensi[d] sine diminutione restituant, cum ea sine gravi sue salutis periculo detinere non possint.

WH 193, Jaffé 14112 + 14110, *post* July 1176–*in* 1177 x *in* 1179.
Tradition: Complete: 1 Dert. 44 (= De); Eber. 15.1 (= Eb); 1 Alc. 46 (= Al); Aur. 51 (= Au 51); Flor. 164 (= Fl); Wig. 5.7 (= W 5.7); Claustr. 181 (= Cr); Cott. 3.10 (= Co); Pet. 2.13.6 (= Pe). **Parts:** Cantab. 55(a) (= Cb); 1 Vict. 85(a) (= V); 1 Par. 152(a) (= Pa); Aur. 73(b) (= Au 73); Bridl. 108(a) (= Bl); Claud. 96(a) (= Cd); Wig. 5.11(a.ii from *si quando*) (= W 5.11); Chelt. 15.7(a), 2.2(b) (= Ch); App. 10.14(a), 2.13(b) (ed. Laurens [Cr] = ApC; cod. Lips. = ApLp; cod. Vind. = ApV; cod. Linc. = ApLn; consensus codd. = Ap); Bamb. 42.13(a: Bamb.DO42.14), 1.2(b) (cod. Bamb. = BbB; cod. Amb. = BbA; cod. Compend. = BbC; cod. Dert. = BbD; consensus codd. = Bb); Erl. 42.14(a), 1.2(b) (= Er); Lips. 47.15(a), 1.2(b) (= L); Cass. 51.14(a), 13.2(b) (cod. Cass. = CsC; cod. Bamb. = CsB; consensus codd. = Cs); Tann. 5.8.5(ai–ii), 5.12.5(aiii), 2.1.2(b) (= T); Brug. 47.1(a), 42.6(b) (cod. Brug. = BgB; cod. Vat. = BgV; consensus codd. = Bg); Frcf.M 51.6 (a: *add marg. supra*), Frcf.FRM 22.9(b) (cod. Frcf. = FrF; cod. Rot. = FrR; cod. Max. = FrM; consensus codd. FRM = Fr); 1 Rot. 31.7(a) (= R); 2 Dun. 69(b) (= Du); Sang. 6.9.6(ai–ii), 6.13.5(aiii), 2.1.2(b) (= S); 1 Comp. 2.20.16(a), 5.2.10(b) (ed.

Bernard of Osma

Agustín = CpA; ed. Friedberg = CpF; consensus edd. = Cp); X 2.28.14(a), 5.3.11(b) (= X).
Printed: App.Cr. (ab); Cass.C (ab); Brug.B (b); 1 Comp.A (ab); X (ab); and from X in Loperráez Corvalán, 1.146–47 (b).

a–a *Sine inscriptione* CrCh(a)ApLp(b)BbC(a)Bg(a)   Alexander III] PaPeR; Alexander Au(51)CoFrFRM(b); *om.* CbVBlCdW(*bis*)Ch(b)Bg(b); Idem *alibi* [Item BbA(a) AOBr]   Toletano] *varr.* tolo. Au 73(b); tholetano T(a); tolletat. ApLp(a); tollet. ApV(a); tolle. ApV(b); toll./tollo./tolo. Bb(b)BACDCsBFrM(a); collo. T(b)Du; tolletano ErFrF   Toletano archiepiscopo *add. marg.* FrM(b) archiepiescopo Toletano *tr.* Cr; (a): ApBbErLCsTFrMSX   archiepiscopo] episcopo: CbVW(5.7 and 11)CoPeCsC(b)FrF(b); *om.* BbA(b); arche CsB(b)   **b–b** principes $Eb^{pc}T^{pc}$; princeps FlPeCrEb^{ac} sui *om.* ChBbD; tui Bg; Anglie Cr   a *om.* Cr   a Bernardo] abernardo Au(73)BbDFrFMDu; aberando ApLpEr; aberrando ApV; t aberiardo BbA; ab Arnardo CsC; abernando L   Bernardo] Berando ApC; Bernhardo BbB; Barnardo CsB; B. DeEbAlAu(51)W(5.7)ChCoPe; h. Cr; *om.* X (Bernardo Fr.ed.) quondam *om.* Au(73)ChBbBACDCsBgCp; *add. supra* Er   Oximensi] oximen.se De; al. Oximensi *add. marg.* ApLn; exomense Al; exomensi Fl; eximense W(5.7)CoPe; eximse Cr; examensi Ch^{pc}; exómense Al; exomensi CsB; exoniensi Au(73)LCsCTS; exonensi BbBFrM(*add. marg.*)Er; exon. BgDuCpA; Certomensi ApC; ceromensi ApLnV; aceromensi ApLp; cerom. (*incert.*: ? $exom.^{ac}$) FrR; exconiensi BbA; xomensi *vel* xoniensi BbD; (xo)niensi (*incert.*) BbC; *om.* FrF   **c–c** idem *om.* X; episcopus idem Eb   episcopus] episcopo BbD; Oxomensis *add.* X   archidiaconum Al; archidiachono BbD   Soriensi FlFrFRM(exonsi *var. marg.* M); Sorienencis De; soyren. Au(51); senonensi ApVln(senosensi *praem.* Ln^{ac}); s'onensi ApLp; Seviensi ApC; exonensi Au(73)BbBLErCp; exhonensi BbA; exon. BgDuS; exoniensi CsT; Soriensi *del. in situ* (exonsi *add. marg.*) FrM; examensi Ch^{pc}; Xonensi BbC; Xoniensi *vel* Xomensi BbD; S. EbAlCrW(5.7)CoPe; *om.* X   **d–d** ecclesia BbA   ecclesie oximensi] exoniensi ecclesie S   oximensi] oxiniensi (*incert.*) De; Oximensi Eb; oximen (*incert.*) Au(51); Oxomensi X(Fr.ed.); exomensi AlFlL; eximensi W(5.7)CoPe; eirmsi Cr; examensi Ch^{pc}; Ceromensi ApCLn; cerom. ApLpV; exoniensi Au(73)CsS; exoni. BgB; exonensi BbBErT^{pc}; exhonensi BbA; xomensi BbC; xinonensi BbD; ceromensi (*incert.*; ? $exonensi^{ac}$) FrR; exonensi FrM; exon. BgVDu; remensi FrF; *om.* Cp.

Abbreviations

Chodorow–Duggan = S. Chodorow and C. Duggan, from the papers of W. Holtzmann, *Decretales ineditae saeculi XII*, *MIC*, 4 (1982).

Holtzmann–Cheney = C. R. Cheney and M. G. Cheney, from the papers of W. Holtzmann, *Studies in the Collections of Twelfth-century Decretals*, *MIC*, 3 (1979).

Jaffé = *Regesta pontificum romanorum*, ed. P. Jaffé, 2nd edn G. Wattenbach, S. Loewenfeld, *et al.* (Leipzig 1885–8: repr. Graz, 1956).

MIC = *Monumenta Iuris Canonici, Series B: Corpus Collectionum* (Biblioteca Apostolica Vaticana).
WH = Walther Holtzmann, projected *Regesta decretalium saeculi XII*.

Sigla of Decretal Collections

Alphabetical list of collections, with folio locations of texts edited here, or their locations in printed editions and analyses. A complete list of all known decretal collections of the twelfth century, with full bibliographical details of editions, analyses and secondary literature, is provided in Holtzmann–Cheney, pp. xx–xxxi, and Chodorow–Duggan, pp. xix–xxxi.

Alan.	Coll. Alani: analysed R. von Heckel, in *ZSRG.K*, 29 (1940), pp. 226–334; S. Kuttner, *Rivista di storia del diritto italiano*, 26 (1953), pp. 37–53, and *Traditio*, 17 (1961), pp. 534–5.
V	Vercelli, Bibl. capitolare, MS LXXXIX, fol. 57r (*Quia requisistis*).
1 Alc.	Alcobacensis prima: Lisbon, Bibl. nac., MS Alcob. 144 (314), fols 14v–15r.
App.	Appendix Concilii Lateranensis:
C.	[*editio princeps*: P. Crabbe, ed., *Concilia omnia tam generalia quam particularia*, ed. (1551), 2.820–944]; Mansi, 22.315–16 and 277.
Lp.	Leipzig, Universitätsbibl., MS 1242, fols 86(WH 27)va–b + 77(WH 8)rb–va.
V	Vienna, Nationalbibl., MS 2172, fols 20(WH 115)ra + 7(WH 90)va
Ln.	Lincoln, Cathedral Chapter Library, MS 121, fols 16v + 2r–v.
Aur.	Aureavallensis: Luxembourg, BN, MS 30, fols 111r–v (= Aur. 51) + 113r–v (= Aur. 73).
Bamb.	Bambergensis: W. Deeters, 'Die Bambergensisgruppe der Dekretalensammlungen des 12. Jhdts' (Inaugural Dissertation ... der Philos. Fakultät die Rheinischen Friedrich Wilhelms-Universität, 1956).
B	Bamberg, Staatsbibl., MS Can. 17 (P. I.II), fols 26ra + 1vb–2ra.
A	Amiens, Bibl. de la Ville, MS 377, fols 112rb–va + 83ra–b.
C	Paris, BN, MS lat. 17971, fols 180vb–181ra + 153ra.
D	Tortosa, Bibl. del cabildo, MS 40, fols 39(WH 111)v + 81 (WH 2)r.
O	Oxford, Oriel College, MS 53, fol. 242ra.
Bridl.	Bridlingtonensis: Oxford, Bodleian Library, MS Bodl. 357 (S.C. 2452), fols 110rb–va.
Brug.	Brugensis:
B	Bruges, Bibl. de la Ville, MSS 378 and 379, fols 63va + 58rb.
V	Città del Vaticano, Bibl. Vat., MS Ottob. lat. 3027, fols 83v + 76r.

Bernard of Osma

Cantab.	Cantabrigiensis: Cambridge, Trinity College, MS R.9.17 (James 819), fol. 91v.
Cass.	Casselana:
C	Kassel, Landesbibl., MS Jur. 15, J. H. Boehmer, ed., *Corpus iuris canonici* (Halle, 1747): cols 289–90 + 199.
B	Bamberg, Staatsbibl., MS Can. 18, fols 37va + 26va.
Chelt.	Cheltenhamensis: London, BL, MS Egerton 2819, fols 76va + 18ra–b.
Claud.	Claudiana: London BL, MS Cotton Claudius A.iv, fol. 208 (*olim* 204)rb.
Claustr.	Claustroneoburgensis: Klosterneuburg, Stiftsbibl., MS 19, fol. 63r–v.
1,2 Comp.	Compilatio prima, secunda:
A	*Antiquae collectiones decretalium*, ed. Antonio Agustín (Lérida, 1576); reissued in *Opera omnia*, 4 (Lucca, 1769).
F	E. Friedberg, *Quinque compilationes antiquae necnon collectio canonum Lipsiensis* (Leipzig, 1882; repr. Graz, 1956).
Cott.	Cottoniana: London, BL, MS Cotton Vitellius E.xiii, fols 226vb–227ra.
1 Dert.	Dertusensis prima: Tortosa, Bibl. del cabildo, MS 144, fol. 18r–v.
2 Dun.	Dunelmensis secunda: Durham, Cathedral Libr., MS C.III.3, fol. 140va–b.
Eber.	Eberbacensis: London, BL, MS Arundel 490, fols 216vb–217ra.
Erl.	Erlangensis: Erlangen, Universitätsbibl., MS 342, fols 302rb + 292rb.
Flor.	Florianensis: St Florian, Stiftsbibl., MS III.5, fol. 179rb.
Frcf.	Francofortana:
F	Frankfurt, Stadt- und Universitätsbibl., MS Barth. 60, fol. 17ra (*Quia requisistis*); fol. 36va (*Consuluit nos*).
R	Paris, BN, MS lat. 3922A, fol. 178va (*Quia requisistis*); fols 185vb–186ra (*Consuluit nos*).
T	Troyes, Bibl. de la Ville, MS 961, fol. 21va–b (*Quia requisistis*).
M	London, BL, MS Egerton 2901 (formerly Phillipps 7369 and 7790), fol. 19v (*Quia requisistis*); fols 73v–74v (*Consuluit nos*).
Fuld.	Fuldensis: Fulda, Landesbibl., MS D.3a, fols 1–88; cf. Heckel, in *ZSRG.K*, 29 (1940), pp. 165–70 and pp. 353–9.
Lips.	Lipsiensis: Leipzig, Univ.-Bibl., MS 975, fols 140va + 118va–b.
1 Par.	Parisiensis prima: Paris, BN, MS lat. 1596, fol. 37v.
Pet.	Petrihusensis: Cambridge, Peterhouse, MS 114, final folio ra–b.
1 Rot.	Rotomagensis prima: Paris, BN, MS lat. 3922A, fol. 166va.
Sang.	Sangermanensis: Paris, BN, MS lat. 12459, fols 68vb + 69vb and 8va.
Tann.	Coll. Tanneri: Oxford, Bodleian Library, MS Tanner 8, pp. 672b + 674a and 602b.

1 Vict.	Victorina prima: Paris, BN, MS lat. 14938, fol. 246va.
Wig.	Wigorniensis: London, BL, MS Royal 10.A.II, fols 39ra–b (= Wig. 5.7) and 40vb (= Wig. 5.11).
X	*Decretales Gregorii IX*: Friedberg, *Corpus iuris canonici*, 2 (1881).

Errata:

p. 78, line 7, recipients' should read recipient's
p. 83, line 21, of should read or

VIII

Improba pestis falsitatis
Forgeries and the problem of forgery in twelfth-century decretal collections

(with special reference to English cases)*

1. Introductory comments

The problem of forged decretals was a matter of deep concern in the Western Church in the later twelfth century, the early-classical period in the history of canon law, of judicial development, jurisdictional centralization and juristic refinement. But it is a problem especially clearly recorded in decretal letters to England, in the English collections which drew so heavily on the archives of English judges delegate, and which in turn were uniquely formative in the wider transmission of decretals in the period.

The treatment of forgery in the literature of Roman and canon law at that time, and in a broader historical perspective, has been admirably analysed in Peter Herde's Römisches und kanonisches Recht bei der Verfolgung des Fälschungsdelikts im Mittelalter[1]. The concept of forgery, as then expressed in canonical commentaries, is clearly seen to extend far beyond the falsification or corruption of documents. It embraced all forms of dishonest or frustratory tactics, false statements by litigants or witnesses, silence or surreptition. The prevalence of such dishonest litigation has been further examined in an important study by Stanley Chodorow, with reference to decretal letters in late twelfth-

---

*) The collation of manuscripts and preparation of texts for this study would scarcely have been possible without access to the materials bequeathed by Walther Holtzmann, and now housed in the Institute of Medieval Canon Law in the University of California at Berkeley. My thanks are due once again to Professor Stephan Kuttner, Director of the Institute, for his exceptional kindness in the course of my many visits. My wife, Dr. Anne Duggan, has also generously helped with the paper's presentation. – For the abbreviations and sigla of decretal collections see below, p. 358–361.

1) Traditio 21 (1965) p. 291–362, esp. p. 319–362.

century collections[2]. Decades earlier, this broader concept had indeed been perfectly defined by the canons of St Peter's college in Wolverhampton, in the opening sentence of a petition to Eugenius III (1145–53), seeking his affirmation of their rights: *Concors decretorum et canonum simulque legum auctoritas nos instruit quod crimen falsitatis committit, non solum qui sciens falsum reddit testimonium, sed etiam qui celator veritatis existit*[3]. The language and date of the letter are significant, its scope of legal learning and reference extending beyond the canon law. The twin themes of forgery and dishonest litigation constantly recur in the decretals.

In a much quoted letter to a pope of the late twelfth century, bishop Stephen of Tournai spoke lamentingly of the *inextricabilis silva decretalium* attributed to Alexander III, and used in courts and teaching. He did not single out the canonists alone for castigation, but in a broad appeal to the pope deplored the contemporary degeneration of theologians, canonists and masters of the *facultates quas liberales appellant*, in that order. The impenetrable forest of decretals was, he said, imputed to Alexander, rather than genuine – *quasi sub nomine sancte recordationis Alexandri pape*. Putative papal letters were being forged and were prevailing in the courts; a *novum volumen* was being read in the schools and used in the courts, welcomed by notaries who rejoiced that their labour would be reduced and their rewards increased by copying these suspect books: *Rursus si ventum fuerit ad iudicia que iure canonico sunt tractanda, vel a vobis commissa, vel ab ordinariis iudicibus cognoscenda, profertur a venditoribus inextricabilis silva decretalium epistolarum, quasi sub nomine sancte recordationis Alexandri pape, et antiquiores sacri canones abiiciuntur, respuuntur, expuuntur. Hoc involucro prolato in medium ea que in conciliis sanctorum patrum salubriter instituta sunt, nec formam conciliis, nec finem negotiis imponunt, prevalentibus epistolis, quas forsitan advocati, et conducticii sub nomine Romanorum pontificum in apothecis sive in cubiculis suis confingunt et conscribunt. Novum volumen ex eis compactum, et in scholis solemniter legitur, et in foro venaliter exponitur, applaudente cetu notariorum, qui in conscribendis opusculis suspectis, et laborem suum gaudent imminui, et mercedem augeri*[4]. The strictures of Stephen, himself a fa-

2) S. CHODOROW, Dishonest litigation in the Church courts, in: Law, church and society. Essays in honor of Stephan Kuttner, ed. K. PENNINGTON – R. SOMERVILLE (1977) p. 186–206.

3) Ed. W. HOLTZMANN, Papsturkunden in England 2 (Abh. Göttingen, Dritte Folge 14–15, 1935–1936) p. 246–247 nr. 76.

4) MIGNE PL 211 c. 516–518 nr. 251, sub annis 1192–1213, with the selectively misleading heading: "Reprehendit nimiam multitudinem decretalium, et professores qui eis

mous canonist and early decretist, were too extreme. The authenticity of many of Alexander's decretals, as found in the collections, can be confirmed in some cases by retracing their texts to the archives of their recipients, or assured in others by their derivation from papal or episcopal registers. But the problem of forged decretals was widespread and serious. Not only can forged texts be sometimes recognized in the collections, even manifest forgeries being transmitted from one to another, but the collections include numerous genuine letters which record the use of forgeries in litigation.

The more systematic collections gave early evidence of their interest in this problem. The earliest extant systematic collection, Parisiensis secunda (not later than 1179), attached the title *De falsariis* to the single letter *Ex tenore litterarum,* to bishop William of Norwich (no. 5 b – e below). It was also used as a rubric for part of the same letter in the technically transitional Worcester archetype (post February 1181). The title was later used in Compilatio secunda, Compilatio tertia, and other well-known collections of the early thirteenth century. The Cheltenham collection, partly derived from the Worcester archetype, further provided the rubric *De sacerdote falsario et sacerdotum vicariis* for the Norwich decretal mentioned above. The title *De crimine falsi* is found in Compilatio prima, Compilatio quarta, and in the official Decretales of 1234, and *De falsatoribus* occurs in Gilbertus. The Peterhouse collection (post 1195) supplied the rubric *De rasura litterarum* for the decretal *Ex litteris quas nobis* (no. 10 below), probably to Canterbury and Worcester. Forgery in its most literal sense and in its wider connotation of deceitful practices was treated under such headings as *De fide instrumentorum, De rescriptis suspectis, De falsis testibus, De dilationibus, De rescriptis per fraudem tacendi impetratis, Non valent littere ante terminum appellationis fraudulenter impetrate*[5].

The earliest primitive collections had often preserved the complete form and diplomatic of the letters, but less importance was attached to the historical elements as a more mature and juristic pattern of composition evolved. The historical matter was excised or abbreviated, and attention was focussed on the principles of law and legal procedure of interest to the canonists, and the longer

---

abutebantur"; see also M. CHENEY, The compromise of Avranches and the spread of canon law in England, English Historical Review 56 (1941) p. 182 – 183, with the suggestion that the *novum volumen* might be Compilatio prima.

5) S. KUTTNER, Index titulorum decretalium ex collectionibus tam privatis quam publicis conscriptus (Ius Romanum Medii Aevi, Subsidia 2, 1977), p. 69, 73, 102, 108, 213, 225 – 226 and 251 – 254.

letters were broken up and their constituent parts distributed through the books and titles of thoroughly systematic works. In the varied and complex lines of evolution, there were exceptions to these generalizations: for example, the author of the primitive Bridlington archetype (not much later than 1181) felt free to abbreviate and freely recompose his texts, to preserve the essential meaning in short space (cf. no. 8 below), whereas the corrector of the systematic Rouen collection and of the Rouen copy of the Frankfurt collection included in his emendations variant readings of even the inscriptions[6]. In the event, a professional re-phrasing or revision cannot be construed as forgery. If that were so, the official Decretales of 1234 could be described as a compilation of forgeries. The authenticity of the Decretales derived not from the original texts, but from the legislative authority of Gregory IX, who commissioned Raymond of Peñafort to assemble something very close to a legal code, which the pope then promulgated for exclusive use in the courts and schools[7].

2. Analysis of selected decretals relating to forgery[8]

From the large number of decretals which relate in some way to the question of forgery, twenty have been chosen here, mostly to English recipients, to provide examples of forged texts and genuine letters recording or alleging the use of forgeries or suspect letters, and in one instance of a forged royal seal. The first two items, attributed to Alexander III, are undoubted forgeries. *Presentium auctoritate* (1), a supposed privilege to John of Garland, is an evident fabrication, as its dispensation for his unchastity makes clear. The hybrid text and unknown conciliar citation of *Sancta Romana* (2), a privilege to the monks of Lenton, disprove its authenticity, despite the harmony of its ruling with contemporary doctrine on priests' sons succeeding in their fathers' churches. The next two texts are not undoubted forgeries, but they are unlikely to be genuine in their extant form. The censure of Gilbert Foliot in *Cum discretionem litterarum* (3) matches in part the tenor of genuine letters on the same subject, which may have provided its sources, but the text is unlikely to preserve the moderate Alexander's language. Likewise, the reproof to the archbishop and suffragans

6) On the work of the Rouen master, see HOLTZMANN-CHENEY p. 142–151 and 162–164.

7) S. KUTTNER, Raymond of Peñafort as editor: the 'decretales' and 'constitutiones' of Gregory IX, Bulletin of Medieval Canon Law, N.S. 12 (1982) p. 65–80.

8) In the comments and summaries which follow, the chancery convention of using plural forms and syntax is retained, though frequently a single document is in question.

of Bordeaux, in *Si vera sunt* (4), for their oppressive procurations, is at the very least an extremely corrupt text, its phrasing at times awkward and uncharacteristic.

There follows a sequence of nine letters of Alexander III to English recipients, in response to consultations or appeals, placed here in chronological order. In a letter of great interest to the collectors and received into numerous collections, *Ex tenore litterarum* (5) to bishop William of Norwich, the pope ordered the deprivation and imprisonment of a priest who had forged papal letters. The decretal *Cum olim G.* (6), to un-named recipients, dealt with a dispute in Dorset, between the rector W. of Sturminster and the deacon G., who had appealed to the pope, alleging forgery in the papal commission to earlier judges who had ruled against him. The precise historical details of this case are established here for the first time.

The next two letters are of quite exceptional interest. Both were addressed to archbishop Richard of Canterbury, and involve a prebend in the church of Gnosall. Until now, the relationship between the letters, the identity of the church, and the recipient of the earlier letter were unknown. In *Cum olim E.* (7), in a dispute between E. and two successive G.'s, the pope ordered that the bishop of Coventry should lose his right to deprive anyone of a benefice (letters 7 and 8 both have variant textual traditions: *auferendi beneficium* and *conferendi beneficium*; the former seems more probable), until he himself made satisfaction to the pope, because he had despoiled E. without judicial process, after appeal and papal confirmation. These details are repeated exactly in the course of *Ex parte venerabilis* (8), as allegations which the pope does not believe he wrote in those terms. If he did so, it was because he was too busy; his letters must always be assumed to imply that the petition rested on truth. *Cum olim E.* is clearly the mandate which Alexander did not think he had so expressed, as the following collation proves:

Cum olim E.	*Ex parte venerabilis*
...*Episcopum autem qui post appellationem et confirmationem nostram eundem E. prebenda illa spoliare presumpsit, auctoritate auferendi beneficium appellatione postposita prives, donec per se vel per nuntium suum et per litteras suas de tanto excessu satisfacturus ad apostolicam sedem accedat. Preterea prenominatum G., si eundem E.*	...*episcopum qui post appellationem eum prebenda spoliaverat auctoritate alicui auferendi beneficium appellatione cessante privares, donec per se vel per nuntium suum aut per litteras suas de tanto excessu satisfacturus ad apostolicam sedem accederet, et prenominatum G., si eundem E. super predicta prebenda presumeret molestare, vinculo ex-*

super iamdicta prebenda molestare presumpserit, vinculo excommunicationis astringas, qua eum teneas usque ad dignam satisfactionem astrictum.

communicationis usque ad dignam satisfactionem astringeres. Verum quoniam non credimus nos ita precise scripsisse, et si taliter scripsimus hoc ex nimia occupatione contigit, et in huiusmodi litteris intelligenda est conditio, etiam si non apponatur, videlicet si preces veritate nitantur...

The mandate *Referente nobis* (9), to the bishop of Worcester and the abbot of Evesham, concerned a dispute between master D. and the clerk G. over the church of *Fossoria.* Alleged papal commissions were successively issued to panels of judges, all heads of religious houses in Wiltshire, except for the bishop of Bath in the adjacent county of Somerset. Because of the unlikely dispensation which the letters contained, in favour of a priest's son, the pope rejects them as worthless – *ineptas litteras.* In contrast, the pope confirmed the authenticity of letters issued in a dispute between Ralph de Alta Ripa and master Alan of Idsall, over the church of *Cambritona.* In *Ex litteris quas* (10), probably to the archbishop of Canterbury and the bishop of Worcester, the pope rejected Ralph's suggestion that the letters were false because of an erasure in the *narratio facti*; the mandate also deals with dishonest litigation and the securing of ex parte judges. Again, in the dispute between the clerks Gwarinus and William, dealt with in *Veniens ad nos* (11) to bishop John and the prior of Norwich, the former alleged that papal commissioners had been secured by misrepresentation. The pope orders the new commissioners to obtain the earlier letters, which he considers suspect, and send them under seal to him, if they find the facts as stated.

Forgery by the well-known English master Hugh of Southwell is recorded in *Ex constanti relatione* (12), to Roger of York and Hugh of Durham. The cardinal legate Hugh Pierleoni had wished to condemn Hugh for the crime, but was prevailed upon by powerful intervention. The pope nevertheless did so, and there is evidence suggesting that his action was effective. The final selected letter of Alexander III, *Recepimus litteras* (13) to the bishop of Durham and the abbots of Bury St Edmunds and St Albans, deals with one phase in the intractable disputes between the archbishops of Canterbury and the monks of St Augustine's. This long and detailed letter, known from archival as well as canonical sources, turns on the archbishop's claim that the monks were using false privileges to assert their right. Of the greatest interest are the pope's detailed and cautious instructions on the circumstances and procedure for the scrutiny of the documents in question.

Lucius III commended the prudence of Baldwin of Worcester, in *Ex litteris tue* (14), for declining to give effect to the judgment of commissioners in a dispute over the chapel of Stretton on Fosse, in which suspect papal letters were used; and he took the opportunity of enunciating a general principle on the rejection of such letters and the detention of those who adduced them[9]. And in a dispute between master A. and the clerk Nicholas over the church of *Drandam*, dealt with in *Constitutus in presentia* (15), in which A. alleged that forged letters were used against him, Lucius remarked that the letters seemed suspect to him because their form was not in harmony with law. The long but incomplete letter of Celestine III to the abbot of Pershore and the prior of Great Malvern, *Cum huius auctoritate* (16), concerns a dispute between the parson and a poor clerk over the vicarage of an unknown church. As for the alleged forged letters used in the dispute, the pope remarks that he does not believe they were issued in this form with his knowledge, though they came from his chancery.

The last four letters record important statements of principle by popes Lucius III, Urban III, Celestine III and Innocent III respectively. All were recognized as of general application, and were received into the famous collections of the period; they deal especially with the apprehension and punishment of forgers. Despite their general reception, the printed editions are incomplete or defective. In *Improba pestis* (17), provoked by the activities of forgers in the English king's lands, Lucius III distinguished the procedures for dealing with clerical and lay forgers of papal letters (not of public letters, as some collections record). The punishment of clerical forgers of the French king's seal are dealt with by Urban III in *Ad audientiam nostram* (18), which affirms at the same time their immunity from penalties of death or amputation. Both letters were sent to archbishop Walter of Rouen, a former royal administrator in England, and briefly bishop of Lincoln. His suffragans and dean received *Per falsarios* (19) from Celestine III, who orders the seizure of those (?) using the letters of forgers whose activities had been discovered in Rome. A letter of Innocent III, *Ad audientiam nostram* (20), to the bishop of Verdun (a single text reads Lon-

9) Mary G. Cheney, Roger, bishop of Worcester 1164–1179 (1980) p. 345 nr. 55 A, for the suggestion that *Ex relatione R.* (Pd Sang. 6.1.21), JL –, WH 484, Lucius III to the abbot of Missenden, the archdeacon of Winchester and the prior of St Frideswide, may be one of the forgeries alleged in this case.

don), deals with suspect letters used by H. *de sancto Stephano.* Since they are ungrammatical, the pope does not believe they were issued with his predecessor's knowledge. The edited version of this letter in X does not reveal that a letter of Celestine III was in question.

3. Decretal texts: Forgeries and their use in litigation

With the publication of the Decretales ineditae, a printed text now exists for every decretal known from the collections, but the editions are often incomplete or defective, based on a limited use of the manuscripts, sometimes with inaccurate historical details or lacking them altogether. The versions offered here are complete, with full details of manuscript locations and existing printings, notes on the collectors' handling of the texts, historical comments, identifications and dates. Because of the extraordinary complexity of the manuscript transmissions and variant readings, it is not always easy to determine the authentic texts. Nor is it feasible to provide within the limits of the present study a full critical apparatus for the texts. The versions below (except for no. 5) are based on all known manuscript sources. Further technical details will be given in the forthcoming Regesta decretalium saeculi XII.

1

Alexander III to John of Garland. Spurious privilege: no prelates or others may place under interdict possessions entrusted to the recipient, or suspend their administrators, or make unwonted exactions without due cause and process. Further, since the recipient could not remain chaste before ordination, and contracted marriage, the pope by clement dispensation grants that this shall not prevent his acquiring an ecclesiastical benefice.

WH 738; JL –. *1159–81.*

Alexander III Johanni de Garlande.

(a) Presentium auctoritate prohibemus ne quis archiepiscopus, episcopus, archidiaconus vel ulla inferior superiorve persona vel possessiones tibi commissas vel earum custodes sive administratores suspendere, vel sub interdicto ponere, vel a te vel a possessionibus quicquam exigere quod indebitum sit, vel extra-

ordinarium, vel priscis et canonicis consuetudinibus contrarium, nisi ex rationabili causa ordine iudiciario specialiter observata, examinata et cognita nullo ausu presumat, et si presumptum fuerit viribus careat, et ipso iure penitus evanescat. *(b)* Quod ideo firmum illibatumque volumus observari, ne hii qui ecclesiarum presunt regimini occasionem licite potestatis ad illicitum et iniquum trahant compendium. *(c)* Preterea cum tu infra sacros ordines positus continere nullatenus posses, matrimonium prout asseris contraxisti, dispensative et misericorditer duximus indulgendum ut hoc nulla ratione tibi preiudicet quominus ecclesiastica beneficia valeas obtinere.

Complete: Brug. 22.3. Parts: 1 Rot. 14.12 (ab + Preterea cum infra sacros ordines positus continere non posses *etc.); 10.14 (*Presentium auctoritate prohibemus ne quis et infra in fine *+ c). Abbreviated:* Presentium auctoritate prohibemus ne quis archiepiscopus et infra *+ (cb): Tann. 7.10.12; Sang. 9.15; 1 Abr. 8.10.3. Pd Brug.*
The printed text has no inscription. The sender is named as Alexander III *in Brug. V and 1 Rot. 14.12,* Alexander *in Brug.B and 1 Rot. 10.14, and* Idem *in Tann. Sang. 1 Abr. The recipient is omitted in Brug. and 1 Rot., but appears as John of Garland (*Garland., Garlandē., Gñd.*) in Tann. Sang. 1 Abr. The privilege is an evident and presumably jocose fabrication, despite its transmission through four English and Anglo-Norman collections. Holtzmann judged it a student jest. The well-known scholar John of Garland was a young man at the time of the letter's first transcription, and was still alive c. 1258 (see A. B. Emden, A biographical Register of the University of Oxford to 1500 2 [1958] p. 743). The name also appears for a parson of Hanningfield in 1182, a canon of St Paul's and a royal justice (possibly the same man) in the 1190s (English Episcopal Acta II: Canterbury 1162–1190, ed. C. R. Cheney-B. E. A. Jones [1986] p. 106–107 nr. 130; and John Le Neve, Fasti Ecclesiae Anglicanae, 1066–1300, 1: St Paul's London, ed. D. A. Greenway [1968] p. 66).*

2

Alexander III to the monks of Lenton. A forged privilege, citing an unknown canon of the council of Agde in 506, forbidding the sons of priests or parsons to celebrate in churches in which their fathers had ministered, or to remain in them. Such priests or sons of priests or parsons may have no further recourse to appeal.

WH 893; JL –. *1174–81 (1159–81).*

Alexander III monachis de Lentona.

Sancta Romana ecclesia pro assuete pietatis officio devotos filios et humiles propensius diligere consuevit et eos et eorum possessiones sue protectionis munimine tamquam pia mater solita est confovere et protegere. Hinc est quod iustis petitionibus vestris gratis assensum prebentes, ex concilio Agatensi de filiis sacerdotum et filiis personarum ecclesiarum hoc decretum statuimus ne celebrent in ecclesiis in quibus celebraverunt patres eorum nec in ipsis aliquatenus permaneant. Mandamus ergo vobis et per apostolica scripta precipimus ut, si huiusmodi sacerdotes vel persone in ecclesiis vestris sint, ex integro eliminentur, et non liceat eis in eisdem diutius perseverare. Inhibemus etiam ne supradicti sacerdotes vel filii sacerdotum vel personarum aliquatenus perquirant appellationis refugium. Qui vero contra hanc paginam nostri decreti ire temptaverit, anathematis spiculo perfodiatur, nisi satisfecerit.

1 Dun. 3.46 only. Pd Decretales ineditae p. 133–134 nr. 78, and HOLTZMANN-CHENEY *p. 95–96.*

The unconventional structure of the letter interweaves the language of different classes of papal documents (privileges, decrees, decretals), and the allusion to a canon of Agde (506) has not been identified. But the doctrine of the letter is in harmony with that in genuine decretals of Alexander III on priests' and parsons' sons succeeding in their fathers' churches. In the period 1174–81, the monks of Lenton had lost their dispute with the priest of Meppershall on this issue, the pope ruling that the legislation of the council of Tours (1163) did not have retrospective effect. The present decretal could record a further attempt by the monks in that dispute (Decretales ineditae p. 134–135).

3

Alexander III to bishop Gilbert of London. The pope laments the frustration of the hopes he had conceived in the translation of the recipient from Hereford to London, which has resulted in the event to the Church's detriment. He rebukes the recipient and other bishops for the neglect of their pastoral responsibilities, specifically in the case of those appealing to the apostolic see for protection.

WH 230; JL –. *1165–70.*

Alexander III Gilberto Lundoniensi episcopo.

Cum discretionem litterarum tuarum et religionem que extrinsecus apparet ad mentem reducimus, intra nos ipsos non modicum conturbamur et spe nostra quam iam pridem de te concepimus nos frustratos dolemus, quoniam de translatione tua in Lundoniis ab Herefordia aliter quam credebamus evenisse videtur, presertim cum quod pro ecclesie commodo fecimus in eius detrimentum appareat gravissime retorqueri. Non enim tu et alii episcopi videmini ea que Dei sunt curare, quoniam cum latratu et baculo lupos deberetis a dominici gregis invasione arcere, increpare quoque et corrigere. Dum ea silentio preteritis, facti estis *canes muti, non valentes latrare*[1] et pastoralis officii negligentes et prorsus obliti oves vobis commissas circumquaque lacerari permittitis, de quibus non nisi lac et lanum queritis. Appellantes siquidem et apostolice sedis omnium oppressorum refugium auxilium invocantes coram vobis tanquam rei maiestatis turpiter rapiuntur. Quibus omnibus favorem prestare videmini, cum nec vel in minimum propter hoc ecclesiastice severitatis gladium exseratis. A quibus etsi timor Dei vos non revocat, sed hominibus magis quam Deo parendum esse censetis. Infamia tamen et populi voce communi debetis penitus retardari et commune hoc crimen in perpetuum evitare. Quia qui ecclesiam Dei persequitur et infestat, beneficio ecclesie non debet sustentari, nec ab ea solacium auxilii accipere, cui amaritudinis abscinthium noscitur propinare[2].

1) Is. 56.10.
2) Cf. Lam. 3.15; Am. 6.13 etc.

1 Par. 33 only. Pd 1 Par.

Though apparently not challenged hitherto, the text of this letter is a probable forgery based on genuine sources. In A memoria tua *(8 June 1165), Alexander had indeed reminded Gilbert Foliot of the expectations which underlay his translation from Hereford to London in 1163, and of their frustration, and ordered him to act with bishop Robert of Hereford in admonishing the king. Somewhat later, in* Sepe nobis *(? 1166), he rebuked the bishop more sharply, but without reference to the translation. Predictably, much stronger language was used in letters written in archbishop Thomas's name, as in* Quod tam crebris *to Alexander in 1169, which referred briefly to Foliot's translation, and in several letters after his absolution in 1170, to cardinal Albert, to the notary Gratian, and to the pope (Materials for the History of Thomas Becket, Archbishop of Canterbury, ed. J. C. ROBERTSON-J. B. SHEPPARD [Rolls Series 67, 5,1881] p. 175–178 nr. 93, p. 294–296 nr. 157; [6, 1882] p. 640–643 nr. 530; [7, 1885] p. 279–283 nr. 662–663, p. 292–294 nr. 666). It is conceivable that* Cum discretionem *records a heightening of the pope's rebukes to Foliot in* A memoria tua *and* Sepe nobis, *but its very bitter language and unrelieved condemnation are uncharacteristic of Alexander III; it is also unlikely that Becket's supporters would have failed to include it in their collections, had it been genuine.*

4

Alexander III to the archbishop of Bordeaux and his suffragans. Reproof and mandate: the pope grieves over the avaricious oppressions alleged against the recipients, who are said to exact excessive procurations from their subject clergy and religious.

Not only bishops, but archdeacons, deans and archpriests offend in the same way, and harassed priests in their turn impose on their subjects what they have themselves suffered from their superiors. The recipients must root out such avarice from God's temple.

WH 920; JL –. *1159–79.*

Alexander III Burdegalensi archiepiscopo et eius suffraganeis.

Si vera sunt que subscriptus epistole textus eloquitur, et mirari cogimur et dolere quod, cum eliminanda sit de templo Dei modis omnibus avaritia, ita se quidam ei subiecisse videntur ut nedum in populo et in ipsis hominibus ecclesiastici ordinis nihil pene aliud inquirere videantur, nisi ut dampnationem gravem super eos exerceant, et spolia ipsorum pro sue familie diripiant voluptate, non attendentes quod apostolus ait. Petrus prohibet dicens: Seniores pascite qui est in vobis gregem Dei providentes non coacti sed spontanee secundum Deum, neque turpis lucri gratia sed voluntarie, neque ut dominantes in clero, sed forma facti[1] gregis ex animo. Dicitur enim quod per dioceses vestras euntes tam immoderatas procurationes quidam extorquent ut uno die sub eorum presentia consumatur quod multis diebus monachis sive canonicis sive aliis clericis in locis ipsis degentibus sufficeret ad vivendum. Preter multa quidem et lauta fercula que requirunt, circa quinque aut septem solidos pro ferratura equorum, totidem libras cere, piperis non modicam quantitatem, diebus singulis sibi postulant ministrari, et nunc procurationibus nunc exactionibus annuis ita subiectas gravant ecclesias, ut non tam difficiles domini seculares inveniantur in rusticos, quam duri pontifices super monachos et canonicos inveniuntur et clerum. Inde siquidem evenit quod dantur preciosa queque pro cibo, et non solum ornatus sed ipse possessiones ecclesiastice distrahuntur, et malis etiam artibus frequenter exquiritur quo episcoporum possit satisfieri voluntati. Presbyteri etenim tot exactionibus fatigati, dum etiam peccata sua pecunia redimere compelluntur, quod a superioribus patiuntur exercent in subditos, et ipsa etiam vendunt ecclesiastica sacramenta, dum non satis est eis quo vel se ipsos exhibeant aut cupiditatem valeant extinguere prelatorum. Non stat tantum in episcopis malum istud, sed archidiaconi etiam et decani et archipresbyteri exactiones suas impudenter exercent. Cum apostolus dicat: *Non requiro datum sed fructum inter vos*[2], contrarium datur et fit, et pro minutio attenditur aut error populi aut dissolutio cleri, dummodo gloriari possint quidam in potestate quam habent, et exurgentibus ecclesiarum ministris lascivientem familiam suam aut ornare vestibus aut lautis valeant cibariis impinguare. Multa posse-mus dicere super hoc et deflere miseriam infelicium temporum hominum, sed parcimus vobis, et de multis pauca proponimus ut ex his que dicuntur recogitentur et corrigantur etiam que tacentur. Eapropter caritatem vestram litteris presentibus ammonemus ut sub districti examinis interminatione precipimus quatinus, et regulis ecclesiasticis et exemplis sanctorum patrum instructi que avaritiam de templo Dei tanquam idolorum servitutum asserunt eliminari debere, intendatis his enormitatibus corrigendis, et primo in vobis deinde quoque in archidiaconibus aliisque ad vestrum ministerium constitutis taliter emendetis ut, que sit quod ordini vestro de nimia cupiditate maculam possit afferre, nec nos districtius ista requirere ac vobis scribere compellamur. Nos enim non poterimus omnino negligere quin acredinem vini curandis vulneribus apponamus, si dulcedinem olei viderimus haberi contemptui, et taliter supradictis reprimendis insolentiis insistemus ut de simulatione ac silentio non debeamus in die Domini iudicari.

1) sancti *MS and* FRIEDBERG; *cf. 1. Petr. 5.1–3.*
2) Philipp. 4.17.

1 Par. 169. Pd 1 Par.

At best the text of this letter is corrupt, and its language is questionable in many respects. FRIEDBERG *noted its corrupt character („ziemlich verderbter Text") but further complicated the problem by printing about twenty variants from the manuscript text, some undoubted errors –* exitus *for* textus; nec . . . nec *for* nunc . . . nunc; tamen *for* tantum; *etc. Moreover, the tone and phrasing of the letter differ from those of other letters of Alexander III on the same problem. If the letter is genuine, it presumably antedates Alexander's legislation on procurations in the Lateran Council of March 1179 (*MANSI *22, c. 219–220, c. 4:* Cum apostolus*).*

5

Alexander III to bishop William of Norwich. After preamble (a), *response that* (b) *the bishop must furnish parsons with legal documents so that, on the death of one of their number, neither his son nor a vicar nor anyone else may hinder the bishop's right of conferring the church on a suitable person;* (c) *if any such person makes a frustratory appeal to the pope and sets too prolix a term, the bishop himself must set the date, and compel him to stand to his judgment if he fails to appear, which provision applies also to one who sets an appropriate term but fails to keep it; and* (d) *persons guilty of similar faults should not be received as witnesses, if brought by either party, if such an issue is transacted in the bishop's presence or that of any other. Man-*

date: (e) *to deprive perpetually of office and benefice that priest who forged the papal letters which the bishop has sent to the pope, and confine him in a strict monastery for his own punishment and as a deterrent to others; and if others are found guilty in the future, he must strictly confine them, pending papal orders.*

WH 488; JL 12253 (abcd), 14146 (e). *1159–March/April 1174.*

Alexander III episcopus servus servorum Dei venerabili fratri Willelmo Norwicensi episcopo, salutem et apostolicam benedictionem.

(a) Ex tenore litterarum tuarum et quorundam relatione accepimus quod multi subditorum tuorum, non suam iustitiam attendentes sed protervitati sue potius insistentes, te litibus et verbis contentiosis ac tediosis afficiunt, et maxime sacerdotum filii et ecclesiarum vicarii, qui defunctis patribus vel dominis suis in ecclesiis et possessionibus eorum spreta sacramentorum aut fidei religione frustratoriis appellationibus se tuentur, et sic locis, quibus aliorum nomine serviebant, auctoritate sua incubare presumunt, antequam in vacantibus ecclesiis persone possint idonee subrogari. Deinde vero, cum in causam trahuntur, in facinus consimile lapsos et cum eis aut aliis talibus coniuratos in testimonium sue pravitatis adducunt, et sic factum quod intendunt verisimiliter monstrare conantur. Quidam etiam nostris apicibus impetratis eos falsare non metuunt, et sic scriptis ad voluntatem suam conversis delegatos a nobis iudices frequentius circumvenire attemptant. Unde quoniam decet nos morbis huiusmodi congruam medelam adhibere et supradictos cavillatores a tam presumptuosis litigiis sicut convenit severius cohercere, sollicitudini tue super significatione presentium respondemus ut *(b)* personas ecclesiarum in tua diocesi consistentium ita tuis et dominorum fundi auctenticis scriptis premunias ut, cum aliquam illarum decedere forte contigerit, decedentis filius vel vicarius seu alius quilibet personatum ecclesie vacantis viro idoneo conferendi tibi iura preripere aliqua caliditate non possit. *(c)* Quod si aliquis talium frustratorie dilationis causa ad nostram audientiam appellaverit et appellationi sue terminum prolixum prefixerit, tu ei diem infra quam sedem apostolicam possit convenienter adire assignes et, si ad illum venire contempserit, tu ipsum ex tunc iudicio tuo super his que in questione vertuntur sine contradictione aliqua stare omni excusatione et appellatione cessante districte compellas. Si autem quisquam appellationi sue terminum congruentem presignat, nec tamen eam ad diem prefixum fuit prosequutus, ipsum nihilominus extunc sententie tue, sicut de alio diximus, appellatione remota parere constringas. *(d)* Verum si coram te vel alio quolibet huiusmodi negotia ventilentur, nolumus ut aliqui morbo consimili laborantes, si

certum sit, aut legitime possint convinci super hiis, si ab alterutra parte adducti fuerint, in testimonium recipiantur. *(e)* Ad hec, de sacerdote illo qui litteras nostras quas nobis misisti falsavit, discretioni tue presentium auctoritate precipimus ut, si inveniri poterit, eum omni officio sacerdotali et beneficio ecclesiastico perpetuo privatum in aliquod monasterium districte religionis retrudas ut ibi tanti facinoris penas luens se talia defleat commisisse, et alii per hoc a consimilibus valeant merito deterreri. Quod si aliquos consimiles ulterius deprehendere poteris, ipsos arctissime custodie sublato appellationis remedio tradas, donec apostolicum mandatum inde suscipias.

Complete: 3 Cant. 6; Font. 3.33; Reg. 43 + 44; Wig. 3.16; Claustr. 132; Chelt. 12.3; Cott. 6.59. Parts: Ambr. 26 (bcde); 1 Alc. 119 (bcd); 1 Vict. 138 (bcd); 1 Par. 93 (bcd) + 184 (e); Aur. 53 (bcd); 1 Berol. 105 (bcde); Flor. 103 (bcde); Cus. 114 (bcde); Wig.alt. 5 (bcde); Belv. 14 (bcde); Bridl. 30 (bcde); Claud. 34 (bcde); 2 Par. 14.1 (bcde); App. 10.5 (bcd) + 26.3 (e); Bamb. 42.3 (bcd) + 11.3 (e); Bamb.C 42.4 (bcd) + 11.3 (e); Bamb.O 42.4 (bcd); Erl. 42.4 (bcd) + 11.3 (e); Lips. 47.4 (bcd) + 11.3 (e); Cass. 51.4 (bcd) + 21.5 (e); Tann. 5.12.1 (bcd) + 2.15.4 (e); Brug. 45.6 (bc) + 36.10 (e); Frcf. 45.3 (b) + 51.7 (cd) + 58.10 (e); 1 Comp. 2.20.4 (bcd) + 5.16.3 (e); Sang. 6.13.1 (bcd); X 2.28.4 (bc) + 2.20.20 (d). Pd Claustr. (ae); App.Cr. (bcde); Cass. (bcde); 1 Comp.A (bcde), 1 Comp.F (e); X (bcd).

The address and salutation are found in Belv., and abbreviated to Alexander episcopus servus servorum Dei Willelmo Norwicensi episcopo S. *in Wig. alt. The death of William Turbe of Norwich on 16 January 1174 fixes the terminus ad quem at c. March/April 1174. The decretal proved of great interest to the collectors. The first appearence of the title* De falsariis *was attached to it in 2 Par. 14.1, and subsequently as a rubric for Wig. 3.16 (e). A full report on the complex transmission of the letter cannot be given within the limits of the present study. The text printed here is based on ten early collections; full technical details will be provided in the Regesta decretalium saeculi XII, in preparation.*

6

Alexander III to unnamed recipients, at least one not a bishop. Mandate: the deacon G. had drawn W., rector of the church of Sturminster, before the chapter of Hemsworth in respect of payment for service, and secured a mandate to the abbot of Bindon and the archdeacon of Dorset to award him expenses when W. did not pursue his appeal to the pope. When despite prohibition W. appealed again, alleging forgery, the judges excommunicated him. The present recipients must secure undertakings from W. and absolve him, award expenses to G. for both journeys, if W.'s failure to prosecute the appeals was unjustified, and reach a just settlement.

WH 284; JL –. *1173–81.*

Alexander III.

Cum olim G. diaconus W. rectorem ecclesie de Strum. super retenta mercede sui servitii coram capitulo de Hemedeswrthe traxisset in causam, idem W. ad nostram audientiam appellavit. Unde memorato G. appellationem prosequente, ille nec venit nec pro se mittere curavit responsalem, qua de causa idem G. ad dilectum filium nostrum abbatem de Bindun. et archidiaconum de Dorsete litteras accepit, quibus iniungebatur ut eundem W. deberent in expensas legittime condempnare, pro eo scilicet quod appellationem non esset prosequutus. Sed licet in eis appellatio esset inhibita, arguens illius litteras falsitatis non probato quod intendebat, idem W. iterum in appellationis vocem prorupit. Ceterum iudices illi, quoniam ad accusationem ipsorum venire contempserat, excommunicationis sententiam in eum protulerunt. Volentes igitur de laboribus predicti G. paterna sollicitudine providere, discretioni vestre per apostolica scripta mandamus quatinus, si verum est quod asseritur, memoratum W. sufficienti ab eo cautione recepta quod vestro super hiis debeat parere mandato eum ab excommunicatonis sententia absolvatis. Deinde nisi legittimum impedimentum ostenderit quare appellationes illas non fuerit prosequutus, eidem G. in necessarias expensas utriusque itineris appellatione postposita condempnetis. Postmodum vero audiatis questiones que hinc inde proposite fuerint, appellatione remota et mediante iusticia terminetis, etc et infra. Testes vero quos idem G. vobis nominabit inducere curetis ut amore iustitie testimonium perhibeant veritati.

Tann. 5.15.2; Sang. 6.15.5; 1 Abr. 6.13.2. Pd Sang.

*Apart from the pope's name, the address is omitted in all three collections; the recipients are unknown, but the mandatory clause shows that at least one was not a bishop. The printed text from Sang. names the abbot of Abingdon (*Abbend.; *1 Abr.*: Habend.*) as the judicial colleague of the archdeacon of Dorset, but the abbot of Bindon (*Bindun.*) is correctly identified in Tann. The church and chapter involved are Sturminster (*Strum̃ *in Tann.,* N. *in Sang.,* Strem. *in 1 Abr.) and Hemsworth (*Hemedeswrthe *in Tann.,* N. *in Sang., and* Hemdeswite *or* Heradeswite *in 1 Abr.). HOLTZMANN proposed Sturminster Newton as the church and, not finding a Hemsworth in Dorset, suggested Henstridge, between Shaftesbury and Sherborne. The solution is almost certainly East and West Hemsworth (*Hemedesworde *in Domesday Book) and Sturminster Marshall, both close to Wimborne and not far from Bindon abbey, all in south Dorset. Since the abbey of Bindon was founded in late September 1172, the earliest date of the letter is 1173.*

7

Alexander III to archbishop Richard of Canterbury. Mandate: when E. complained that he was despoiled of a prebend in the church of Gnosall after appeal and without judicial process, the pope committed the case first to the bishop of London, and again in the same form to the bishop and the abbot of St Albans, when the adversary G. appealed. The pope confirmed their judgment in favour of E., who gained possession. But after G.'s death, a certain clerk G. secured a mandate from the pope, without mention of the preceding process and his own free abjuration of the prebend, on the basis of which the bishop of Coventry despoiled E. of the prebend. The pope orders the present recipient to restore to E. the prebend, its fruits and his expenses, notwithstanding letters obtained by G. The bishop who despoiled E. after appeal and papal confirmation must be deprived of the right of taking a benefice from anyone, until he makes satisfaction to the pope, in person or through his representative and letters. If G. presumes to molest E., he must be excommunicated until he makes amends.

WH 282; JL –. *1174–early 1175.*

Alexander III Cantuariensi archiepiscopo.

(a) Cum olim E., ad presentiam nostram accedens, proposita nobis conquestione monstrasset quod prebenda ecclesie [de] North. post appellationem et absque ordine iudiciario esset spoliatus, venerabili fratri nostro Londoniensi episcopo per scripta nostra mandavimus ut, si res ita se haberet, illi prelibatam prebendam faceret restitui, et postmodum, si G. qui eandem prebendam detinebat experiri vellet, causam audiret et appellatione remota fine debito terminaret. Qui, cum non esset expressum in litteris nostris quod restitutio fieret appellatione remota, statim in vocem appellationis prorupit, et episcopus causam ipsam ad nostram examen remisit. Nos vero tergiversationem et versutiam alterius partis attendentes, eidem episcopo et dilecto filio nostro abbati sancti Albani causam ipsam sub eadem forma commisimus terminandam. Qui siquidem convocata utraque parte de causa plenius cognoscentes, prefato E. prelibatam prebendam adiudicaverunt, et restitui et pacifice dimitti iusserunt. Quorum sententiam ratam habentes et firmam, auctoritate apostolica confirmavimus et scripti nostri patrocinio curavimus prout decuit munire. *(b)* Cumque defuncto prefato G., ipsius prebende predictus E. possessionem haberet et aliquanto tempore tenuisset, accessit quidam clericus G. nomine ad presentiam nostram, et nulla facta mentione de ipsius cause progressu, a nobis cum supra-

dictam prebendam spontanee abiurasset litteras impetravit, quarum occasione Conventrensis episcopus, non attendens quomodo causa fuerat decisa et sententia confirmata memoratum E. prelibata prebenda inconsulte nimis et inprovide spoliavit, et propter hoc idem E. coactus est denuo non sine rerum dispendio et persone discrimine ad nos laborare. Inde est quod nos consideratis angustiis et anxietatibus suis et intellectis fraudulentis machinationibus et versutiis quibus videtur iniuste vexatus, ipsum ad te duximus remittendum, fraternitati tue per apostolica scripta precipiendo mandantes ut supradicto E. prelibatam prebendam cum fructibus inde perceptis et expensis quas nunc ad nos veniens coactus est facere, omni occasione et contradictione et appellatione cessante, nostra et tua facias auctoritate restitui et quiete pacificeque dimitti, et si quid minus est de prescripta sententia studiosius adimpleri, non obstantibus litteris quas idem G. taliter impetravit. Episcopum autem qui post appellationem et confirmationem nostram eundem E. prebenda illa spoliare presumpsit, auctoritate auferendi beneficium appellatione postposita prives, donec per se vel per nuntium suum et per litteras suas de tanto excessu satisfacturus ad apostolicam sedem accedat. Preterea prenominatum G., si eundem E. super iamdicta prebenda molestare presumpserit, vinculo excommunicationis astringas, qua eum teneas usque ad dignam satisfactionem astrictum.

Complete: 3 Cant. 16; 1 Dun. 2.9; Reg. 83; Chelt. 6.2; Cott. 3.84; Pet. 2.31.3. Parts: Tann. 5.14.4 (a), 5.1.16 (b); 2 Dun. 104 (b); Sang. 6.15.3 (a), 6.1.22 (b); 1 Abr. 6.12.1 (a), 6.1.13 (b). Pd Sang.

The sender is named Alexander III *in Reg., Tann., Sang., 1 Abr. for (b); and as* Idem *in 3 Cant., 1 Dun., Tann., Sang., 1 Abr. for (a). In Reg., Chelt., Cott., Pet. the text stops short at* veniat *(*accedat: *Reg.), and omits the final sentence* Preterea… astrictum. *Neither the recipient nor the church has hitherto been identified. The letter was sent in fact to the archbishop (Richard) of Canterbury, as recorded in the heading for (b) in Sang.:* Alexander III Cantuariensi archiepiscopo. Pars capituli Cum olim, infra De officio eius ad quem appellatur *(= Tann. 5.14:* Quod sit officium eius ad quem appellatur; *cap. 4:* Idem. Cum olim E.*), and is confirmed by comparison with* Ex parte venerabilis *(see infra prox.), which clearly deals with the same case, and also determines the date of* Cum olim E. *Holtzmann proposed Northam as the place of the church (*North. *in Cott., Pet.; om. in 3 Cant.;* N. *elsewhere), but it was in fact the secular college of Gnosall in Staffordshire, which had a dean and four prebendaries, and of which the bishop of Coventry became titular dean (cf. J. H. Denton, English royal free chapels, 1100–1300 [1970] p. 69–71). The bishop involved in the case was bishop (Richard Peche, 1161–82) of Coventry, as named in the early collections (Reg., 1 Dun., 3 Cant.* [convenitur!]; *om. Chelt., Cott., Pet., etc.), but not in the printed text.*

8

Alexander III to archbishop Richard of Canterbury. Mandate to confirm an earlier sentence of bishop Richard of Coventry in the dispute between Master G. and the clerk E. over a prebend in the church of Gnosall, if he finds the bishop's report correct, namely that as papal commissioner he had ruled in favour of G., but E. on appeal brought back a mandate to the present recipient to restore him without judicial process, and remove the bishop's authority of depriving anyone of a benefice, until he made satisfaction to the pope, and to excommunicate G. if he presumed to molest E. The pope does not believe that he wrote precisely this. If in fact he did so, it was through excessive preoccupation; his letters must be always be assumed to imply 'if the petition is based on truth', even if not explicitly stated.

WH 471; JL 14317. *Ferentino 16 July 1175.*

Alexander III fratri Ricardo Cantuariensi archiepiscopo.

(a) Ex parte venerabilis fratris nostri R. Coventrensis episcopi nostris est auribus intimatum quod, cum de causa que inter magistrum G. et E. clericum super prebenda de Gnoweshale vertebatur diligenter cognovisset et eidem G. secundum tenorem litterarum nostrarum in quibus continebatur quod, si constaret predictum E. de periurio esse convictum et prebende illi perpetuo renuntiasse, ab eadem prebenda appellatione cessante ammoveretur, eo cognito et probato cum prelibatam prebendam G. adiudicasset, predictus E. in vocem appellationis prorupit, et ad nos veniens ad te secundum hunc tenorem litteras reportavit quod ei prebendam precise et absque cause cognitione restitueres, *(b)* et episcopum qui post appellationem eum prebenda spoliaverat auctoritate alicui auferendi beneficium appellatione cessante privares, donec per se vel per nuntium aut per litteras suas de tanto excessu satisfacturus ad sedem apostolicam accederet, et prenominatum G. si eundem E. super prebenda presumeret molestare vinculo excommunicationis usque ad dignam satisfactionem astringeres. *(c)* Verum quoniam non credimus nos ita precise scripsisse, et si taliter scripsimus hoc ex nimia occupatione contigit, et in huiusmodi litteris intelligenda est conditio, etiam si non apponatur, videlicet si preces veritate nitantur, fraternitati tue per apostolica scripta precipiendo mandamus quatinus, inspecto tenore litterarum nostrarum quas predicto episcopo direximus, si inveneris quod ei secundum predictum modum scripsimus et in litteris nostris fuit appellatio inhibita et in litteris quas tibi prefatus E. clericus reportavit non fuit habita mentio de forma priorum litterarum, sententiam prefati episcopi omni

occasione et appellatione remota confirmes et sepedictum E. cum litteris nostris quas tibi detulit ad presentiam nostram venire compellas.

Datum Ferentini xvii. Kalendas Augusti.

*Complete: Cus. 49; 1 Cant. 3; Roff. 55; 1 Dun. 3.52; Font. 1.49; Reg. 97; Bridl. 67 (freely rendered); Wig. 7.16; Claustr. 207; Chelt. 6.10; Cott. 3.68; Pet. 2.23.17; App. 7.18; Bamb. 33.18; Erl. 33.19; Lips. 35.18; Cass. 42.19; Tann. 4.3.19; Brug. 37.3; Frcf. 32.7; 1 Comp. 1.2.2; Sang. 5.3.21; X 1.3.2. Parts: 1 Berol. 58 (*Ex parte venerabilis fratris nostri et infra*) + (c) only; X 1.3.2 (ac). Pd App. Cr.; Cass. C; 1 Comp. A; X (ac).*

The letter must be read with Cum olim E. *(supra prox.), and is discussed in the introduction above. 1 Berol. preserves only the opening phrase of (a) and lacks (b); (b) is also omitted in X; much of the phrasing is freely reconstructed in Bridl., and Frcf. R is a much edited and corrected text. The inscription is omitted in 1 Cant., Font., Claustr. The sender is named* Alexander III *in 1 Berol., Cus., Reg., Cott., Pet.; omitted in Bridl., Wig., Chelt.; and* Idem *elsewhere. All inscriptions identify the recipient archbishop (*R. *in Cus., Reg., App. Cr. Lp. V, Bamb. C) of Canterbury, except that Frcf. F has the bishop of Exeter, and Frcf. RTM are corrected to Canterbury from* Luxom̄si *or* Luxoniensi. *The date is provided by 1 Cant. and abbreviated in 1 Dun. The identity of the church is deduced from* Gnoeshal. *in Wig.,* Gnoweshale *in Cott., Pet.,* Gnoushale *in Tann., and* Nosselauá *in Reg. (variants include* Norh., North., Norhal., Norhale, Norshal., Cerno welhul. *[!Cus.],* Enorvelham *and* Enowelaham *[Brug.]). The initials of litigants are widely confused in the manuscript transmission (including* G. *and* E., *which are accepted as correct,* H., He. *and* F.*).*

9

Alexander III or Lucius III to the bishop of Worcester and the abbot of Evesham. Mandate: with reference to the alleged papal commissions addressed firstly to the bishop of Bath, the abbot of Stanley and the prior of Monkton Farleigh, and then to the bishop of Worcester, the abbot of Stanley and the prior of Bradenstoke, in the dispute between the plaintiff Master D. and the clerk G. over the church of Fossoria, *the pope orders the recipients to silence G. in respect of such absurd letters, and compel him to appear before the pope with the letters in question. The judges who had received them must declare the truth of the matter without fear or favour.*

WH 853; JL –. *c. Jan. 1175–81 × 84.*

Alexander III (*vel* Lucius III) Wigorniensi episcopo et abbati de Evesham.

Referente nobis dilecto filio nostro magistro D. presentium latore didiscimus quod clericus quidam G. nomine in repetitione ecclesie de Fossoria a multis retro temporibus eum fatigavit, licet autem tactis sacrosanctis evangeliis illam abiuraverit, et filius creditur fuisse presbyteri qui tanquam persona in eadem ecclesia ministravit. Ipse namquam, quod sine admiratione non dicimus, ad venerabilem fratrem nostrum Batoniensem episcopum et dilectos filios nostros abbatem de Stanlega et priorem de Ferlega litteras dicitur apostolicas impetrasse, in quibus continebatur quod non obesset ei si presbyteri filius extitisset et quod haberent eum a iuramento absolutum. Cumque istarum litterarum auctoritate, sicut nec dignum erat nihil assequi potuisset et tandem quasdam litteras sub nostro nomine conscriptas tibi, frater episcope, et dilectis filiis nostris abbati de Stanlega et priori de Bradenestoke dicitur porrexisse, in quibus continebatur eum a iuramento quod fecerat absolutum et quod nihil ei obesset si, ut dictum est, filius extiterit sacerdotis. Quia vero non est verisimile tales a nobis litteras cum huiusmodi dispensationibus emanasse, discretioni vestre per apostolica scripta mandamus quatinus, si de hiis vobis constiterit, prefato G. super ecclesia de qua tam ineptas litteras impetravit sine appellationis obstaculo silentium imponatis, per excommunicationis sententiam eum compellentes ut cum litteris illis quarum fecimus mentionem sub sigillis vestris debita cautela signatis nostro se conspectui representet. Iudices autem ad quos littere ille pervenerunt nostra auctoritate precipiendo firmiter iniungatis ut nobis et vobis veritatem negotii, sive predictus G. iudicio pareat sive declinet examen, postposita cuiuslibet persone gratia vel favore non negligant intimare.

Cott. 5.66; Tann. 6.1.10; Brug. 37.1; Sang. 7.12; 1 Abr. 7.1.5; 2 Dun. 118; cited: Pet. 2.28. Pd incomplete: Brug.

The text is complete only in Cott.; all other collections lack the final passage Iudices ... intimare. *The Pet. codices now lack the folios which included the letter, but it is cited by cross-reference in cod. 203, fol. 258 va:* De interpretatione rescriptorum ... infra libro .iiii. de falsariis. Fraternitatis. Accepimus. Referente nobis dilecto. *The inscription is omitted in Cott. The sender is named as* Alexander (III) *in Brug. BV, as* Lucius III *in 2 Dun., and* Idem *elsewhere (following* Lucius III *in Tann., Sang.); the bishop of Worcester is named as sole recipient in Tann. (*eidem *after* Wigorniensi episcopo, *6.1.9), 2 Dun., and with the abbot of Evesham in Brug. (*vesham *in V); the abbot of Evesham (*Euehem*) appears as sole recipient in Sang., and the abbot of Einesham in 1 Abr., but the plural forms of the letter require more than a single recipient, one not a bishop.*

The decretal has been hitherto attributed to Alexander III (see Cheney, *Roger of Worcester p. 356–357 nr. 77, c. January 1175 – 30 August 1181), which may well be correct. But the letter first appeared in collections after Alexander's death, and the manuscript transmission allows the possibility that Lucius III was the sender (cf. paragraph supra prox.). In the second panel of judges the abbot of Stanley (*Stranguela *and* Strangela *in Brug. BV;* Strangula Friedberg *edn) is replaced in some collections (Tann., Sang., 1 Abr., 2 Dun.) by the abbot of* uesteb. *or* uestl. *or* nesteb., *suggesting perhaps Westbury, but there was no abbot of Westbury in the period. The church in question (*Fast'one, Fossoria, Fossona, Fa.*) has not yet been identified, but was perhaps one of the many places on the Fosse Way in south-west England.*

10

Alexander III to the archbishop of Canterbury and the bishop of Worcester. Mandate to quash anything done to Master Alan of Idsall's prejudice through papal letters secured by Ralph de Alta Ripa in concealment of preceding stages of their dispute over the chapel of Cambritona, *to award expenses to Alan, and proceed to a canonical verdict on the basis of the pope's earlier mandate. The authenticity of that mandate had been challenged by Ralph because of an erasure in the* narratio facti, *but the present recipients had proceeded to judgment because the form of the letter was consonant with reason. Ralph had then secured a commission to the bishops of Norwich and London, but Alan appealed against their appointment because of their close personal links with Ralph. From an inspection of the letters, the pope rules that they cannot be judged forgeries or even suspect because of the erasure, since even* privilegia *have erasures in their lists of possessions, and* littere *if there is an error in a matter of fact; nor is the erasure in a suspect position in the letter in question. Under his own seal the pope returns the original mandate with its erasures, ordering the commissioners to hear and resolve the issue.*

WH 425; JL 14142. *c. March 1176–1181.*

Alexander III Cantuariensi archiepiscopo et Wigorniensi episcopo.

(a) Ex litteris quas nobis vestra fraternitas destinavit evidenter accepimus quod, cum causam que inter magistrum Alanum de Hideshale et Radulfum de Altaripa super capella de Cambritona vertitur de mandato nostro suscepissetis terminandam et litteras nostras in communi audientia perlegi fecissetis, predictus R. earum sibi postulavit copiam exhiberi, qui siquidem litteris ipsis diligenter inspectis eas arguit falsitatis, hac de causa videlicet quia in narratione facti abrase sunt ubi scriptum est ‚Iure parrochiali', *(b)* asserens se probaturum in presentia nostra quod tales littere de cancelleria nostra non emanassent. Vos autem videntes formam litterarum a rationis tramite minime discrepare, ab executione sententie cause desistere noluistis, prefato R. iuramentum deferentes quod nec subterfugii nec frustratorie dilationis causa hec allegasset, sed quia ita esse credebat, iuramento autem ad diem prefixum non prestito memoratum A. in possessionem causa rei servande iudicastis induci, et quia quidam laicus serviens predicti R. vestro iudicio restitit excommunicatus est, et ecclesia sub interdicto conclusa. Tandem cum predictus R. ad presentiam nostram accedens et tacens prout dicitur quod in priori commissione appellatio fuisset inhibita, nec mentionem faciens argutionis litterarum aut iuramenti ei delati et non pre-

stiti, seu sententie missionis in possessionem causa rei servande, litteras ad venerabiles fratres nostros Lundoniensem et Norwicensem episcopos impetravit in hunc scilicet modum quod, si quid in preiudicium memorati R. occasione prioris commissionis factum fuisset, in irritum duceretur. Cumque prefatus A. citatus a predicto Norwicensi, qui suas et Lundoniensis episcopi vices agebat, coram ipso litteras ipsas diceret veritate tacita impetratas, et petens sibi fieri executionem prioris sententie et Norwicensis episcopi suspitionem pretendens, cui prefatus R. multa familiaritate coniunctus, et Lundoniensis episcopi nepos esse et panem eius cotidie commedere dicitur, ad nostram audientiam appellavit. Unde quoniam nemini debet propria fraus prodesse aut patrocinium ministrare, *(c)* nos inspicientes litteras nostras et videntes quod propter abrasionem illam non possent iudicari false nec etiam suspecte haberi, presertim cum etiam privilegia in possessionibus abradantur et littere in narratione si erratum est de facto incunctanter possint abradi, *(d)* nec littere ipse in loco suspecto fuerint abrase, fraternitati vestre per apostolica scripta mandamus atque precipimus quatinus, si quid factum fuerit in preiudicium memorati A. occasione litterarum quas sepedictus R. a nobis impetravit, non facta mentione de redargutione abrasarum litterarum, nec de sententia missionis in possessionem causa rei servande, nec de appellatione inhibita, aut de iuramento sibi delato et non prestito, occasione et appellatione postposita in irritum revocetis, et sententiam nostram faciatis inviolabiliter observari et eundem R. in expensas portitoris litterarum pro eo quod a probatione sua desistit condemnetis. Postea vero utraque parte ante vos constituta causam audiatis et secundum tenorem abrasarum litterarum quas vobis sub sigillo nostro clausas remittimus fine canonico terminetis, nullis litteris preiudicantibus iusticie et veritati si que fuerint harum tenore tacito impetrate. Si autem temeritatem et fraudem illius vellemus attendere et eum de suis meritis iudicare, illi super eadem causa silentium faceremus imponi, ut alii qui audirent sedem apostolicam pavescerent tali modo circumvenire, cui deberet quod veritati innititur remoto falsitatis obstaculo suaderi.

Complete: Roff. 75; 1 Rot. 17.10. Parts: Bamb. 0 57.1, Erl. 39.15, Tann. 6.2.4 (= Tann. B), 2 Clar. 52, Crac. 58, Luc. 29, Mon. 31, Lamb. 34, 2 Alc. 10, Gilb. Br. 2.15.1, Fuld. 2.19.1, 2 Comp. 2.14.1, X 2.22.3 have only (a), etc. et infra *(om. in X), (c); in (d), Claud. 207, Claustr. 308, Chelt. 4.8, Cott. 3.81, Pet. 2.29.1, App. Cr. 49.3, Tann. 4.4.1 (= Tann. A), Sang. 5.3.37, 1 Abr. 5.4.1, 2 Dun. 86 abbreviate* preiudicantibus iustitie … impetrate *to* obstantibus etc. *(App. Cr. om.* etc.*), and stop short at* faceremus imponi *(Claud. at* tali modo circumvenire*). Pd App. Cr. with minor abbreviations in (d); 2 Comp. A (ac); X (ac).*

The inscription is omitted in Claustr., Chelt., Cott., Pet., App. The sender occurs as Idem *in Roff., Crac., Mon., 2 Alc., X, and elsewhere as* Alexander III *(om.* III *1 Rot.). Canterbury and Worcester are named recipients in Claud.; Worcester and Coventry in Roff., Erl., Bamb. O, 1 Rot., 2 Clar., Crac., Luc. Mon., 2 Alc.; London and Coventry in Tann., Sang., 1 Abr., 2 Dun.; and Coventry alone in Lamb. The recipients are omitted in Tann. B, Gilb., Fuld., 2 Comp., X. The order of precedence is wrong for Worcester and Coventry; the subject-matter rules out London, and also a single recipient. The Canterbury and Worcester form is the ony one which raises no problem. The litigants were the well-known master Ralph de Alta Ripa and probably master Alan of Idsall (CHENEY, Roger of Worcester, p. 340–341 nr. 49). Ralph, who was clerk to his uncle Gilbert of London, later canon of St. Paul's, Master of the Schools, archdeacon of Colchester, royal clerk and justice, died at Acre in 1190 or 1191 (Adrian MOREY – Christopher N. L. BROOKE, Gilbert Foliot and his Letters [1965] passim, esp. p. 274; Le Neve: St. Paul's p. 19, 26, 32, 49). Alan's place-name appears as* Hiddeshal., Hidesleshale, Hidesh., Hillehal., Hilesdale *etc; as* Billesdale *(Claud.) and in various corrupt forms. The church of* Cambritona, Cambrintona, Cambringt., Camb., Cabitun., Capitun., Kabituñ., Kabicim., *etc. has not been identified, though HOLTZMANN suggested Comberton.*

11

Alexander III to bishop John and the prior of Norwich. Mandate: in the dispute between the clerks Gwarinus and William over a debt and the expenses of an appeal, the abbots of Coggeshall and Crowland declined to accept Gwarinus's charge that their commission was obtained by misrepresentation, and proceeded to judgment despite his appeal. If the recipients find the facts as stated, they must quash the judges' sentence, restore the situation as it stood before the appeal, compel William to make restitution if he failed to give effect to a compact between himself and Gwarinus concerning the promotion of a certain petition, and annul any sentence passed on Gwarinus after he set out for the curia. They must secure the letters of commission to the earlier judges and, if they find them as described by the pope in his sealed letters to them, they must send them under their seals to him, since he considers them suspect.

WH 1062; JL –. *1176–81.*

Alexander III Johanni episcopo et priori Norwicensi.

(a) Veniens ad nos Gwarinus clericus presentium lator nobis proposuit quod Willelmus clericus de Coggeshale et de Croilande abbatibus sub nomine nostro litteras presentavit ut, si idem G. ei redditus trium marcarum argenti quas sibi annuatim solvere interposita fide dicitur promisisse solvere nollet, eum ad solutionem ipsius pecunie cogere non differrent. Continebatur etiam in litteris ipsis

quod compellerent prefatum G. expensas memorato W. restituere, quas fecerat cum pro ipso veniendo usque ad nos laborem assumpsit. Ceterum constanter nobis et sollicite retulit quod, cum prefatus W. venturus olim pro suis negotiis ad presentiam nostram ab eodem G. suscepisset petitionem quandam apud nos promovendam, propter hoc quinquaginta solidos et unum palefridum recepit ab eo, ita quod his contentus esset aut, si petitionem ipsam non manciparet effectui, sibi equum et pecuniam restitueret. Tandem vero idem W. litteras supradictas in quibus inhibita erat appellatio exhibuit predictis abbatibus, coram quibus prefatus G. vocatus in causam probationem optulit quod eedem littere falsa suggestione impetrate fuissent. Sed quia idem abbates exceptiones eius repellentes volebant in causa procedere, ad nostram audientiam appellavit. Idem vero abbates post appellationem memoratum W. in possessionem redditum trium marcarum, quas habebat prefatus G., causa rei servande inducendum iudicaverunt, et ipsum G. in solutionem centum solidorum eidem W. pro expensis quas fecerat ad nos veniendo solius iuramento recepto per sententiam condempnaverunt. Inde est quod discretioni vestre per apostolica scripta precipiendo mandamus quatinus partibus ante vos convocatis inquiratis super hoc diligentius veritatem et, si vobis constiterit predictos abbates in causa presertim post appellationem taliter processisse, sententiam eorum in hac parte contradictione et appellatione cessante cassetis, et omnia reducatis in eum statum in quo tempore appellationis fuisse noscuntur. *(b)* Postea vero que hinc inde proposita fuerint diligentius audiatis et exinde quod iustum fuerit iudicetis. Porro si inter predictos G. et W. talis pactio intercesserit quod, si idem W. petitionem prefati G. quam suscepit promovendam non manciparet effectui, ei prefatum equum et pecuniam restitueret, ipsum ad hec predicto G. restituenda si petitionem illam non mancipavit effectui appellatione remota ecclesiastica districtione cogatis. Si qua vero sententia in predictum G. lata est postquam iter arripuit ad nos veniendi, eam appellatione cessante auctoritate nostra denuncietis irritam et inanem. Litteras autem predictibus iudicibus super hoc exhibitas iuri et veritati nullum volumus preiudicium facere, sed potius volumus et mandamus ut litteras ipsas ab eisdem iudicibus requiratis, et si tales sunt littere bullate quale est rescriptum quod vobis sub bulla nostra mittimus, litteras ipsas, quoniam eas suspectas habemus, sub sigillis vestris ad nos transmittatis. Porro si his exequendis et cetera.

Complete (except that only Wig. and Chelt. have the conclusion Porro si his exequendis *[+* etc. *in Wig]): Bridl. 151; Wig. 7.76; Chelt. 4.19; Tann. 4.5.15; Sang. 5.4.14; 1 Abr. 5.5.11. Part (a) only: Cott. 3.62; Pet. 2.23.15. Pd Sang.*

The inscription is omitted in Chelt. and Cott.; Alexander (III) *is named as sender in Pet., which otherwise omits the inscription; and Tann., Sang., 1 Abr. have* Idem. *Bridl. and Wig. read* episcopo et priori Norwicensi, *and Tann., Sang., 1 Abr. have* Norwicensi episcopo et priori eiusdem loci; *the bishop is identified as Jo(hn) in Wig. Since John of Oxford was not consecrated bishop of Norwich until December 1175, the earliest date of the letter is 1176. If the order of precedence of the earlier commissioners is correct, they were Odo of Coggeshall (1169–76) and Robert of Crowland (1175–90), within the period 1175–76.*

12

Alexander III to archbishop Roger of York and bishop Hugh of Durham. Mandate to despoil Master Hugh of Southwell of the churches of Epperstone and Shelford. The cardinal legate Hugh Pierleoni had wished to condemn Hugh on a charge of forgery, but had deferred to his appeal on the intervention of powerful persons.

WH 404; JL –. *post April 1177.*

Alexander III Rogero Eboracensi archiepiscopo et Hugoni Dunelmensi episcopo.

Ex constanti relatione dilecti filii nostri Hugonis sancti Angeli diaconi cardinalis et ex litteris quas idem cardinalis nobis exhibuit evidenter cognovimus quod magister Hugo de Suellis litteras tibi, frater archiepiscope, falsas exhibuit. Verum cum idem Hugo diceret litteras illas se tibi non reddidisse, tandem sufficientia testium est probatum quod easdem litteras tibi reddiderit et, cum idem cardinalis ipsum vellet sicut falsarium condempnare, idem Hugo ad nostram audientiam appellavit, cui appellationi idem cardinalis ita duxit quod grave gerimus deferendum, quod postmodum magnarum personarum supplicatione inductus eidem Hugoni ad tempus pepercit. Quoniam igitur decet nos tam gravem excessum durius vindicare, ut alii exemplo pene illius similia attemptare formident, fraternitati vestre per apostolica scripta precipiendo mandamus quatinus, predictum Hugonem ecclesiis de Epperstone et de Shelford contradictione et appellatione cessante spoliantes, perpetuum ei silentium super eisdem ecclesiis imponatis, et ipsum nullius contradictione vel appellatione obstante nichilominus in aliquo monasterio recludetis, ubi possit quod tam nequiter egit lamentis penitentie emendare.

Bridl. 152 only. Pd Decretales ineditae p. 130–132 nr. 76; and G. V. Scammell, Hugh du Puiset, Bishop of Durham (1956) p. 251–252.

*Cardinal Hugh Pierleoni was papal legate in England from October 1175 until July 1176. He apparently did not reach the pope until April 1177. The language of the decretal suggests that he reported the details of this case to the pope in person, and therefore in or after April 1177. Equally, the last recorded appearances of the well-known master Hugh of Southwell are in witness lists in late May 1177 (*CHENEY, *Roger of Worcester, p. 340 nr. 47 A). The case is fully discussed in Decretales ineditae p. 131–132.*

13

Alexander III to the bishop of Durham and the abbots of Bury St Edmunds and St Albans. Advice and mandate: having rehearsed the process of the dispute between the archbishop of Canterbury and the abbot and monks of St Augustine's, concerning monastic privilegia *which the archbishop declares to be forged, the case having been commissioned to the bishops of Hereford and Worcester (then abbot of Ford) and Master Peter of Melide, the pope deems it prudent that the documents should not be sent to the curia, nor shown all at once to the archbishop. He should inspect them one at a time in a place mutually satisfactory, and copy them if necessary, so that properly instructed he or his representative could argue his case in the curia by the appointed term. In the event of non-appearance, silence shall be imposed on him and his successors in this matter, and the privileges shall meanwhile be observed. By the appointed date the recipients must send the pope transcripts of documents shown to them and their own reports under seals. The archbishop must be content to inspect a maximum of twelve privileges. The recipients must quash sentences imposed after the monks' appeal, and send under suspension those officials who forbad papal letters to be obeyed or received. In the event of resistance, they must receive witnesses and attestations and send them to the pope. A more severe sentence will follow conviction in the papal presence.*

WH 846; JL 14365. *Tusculum 23 Jan. 1181.*

Alexander episcopus servus servorum Dei venerabili fratri Dunelmensi episcopo et dilectis filiis sancti Eadmundi et sancti Albani abbatibus, salutem et apostolicam benedictionem.

(a) Recepimus litteras quas dilecti filii nostri R. abbas et fratres sancti Augustini contra venerabilem fratrem nostrum R. Cantuariensem archiepiscopum apostolice sedis legatum miserunt, ex quarum tenore perpendimus quod, cum fratribus nostris venerabilibus Herefordensi et Wigorniensi episcopis, tunc Fordensi abbati, et bone memorie magistro P. de Melide fuisset mandatum a

nobis ut, si prefatus archiepiscopus privilegia, quibus idem abbas et fratres se ab eius credunt impetitionem defendi, vellet redarguere falsitatis, ea sibi facerent quamtocius exhiberi, et que proponerentur hinc inde sublato appellationis remedio diligentius audientes eadem privilegia facerent fideliter et studiose conscribi, primo iudicium Cantuarie absente prefato Herefordense fuit in ecclesia sancti Gregorii celebratum, que sub muro civitatis posita quasi thalamus prefati archiepiscopi reputatur. Confluxerat autem illuc tota sinodus fere que celebratur eo die, et erant vici platee et atria plena nimis, ut asserunt fratres ipsi, hominibus temerariis ad dispendium eorum paratis. Unde, cum rogati fuissent ut omnia privilegia quecumque a tempore beati Gregorii penes ipsos essent exhiberent, adversario responderunt in mandato non omnia contineri, sed quedam illa dumtaxat que arguere vellet, nec mandatum fuisse ut adversario exhiberentur sed iudicibus, nec de loco expresse in mandato aliquid habebatur. Tandem ad instantiam iudicum, tamquam hoc de voluntate archiepiscopi peterent, concesserunt ut cum tribus clericis et tribus monachis ipse septimus apud beatum Augustinum videret illorum privilegia et contractaret. Sed, cum hoc renuisset eisdem postulantibus, annuerunt secundo ut cum sex clericis et sex monachis ipse terciusdecimus, una cum iudicibus, copiam privilegiorum haberet; sed hoc archiepiscopus respuit, non propter laborem, cum ecclesia ipsa a loco iudicii vix iactu lapilli distare dicatur. Inde utique fuit quod, videntes in duobus mandati fines excedi a iudicibus precipientibus citra formam mandati omnia privilegia adversario exhiberi, cernentes quoque superhabundantem concessionem ab archiepiscopo memorato contempni, ad appellationis remedium confugerunt. Iudices tamen eis diem nihilominus prorogarunt Lundoniis crastino post festum sancti Laurencii, ubi peremptorio die conventi sub iudicibus tribus, post appellationem interpositam, statim audientes terminum prescriptum appellationis remedium innovarunt, causas eius multiplices exponentes. Adiecit preterea nuntius predicti abbatis et fratrum quod, post appellationem interpositam, archiepiscopus quosdam clericorum eorundem fratrum suspensioni et aliquas ecclesias ipsorum interdicto pro sue voluntatis arbitrio subiecit, et quod officialium eius quidam litteris apostolicis obediri easque recipi, quod gravius et mirabilius gerimus, vetuissent. Econtrario autem, nuntii archiepiscopi constanter inficiantes que contra dominum suum nuntius iamdictus obiecerat, litteras delegatorum iudicum presentarunt apertius continentes quod, cum prefatus archiepiscopus secundum formam mandati apostolici instanter peteret instrumentorum sibi copiam exhiberi, certa designans privilegia que volebat arguere falsitatis, pars fratrum ipsorum suis defensionibus utens quantum potuit privilegiorum exhibitionem vitavit. Sed cum de consilio virorum prudentium, quorum habebant copiam, iudices delegati interlocuti fuissent privilegia exhibenda, que nominatim archiepiscopus petierat accusanda, et firmiter iniunxissent auctoritate qua fungebantur fratribus prenominatis quatinus exhiberent eis privilegia illa, ut per eos eorundem privilegiorum inspiciendorum archiepiscopo copia fieret, licet in litteris commissionis appellationis remedium tolleretur, et plenariam fratribus securitatem promitterent integra et illibata privilegia ipsa reddendi, ad nostram tàmen audientiam appellarunt. *(b)* Nos itaque attendentes tempus ad prosequendam appellationem prescriptam nullatenus expectandum, cum privilegia nisi inspecta argui non valeant falsitatis, et difficile sit et periculosum ea apud sedem apostolicam exhiberi, de communi fratrum nostrorum consilio censuimus ut coram vobis exhibeantur privilegia, que archiepiscopus dixerit arguenda, in claustro predictorum fratrum vel in alio loco ipsis omnino securo et illi congruo, ad arbitrium vestrum, usque ad proximum festum nativitatis beati Johannis baptiste. *(c)* Nolumus autem exhiberi omnia simul sed, uno exhibito et ipsius inspiciendi et transcribendi, si necesse fuerit, copia prestita, reddatur illud fratribus ipsis et aliud presentetur. Deinde usque ad festum purificationis beati Marie sequentis anni archiepiscopus sufficienter instructus ad redarguenda privilegia supradicta per se vel per sufficientem responsalem ad apostolicam sedem accedat. *(d)* Si vero nec venerit nec sufficientem miserit responsalem, ei suisque successoribus perpetuum silentium sit impositum privilegia ipsa ulterius arguendi. *(e)* Interim autem nolumus privilegia ipsa vacillare, sed precipimus sententiam, que super statu monasterii lata est, inviolabiliter observari. *(f)* Mandamus etiam ut sententia, in clericos eiusdem monasterii vel ecclesias post appellationem prolata, denuncietur publice non tenere, et qui prohibuerunt litteris apostolicis obediri aut eas recipi compellantur suspensi ad sedem apostolicam laborare. Quia igitur quanto amplius de prudentia vestra et honestate confidimus, tanto studiosius et fidelius decet vos commissum experientie vestre negotium ventilare, discretioni vestre mandamus atque precipimus quatinus in facto iuxta formam quam prescripsimus omni gratia et timore postposito sublato appellationis diffugio procedatis et in prescripto festo purificationis rescripta privilegiorum, que vobis exhibita fuerint, cum litteris vestris rei veritatem continentibus sub sigillis vestris nobis transmittatis inclusa. Ne autem contentio pre multitudine oriatur, *(g)* iubemus ut archiepiscopum in inspectione privilegiorum duodecim numerum excedere non sinatis, sed eum cum duodecim inter clericos et monachos faciatis esse contentum. *(h)* Sententiam quoque, si quam in clericos vel ecclesias monasterii constiterit post appellationem interpositam promulgatam, nullius appellatione obstante denuntietis publice non tenere. *(i)* Archiepiscopo preterea districtius auctoritate apostolica iniungatis ut officiales suos, qui obediri litteris nostris aut eas recipi vetuisse dicuntur, si res ita se habet, suspensos ad apostolicam sedem dilatione et appellatione cessante transmittat. Si vero negaverint et monachi duxerint insistendum, appellatione cessante recipiatis testes et, attestationes studiosius conscribentes, in prescripto festo nobis transmittatis inclusas, alioquin, si in hoc fuerint in auditorio nostro convicti, duriorem sententiam reportabunt. [Si autem omnes his exequendis nequiveritis interesse, duo vestrum ea nihilominus exequantur.

Data Tusculani x. kal. Februarii.]

Complete: Wig. 7.59; Cott. 7.59; Tann. 6.1.6; Sang. 7.7. The letter with complete address and date is also found in Thomas of Elmham, Historia monasterii sancti Augustini Cantuariensis, ed. Charles HARDWICK *(Rolls Series 8, 1858) p. 442–446 nr. 75. Parts: Claustr. 291 omits (i), concluding* Archiepiscopus preterea etc.; *2 Dun. 117 omits (d); Alan. 2.12.1, Fuld. 2.19.4, 2 Comp. 2.14.2 abbreviate (a) to* accepimus ... misit (miserunt) etc. et infra *+ (bdegh); X 2.22.4 has shortened versions of (a) to* transmisit (miserunt) et infra, *and of (b) from* cum privilegia *+ (deg). A shortened version of the letter is also preserved in Chronica W. Thorne monachi sancti Augustini Cantuariensis (Historiae Anglicanae scriptores decem, ed. Roger* TWYSDEN, *1652) p. 1832–1833: abbrev. (a) + (bcdefg). Pd: Thomas of Elmham; abbreviated: William Thorne.*

The full address is supplied in Elmham. It is lacking in Claustr., Cott., Sang. Alexander III *is correctly named in 2 Comp., but omitted in Wig., and designated elsewhere as* Idem, *except that Alan. has Innocent III. In the decretal collections, only Wig. has the correct identification of the recipients; in Alan., Fuld., 2 Comp., X, the letter is incorrectly addressed to the archbishop of York (*Ebroacensi *in Alan.). The text is prefaced in Thorne by:* dominus vero papa commisit causam predictam Eboracensi et Dunelmensi episcopis et sancti Edmundi et sancti Albani abbatibus. *The intended recipients were bishop Hugh of Durham and abbots Hugh of Bury St Edmunds and Simon of St Albans, but the abbot Hugh was already dead (14 or 15 November 1180), when the decretal was issued on 23 January 1181. His name was dropped in Alexander's subsequent letter to the commissioners on 23 March 1181 (*Cum super questionem falsi: *Elmham p. 441–442 nr. 74). According to Gervase of Canterbury, a meeting was convened in London on 26 June 1181, to investigate the dispute in accordance with the papal mandate (The Historical Works of Gervase of Canterbury, ed. William* STUBBS *[Rolls Series 73, 2 1880] p. 296–297); and Elmham includes Henry II's confirmation of a composition reached between the parties on 8 March 1182, at Poitiers (p. 449–452 nr. 80). The letter is important in the history of the collections, since its presence in the archetype of the Worcester family fixes the terminus a quo of that collection in March 1181 at the earliest. A parallel letter from the pope to the abbot and monks of St Augustine's, on the same date, is preserved in a cartulary of the monastery: Papsturkunden in England 1 (1931) 470–473 nr. 201.*

14

Lucius III to bishop Baldwin of Worcester. Commendation and mandate: the pope commends the bishop's prudence in declining to give effect to a judgment by the abbot of Missenden, the prior of Canon's Ashby and Master Ambrose in favour of G. against the present plaintiff A. in respect of the chapel of Stretton on Fosse. Since G. lacked sealed letters to authorize the judgment, the bishop refused to act on a certain rescript offered by G., who also harassed A. with letters shown to be forged. If the charges are proven, the bishop must rule in favour of A., and imprison G., if found guilty of forgery. Whenever putative papal letters are suspected by the bishop, he must give them no credence, and detain whoever presented them.

WH 432; JL 15204. *Velletri 1182–83.*

Lucius episcopus servus servorum Dei venerabili fratri Balduino Wigorniensi episcopo salutem et apostolicam benedictionem.

(a) Ex litteris tue fraternitatis acceptis, tam eorum tenore quam ex relatione A. latoris presentium, intelleximus quod, cum bone memorie Rogero predecessori tuo ad capellam de Stratam ab eo qui ius presentandi habebat fuisset canonice presentatus, G. qui filius eius proponitur qui in eadem proximus ministravit ad presentiam ipsius accessit, asserens se in eadem capella fuisse rationabiliter ordinatum, et institutionem illius fieri non permisit. Unde idem antecessor tuus, donec inter eos querimonia finiretur, prefato A. proventus illius capelle promisit atque concessit. Cum tempore procedente ex parte dilectorum filiorum nostrorum abbatis de Messendene et prioris de Essebi et magistri Ambrosii fuissent tibi littere presentate, quibus mandabatur ut sententiam quam tulerant pro memorato G. super capella illa de mandato apostolico executioni mandares, litteras quarum auctoritate sententiam tulerant expetiisti. Sed cum prenominatus G. litteras bullatas non haberet, rescriptum quoddam ostendit qua de causa distulisti quod iudicatum fuerat adimplere. Predictus vero G. aliarum litterarum optentu, que nihilominus false sunt invente, memoratum A. presumpsit indebite molestare, licet autem prefato A. fide mediante promiserat quod eum super prefata capella inquietare de cetero non deberet. Volentes igitur eidem A. in suo iure adesse, *(b)* fraternitati tue per apostolica scripta mandamus quatinus, si tibi constiterit eum ad prefatam capellam canonice vocatum et memoratum G. fide media promisisse illum super eadem capella se minime vexaturum, vel filium fuisse illius qui sicut dicitur in eadem proximo ministravit, eum si alias idoneus fuerit in capella illa sublato appellationis remedio resti-

tuere non omittas. Prefatum vero G. ad presentiam tuam convocatum, si de falsitate coram te probari poterit, in aliquo monasterio appellatione remota retrudas, in quo reatum suum valeat expiare, iniungens iudicibus ex parte nostra ut falsarum tibi exibeant copiam litterarum. *(c)* Super eo autem quod sententiam auctoritate falsarum litterarum noluisti executioni mandare, tuam plurimum prudentiam commendamus, mandantes ut, quotiens aliqua scripta sub nostro nomine destinata redarguenda videris falsitatis, nullam eis fidem adhibeas, et quod per ipsa mandatum fuerit non observes, sed eum qui presentavit retineri facias.

Datum Velletri.

Complete: Tann. 6.1.9; Sang. 7.11 (= Sang. A); 1 Abr. 7.1.4. Parts: (b) abbreviated to fraternitati tue per apostolica scripta mandamus quatinus G. clericum ad tuam presentiam convocatis, si de falsitate ... expirare *+ (c): Wig. 7.82;* fraternitatis tue litteris susceptis et infra *+ (c): Chelt. 14.15, Cott. 5.63, Sang. 5.2.11 (= Sang. B);* Pars capituli Ex litteris *+ (c): 2 Dun. 174, Alan. 2.15.4, 2 Comp. 2.18.4; (c) only: Claud. 157, X 5.20.2. Pd Sang.; incipit + (c): 2 Comp. A; (c) only: X; and (b) abbrev. + (c), from Wig. in P. M. Baumgarten, Papal letters relating to England, 1133–1187, English Historical Review 9 (1894) p. 534–535.*

The full inscription is found only in Wig., which alone also preserves the abbreviated date. The inscription is omitted in Chelt.; elsewhere Lucius III *is named as sender in all collections, except that* Cott. *names* Alexander III, *and the bishop of Worcester is identified as recipient, except for his omission in 1 Abr.; he is identified as* B*(aldwin) in Wig. and Claud. Though abbreviated, the version in Wig. is of particular interest, with its full inscription, shortened date and initial* B. *for the bishop. It is an addition in situ to Book 7, written in a different hand from the main transcription. The associations of Baldwin with the codex are well known, and this is one of its several additions addressed to him. For the dispute in question, see Cheney, Roger of Worcester p. 73–74, 329 nr. 26 and 26 A, p. 341 nr. 49 A (the present letter), p. 345 nr. 55 A, and p. 365–366 nr. 93 A.*

15

Lucius III to unnamed recipients, at least one not a bishop. Mandate to resolve the dispute between Master A. and the clerk Nicholas over the church of Drandam, *to investigate A.'s charge that Nicholas used forged letters against him in the presence of the abbots of Fountains and Rievaulx, and that the judges did not defer to his appeal. The letters had seemed suspect to the pope when he saw them.*

WH 168: JL –. *1181–85.*

Lucius III.

Constitutus in presentia nostra dilectus filius noster magister A. sua nobis conquestione monstravit quod, cum ecclesiam de Drandam canonice fuisset adeptus, Nicholaus clericus coram dilectis filiis nostris de Fontibus et de Rivaus abbatibus super prefata ecclesia eum per falsas litteras impetivit. Testibus autem contra generalem recognitionem in capitulo factam pro parte altera introductis et eorum dictis in scripta redactis et publicatis, cum iam dictus A. copiam sibi attestationum fieri et inducias de vita testium inquirenda sibi peteret indulgeri, predicti iudices hoc facere recusabant. Cum autem ipse A. de falso litteras arguisset et de ipsa falsitate in nostra presentia comprobanda cautionem iuratoriam optulisset, iudices eum super hoc audire noluerunt et ideo ab ipso est ad audientiam nostram appellatum, sed ab eis ad sententiam nihilominus est processum. Verum cum iamdictus A. ad presentiam nostram accessisset, litteras ipsas sub sigillis iudicum transmissas nobis exhibuit, que utique suspecte videbantur habende, eo quod formam iuri minus consentaneam habebant. Inde est quod discretioni vestre per apostolica scripta precipiendo mandamus quatinus litteras memoratas exhiberi vobis a iudicibus auctoritate apostolica faciatis et, si vobis de ipsarum falsitate constiterit vel iudices interposite appellationi non detulisse noveritis, quicquid ab ipsis auctoritate dictarum litterarum et in preiudicium appellationis factum esse claruerit, appellatione cessante in irritum revocetis et tam de dampnis illatis quam de fructibus perceptis memorato A. iusticie plenitudinem per censuram ecclesiasticam exhibere curetis, deinde inter partes causam audiatis et fine canonico terminetis.

Tann. 4.5.10; Sang. 5.4.10; 1 Abr. 5.5.7; 2 Dun. 96. Pd Sang.

Lucius III *is named as sender in all four manuscripts, but otherwise the inscription is lost. The form of the letter requires a plurality of recipients, at least one not a bishop. The church of* Drandam *(Tann., 2 Dun.).* Drandham *(Sang.), or* Trandan *(1 Abr.) has not been identified, but the earlier commission to the Cistercian abbots of Fountains and Rievaulx suggests a location in Yorkshire. The plaintiff master A.'s adversary is named Nicholas in Tann.* (Nich.; Ni. *in 2 Dun.;* N. *in Sang., 1 Abr.).*

16

Celestine III to the abbot of Pershore and the prior of Great Malvern. Mandate to restore a disputed vicarage and its fruits to the poor clerk N., if he was despoiled by the priest and parson N. in the circumstances alleged, and proceed to investigate and canonically resolve any issue arising. If the priest had assented to the clerk in the vicarage, he must vex him no further and pay the expenses of his journey to the curia. On the charge of forged papal letters, the pope declares on inspection that he does not believe they were issued in this form with his knowledge, though they clearly came from his chancery. [The opening part of this long and complicated letter is missing; two earlier panels of judges had been appointed to deal with the case.]

WH 248; JL –. *1191–98.*

Celestinus III abbati de Persovere et priori de Malvernia.

Cum huius auctoritate mandati utraque pars in eorundem iudicum presentia constituta fuisset, N. presbiter litteras nostras falsas civiliter accusavit. Unde iuratoria cautione ab illo accepta quod de questione falsi prosequenda illorum rationabili staret arbitrio, idem iudices ab N. clerico, quod portitorem coram eis exhiberet vel eorum iudicio staret, iuramentum receperunt. Eodem vero clerico die super hoc prefixo portitorem non exhibente, inter ipsum et adversarium suum, dum uterque alterum sibi suspectum esse proponeret, de communi portitore qui litteras ipsas ad Romanam ecclesiam deferret non potuit convenire. Cumque a predicto N. clerico proponeretur se expensas communi portitori prestare non posse, et dictus N. presbiter postulasset ut per ipsos iudices vel alios idoneos viros portitor eligeretur et ipse propter paupertatem predicti N. clerici expensas portitori prestaret, idem clericus asseruit eundem presbiterum ideo sibi magis esse suspectum, quia portitorem si communis eligeretur pecunia potentis adversarii timebat posse corrumpi. Propter quod prefati iudices de prudentium virorum consilio ipsas litteras sub eorum sigillis inclusas eidem N. clerico nobis deferendas tradiderunt, quia coram eis corporaliter prestitit iuramentum quod eas sine dolo apostolico conspectui presentaret, honus defensionis super periculo cause sue subiturus, si illarum litterarum portitorem, qui tunc sicut asseruit iter ad curiam Romanam veniendi arripuit, in presentia nostra non posset exhibere. Et licet eum presbiter, qui se illorum iudicio staturum iuraverat, de falso prosequendo cautionem nisi littere sibi aut communi portitori traderentur in eorum presentia exponere voluisset, ipsi nichilominus diem in quo in presentia nostra utraque pars appareret, scilicet dominica qua cantatur ‚Quasimodo geniti' eis prefigentes, transcriptum illarum litterarum cum litteris suis rei veritatem continentibus utrique parti per se vel per alium nostro conspectui tradiderunt proferendum. Sed N. clericus multum se gravari sentiens, pro eo quod dies adeo prolixus ei fuerat statutus, confestim ad eorundem iudicium accessit et statutum ab eis terminum abbreviari et diem artiorem prefigi humiliter postulavit. Unde diem artiorem, dominicam scilicet qua cantatur ,Invocavit me' utrique parti prefixerunt, iam dicto N. presbitero per litteras suas firmiter precipientes ut eodem die simul cum adversario suo coram nobis appareret. Verum cum nuntius prefati N. clerici termino a memoratis iudicibus statuto posterius se cum litteris ipsius nostro aspectui presentasset et per quadraginta dies in curia nostra moram fecisset, iamdictus N. [presbiter] per se vel per alium coram nobis non apparuit. Unde prescriptas litteras coram nobis perlegi fecimus et, licet non credamus litteras ipsas de nostra intentione sub huiusmodi forma a nobis fuisse obtentas, tamen ex illarum inspectione nobis plenius constat eas de cancellaria nostra emanasse. Idem quoque pauper clericus transmissa nobis conquestione monstravit quod, cum posteriores iudices litteris suis, in quibus mandatum apostolicum sibi directum continebatur, prioribus iudicibus cause processum inhibuissent, ipsi nichilominus in ipsa procedere voluerunt, nisi idem clericus illud autenticum scriptum exhiberet; unde taliter compulsus fidem prestitit quod illud alio die exhiberet. Qui vero iudices, cum idem rescriptum die statuta eis exhibitum impressissent et idem clericus illud in iure exhibere et adversario suo coram eis copiam inspiciendi facere renuit, post appellationem memorati clerici super hoc ad nos interpositam contra ipsum absentem super eadem vicaria sententiam protulerunt. Adiecit preterea memoratus clericus quod, priusquam presbiter dictus in personatum prescripte ecclesie per officiales diocesiani episcopi inductus fuisset, ei ab eisdem officialibus fuit expressum quod in vita eiusdem N. clerici de ipsa ecclesia non amplius quam duorum aureorum perciperet pensionem. Et licet idem presbiter, tamquam de predicta pensione contentus illi clerico super eadem vicaria, prout in autenticis litteris bone memorie W. quondam diocesiani episcopi nec non et eiusdem ecclesie patroni que coram eisdem officialibus in iure perlecte fuerant continebatur, assensum prebuisset et ei in illorum presentia constituto nullam super hoc quod filius in eadem ecclesia proximo ministrantis esse dicatur vel quolibet alio quominus eandem vicariam possideret movisset questionem, ipsum nullatenus post appellationem eiusdem clerici ad nos interpositam ab eadem vicaria violenter eiecit. Unde discretioni vestre per apostolica scripta mandamus quatinus, si prefatum N. clericum prout dictum est spoliatum fuisse noveritis, prescriptam vicariam cum fructibus a tempore spoliationis inde perceptis ante litis ingressum, auctoritate nostra suffulti contradictione et appellatione cessante litteris ad prefatos iudices impetratis nequaquam obstantibus vel sententia a prioribus iudicibus taliter lata non obstante, eidem clerico restitui[a] faciatis. Restitutione autem facta, siquidem postmodum dignum videritis questione, audiatis causam et eam appellatione remota fine canonico terminetis, ita siquidem quod, si inveneritis predictum presbiterum eidem clerico prout superius narratum est super predicta vicaria[b] assensum prebuisse, ipsum ab indebita prenominati clerici de cetero vexatione desistere sublato appellationis obstaculo ecclesiastica districtione cogatis, eum nichilominus expensas quas nuntius memorati N. clerici per illius presbiteri iniquitatem nunc ad nos veniendo fecisse dinoscitur, eidem clerico appellatione postposita sicut iustum fuerit reddere compellatis. Si vero idem presbiter vel alius vobis restiterit quominus mandatum apostolicum adimplere possitis, eum a sua presumptione appellatione remota censura ecclesiastica compescatis.

a) clerico restitui] clerico prout superius narratum est, super predictam vicariam restitui *in SINGER's edition; but* prout ... vicariam *has* vac – at *superscript for deletion.*
b) predicta vicaria] *corrected in cod. from* predictam vicariam.

Sang. 5.12.11. Pd Sang.

The sender is designated Idem *following* Celestinus III Wintoniensi et Cicestrensi episcopis. Sicut dilecti filii, *JL –, WH 930, 1191–1198. The recipients were abbot Simon of Pershore (*Persouer.*) and prior Walter of Great Malvern (*Ma.*), a dependency of Westminster (see CHENEY, Roger of Worcester, p. 374–376); the* quondam *diocesan bishop* W., *mentioned in the letter, was William of Northolt, bishop of Worcester, 1186–1190.*

17

Lucius III to archbishop Walter of Rouen. Mandate: the authenticity of papal letters has been brought into question by the activities of forgers in the English king's lands. Clerical forgers discovered by the recipient must be deprived of office and benefice, and imprisoned pending papal orders. Lay offenders must be delivered to the English king for judgment.

WH 546; JL 15207. *Verona 16 Oct. 1185.*

Lucius III Waltero Rothomagensi archiepiscopo.

Improba pestis falsitatis quam falsarii quidam in terra karissimi in Christo filii nostri illustris Henrici Anglorum regis morantes ad confingendas litteras apostolicas invenerunt in communem nosciter excrevisse perniciem, ita ut litterarum nostrarum auctoritas in aliquibus locis quadam dubitatione iam fluctuet, nisi tante presumptionis excessum censura sicut convenit emendet. Unde nos de tua presertim industria confidentes executionem rei huiusmodi tibi duximus committendam per apostolica tibi scripta precipiendo mandamus quatinus falsarios ipsos qualicumque casu Deo volente reperire poteris, si clerici sunt, ab ordine et beneficio si quid habent absque ulla dilatione et appellatione privatos sub districta facias custodia detineri, donec quid de ipsis agendum sit plenius tibi ex nostra responsione mandetur. Si quos vero laicos deprehenderis inter eos, karissimo in Christo filio nostro illustri Anglorum regi tradas, illos pro meritis iudicandos, ut iudicio videlicet tam ecclesiastico quam mundano pestis illa que communiter omnibus pernitiosa dinoscitur cum suis actoribus condempnetur.

Data Verone xvii. kalendas Novembris.

Paris, BN lat. MS 3922 A, fol. 145 v; 1 Rot. 17.9; Gilb. 5.7.1; Fuld. 5.14.6; Est. 5.9.1; 2 Comp. 5.9.1. Pd 2 Comp. AF, Mansi 22 c. 482–483, Ordo iudiciorum, ed. A. P. Royer-Collard (1837) p. 21–22.

The inscription is determined by Idem eidem *in 1 Rot. (following* Ad hoc sumus, *JL 15208, WH –); the copy in BN lat MS 3922 A, fol. 145 v, lacks inscription, and all other copies have only* Lucius III. *The date is also supplied by 1 Rot., but BN lat. 3922 A, fol. 145 r, has the same date for* Ad hoc te credimus, *1 Rot. 19.4, JL –, WH 71, likewise of Lucius III to archbishop Walter of Coutances. It is possible that the attachment of the same date to two letters to the same recipient in the same codex is due to scribal error. The date has hitherto been given as 16 October 1184–1185, but Walter's translation from Lincoln to Rouen in the summer of 1184 was not confirmed until 17 November; the year of the decretal is therefore presumably 1185. The later collections and therefore the printed text refer to the forgery of public letters (*litteras publicas*), but the earliest copies in the Rouen codex show that the forgery of papal letters (*litteras apostolicas*) was in question. The text of 2 Comp. attaches the initial* R. *to the English king's title, but Lucius III died in 1185 and Richard did not succeed until 1189.*

18

Urban III to archbishop Walter of Rouen. Response to the archbishop's enquiry: clerical forgers of the French king's seal must be degraded and branded, and compelled to leave the province, but they must not be punished with the loss of limb or to the risk of death, and they must be allowed to depart.

WH 39; JL 15752. *1185–87.*

Urbanus III Waltero Rothomagensi archiepiscopo.

Ad audientiam nostram te significante pervenit quod, cum quosdam perversos clericos qui falsaverant sigillum carissimi in Christo filii nostri Phillipi illustris regis Francorum carcerali custodie mancipaveris, quid faciendum tibi sit de ipsis a sede apostolica duxisti inquirendum. Unde nos fraternitati tue de fratrum nostrorum consilio respondemus ut eis nec membrum auferri nec penam infligi facias per quam periculum possint mortis incurrere, sed eis prius a suis ordinibus degradatis in signum maleficii caracterem aliquem imprimi facias, quo inter alios cognoscantur et provinciam ipsam eos abiurare compellas et abire permittas.

1 Rot. 17.16; Gilb. 5.7.2; Fuld. 5.14.7; Est. 5.9.2; 2 Comp. 5.9.2; X 5.20.3. Pd 2 Comp. A; and abbreviated in X.

All collections name Urban III as the sender but only 1 Rot. identified archbishop W(alter) of Rouen as the recipient. Whereas king Philip of France appears generally as the king whose seal was forged, Est. names him as king H(enry) of the English.

19

Celestine III to the suffragans and dean of Rouen. Mandate: fearing that the letters of forgers recently found in Rome may be received as genuine, the pope orders the recipients to seize the (?) users of any such letters they can discover, by examination of the seal and curial style, pending papal instructions, and cancel anything done by the letters' use. [ambiguous, perhaps defective, text.]

WH 695; JL 17645. *Lateran 21 Dec. 1191.*

Celestine III suffraganeis et decano Rothomagensi.

Per falsarios qui nuper sunt in urbe reperti quedam sunt littere destinate quas timemus tamquam veras ab aliquibus admitti. Ideoque fraternitati vestre per apostolica scripta precipiendo mandamus quatinus, si quos tales valueritis invenire, quos cognoscere poteritis ex comparatione bulle et qualitate stili, faciatis eos omni dilatione postposita capi et tamdiu sub arcta custodia detineri, donec id nobis fuerit intimatum, ut quid exinde fieri debeat vobis significare possimus. Quicquid enim occasione illarum litterarum factum fuerit in irritum volumus revocari.

Datum Laterani xii. kalendas Januarii, pontificatus nostri anno primo.

Luc. 78; Hal. 49; Mon. 39; 2 Berol. 15; Crac. 100; Gilb. 5.7.3; Fuld. 5.14.8; 2 Comp. 5.9.3. Pd Luc., 2 Comp. AF.

The inscription is omitted in Mon.; elsewhere the collections name Celestine III as sender, except that his number is omitted in Hal. and Crac., and 2 Berol. has Idem; *the suffragans and dean of Rouen are identified in Luc., Hal., Crac., with the place-name defaced in 2 Berol. (which is largely illegible to* [cognos]cere poteritis*). The recipients are omitted in Gilb.,*

*Fuld., 2 Comp. The date is provided in 2 Berol. and Crac., and abbreviated in Hal. and Mon. Crac. provides an alternative reading of Canterbury (*vel Cantuarien.*) for Rouen. The problems of text and interpretation arising from the extant versions of the letter will be discussed in a separate study.*

20

Innocent III to the bishop of Verdun. Response to the bishop's consultation: concerning the putative papal letters presented to the bishop of Verdun by H. de sancto Stephano *on his own behalf, which the bishop considered suspect, the pope does not believe they were issued with his predecessor's knowledge, since they are ungrammatical.*

[WH 39 A; JL 15209] *(?) 1198–1201*

Innocentius III Virudenensi episcopo consulente.

Ad audientiam nostram te significante pervenit quod H. de sancto Stephano super absolutione sua litteras tibi ut prima facie videbatur apostolicas presentavit, quas quoniam habuisti suspectas nec de cancellaria ecclesie Romane emanasse putasti ad nos remittere curasti, consulens apostolicum nostrum, unde devotionem tuam in Domino commendamus, utrum occasione ipsarum prefatum virum debeas habere absolutum. Nos igitur litteris ipsis diligenter inspectis taliter tibi duximus respondendum quod, cum eas non credamus de predecessoris nostri conscientia emanasse, nullam eis fidem te volumus adhibere, cum manifestum contineant in constructione peccatum.

Complete: Sang. ap. 2; Tann. cod. fol. 591 r; Hal. 67; Mon. 96; 2 Berol. 25; Crac. 10; 1 Comp. Rot. 1.1.9; Gilb. W 1.2.3; Fuld. 1.2.3; 2 Alc. 3; 2 Comp. 1.2.5. Abbreviated in X 1.3.11. Pd 2 Comp. A; incomplete and paraphrased in X.

This letter of Innocent III is wrongly assigned to Lucius III in 2 Comp., and thence registered as JL 15209. The inscription is lacking in 2 Berol. (but Innocentius III Virdunensi episcopo *is attached in error to the preceding chapter), Crac., and 1 Comp. Rot. Innocent III is named in 2 Berol. (misplaced), Tann. cod. fol. 591 r, Sang. ap., Mon., Gilb. Br., and 2 Alc.; Hal. and X have* Idem. *The recipient is uniquely named bishop of London in Tann. cod. (see also The Letters of pope Innocent III [1198–1216] concerning England and Wales, ed. C. R. Cheney and M. Cheney [1967] p. 59 nr. 359, with the comment that the presence of the letter in Hal. suggests a date not later than 1201), but as bishop of Verdun in Sang. (*Vidun.: *Singer and WH read* Mdun.*), Mon. (*Virdun*) and 2 Alc. (*Viridenensi*), and misplaced in 2 Berol. (*Virdunensi*). Only an abbreviated and partly rephrased version survived in X, which omits* quas quoniam ... absolutum *(supplied in Friedberg's edition), and* *renders* Nos igitur . . . peccatum *as* Quibus quoniam manifestum continent in constructione peccatum, fidem te nolumus adhibere. *The balance of evidence suggests that Innocent III was responding in this letter to the bishop of Verdun who had challenged the authenticity of letters attributed to Celestine III. The identity of* H. de sancto Stephano *has not been established.*

Abbreviations

Canones-Sammlungen	=	*Emil* FRIEDBERG, *Die Canones-Sammlungen zwischen Gratian und Bernhard von Pavia (1897).*
CHENEY, *Roger of Worcester*	=	*Mary G.* CHENEY, *Roger, bishop of Worcester 1164–1179 (1980).*
Decretales ineditae	=	*Stanley* CHODOROW *and Charles* DUGGAN, *from the papers of W.* HOLTZMANN, *Decretales ineditae saeculi XII (MIC 4, 1982).*
DEETERS, *Bambergensisgruppe*	=	*Walter* DEETERS, *Die Bambergensisgruppe der Dekretalensammlungen des 12. Jahrhunderts (phil. Diss. Bonn 1954).*
DUGGAN, *Decretals of Alexander III*	=	*Charles* DUGGAN, *Decretals of Alexander III to England, in Miscellanea Rolando Bandinelli, papa Alessandro III, ed. F.* LIOTTA *(1986) p. 85–151.*
DUGGAN, *Decretal Collections*	=	*Charles* DUGGAN, *Twelfth-Century decretal collections and their importance in English history (University of London Historical Studies 12, 1963).*
HOLTZMANN-CHENEY	=	*Christopher R.* CHENEY *and Mary G.* CHENEY, *from the papers of W.* HOLTZMANN, *Studies in the collections of twelfth-century decretals (MIC 3, 1979).*
MANSI	=	*Sanctorum conciliorum nova et amplissima collectio, ed. J. D.* MANSI *(1759–1798).*
MIC	=	*Monumenta Iuris Canonici, Series B: Corpus Collectionum.*
Pd	=	*printed in*
SINGER, *Neue Beiträge*	=	*H.* SINGER, *Neue Beiträge über die Dekretalensammlungen vor und nach Bernhard von Pavia (SB Wien, 171, 1, 1913).*
WH	=	*Walther* HOLTZMANN, *Regesta decretalium saeculi XII (see Decretales ineditae, p. vii).*

Sigla of Decretal Collections

The complete list of all known decretal collections of the twelfth century, with full bibliographical details of editions, analyses and secondary literature, is provided in HOLTZMANN-CHENEY, *p. xx–xxxi, and Decretales ineditae p. xix–xxxi.*

1 Abr.	=	*Abrincensis Prima:* SINGER, *Neue Beiträge p. 355–400.*
Alan.	=	*Coll. Alani: R.* VON HECKEL, *ZRG Kan. 29 (1940) p. 226–334.*
1 Alc.	=	*Alcobacensis prima:* HOLTZMANN-CHENEY, *p. 8–25;* DUGGAN, *Studia Gratiana 14 (1967) p. 51–71;* IDEM, *Decretals of Alexander III p. 87–106.*

2 Alc.	=	*Alcobacensis secunda:* HOLTZMANN-CHENEY, *p. 297–299.*
Ambr.	=	*Ambrosiana:* HOLTZMANN-CHENEY, *p. 35–42.*
App.	=	*Appendix Concilii Lateranensis:*
Cr.	=	*editio princeps: Concilia omnia tam generalia quam particularia, ed. P.* CRABBE *(1551), 2 p. 820–944;* MANSI, *22 c. 248–453.*
Lp.	=	*Leipzig, Universitätsbibliothek 1242, fols. 73 v–110 v.*
V	=	*Vienna, Nationalbibliothek 2172, fols. 2 r–52 v.*
Ln.	=	*Lincoln, Cathedral Chapter Library 121, fols. 1 r–61 r:* HOLTZMANN-CHENEY, *p. 124–127.*
Aur.	=	*Aureavallensis: W.* HOLTZMANN, *ZRG Kan. 16 (1927) p. 77–115.*
Bamb.	=	*Bambergensis:* DEETERS, *Bambergensisgruppe:*
B	=	*Bamberg, Staatsbibliothek Can. 17 (P. I. 11), fols. 1 v–47 r.*
C	=	*Paris, Bibliothèque Nationale lat. 17971, fols. 153–184: as Compendiensis,* SINGER, *Neue Beiträge p. 8–67.*
O	=	*Oxford, Oriel College 53, fols. 340–349 v (olim 240–249).*
Belv.	=	*Belverensis:* DUGGAN, *Decretal Collections p. 71–73, 154–162 (numerical concordance with WH: 212).*
1 Berol.	=	*Berolinensis Prima: J.* JUNCKER, *ZRG Kan. 13 (1924) p. 284–426.*
2 Berol.	=	*Berolinensis Secunda:* HOLTZMANN-CHENEY, *p. 272-278.*
Bridl.	=	*Bridlingtonensis: Oxford, Bodleian Library Bodley 357 (S. C. 2452), fols. 80 r–133 v.*
Brug. B	=	*Brugensis: Canones-Sammlungen, p. 136–170.*
V	=	*Città del Vaticano, Bibl. Vat. Ottob. lat. 3027, fols. 1–111; W.* HOLTZMANN, *Über die vatikanische Handschrift der ‚Collectio Brugensis', in Collectanea Vaticana in honorem Anselmi M. Card. Albareda 1 (Studi e Testi 219, 1962) p. 391–414.*
1, 3 Cant.	=	*Cantuariensis prima, tertia:* DUGGAN, *Decretal Collections p. 73–76, 162–171, and pl. III (numerical concordance with WH: 212).*
Cass.	=	*Casselana: J. H.* BOEHMER, *Corpus iuris canonici 2 (1747) appendix p. 181–348;* DEETERS, *Bambergensisgruppe p. 7–9.*
Chelt.	=	*Cheltenhamensis: London, British Library Egerton 2819, fols. 11 r–102 r.*
2 Clar.	=	*Claravallensis Secunda:* HOLTZMANN-CHENEY, *p. 284–290.*
Claud.	=	*Claudiana: London British Library Cotton Claudius A. iv, fols. 193 r–220 r (olim 189 r–216 r);* HOLTZMANN-CHENEY, *p. 132–134.*
Claustr.	=	*Claustroneoburgensis: F.* SCHÖNSTEINER, *Jahrbuch des Stiftes Klosterneuburg 2 (1909) p. 1–154.*
1, 2 Comp.	=	*Compilatio prima, secunda:*
A	=	*Antiquae collectiones decretalium, ed. Antonio* AUGUSTÍN *(1576); reissued in Opera omnia 4 (1769).*

F	= *E. FRIEDBERG, Quinque compilationes antiquae necnon collectio canonum Lipsiensis (1882).*
1 Comp. Rot.	= *Compilatio prima, abbreviation with additions in Paris, Bibliothèque Nationale lat. 3922A, fols. 211r–227v: Stephan KUTTNER, Repertorium der Kanonistik: Prodromus corporis glossarum 1 (Studi e Testi 71, 1937) p. 313–314; HOLTZMANN-CHENEY, p. 138–139.*
Cott.	= *Cottoniana: London, British Library Cotton Vitellius E. xiii, fols. 204r–288r.*
Crac.	= *Cracoviensis: Cracow, Kapit. Katedr. 89, p. 129–147, 150–151; analyzed A. VETULANI, Studia źródłoznawcze/ Commentationes 8 (1963) p. 49–80.*
Cus.	= *Cusana: HOLTZMANN-CHENEY, p. 66–74.*
1 Dun.	= *Dunelmensis prima: HOLTZMANN-CHENEY, p. 75–99; DUGGAN, A Durham canonical manuscript of the late twelfth century, Studies in Church History 2 (1965) p. 179–185.*
2 Dun.	= *Dunelmensis secunda: HOLTZMANN-CHENEY, p. 300–318.*
Erl.	= *Erlangensis: Erlangen, Universitätsbibliothek 342, fols. 291–306: DEETERS, Bambergensisgruppe p. 9–10.*
Est.	= *Estensis: Modena, Bibl. Esten. α.R.4.16 (Lat. 968, olim XII.L.8), fols. 78r–117v.*
Flor.	= *Florianensis: HOLTZMANN-CHENEY, p. 43–63.*
Font.	= *Fontanensis: HOLTZMANN-CHENEY, p. 100–115.*
Frcf.	= *Francofortana:*
F	= *Frankfurt, Stadt- und Universitätsbibliothek, Barth. 60, fols. 2r–85r: S. KUTTNER, ZRG Kan. 22 (1933) p. 370–380.*
R	= *Paris, Bibliothèque Nationale lat. 3922A, fols. 173r–209r: HOLTZMANN-CHENEY, p. 160–168.*
T	= *Trecensis: Troyes, Bibliothèque de la Ville 961, fols. 1r–96v.*
M	= *St Maximin: London, British Library Egerton 2901, fols. 1r–97v.*
Fuld.	= *Fuldensis: HECKEL, ZRG Kan. 29 (1940) p. 165–170 and 353–359.*
Gilb.	= *Coll. Gilberti: HECKEL, p. 180–225.*
W	= *Fulda, Landesbibliothek D. 14, fols. 2–31v, and D. 5, fols. 84–139r: HECKEL, p. 120–121 and 124–125.*
Br.	= *Brussels, Bibliothèque Royale 1407–1409 (Cat. 2560), fols. 93–148v.*
Hal.	= *Hallensis: HOLTZMANN-CHENEY, p. 233–242.*
Lamb.	= *Lambethana: HOLTZMANN-CHENEY, p. 217–218.*
Lips.	= *Lipsiensis: E. FRIEDBERG, Quinque compilationes antiquae (1882) p. 189–208; DEETERS, Bambergensisgruppe p. 10–11.*
Luc.	= *Lucensis: HOLTZMANN-CHENEY, p. 243–271.*
Mon.	= *Monacensis: HOLTZMANN-CHENEY, p. 221–232.*
1 Par	= *Parisiensis prima: Canones-Sammlungen, p. 45–63.*

2 Par.	=	*Parisiensis secunda: Canones-Sammlungen, p. 21–45.*
Pet.	=	*Petrihusensis: Cambridge, Peterhouse 193, final quire; 114, first and final quires; 193, first quire; 203, final quire; 180, first and final quires.*
Reg.	=	*Regalis: London, British Library Royal 15 B. iv, fols. 107v–118v.*
Roff.	=	*Roffensis: DUGGAN, Decretal Collections p. 173–187 (numerical concordance with WH p. 212).*
1 Rot.	=	*Rotomagensis prima: HOLTZMANN-CHENEY, p. 160–207.*
Sang.	=	*Sangermanensis: SINGER, Neue Beiträge p. 68–354.*
Tann.	=	*Coll. Tanneri: W. HOLTZMANN, in Festschrift zur Feier des 200jähr. Bestehens der Akad. der Wissenschaften in Göttingen (1951) p. 83–145.*
1 Vict.	=	*Victorina prima: HOLTZMANN-CHENEY, p. 26–34.*
Wig.	=	*Wigorniensis: H. E. LOHMANN, Die Collectio Wigorniensis, ZRG Kan. 22 (1933) p. 36–187.*
Wig. alt.	=	*Wigorniensis altera: DUGGAN, Decretal Collections p. 152–154 and pl. I.*
X	=	*Decretales Gregorii IX: FRIEDBERG, Corpus iuris canonici 2 (1881).*

IX

EQUITY AND COMPASSION IN PAPAL MARRIAGE DECRETALS TO ENGLAND*

The sources of canon law in the twelfth century are rich in material concerning marriage and human sexual relations. Conciliar legislation, judicial rulings on individual cases and academic treatises, many still known in manuscript only, together confront the scholar with a vast and intricate maze of doctrinal definitions, analyses and speculations. The period was one of the most intellectually creative phases in the history of canon law, alike for marriage questions and for many other themes, in which principles were by degrees clarified to form a moral, ethical and contractual system of marriage law with enduring consequences, many indeed effective even today. It is not proposed here to deal with the canon law of marriage in its juristic or theological essence or evolution, a task on which numerous scholars have long been and are still engaged, but rather to discuss the ways in which the law was applied or abrogated in specific circumstances. In this way we may hope to disclose facets of human society and the flexibility of the papal curia

* The footnotes of this paper are directed almost wholly to the texts of decretal letters, since the language and tenor of the papal judgments are the primary interest of the present study. Each letter is identified by a WH number, following the system of numeration adopted by the late Walther Holtzmann. A forthcoming *regesta* of all twelfth-century decretals and a volume of texts previously unprinted are based on the Holtzmann files, now deposited at the Institute of Medieval Canon Law in the University of California at Berkeley. WH references used here provide the location of each item in the *regesta* and in the volume of texts, the latter being designated 'new edition' in the notes below. All letters addressed to the British Isles in these projected volumes have been assigned to the present writer, and all others to Professor Stanley Chodorow. It would not be possible to express sufficient thanks to Professor Stephan Kuttner, President of the Institute, for providing congenial access to the Holtzmann papers through many years, and for directing these projects towards their completion. Additionally, the footnotes cite a JL number for each letter if it is listed in the *Regesta Pontificum Romanorum* (ed. P. Jaffé, S. Loewenfeld *et al.*, II, Leipzig, 1888), and an *X* number if it is found in the *Decretales Gregorii IX* (*Corpus Iuris Canonici*, II, ed. E. Friedberg, Leipzig, 1881). The abbreviations *1 Comp.* and *2 Comp.* note decretal locations in *Compilatio I* or *Compilatio II* (*Quinque Compilationes Antiquae necnon Compilatio Lipsiensis*, ed. E. Friedberg, Leipzig, 1882), if the texts were transmitted to either of those collections, but did not survive into the official collection of Gregory IX. The most accurate dating at present available for each letter is also given.

in matching its judgments to the context of each dispute. It is an axiomatic function of the papal office to dispense justice in its most perfect sense, to declare the law unambiguously, and to administer it with discrimination and humanity. Towards the mid-twelfth century, Gratian summed up the papal rights of law-giving and dispensation, in asserting that the *prima sedes* has the right to lay down laws, but is not itself bound by them. As the framer of laws, it has the right to dispense from them; but it is the mother of justice, and therefore should not deviate from reason and equity[1]. It is the main conclusion of this essay that the popes of the later twelfth century, from Alexander III to Celestine III, applied the laws of marriage with these high and difficult ideals in mind.

The evidence on which this judgment is based is found chiefly in the many collections of decretal letters, originating in the 1170s and culminating in the official *Decretales* of Gregory IX in 1234. It is well known that one of the five component books of that authoritative work is devoted wholly to marriage, its opening section entitled '*De sponsalibus et matrimoniis*', following the pattern of Bernard of Pavia's *Compilatio Prima* of 1190. Indeed, from the earliest phase of decretal compilation, collectors had recognized the importance of the most recent papal rulings on marriage questions, and brought them together in a coherent and orderly sequence. For instance, the primitive Worcester Collection of *c.* 1181 was devised in seven books, of which the first was named '*De statu et iure coniugii sive contracti sive contrahendi*'[2]. But not all relevant matter was assembled under these headings. The large problems of clerical marriage or concubinage

[1] *Decretum*, C. XXV, qu. 1, *dict.* post c. 16. The juristic concepts of equity and reason, *aequitas* and *ratio*, are not analysed here, though they are a necessary backcloth. Cf. the excellent study by G. Lesage, 'La "Ratio canonica" d'après Alexandre III', *Proceedings of the Fourth International Congress of Medieval Canon Law*, ed. S. Kuttner, in *Monumenta Iuris Canonici, Series C: Subsidia*, 5 (Città del Vaticano, 1976), p. 95-106; see also P.G. Caron, '"Aequitas et interpretatio" dans la doctrine canonique aux xiiie et xive siècles', *Proceedings of the Third International Congress of Medieval Canon Law*, ed. S. Kuttner, in *MIC, Series C: Subsidia*, 4 (1971), p. 131-41; and R. Weigand, 'Kanonistische Ehetraktate aus dem 12. Jahrhundert', *ibid.*, p. 59-79. The fundamental works by A. Esmein and J. Dauvillier provide a general survey of the canon law of marriage in the period, and valuable insights for the present essay are found in the publications of professors C.N.L. Brooke, J.A. Brundage, C. Donahue, G. Fransen, R. Helmholz, J.T. Noonan, and other scholars; cf. esp. R. Weigand, *Die bedingte Eheschliessung im kanonischen Rechts*, 1 (München, 1963), with an important bibliography of sources and secondary literature.

[2] H.-E. Lohmann, 'Die Collectio Wigorniensis', *Zeitschrift der Savigny-Stiftung für Rechtsgeschichte, Kan. Abt.*, 22 (1933), p. 39-40 and 79-89.

and that of family inheritance of churches are dealt with in sections concerned with the state of the clergy, or the state and rights of churches. Moreover, as collectors became more juristically skilled, they selected and truncated material rather drastically, dissected or edited the letters, and frequently omitted some or even all historical details, intent simply on preserving definitions of legal principle or procedure. The familiar printed editions of famous collections are therefore less useful for our purpose. They omit many letters known in the earlier collections, and the excerpts which they retain frequently have no knowledge of those papal phrases and finely balanced judgments which record the pope's humanity, common sense or caution in a specific dilemma. It was common enough for a decretal to embody a clear definition of law, but also to dispense from its enforcement in the case in hand. Through generations of textual transmission, an excerpted statement of the point of law might survive, at times without trace of the human context, or alternatively the full scope of the original letter might be lost. Two examples from the Gregorian collection will suffice to illustrate respectively these defects. *Proposuit nobis*, from Alexander III to Bartholomew of Exeter, expressly recorded the pope's compassion in dispensing from the general law in the case of a certain son succeeding in his father's church. Its revealing phrase '*interna mentis affectione compatimur*' did not survive transmission into the official collection, although in this instance Friedberg's edition reinserted the passage which he recovered from earlier sources[3]. Again, *Preterea de his*, from Alexander to the bishop of Winchester, records in the 1234 collection that an appeal to the apostolic see should not be exploited as a protection for subsequent transgression[4]. But this chapter was simply one paragraph of the longer letter *Suggestum est*

[3] Cf. n. 25, below. In his edition of *X*, Friedberg prints such reconstructions in italic. At the same time, his inscription for this letter is inaccurate, giving 'Idem (*scil.* Alexander III) Oxonensi episcopo', a typical misreading for 'Exoniensi'. The details of the same letter are also faulty in the most accessible edition of the early systematic collection *Appendix Concilii Lateranensis*, which has the abbreviated address 'Idem B.' only, and the internal reading 'in tanta mentis affectione compatimur' for the phrase in question (cf. J.D. Mansi, ed., *Sacrorum conciliorum nova et amplissima collectio*, XXII [Venetiis 1778], col. 354: *App.* 19.6). The correct forms are found in the Lincoln MS of the *Appendix* (Lincoln Chapter Library MS 121, fol. 29r) and in other collections. The primitive collection *Alcobacensis prima* (Lisbon, Bibl. nac. cod. Alcob. 144 [314], fol. 27r: *1 Alc.* 79), completed in Portugal not much later than 1181, has been used for the present discussion. Similar textual problems could be cited for many of the decretals examined in this paper, for which the extracts cited are transcribed from the original manuscripts.

[4] *X* 2.28.22, JL 14152, 1159-81.

nobis, whose opening topic related to clerical marriage and even priestly concubinage in the Winchester diocese. That section is not found in the official corpus, yet it contains a papal admonition of much interest for our present purpose. Alexander counselled prudence and discretion in all such matters — '*In quibus omnibus cum ea cautela et providentia et maturitate procedere te convenit quod circumspectio tue sollicitudinis valeat commendabilis apparere*'[5].

Our enquiry must therefore be pressed back into the many earlier collections. But, to confine the material within manageable limits, decretal letters to England only will be considered here. On the other hand, the description 'marriage decretal' is very broadly applied and includes all social conditions or relationships which have a sexual aspect or implication — marriage questions in their normal connotation, illicit or extra-marital associations, inheritance disputes, illegitimacy, the age of consent, clandestine marriages, clerical liaisons, and so forth. In round numbers about 80 decretals to England deal with such problems or at least make some significant reference to them, of which barely half survived into the official *Decretales*, some in an extremely attenuated form. The recovery of evidence is therefore very substantial, and provides nine marriage decretals hitherto unprinted[6]. Moreover, more than 50 further letters to England concern the sons of priests or clerks, and three of these are previously unpublished texts[7]. Against the fact that about 1100 decretals are known from the collections of the period for the whole of Western Christendom and on all subjects, this harvest of English marriage cases and evidence of clerical liaisons is of crucial value, alike for social and legal history[8].

[5] WH 1004; otherwise as n. 4, above: *Suggestum est nobis* is not known either in *X* or JL, but was printed by Friedberg in his analysis of the primitive French collection *Parisiensis prima* (cf. *Die Canones-Sammlungen zwischen Gratian und Bernhard von Pavia*, Leipzig 1897, p. 55: *1 Par.* 52), and has been later found in other collections: cf. Lohmann, *Collectio Wigorniensis*, p. 102-03, no. 3.14, and p. 75-6. *Preterea de his* is found with variant incipits in many collections: cf. Lohmann, *ibid.*, p. 103.

[6] In addition to hitherto unprinted decretals discussed below, cf. WH 26 and 937; all will appear in the new edition.

[7] Cf. WH 893, 923 and 1054; these also will appear in the new edition.

[8] From the large secondary literature useful for the work in hand, see esp. A. Morey, *Bartholomew of Exeter: Bishop and Canonist* (Cambridge, 1937); W. Holtzmann and E.W. Kemp, ed., *Papal Decretals relating to the Diocese of Lincoln in the Twelfth Century*, in *Lincoln Record Society*, 47 (1954); A. Morey and C.N.L. Brooke, *Gilbert Foliot and his Letters* (Cambridge, 1965); and J.E. Sayers. *Papal Judges Delegate in the Province of Canterbury* (London, 1971). Cf. C. Duggan, *Twelfth-Century Decretal Collections and their Importance in English History* (London, 1963). There is a list of decretals to Gilbert Foliot in Morey and Brooke, ed., *The Letters and Charters of*

Numerous decretals deal with the sensitive problems of clerical incontinence or of clerks' sons holding ecclesiastical benefices. Their context is above all the insistence of the reformed papacy on clerical celibacy and the related question of inheritance of benefices and church property. Certainly, there is evidence of widespread abuse in the English Church, and of a sustained effort to counter its effects[9]. But it may not be taken for granted that the weight of evidence proves that the abuse was more prevalent in the English Church than elsewhere, since it is now generally accepted that the extant decretals reflect in their regional ratios the provenance of the canonical collections, rather than the numbers actually sent out from the curia[10]. Nor can it be assumed that the sons of clerks were all the result of invalid or illicit unions. Even so, general and individual condemnations of unlawful liaisons or uncanonical successions provide a formidable proportion of all surviving English decretals, and these recorded cases are presumably but a fraction of the total number. There can be no doubt that large numbers of English clerks lived the lives of married laymen. If this were not already known from narrative sources, it would be clearly revealed by the canonical collections. Concubinage without a form of marriage was unacceptable for all clergy, but a valid marriage was possible for clerks in minor orders. Alexander III expressed a general censure in two letters to archbishop Richard of Canterbury. *Cum in Cantuariensi* mandated the Archbishop to discipline the many clerks keeping concubines in their houses. If such were obstinate, they must be despoiled of their churches[11]. More strongly still, *Sicut ad extirpanda* was addressed jointly to Canterbury and its suffragans. The depraved and hateful custom of clerks keeping concubines has long been a scandal in England. Such clerks in the subdiaconate or above must put away the women within forty days, or be suspended from benefice, and finally

Gilbert Foliot (Cambridge, 1967), p. 525-29. See now Mary G. Cheney, *Roger, Bishop of Worcester, 1164-1179* (Oxford, 1980); cf. also *eadem*, 'Pope Alexander III and Roger, Bishop of Worcester, 1164-79: The Exchange of Ideas', *Proceedings of the Fourth International Congress of MCL*, p. 207-27. Dom Adrian Morey's work on Alexander III's marriage decretals to Bartholomew of Exeter is particulary valuable; the thesis of the present essay accords with Morey's acceptance of the view that 'leniency and commonsense' characterized Alexander's judgments: cf. *op. cit.*, p. 66-72 *et passim*.

[9] Cf. C.N.L. Brooke, 'Gregorian Reform in Action: Clerical Marriage in England, 1050-1200' in *Cambridge Historical Journal*, 12 (1956), p. 1-21; cf. M. Cheney, 'Pope Alexander III', p. 211-13.

[10] Cf. Duggan, *Decretal Collections*, p. 140-51, *et alibi*.

[11] WH 255(a), JL 13810, *1 Comp*. 3.2.9, 1174-79.

perpetually deprived if they do not comply. Below the subdiaconate, those who have married must relinquish their benefices and retain their wives[12]. The decretal *Ad aures nostras*, to the bishop of London, dealt with the problem in its second paragraph. Clerks, either in holy orders or minor orders, must put away their concubines. If they fail to do so at the second or third warning, and do not undertake not to take them back, they must be deprived of their churches or portions and must not be allowed to celebrate[13].

A two-fold distinction has thus been made between major and minor orders, and between marriage and concubinage in minor orders. Since no valid marriage was possible in or above the subdiaconate, all liaisons of clerks in those ranks were illicit and involved concubinage, and therefore the women must be put away. But below the subdiaconate, whereas all concubinage was likewise illicit, valid marriage could be contracted. Clerks in minor orders who were married must remain in the married state and relinquish their churches. This distinction is drawn in several extant letters of Alexander III, in addition to those already mentioned, including mandates to the bishops of Winchester and Worcester, and a further letter to the bishop of London[14]. The hitherto unprinted decretal *De clericis concubinariis*, to bishop Robert of Hereford, adds the sound advice that dismissed concubines may not remain in the parish of the offence or nearby, where access may readily be had to them, and is very explicit in its distinct instructions concerning the marriage or concubinage of clerks in minor orders[15]. Still further letters of Alexander III leave the law in no doubt, but reveal his concern and circumspection. *Universalis ecclesie*, to Gilbert Foliot of London, speaks of the very many clerics in the bishop's diocese who took wives while in the rank of acolyte or under, but presumed to retain their churches. Therefore, in this married state, they are divided in their interests, and should understand that they cannot both please their wives and perform their liturgical duties, since they are unable to give their undivided attention to divine service. The bishop must remedy this situation, and compel them to put aside their churches, which should be granted to suitable persons

[12] WH 927, JL 13813, *X* 3.2.4 and 3.3.1, 1174-81.

[13] WH 45(b), JL 13992, *X* 3.2.6, 1163-81.

[14] Cf. WH 589(a) and (c), JL 12254, *1 Comp.* 3.3.4 and 3.2.6, 26 November 1164: to Roger of Worcester; WH 961, JL 14222, 1163-81: to Gilbert Foliot of London; WH 1004(a), 1159-81: to the bishop of Winchester: cf. nn. 4 and 5, above.

[15] WH 332(a), new edition, 1164-67 or 1174-81.

in holy orders. The clerks in question may retain '*sub dissimulatione*' a simple benefice held in those churches, but they may not have churches in their care[16]. The pope's regard for public propriety and the avoidance of scandal is clear from his letter *Ex parte prioris* to the bishop of Worcester, in which he condemns the alleged behaviour of a priest who keeps a concubine and frequents taverns like a layman — '*quia indecens et rationi contrarium est, ut hii qui altario serviunt feminarum complexibus maculentur aut per tabernas discurrant, cum eos sobrios et castos esse opporteat*'[17]. With a wise attention to circumstances, he instructed Bartholomew of Exeter in the decretal *Significatum est nobis*. It is evident that the behaviour of certain subdeacons of the Exeter diocese or living there is contrary to law, since they have presumed to contract marriages and live with their wives like laymen, but the bishop should carefully discover what manner of lives they had previously led, and what kind of lives could be expected of them if they put away their wives. He should compel those who were honourable and might live chastely again to dismiss the women. But, if they were previously dissolute, and likely to fall into worse behaviour under constraint, their offence could be dissimulated to avoid a graver fault. The latter may not, however, celebrate divine office or receive benefices, and if they hold parsonages they must either put away their wives or resign their churches[18]. In such cases the law was not in doubt but the pope was faced with a most serious dilemma, in which he strove to ensure the maximum attainable virtue and the least deterioration.

An unusually hazardous problem was raised by Robert Foliot of Hereford, on which Alexander advised him in *Super eo quod*, a letter dealing with a series of questions put to him by the bishop. The latter reported that he could not deal with the abuse resulting from long-standing grants of benefices made by his predecessors to married clerks in inferior orders. Great danger, even to the shedding of blood, might result from the attempt to deprive them. A violent and ill-disciplined society was in question, and doubtless the geographical location of the Hereford diocese is the context, especially since the letter included an earlier reference to the uncanonical customs of the bishops of Scotland and Wales. The extreme difficulties permit discretion —

[16] WH 1041, JL 14267, *1 Comp.* 3.3.2, 1 March 1171-81.

[17] WH 464, JL 14135, *1 Comp.* 3.2.11, 1164-79.

[18] WH 962, JL 13904, *1 Comp.* 4.6.3, 1162-81; cf. Morey, *Bartholomew of Exeter*, p. 92.

'*quia ibi natio et gens barbara est et multitudo in causa, eos sub dissimulatione sustineas*'. But the bishop must take care that benefices are not conferred on married clerks in future, and no such clerks are to be admitted to sacred orders or the administration of churches, unless they have taken a vow of perpetual chastity and have had no more than one wife — '*qui unicam et virginem habuerint uxorem*'[19].

The very large number of decretals which refer to the sons of priests or clerks affords further evidence of the prevalence of clerical marriage or cohabitation, and so the status of the sons of the clergy provides a reflected vision of their parents' relationships. Most decretals in this category are not, however, concerned with the morality or legality of the liaisons, but more typically with their consequences, especially in respect of benefice inheritance, eligibility for ordination, and fitness of character for celebration of the divine office. The matter arises most commonly in disputed benefices, but it must not be supposed that all accusations of clerical parentage were truthful. Such allegations were a useful weapon in litigation, especially if coupled with the charge that the clerical father had previously ministered in the church in question. Thus, in *Conquerente nobis*, Alexander III wrote to bishop Roger of Worcester in favour of the clerk Milo against the priest Roger over the church of St Mary at Droitwich, on the grounds that Roger was the son of a priest and born in the priesthood, his father having ministered in the same church[20]. Milo enjoyed the favour of the patron, and the pope ordered that he should secure possession of the church if he was otherwise suitable. But bishop Roger's diligent enquiries established the charges as false, that Roger was not born in the priesthood, nor was it established that his father had been vicar or parson in the church disputed. So Alexander wrote to him again, and in the revised judgment *Intelleximus ex litteris* reversed his decision, now in Roger's favour, despite the fact that Milo had the support of the '*dominus fundi*'. The case is of unusual interest, since the overturned judgment was widely received in decretal collections and was finally transmitted into the official collection of 1234, whereas the revised decision is found only in the primitive Worcester Collection of *c.* 1181[21]. The legal definition is not in dispute. The later collectors accepted the formulation of the first

[19] WH 1017(f), JL 13946, *X* 3.3.2, 1174-81.
[20] WH 143, JL 14138, *X* 1.17.4, 1164-79.
[21] WH 577, 1164-79; cf. Lohmann, *Collectio Wigorniensis*, p. 115: no. 4.39.

judgment as valid, as indeed it was, doubtless unaware of the fraudulent charges which gave rise to it.

It is not surprising that Alexander III and his successors condemned the possession of churches as if by hereditary right, since the principle was well established in canonical tradition and reinforced by more recent conciliar legislation. Alexander's view is perhaps nowhere more clearly expressed than in his letter *Ex parte Matthei*, to bishop Bartholomew of Exeter — '*quia non est consentaneum rationi, ut filii parentibus in ecclesiis succedere debeant, cum sanctuarium Dei non possit iure hereditario possideri*'[22]. On another occasion, he mandated bishop Gilbert of London and at least one other colleague to root out the practice in their areas, having heard of clerks within the recipients' jurisdiction, who were sons of priests and born in the priesthood, yet ministered in their fathers' churches — '*successiones huiusmodi ab ecclesie Dei limina sunt penitus extirpande*'. This decretal, *Ad audientiam nostram*, declared that priests' sons who have been ordained to the priesthood may not celebrate unless they have first ministered in a religious community, and Alexander's letter *Quod super his*, to bishop Hugh of Durham, ordered in a similar sense that priests' sons cannot be promoted to the diaconate or priesthood unless their lives have been tested in a monastery or house of canons regular, and they have worn the religious habit[23]. Nevertheless, there was room for flexibility and compassion for the human predicaments which were sometimes brought to light. Alexander III decided in favour of a priest who claimed that he had held his church for thirty years, and that he was not the son of a priest, whereas the papal decree of prohibition had been promulgated against priests' sons. Alexander's reply, *Significavit nobis*, to bishops Bartholomew of Exeter and Richard of Winchester, exonerated the priest from a retrospective penalty, asserting that new constitutions give shape only to future affairs, and ordered that the priest should not be harassed further if he had held the church a long time before the council of Tours and was otherwise suitable[24]. Still more striking, as an example of individual dispensation, is the same pope's *Proposuit nobis*, to Bartholomew of Exeter. The pope commends the bishop's prudence in declining to entrust the cure of

[22] WH 460, 1174-80.

[23] WH 29, JL 14223, 1163-81; and WH 823, JL 13869, *1 Comp*. 1.9.5, 1159-81.

[24] WH 974, JL 14224, 1174-81; cf. Morey, *Bartholomew of Exeter*, p. 56. Some collections name the bishops of Exeter and Worcester as the recipients; the church in question was that of Meppershall in Bedfordshire.

souls to a certain clerk who was a priest's son, though the clerk was presented to the church by the '*dominus fundi*'. But he looks with affectionate compassion on the clerk who had laboured to come to present his case in the curia, and decides that it is not fitting that an ordained subdeacon should have no share in a benefice. The bishop should find some honest priest with the consent of the clerk to serve in the church, but the clerk should also serve there in his order for the rest of his life and receive half of all its benefices[25]. A similar clemency is recorded in the letter *Ex parte R.*, undoubtedly English in provenance but of unknown address. A poor clerk had complained to the pope that he was harassed by a certain G. Ruffus, who may be fairly conjectured as dean Guy of Waltham, on a charge that he was the son of the previous minister in his church, which he has possessed for almost thirty years. His accuser has ample means, whereas he has none other, and is seriously disabled, having lost the sight of an eye and the hearing of one ear. Alexander states that it is right for him to show compassion to ecclesiastics, especially if burdened by continuing infirmity. If therefore the clerk has held the church so long, since he has no other benefice and is gravely disabled, he should be given possession[26]. It is clear that the pope was more frequently concerned to stress that hereditary right to churches should be broken, than that a judgment should be delivered against the person involved, as is evident from such letters as *Significavit nobis*, from Alexander III or Lucius III, to the abbots of Leicester and Rufford and the jurist Vacarius. The pope permitted the son to hold the church, provided that another incumbent, even his brother, had intervened between the father and the son — '*id ei misericorditer indulgemus, si inter ipsum et illum qui pater suus dicebatur fratris sui vel alicuius alterius intercesserit persone mediatio*'[27].

Many intricate marriage disputes were brought to the papal curia; requiring a definition of marital status or conjugal obligations. Among the English cases, a significant number involved powerful English families, frequently reflecting dynastic and territorial interests. Projected marriage alliances or inheritance rights could depend on papal rulings concerning legitimacy, the validity of an existing marriage, the impediments of affinity or consanguinity and so forth. The identity

[25] WH 751, JL 14217, *X* 1.17.6, 1162-81; cf. at n. 3, above. The church in this case was that of Aylesbeare in Devon.

[26] WH 465, 1159-81(?).

[27] WH 975, 1159-81 or 1181-85.

of the litigants is not always clear from the printed editions, but the following have been positively identified in papal letters subsumed into collections of canon law: Richard of Anstey, Hugh de Ralegh, earl Roger of Hereford and earl Hugh de Lacy, Mary, daughter of Gilbert of St Leger, members of the Arderne family, William FitzGodric (linked by marriage with the Lacy of Pontefract dynasty), and William I and William III de Roumare, earls of Lincoln. In addition, many noble men and women, knights and other persons of rank appear, often no longer identifiably, and it is a matter of great interest that the marriage disputes of the English upper classes contributed so substantially to the corpus of decretal law. Some of these papal rulings have an important place in the central history of marriage law, as witnessed by Innocent II's *Super eo quod* to Henry of Winchester in the well-known Anstey case, the pope defining that with the intervention of lawful consent the parties are married immediately from that moment when each willingly agreed to be the spouse of the other[28]. Others more readily suit our present theme, in recording papal concern to reach a workable compromise in the actual circumstances. Two letters of Alexander III to Roger of York concern the marriage of William FitzGodric to Aubrey de Lisours, the Lacy of Pontefract heiress, the canonical issue revolving round an earlier betrothal between William and Aubrey's daughter, allegedly below the age of consent at that time. It is evident that powerful material interests were at stake, one decretal asserting that the English king had given the mother in marriage to William. The pope was placed in some difficulty, as a result of conflicting testimony, the obduracy of the parties, and the extreme pressures brought to bear on the case. He affirmed the various points of law arising — in the earlier letter, *Ex litteris fraternitatis*, he ruled against the second union, and in the later mandate, *Accessit ad presentiam*, he declared that betrothals and marriages were not possible before the age of seven, especially if consent has not followed. But his final judgment is that William and Aubrey may remain united, lest the discord which had been quietened between the families should be recreated — '*id dissimulare poteris et equanimiter tolerare*'. Moreover, the marriage being tolerated by the Church, the children of the marriage cannot be deprived of their inheritance — '*a successione*

[28] WH 1016, JL 8274, *1 Comp.* 4.1.10, 1139-41; cf. P.M. Barnes, 'The Anstey Case' in *Medieval Miscellany for Doris Mary Stenton*, Pipe Roll Society, new series, 36 (1962), 1-24.

paterne vel materne hereditatis'[29]. The case of Hugh de Ralegh, sheriff of Devon, is no less interesting. In a decretal *Pervenit ad audientiam*, to Bartholomew of Exeter, Alexander dealt with a charge of consanguinity which had been brought against the marriage of Hugh and his wife Muriel. Remarking that this is a matter of great discretion, the pope orders the bishop to summon the parties before him, if persons have come forward who wish to and are able to question the legitimacy of the marriage. He should discover how long Hugh and Muriel had lived together, and whether their accusers had kept silence at the time of the marriage. It would be a grave matter to hear their complaints now, if they were knowingly silent at the time of the union. It is more tolerable to leave together those who have been joined against the laws of men than to separate, against the laws of God, those who have been lawfully united. But, if the marriage was recent and the accusers did not know of it at the appropriate time, local evidence should be carefully weighed, and a decision reached in harmony with the law[30]. Two further letters concern the case of Mary, daughter of Gilbert of St Leger — *Ex litteris quas*, to archbishop Richard of Canterbury, and *Ex litteris venerabilis*, to his suffragan bishops of Winchester, Bath and Hereford, to whom the case was commissioned. Gilbert had betrothed Mary to a certain R. in her absence, and later a marriage was contracted in her presence '*per verba presentis temporis*', so that nothing was lacking save the solemnities '*in facie ecclesie*', it being then Lent. The young man seemingly changed his mind later and solemnly married Matilda, daughter of Hugh of Polstead, despite the ban of archbishop Richard. The matter was brought to judgment. The young man confessed the facts of the case, claiming that he proceeded to the marriage with Matilda '*prava quorundam suggestione seductum*'; but Mary asserted that the complaint had been brought by her father against her will, and Matilda demanded that R. be restored to her. The women were said to be related, and fears of adultery and incest arose. Mary appealed to the pope, and relying on this protection married W., in spite of threatened excommunication. Alexander says that he cannot solve this case in the absence of the parties, and so entrusts it to his commissioners,

[29] WH 12, JL 13887, *X* 4.2.5, *c.* 1175; and WH 420, new edition, *c.* 1168-75. The dispute and the probable dates of the letters are discussed in the forthcoming edition of new texts.

[30] WH 701, JL 14214, *1 Comp.* 4.19.3, 1162-67; cf. Morey, *Bartholomew of Exeter*, p. 67-68.

enjoining that the second marriage shall be observed, if the promise of Mary and R. is the only impediment. Second vows should not be taken against the Church's prohibition, but it is not fitting — '*non est tamen conveniens*' — that a solemn sacrament of marriage be dissolved for that reason alone. Once more Alexander sought to tread an equitable path through conflicting claims and interests, and it may well be judged in this instance that his '*conveniens*' solution was indeed the most appropriate in human terms and in harmony with canonical equity[31]. Still further but mutually unrelated commissions involved the great family de Roumare. In *Significavit nobis* Alexander III appointed the abbot of Fountains and the jurist Vacarius to settle a dispute in which the deceased William I de Roumare was alleged to have constrained the plaintiff with prison and chains to swear to marry the lady Ha. He later escaped and married another, who bore him sons. But, at the instigation of Ha., he was compelled to swear that he would separate from the other woman, pending ecclesiastical judgment. Now, Ha. has since died, and he dares not return to the second. The judges are instructed to reach a judgment appropriate to the facts established by their enquiry[32]. A second letter, *Comes Willelmus*, was sent by Celestine III to Hugh of Lincoln. Earl William III de Roumare had secretly confessed that his wife had been instigated by others to suggest that their marriage was suspect by reason of consanguinity, and therefore sought an annulment. He was so incensed by his wife's contempt of him, although he did not believe the charge, that he neither denied it nor appealed to the pope, and a separation ensued. Both parties subsequently married other persons, but now the earl is smitten in conscience and has asked the bishop's advice. The pope notes the earl's scruple of conscience, but declares that he should not now abandon the second or deny her conjugal rights. He must do penance as enjoined by the bishop, and in relations with the second consort accept that she has the right to require the conjugal debt from him, yet he has lost the right to demand it of her[33]. It may be wondered what reliance the pope felt able to place on the testimony

[31] WH 426(a), JL 13793, *X* 4.1.7, 5 February 1175-81; and WH 439, JL 14311, *X* 4.16.2, 5 February 1175-81.

[32] WH 973, JL 13937, *X* 4.7.2, 30 June 1177; cf. Holtzmann and Kemp, *Decretals to Lincoln*, p. 20-21, no. 8, where Oliver Angevinus is conjectured as the identity of the plaintiff.

[33] WH 133, JL 16611, *2 Comp.* 4.13.2, 15 April-25 October 1191; cf. Holtzmann and Kemp, *Decretals to Lincoln*, p. 56-57, no. 23, where the two women are identified as Alice and Philippa, the latter being the daughter of Jean I, count of Alençon.

in such a case, or how he assessed the motivation of the plaintiff, or indeed what hope he held of the implementation of his judgment in the case of so powerful an impetrant.

We should not expect to find a general disquisition on love and marriage in papal decretals, yet there is ample evidence of the importance attached by the popes to marital affection, to mutual responsibilities, to care for children, to a fair solution if alienation arises, to the eradication of abuse, and at least to discretion in potentially scandalous situations. Alexander III expressed a broad concern for the welfare of wives in the decretal *Relatum est auribus*, to the archbishop of Canterbury and his suffragans generally. He has heard that there are such in the Canterbury province who abandon their wives and adhere to concubines, and even attempt to defend and foster their fault by appeals. They must be constrained to take back their wives and treat them with marital affection[34]. Thus the general law was stated, but a better insight into its application and the many complications arising is provided by a consideration of cases. Bartholomew of Exeter received many letters from Alexander III to aid the solution of particular marriage disputes. In *Ex presentium latoris* the pope advised him in the affair of one of his subjects who confessed to adultery with the wife of another, repeated the offence after accepting penance, married the woman after her husband's death, and still retains her as his wife. Alexander was well aware of the possibility of collusion in such a chain of events, and instructed the bishop accordingly. If he finds that either party was involved in any way with the husband's death, or if the man promised marriage before that event, the two must be separated forthwith. Otherwise, the bishop may go forward to a canonical settlement[35]. Another of Alexander's letters, *Super eo quod*, instructed Bartholomew on a number of marriage questions. If a certain subject of the bishop has married a woman whose mother or sister he had already known, are they both bound to the conjugal debt? Further, what is to be done if the man has confessed his fault in secret, since it cannot be proven and he does not wish to remain continent? The bishop is admonished to advise the man to persuade his wife to observe continence so that they may both remain in that state. If they cannot be so induced, the man must accept penance and also render his wife her due. A further question concerns those who

[34] WH 868(a), JL 13823, *1 Comp.* 2.20.21, 1174-81.

[35] WH 474, JL 13900, 1162-81.

have made a pure and unconditional promise to marry and have taken an oath. They must be exhorted by every means to fulfil their promise and be joined in marriage. If, however, they wish mutually to remit their promise, lest worse befall — as if one takes a partner whom he or she will always hate — this can be accepted with patient toleration [36]. Yet again, in *Veniens ad nos*, Alexander discussed the case of Bartholomew's subject R., who confessed that he had married the cousin of a woman he had already known, and has tearfully asked the pope to advise him for the good of his soul. The pope declares that if the facts are so, or if others come forward who wish to and can prove them so, and if the sin was public and notorious, he should be induced to enter the religious life; failing this, he must accept penance and be separated from both women without hope of marriage. But if the bishop knows his sin was secret, he may remain with her whom he took as wife '*in facie ecclesie*', accepting a suitable penance [37]. In all such cases Alexander was anxious to reach a just and feasible solution, combining pastoral care with the public good of Christian society. His insistence on an equitable judgment is seen still more strikingly in the decretal *Singulorum consultationibus*, to abbot Simon of St Albans, concerning a man who, being already married, joined with another who was unaware of his earlier marriage. He lived long with the second, and she bore him several sons. But on the death of his wife he attempted to abandon the second woman, alleging that their union was unlawful. The pope agreed that such was indeed the law, since no one could have as his wife the one with whom he had committed adultery, especially her to whom he gave his promise while his wife was still alive; but it was unfitting for that man to seek advantage from an offence which he had knowingly committed. The innocent woman could seek a separation, but not the man, lest he would seem to benefit from his sin — '*cum de suo delicto videretur commodum reportare*' [38].

A similar concern for protective justice is revealed in the same pope's letter *Ex parte Emme*, to the abbots of Bury St Edmunds and Ramsey. Andreas and Emma had sworn mutual oaths in the presence of clergy and laity, and had thereafter lived together and had children. But Andreas deserted his family, and the judges are mandated to compel

[36] WH 1013(a) and (c), JL 13907 and 13903, *2 Comp.* 4.7.1 and *X* 4.1.2, 1162-81, possibly 1164-65.

[37] WH 1069, JL 14215, 1162-81; cf. Lohmann, *Collectio Wigorniensis*, p. 81, no. 1.11.

[38] WH 989, JL 12636, *X* 4.7.1, 1167-81.

him to regard his salvation, put away the '*superinducta*', return to his wife, treat her with due affection, and expiate his guilt with penance. If he resists, the culprits must both be excommunicated and avoided by all, until satisfaction is made[39]. It will be noted that some decisions of Alexander III were influenced by the important distinction between the *forum internum* and the *forum externum*, more specifically distinguishing whether the offence was brought to light by private confession or was public knowledge. The papal judgment could be adapted according to such considerations. The pope was likewise concerned to determine whether or not the offence was known or alleged by the culprit's admission alone, since it might sometimes suit a litigant's case to impute an impediment against himself. A letter touching this problem was sent by Clement III to the Confessor of the Salisbury diocese. In *Ex litteris tue*, Clement recorded that the man G. had confessed and sought penance from the recipient, in respect of his offence with his spouse's sister, after he had been betrothed to the girl below marriageable age and had lived at her father's house. When the girl's parents later required him to marry his betrothed, he confessed his fault to them, but the local archdeacon compelled him, against his will, to be united with his spouse. The Confessor forbade him access to either, and consulted the pope. The latter declared that the man should not abstain from his spouse merely on the grounds of his own confession of the fault[40]. A prolonged and difficult problem was later put to Celestine III, as recorded in his answer *Cum haberet uxorem*, to Hugh of Lincoln. Though lawfully married to Alice, John had committed adultery with Maxilla. He confessed his fault publicly, and in lawful form abjured the latter, but subsequently disregarded his oath and went through a form of marriage with Maxilla, while Alice was still alive. When Alice died, John and Maxilla continued to live together for ten years and had ten children. The question is — can they remain together, or if separated can they contract other marriages? The pope declares that they must be separated, and accept penance and perpetual continence. They are both advanced in years, and their public adultery and perjury have been a grave scandal in the Church. The length of their cohabitation and the number of their children only increase their fault; but the bishop must compel them to provide for their children, as far as their

[39] WH 457, JL 13872, *X* 4.1.9, 1159-81.

[40] WH 427, JL 16624, 16 September 1189.

means allow[41]. Such cases raised most serious problems. Celestine could hardly rule in conflict with the clear decisions of earlier popes and councils, some of which he cites in his judgment. He had also to bear in mind the public disgrace and disturbance to the Church. But the children were blameless and therefore must be cared for. Elsewhere, Celestine underlined the necessity of securing reliable evidence in matrimonial cases. In the decretal *Si matrimonii causa*, to Hubert Walter of Canterbury, he insisted that the accuser in a criminal marriage suit should not be represented by a proctor. It is right that the accuser should confront the accused, and subject himself to liability. The procedure is not necessary in a non-criminal matter, but is safer so to act, so that a definitive conclusion can be reached in the presence of both[42].

The pope was frequently asked to define the law or make a particular judgment on the question of legitimacy. The problems arose most commonly where property rights and inheritance were disputed, and the importance of this subject for the relations between secular and ecclesiastical jurisdiction is well known[43]. Many papal marriage decretals to England dealt either primarily or coincidentally with contested legitimacy, and at times made clear the appropriate functions of the two jurisdictions. Alexander III wrote to Bartholomew of Exeter and the abbot of Ford, in *Lator presentium R.*, concerning a dispute between R. and Hugh over the property of R.'s grandfather. The latter had evidently had two wives by whom respectively the father of R. and his uncle Hugh were born. Hugh contended that R.'s father was not of legitimate birth, so R. could claim nothing by hereditary right from his grandfather's estate. When the matter was brought to judgment, Hugh's evasive tactics prompted R. to appeal to the pope. The latter orders the judges to reach an expeditious decision on the matter of legitimacy, and then inform the secular lord so that the question of inheritance can be decided, a particularly clear statement of the separate jurisdictions — '*extunc seculari domino sub cuius iudicio causam de hereditate intrarunt significetis, ut pro questione nativitatis non dimittat, quin causam super hereditate audiat et decidat*'[44]. It is interesting to notice an emphasis in Alexander's rulings that prompt

[41] WH 243, JL 17678, *X* 4.7.5, 28 June - 25 December 1192.

[42] WH 908, JL 17615, *2 Comp.* 1.18.2, 1193-98.

[43] Cf. the various studies by R.H. Helmholz, esp. 'Bastardy Litigation in Medieval England', *American Journal of Legal History*, 13 (1969), p. 360-83.

[44] WH 604, JL 14218, *X* 4.17.5, 1175-80.

judgments be reached to avert frustratory delays and to facilitate just inheritance, as made very clearly in a hitherto unprinted letter to the same bishop of Exeter. The plaintiff W. took his case to the pope, alleging that Bartholomew had declined to accept proofs of his legitimacy. In the reply *Ex parte W.*, Alexander mandates the bishop to adjudicate between W. and his relation and adversary F., reminding the bishop of the pope's own duty to do justice to all and not appear to deny justice to anyone. If W. can establish his case, he is to be declared legitimate, so that he may then through the administration of secular justice secure his inheritance — '*ipsum W. auctoritate nostra legitimum denuntietis, qui postmodum per iustitiam secularem suam super memorata hereditate iustitiam consequatur*'[45]. In a dispute over the Arderne inheritance, Alexander had evidently crossed the border of the two jurisdictions and had given offence to the English king — '*qui sicut accepimus commotus est et turbatus*'. He therefore conceded in *Causam que inter*, to bishops Gilbert of London and Richard of Winchester, that the question of possession was within the king's right, mandating them nevertheless to reach a judgment on the antecedent question, namely whether or not the mother of R. was of legitimate birth. And with significant implication he observes that it is strange that the woman's status should be called in question now, after her death, when no accusation was made while she was alive. The case was not then resolved, and later commissioners were appointed. *Causam que vertitur*, to the bishops of Exeter and Winchester, and the abbot of Ford, records a further phase of this complicated dispute, revolving around the alleged illegitimacy of Agatha, mother of one of the parties. In this instance the commissioners are instructed to disregard previous or later documents leaving the question of possession to the king's court. They are to go forward without delay to judgment[46].

Although such litigation recorded material and property interests as the primary motive of the contestants, the papal replies reveal a concern with swift justice, and incidentally stress the serious and solemn nature of the marriage bond and its indissolubility. Indeed, so powerful is

[45] WH 473, new edition, 1162-81.

[46] WH 120, JL 14002, *X* 4.17.7, Oct. 1178; and WH 123, JL 13932, *X* 1,29.17, 2.14.3, and 4.17.4, *ex* 1178-81. Cf. Morey, *Bartholomew of Exeter*, p. 68-70, for a reconstruction of the Arderne (or de Ardenna) dispute, where a link is suggested with 'the great Bohun *v.* Arderne case of 1199'; cf. now C. Duggan and A. Duggan, 'Ralph de Diceto, Henry II and Becket', in *Authority and Power* (presented to Walter Ullmann), ed. B. Tierney and P. Linehan (Cambridge, 1980), p. 75-76 and 79-80.

the bond that it has a retrospective force, and confers legitimacy on children born before the marriage. The '*legitimatio per subsequens matrimonium*' is a very familiar principle in Roman and canon law, but marked a striking contrast with English secular law and interests. It may well be thought that the canon law accepted a more humane view in respect of the children born in such circumstances, a compassionate regard which was not received by English law until the twentieth century[47]. At the same time, Alexander's decretals place the emphasis of retrospective legitimation in the intrinsic quality of the later valid marriage. The matter was succinctly expressed in *Meminimus nos*, yet another decretal to Bartholomew of Exeter. An inheritance dispute had arisen between R. and P., in which it was alleged that the former's father and mother had married after his birth, and the pope had ruled that R. should be declared legitimate and not debarred from his inheritance — '*Tanta est vis matrimonii, ut qui antea sunt geniti post contractum matrimonium legitimi habeantur*'. However, the further charge was made that the father had begotten R. in adultery, while his previous wife was still alive, so the pope mandates that, if such was indeed the case, R. should be declared illegitimate — '*spurium*' — and deprived of the inheritance, especially if his mother was involved in the death of the first wife, since a lawful marriage could not be contracted between them[48]. The principle of retrospective legitimation was stated here in a classical formulation, but it was not effective if the parents' union was adulterous and an impediment to a subsequent valid marriage.

Inevitably, some legitimacy disputes were so complex and intractable, and the evidence so conflicting, that it was difficult for the pope to reach a verdict completely consonant with the law. The case of William Fitz Godric and the Lacy of Pontefract heiress has already been outlined above. In that case, Alexander agreed with evident misgivings to recognize the marriage of William and Aubrey, although William had been previously betrothed to Aubrey's daughter. The dubious union was tolerated in the interests of peace and harmony, and the children of the marriage were not deprived of their inheritance[49]. The status and material welfare of the children of doubtful unions were of concern to the pope, but in particularly notorious or flagrant cases it was

[47] Cf. Helmholz's concluding sentence, *Bastardy Litigation*', p. 383: 'It is difficult not to wonder what Grosseteste's reaction would be to the delay'.

[48] WH 650, JL 13917, 1162-81.

[49] Cf. n. 29, above.

impossible to reach a judicial verdict to their advantage. Such a predicament was discussed by Alexander in his decretal *Referente nobis*, to archbishop Roger of York. The man G. was betrothed to a certain girl, but later put off the betrothed and clandestinely married her sister, by whom he had a child. The marriage was challenged, but the man died and an inheritance dispute arose between his brothers in their own interests and the woman's parents on behalf of the issue of the marriage. The archbishop was unwilling to decide the matter, and referred the question to the pope. The verdict hinged on the validity of the contested marriage and the legitimacy or otherwise of the child. Alexander declared that the justice of public honour prevented the recognition of the marriage. If such an illegal marriage was contracted, the parties should have been separated, and since the son may not be excused by permission of the Church or through the ignorance of the parents, he cannot be admitted as heir to the parental property[50]. The pope could not easily have decided differently, though it has been noted above that Celestine III ordered in a later judgment that provision be made for children whom he could not declare legitimate. In that case also, the pope observed that the illicit union could not be overlooked, in view of its public notoriety. Celestine III was certainly open to humane decisions, as witnessed in a further letter to the bishop of Lincoln and a certain abbot. In the decretal *Pervenit ad nos* he dealt with the complaints of the widow Lucy who was harassed by William Panes and his son, after her parents' deaths. Lucy asserted that her parents had been lawfully married, and lived without accusation for a long time. But now William and his son accuse her parents of having conceived her illegitimately, and seek to deprive her of her inheritance on a charge of illegitimacy. The pope briefly orders the recipients, if they find the facts as stated, to pronounce her legitimate and free her from vexation[51]. A materialistic and acquisitive society can be discerned in the actions and claims which gave rise to these disputes. The popes recognized the possible motives and potential deceptions of the impetrants, as well as the sensitive aspects of the human relationships involved. Respect for truth and justice should not be diminished, but the rigour of the law could in many directions be softened with the oil

[50] WH 854, JL 17623, *X* 4.17.10, 1159-81; previously attributed incorrectly to Celestine III, 1191-98. Cf. also n. 41, above.

[51] WH 724, JL 17633, *X* 4.17.11, 21 January-12 March 1193. Lucy was the widow of Tinchebrai.

of clemency — '*et iustitie rigorem oleo misericordie temperare*'[52]. And, in a different context, the pope's dispensing power from the canonical bar of illegitimacy is typically stated in the decretal *Dignum est*. to Richard FitzNeal, distinguished royal servant and son of bishop Nigel of Ely. Alexander writes that it is fitting for the pope to grant favour and grace to those who are learned and of good character — '*prerogativam favoris et gratie nostre obtineant*'. Many have told him of the recipient's qualities, as to his learning and character, and so he grants that his illegitimacy will not be a bar to his advance to ecclesiastical rank or benefice. But this is a gift of special favour — '*que tibi de speciali beneficio indulgemus*', and may not be used as a precedent in the future[53].

Several decretals to England treat of marriages arranged before either one party or both had reached the age of consent. It is already clear that many marriage disputes brought into the papal curia resulted from dynastic and territorial ambitions, or concerned hereditary rights. Such motives sometimes also prompted litigation involving the age of consent. The marriage treaty and the arranged marriage are very familiar features in human society, and were very noticeably so in Western Europe in the twelfth century. The son of Henry II and the daughter of Louis VII were married with the consent of papal legates in 1160, when the parties were respectively seven and three[54]. In strict law, such a marriage could not be contracted, but it is doubtful how far the popes could succeed in making the law effective against powerful secular pressures. Nevertheless, papal guidance on the general law and judgments in individual cases exerted a moderating and humanizing influence. Bishop Reginald of Bath consulted Alexander III on various problems which could arise in connexion with the age of consent, and received a well-judged response in the decretal *A nobis tua*. The bishop asked if it was lawful for both or either party to withdraw before the appropriate age from a marriage agreed to before that age.

[52] The phrase is taken from WH 1073, 1164-79: *Veniens ad presentiam*, not a marriage decretal; cf. Lohmann, *Collectio Wigorniensis*, p. 107, no. 3.38 = 2.31(b).

[53] WH 346, JL 14183, *I Comp*. 1.9.(9), 1159-81; for the identification of the recipient as Richard FitzNeal, see Duggan and Duggan, 'Ralph de Diceto, Henry II and Becket', p. 76-77 and 80.

[54] Cf. *Radulfi de Diceto decani Lundoniensis opera historica: Ymagines historiarum*, ed. W. Stubbs, Rolls Series (London, 1876). I, p. 303-04. The present section on the age of consent does not attempt to rationalize the individual rulings concerning the determining age, and indeed the manuscripts are themselves sometimes inconsistent in detail.

The pope replied that they did not have the power of consent at that time, so therefore must await the lawful age, and then either confirm the marriage or separate if both so wished, unless they had meanwhile consummated the union. But, concerning the woman, herself of age, who married a partner below the age of consent, it is not possible for her to withdraw her consent, unless he does not wish to consent to her when he has come of age[55]. The marriage of William FitzGodric has been cited twice already. One of the several aspects of that complex case was the age of the daughter to whom William was betrothed before marrying her mother. Although the pope finally ruled in favour of tolerating their marriage, he was much concerned with the daughter's age at the time of the betrothal. In moving towards his verdict, he declared that the marriage of William and Aubrey should be observed if the daughter had been below the age of seven and had later declined the union — '*quia ... desponsationes et matrimonia ante vii. annum fieri non possunt, presertim si consensus postea non accedit*'. On the other hand, the marriage was '*inhonestum*' if the girl had reached the age of seven, in spite of William's renunciation and her own unwillingness[56]. The relevant letters were sent to Roger of York, who was also the recipient of Alexander's *Ex litteris tue*, a decretal not previously published. A certain Walter had confessed to illicit knowledge of the mother of a girl to whom he had been betrothed, but claimed that he had not known the girl herself, since she was not yet ten years old. The pope approached this problem with great prudence. He could not and should not judge of matters concealed within the heart — '*non possumus nec debemus de occultis cordium iudicare*'. Nevertheless, he decided that Walter should have access to neither woman. By indulgence, and after penance, he should be allowed to marry another — '*propter fragilitatem carnis humane*'. As for the girl, no stain attaches to her in this matter, and so she may freely marry whomsoever she wishes[57].

In many instances the pope was unsure of the truth of the pleas entered before him, yet he made clear his advice in either direction when appointing the judges delegate. In *Litteras tue* to Robert Foliot of Hereford, he reviewed the alleged marriage of a man of full age — '*perfecte etatis*' — with a girl still in the cradle — '*in cunabulis*'.

[55] WH 4(a) and (b), JL 13765 and 13767, *X* 4.2.8 and 4.2.7, 1174-81.

[56] Cf. n. 29, above.

[57] WH 432a, new edition, 1159-81.

In the course of time the man knew the girl's mother and accepted her as his wife, and the bishop was uncertain how to deal with this situation. Alexander replied that, if the man had accepted the girl's mother before the daughter had reached the age of seven, their marriage should not be dissolved, since betrothals in the cradle were null. But if the girl had completed her seventh year at the time of the mother's marriage, they should be separated and the man must be refused marriage to either[58]. In a further instance, the pope was seemingly not disposed to accept an accusation that the girl in the marriage dispute was under age at the material time. In *Lator presentium Willelmus*, to the bishop and two archdeacons of Norwich, Alexander discussed the case of William, who claimed that he had lawfully married Juliana (or Julia) '*in facie ecclesie*'. But a scandal had later arisen between them, and William had withdrawn from relations with her. The woman's family had borne this ill, and alleged that he had married her against her will and when she was under age. Since, as it was also alleged, their protest suited William's interest — '*vitam cupiebat agere dissolutam*', they were separated by mutual efforts. The pope defended the bond of marriage against this unlawful procedure, for they had been separated without good reason — '*minus rationabiliter*'. Canonically contracted marriages must not be lightly dissolved. The judges must take appropriate action to make the parties stay together, if their separation had been judicially improper and if the Church had been deceived in the matter — '*ecclesiamque fuisse deceptam*'[59]. On yet another occasion, Alexander wrote to the bishop of Chichester, concerning the case of a certain burgher of Hastings. The decretal *Suggestum fuit nobis* includes much of interest on marriage problems, including the age of consent. The man in question had put away a concubine, who had borne him children, and married a girl below the age of twelve. The concubine then provoked such discord that he could no longer look kindly on the girl or stay where she was, or be induced to take her back. However, when about to set out for Jerusalem, he promised the girl's father he would return in two years. Many years had now elapsed, and no reliable report could be had of him. The woman did not wish to remain continent, and her family brought a charge of consanguinity against the union. The pope therefore orders the bishop to advise the woman to wait, and the bishop should also make

[58] WH 631, JL 13947, *X* 4.2.4, 6 March 1177.

[59] WH 605, JL 14036, *X* 2.27.7, 1159-81.

most earnest enquiries about the man. But if these enquiries prove fruitless, and less worse befalls, the woman may be granted the freedom of marrying whom she wishes. The charge of consanguinity against the marriage should be heard, if the man returns[60].

In some such cases, Alexander frankly confessed that he did not know whom to believe. He commissioned a particularly confusing suit to Roger of Worcester and the abbot of Evesham, in the mandate *Recepta questione*. The dispute arose from a complaint by the woman A. that she had been united to H. while she was under age and in his father's custody. But, on reaching the age of discretion, she renounced H. and was taken in marriage by B. Among the welter of charge and counter-charge, the witnesses for B. swore that A. was five years old when espoused to H., and that she fled as soon as she could, and came willingly to B. Against which, witnesses for H. swore that she was 14 years old when she was betrothed to him, that she lived with him without objection for more than a year, and was taken furtively from him. Alexander could not establish the truth here — '*nescimus cui partium fides sit potius adhibenda*'. In instructing the judges, he places the determining age at 12 years. If she was 14 or 12 when H. married her and she consented, B. must restore her. But if she was not yet 12, did not consent and left as soon as possible, she shall remain with B. without objection — '*nisi rationabilis causa obstiterit*'[61].

The problem of clandestine marriages has been mentioned above, and has been the subject of recent scholarly debate. There can be no doubt that the popes in the period recognized that valid marriages could be contracted clandestinely. Alexander III made this clear by implication in an unprinted letter to an unidentified bishop, *Si quando fratres*. If marriages have been contracted in secret and the parties then wish to have their marriages publicly declared '*in facie ecclesie*', in accordance with custom — '*prout moris est*', this is permitted, and the children should be declared legitimate, unless there is some clear and reasonable objection[62]. Such was the general law, but it is not easy to agree with the suggestion that Alexander 'was probably aware that

[60] WH 1006, 1159-81.

[61] WH 847, ? 1175-79.

[62] The quotation is not from an English decretal: cf. WH 911a, *Si quando fratres*, Alexander III to the bishop 'Belarensi' (see new edition); the subject matter of this new letter is related to that of *Quod nobis ex parte*, to the bishop of Beauvais: WH 819, JL 13774, 18 October 1170-19 September 1171.

his decisions would promote clandestine marriages', or that, however he may have disapproved of them, he was willing to accept the price to ensure a freer marriage[63]. This theory is not supported by a letter of Alexander III to archbishop Roger of York, *Solet frequenter*, concerning the vexatious pressure of litigation in the archbishopric as a result of clandestine marriages. Such unions frequently occurred there, and in disputes arising the parties contradicted one another's evidence. Matters are therefore rendered nugatory through lack of witnesses, which should be confirmed by ecclesiastical authority, if contracted in public. The pope mandates the archbishop to make a general prohibition, under pain of perpetual anathema, that marriages do not take place in future in secret — '*in absconso*' — but publicly in the presence of suitable witnesses, so that the matter be worthily confirmed and the contracting parties may not be beset with such ambiguity — '*nec contrahentes tam ambigua possint questione pulsari*'[64]. It would be difficult to imagine a more categorical condemnation of the practice.

Several English marriage decretals touch on the religious life, or involve religious communities in some way. At times a problem arose when a man in danger of death took the religious habit or entered a community and then recovered. Alexander III advised the abbot of St John of Croxton in such a predicament, in the previously unprinted decretal *Devotionis tue*. Such a man had entered the religious life with his wife's consent, but on his restoration to health she changed her mind and wished to have him back. The pope's verdict was that if the decision had been taken, or confirmed, with full understanding, and if the wife had vowed chastity, the arrangement should stand, so that he remained in religion and she observed her vow — '*alioquin quoniam ipsi una caro sunt effecti, non debet una pars in seculo remanere, et altera ad religionem transire*'[65]. A rather different situation was discussed by Alexander in *Ex parte mulieris*, to the prior and community of Dunstable. In this case the wife had been unwilling to agree and merely consented when her husband's life had been despaired of. She gave him to the community '*cum gemitu et nimia cordis amaritudine*'. This man also recovered, after taking the habit, but the canons of Dunstable were unwilling to restore him at the wife's request. Again, '*cum vir et*

[63] Cf. C. Donahue, 'The Policy of Alexander the Third's Consent Theory of Marriage', *Proceedings of the Fourth International Congress of MCL*, p. 251-81 (esp. 270-79).

[64] WH 990, JL 14162, *1 Comp.* 4.4.(4), 1159-81; cf. also n. 50, above.

[65] WH 343a, new edition, 1162-81.

mulier una caro sint', it is improper for one to remain in the world and the other to enter religion. The pope understood that the wife had not accepted the religious habit, or promised to do so, and therefore her husband should be restored to her[66]. The essential difference between the two cases was the wife's standing. In the former instance she had willingly committed herself to chastity, whereas in the latter she had acted under constraint and took no vow. A variant problem was put by Robert Foliot of Hereford to Alexander III, to which the latter replied in *Super eo quod.* A certain married man had entered a monastery and had perhaps even been professed, in the presence of priests and monks and with his wife's consent, but without his bishop's knowledge, and the wife remained in secular life and habit and took no vow. Alexander decided that, if the wife remained in this state, the man should be recalled from the community by the bishop, 'because they are one flesh'. But she should be diligently exhorted to assume the religious life and take a vow of chastity[67]. The pope clearly leaned in this case to the solution of perpetual continence for both, yet conceded the woman's right to have her husband restored. Yet another related problem was raised by Bartholomew of Exeter. An educated nobleman — '*literatus et nobilis*' — had sworn before witnesses with '*verba de presenti*' to marry a certain girl within two years. Later he wished to enter the religious life and sought the bishop's permission to assume the monastic habit before the marriage contract, knowing that it was open to him to assume a stricter monastic life after the contract and even against her will, provided that this were done within two months, in accordance with ancient canons restated by Alexander. The pope's reply *Commissum* ruled that it is better for him to keep his oath and fulfil the contract. Then he could enter the religious life, provided they had not physically been united after the first betrothal. The letter gives no guidance on the girl's position or status[68]. A curious case was commissioned by Alexander III to bishop John of Norwich and his archdeacon, concerning an accusation of invalid marriage. In *Querelam R. nobilis*, the pope recorded that the marriage of the noble lady R. with the knight M. was challenged on the grounds that she had been

[66] WH 466, new edition, 1162-81. The man in question was Walter of Odell in Bedfordshire.

[67] WH 1017(d), JL 13946, *X* 3.32.1, 1174-81.

[68] WH 135, JL 13905, *X* 4.1.16, 1162-81. Alexander's phrasing is of interest: 'iuxta veterum canonum statuta nostra constitutione innovata, ad arctioris vitae religionem posset transire'. Morey remarks that 'this was a somewhat epoch-making decision and was so regarded at a later period': cf. *Bartholomew of Exeter*, p. 71 and n. 4.

a professed nun, having taken the habit. This action was said to result from envy, and the woman replied that she had simply been within the nuns' care for her education — '*tantum causa custodie inter moniales fuit aliquando tempore educata*'. In her absence and without her knowledge, the dean of the district had judged against the marriage, and compelled the man to abjure his wife's company. The commissioners are mandated to investigate the case diligently and carefully. If it is not manifest and public that the woman had been a professed nun, her husband must be restored to her, and the culpable dean be sent to the pope. Subsequently, they may consider any challenge which may be made against the marriage[69]. The pope's compassion is revealed in another newly edited letter concerning the nuns of Cheshunt. In *Ex parte Adeline*, Alexander mandated the bishop of London to take action against the nuns who had treated the plaintiff Adeline in a most inhuman manner. Adeline had become pregnant, and entered the community, took the habit and proposed to serve God there, paying incidentally a substantial sum of money. But after her child's birth, the nuns expelled her and kept the money. Not surprisingly, the pope condemned this harsh action — '*valde inhumanum est ut mulier ipsa immisericorditer tractetur*', and was much concerned at the stress and risks which such a one might suffer in consequence. The bishop must compel the nuns to take her back, or within 15 days return her money in full, so that with God's mercy she could provide for her soul's salvation in another place — '*ut sibi possit in alio loco competentius providere, et animum suum Domino miserante salvare*'[70].

The popes did not cease to proclaim the indissolubility of a validly contracted marriage — '*sine iudicio ecclesie matrimonium nulla potest ratione dissolvi nec ei ad secunda vota migrandi licentia debet aliquatenus indulgeri, quia sacra testante scriptura vir non potest uxorem nisi causa fornicationis dimittere, et tunc aut ei debet reconciliari aut ea superstite continere*'[71]. It cannot be thought that this high ideal was easy, yet how could the pope diverge from such explicit scriptural teaching. Many cases brought before him were so obscured by perjured testimony that a perfect judgment on the specific question could not be reached with certainty. Others disclosed a human predicament of such com-

[69] WH 788, 1176-81.

[70] WH 449, new edition, 1163-81.

[71] The quotation is not from an English decretal, but its scriptural authority is very familiar: cf. WH 749, *Proposuisti nobis*, Alexander III to the archbishop of Tyre, 1166 or 1178-79.

plexity that a verdict falling short of the fulness of justice and virtue could be tolerated. In attaining as nearly as possible to a moral idealism set clearly before the faithful, some papal rulings required an almost heroic virtue, while others frankly recognized that a pragmatic judgment could be given without prejudice to principle. In some such cases the principles were left inviolate, while a human problem was resolved on grounds of reason and common sense, or to avert a graver situation. Alexander III's letter *Pervenit ad nos* to archbishop Richard and the Canterbury suffragans may serve as a concluding statement of the perfect affection ideally required in Christian marriage. By general custom, persons afflicted by the disease of leprosy are separated from the community and set apart in isolated places, but the pope has heard that in some such cases wives are not following their afflicted husbands, or husbands their wives. They are one flesh and should not remain without the other, so they must be constrained to follow them and minister to them with conjugal affection[72]. The devotion and self-denial required by such papal admonitions contrast sharply with the self-interest and tortuous litigation recorded in some of the marriage cases briefly surveyed in this essay. It was the pope's concern to harmonize Christian morality and virtuous ideals with the imperfect society resulting from fragile human nature. His authority as judge and teacher was exercised with discretion and pastoral care.

The conference paper ended at this point, but a short additional comment may be useful in the light of questions subsequently raised. The words equity and compassion were not conjoined in the title with a strictly technical significance. The meaning of compassion is self-explanatory, and the term equity implies a sense of fair judgments and that higher concept of justice which a rigid application of enacted laws sometimes impedes. The canonical principles of *aequitas* and *ratio* can be further explored in the professional studies noted above[73]. A query arose concerning political or social influence exerted to secure a favourable verdict in marriage disputes. It is readily agreed that such interventions occurred, and were doubtless sometimes successful. Indeed, that point is evident in several cases discussed within the paper, but it cannot therefore be assumed that the justice and humanity attested by the papal judgments cited is called in

[72] WH 713, JL 13794, *X* 4.8.1, 1174-81; in several collections (including *X*) the decretal has a singular address and style, to the archbishop alone, without his suffragans.

[73] Cf. n. 1, above.

question. It would be quite unrealistic and unfounded to impute duplicity or insincerity to the papal language of justice, and clearly so in those cases which did not involve powerful or wealthy litigants. The status and treatment of women gave rise to further questions, particularly concerning the dismissal of clerical concubines, which was thought to be inhuman. Again, there is an element of unreality in such an approach, however compassionately inspired. There are limits to which any pope can go, in adapting his judgments to human situations, and such limits stop short of distorting the moral law as he receives it. It would be inconceivable that a pope should condone public scandal in clerical standards of behaviour. At the same time, where vital moral principles were not at stake, it is noteworthy that many papal verdicts worked to the advantage or protection of the women involved. This important effect of the canon law of marriage is sometimes overlooked. It is a familiar opinion that the Church's marriage law has been too inflexible. The only substance for such a charge lies in the fact that there are immutable principles, valid for the Church in all ages, based on unambiguous scriptural teaching. Certainly, no pope could contradict these, though the cases discussed above reveal a notable openness to discretion and dispensation. Finally, it has been recently suggested that Alexander III's doctrine of marriage reflected some assimilation of the notions of romantic and courtly love, so prevalent in the period[74]. Such a theory is quite without foundation. The conventions of courtly love are distinct from, and even hostile to, the papal concern with law, unobscured but applied with Christian charity[75].

Errata:
p. 69, line 4, Roger of Hereford and earl Hugh de Lacy
should read Roger of Hereford and Hugh de Lacy
p. 75, line 12, but is safer *should read* but it is safer

[74] Donahue, 'The Policy of Alexander', p. 277-79.

[75] Cf. Lesage, 'Ratio Canonica', p. 106: 'la *ratio canonica* s'identifie chez lui avec l'esprit authentiquement chrétien qui doit animer le droit, la discipline et les institutions ecclésiastiques'.

* For decretals designated 'new edition' here, see the forthcoming *Decretales ineditae saeculi xii*, Monumenta Iuris Canonici, Series B, Corpus Collectionum, 4 (Vatican City, in press): from the papers of Walther Holtzmann, edited and revised by S. Chodorow and C. Duggan.

ADDENDA

I. For further discussions of the decretal collections and judges delegate, see my chapters in the forthcoming *The History of Medieval Canon Law in the Classical Period, 1140-1234*, edd. K. Pennington and Wilfried Hartmann, Catholic University Press of America.

II. For a new edition of the Becket letters, see *The Correspondence of Archbishop Thomas Becket*, ed. and trans. Anne J. Duggan, Oxford Medieval Texts (in press).

VII. For the argument that the bishop of Osma involved in *Quia requisistis* was John rather than Bernard, see Peter Linehan, 'Royal influence and papal authority in the Diocese of Osma: A note on "Quia requisistis" (JL 13728)', *Bulletin of Medieval Canon Law*, New Series, 20 (1990), 31–41.

INDEX

Where two or more decretal letters with the same incipit are listed in the Index below, their numbers in Jaffé-Loewenfeld's Regesta Pontificum Romanorum ad annum 1198, 2 Vols. (Leipzig, 1885–88) (JL), *or, failing that, in Walther Holtzmann's unpublished* Registrum decretalium (WH) *are supplied in brackets.*